Strategies and Tactics of Behavioral Research

Third Edition

James M. Johnston
Auburn University

Henry S. Pennypacker
University of Florida

Routledge
Taylor & Francis Group

NEW YORK AND HOVE

Published in 2009
by Routledge
270 Madison Avenue
New York, NY 10016
www.psypress.com

Published in Great Britain
by Routledge
27 Church Road
Hove, East Sussex BN3 2FA

Routledge is an imprint of the Taylor & Francis Group, an informa business

Typeset by RefineCatch Limited, Bungay, Suffolk, UK
Printed and bound by Sheridan Books, Inc. in the USA on acid-free paper
Cover design by Design Deluxe

10 9 8 7 6 5 4 3 2 1

Library of Congress Cataloging-in-Publication Data
Johnston, James M.
  Strategies and tactics of behavioral research / James M. Johnston and
Henry S. Pennypacker, Jr. – 3rd ed.
    p. cm.
  Includes bibliographical references and index.
  1. Psychology—Research—Methodology.   I. Pennypacker, H. S. (Henry S.)   II. Title.
  BF76.5.J63 2008
  150.72—dc22   2008019278

ISBN: 978-0-8058-5882-2 (hbk)

To
Ogden Lindsley
and
Murray Sidman

Giants of our field upon whose
shoulders we proudly stand

Contents

List of Boxes

Preface

Our decision to write a third edition of *Strategies and Tactics of Behavioral Research* arose from our experiences, as well as those of many colleagues, in helping students to understand this material. We discovered many ways of improving our discussion of this approach to studying individual behavior, but we also saw that the audience for our text was changing. We had written the second edition primarily for doctoral students in psychology, education, and other academic fields specializing in the experimental study of behavior. However, we also observed considerable growth in Master's programs, especially those preparing practitioners working toward newly established credentials in the field of Applied Behavior Analysis.

We have written this third edition, no longer accompanied by a readings volume, to meet these changing needs. Although the core content and chapter divisions of the second edition remain relatively untouched, we have discarded many of the secondary issues and digressions that encumbered discussions in the previous edition. Instead, we have focused on describing and explaining the primary material in a straightforward and relatively simple narrative. We have composed both sentences and paragraphs with unwavering attention to the needs of student readers.

Because many students learning this material may be planning careers as practitioners rather than as researchers, this third edition considers the relevance of methodological procedures and decisions for the delivery of professional services. This is not a stretch, of course. Many methodological requirements of professional practice originated in behavioral research methods, and the fact that the Behavior Analyst Certification Board[fi] mandates coursework in this area clarifies the need to address the role of research methods in service scenarios.

Aside from substantive and literary revisions, we have also added a number of features that will make the volume more effective as a textbook. New terms are now identified in bold face type and are formally defined in indented tinted boxes, as well as in the glossary at the end of the book. There are now many tables that summarize the main points of a discussion, and they are joined by considerably more figures, including figures adapted from journal articles. Chapter end matter now includes not only study guides, but a chapter summary, suggested readings, discussion topics, and exercises. This material is also available on an instructor's website, www.psypress.com/behavioral-research, which further includes lecture outlines and test items.

In sum, although the chapter topics are unchanged from the second edition, this third edition otherwise provides a very different experience for student and instructor. Substantial improvements in clarity of exposition and the addition of new learning aids offer a more appealing learning opportunity, and instructors will find it easier to take advantage of students' interests. Incorporating the methodological interests of practitioners into each chapter extends this appeal to a growing professional discipline, a field partly defined by its respect for the highest standards of scientific practice.

We would like to thank our many students and colleagues who have offered valuable feedback along the way. We would especially like to thank Ryan Zayac at Central Washington University, who prepared many of the supplementary materials, and Wayne Fuqua at Western Michigan University, who served as a reviewer.

Finally, as with the second edition, the first author has assumed primary responsibility for this edition, although with the active intellectual support and guidance of the second author. Our contributions to the foundations on which the third edition is based remain thoroughly intertwined.

—*James M. Johnston*
—*Henry S. Pennypacker*

Those who fall in love with practice without science are like a sailor who enters a ship without a helm or a compass, and who never can be certain whither he is going.

—Leonardo da Vinci

PART ONE

THE NATURAL SCIENCE
OF BEHAVIOR

CHAPTER ONE

Science and Scientific Behavior

The chief problem of science is the scientist
—D. L. Watson

INTRODUCTION

The scientific achievements of the 20th and now the 21st century have changed our lives in profound ways, and many people have come to revere science as an almost magical endeavor. We have grown confident that, given enough time and money, science can solve most of life's problems, and we may be right. Those who devote their lives to doing research are held in high regard, and scientific careers are now rewarding not just professionally but financially.

And yet, most people do not understand how science really works. The average citizen does not have contact with the daily activities of scientists, so it is not surprising that it is hard to appreciate how scientific pursuits are different from everyday interests. A newspaper article about a scientific discovery inevitably stops short of explaining exactly how it was accomplished or describing the years of research that made the breakthrough possible.

Even researchers are likely to "miss the forest for the trees" as they focus on their own areas of interest. Most scientists are trained in the research literature and methods of their own specialties. They usually do not appreciate the underlying features of experimental methods common to all disciplines that make science a special way of learning about the world. There are some writers who specialize in studying science as an industry or enterprise, and a few others focus on science from a philosophical point of view. However, the critical essence of science—the features that are fundamental to its effectiveness—often eludes these writers too.

SCIENTISTS AS BEHAVING ORGANISMS

Are Scientists Different?

Understanding the essential features of a scientific search for nature's secrets requires looking at the behavior of scientists is a particular way. This perspective is based on appreciating the fundamental processes underlying how human behavior actually works, which is itself the product of a field of scientific study. This point of view is very different from how we are taught by the culture to view human behavior. For instance, although we learn to talk about what is going on "in the scientist's head," this only distracts us from noticing more important relationships between scientists' behavior and their daily work environments.

The key to understanding how science works lies in acknowledging that scientists are behaving organisms. As such, there is no evidence that scientists are generally different from other people. In other words, they are not any smarter or more logical than others who earn advanced degrees (Mahoney, 1976).

It is also important to recognize that the behavior of scientists, just like the behavior of all human and nonhuman animals, is as much a part of nature as any other scientific subject matter and can be approached with the same experimental tools. In fact, the scientific study of behavior over the past 100 years or so has revealed many now well-established laws about the variables that determine an organism's behavior. This research has shown that, in addition to whatever genetic endowment each individual is born with, the major influence on behavior is each person's moment by moment experiences as he or she goes through life.

BOX 1.1

Are Scientists Different?

In a somewhat humorously disrespectful book, titled *Scientist as Subject: The Psychological Imperative* (1976), Michael Mahoney delights in puncturing many illusions about scientists. For instance, he argues that scientists are not more intelligent than others, often illogical in their work, often selective and biased in their treatment of data, passionate in their prejudices, frequently dogmatic in their opinions, sometimes selfish and ambitious in pursuing personal recognition and defending territory, often secretive about their findings, and fond of spinning "truths" in hypotheses and theories before the data warrant. His general point is that scientists are not special, but just like the rest of us.

This list of shortcomings should suggest that, however well science usually works, it can go awry. Although it is relatively uncommon, scientists are sometimes dishonest with themselves (when they interpret data in a way they know is incorrect) or with their peers (when they publish findings they know are false). Fortunately, science has some effective self-corrective mechanisms. In brief, scientific research includes a public component that keeps innocent bias and blatant dishonesty at a minimum. Scientists must publish complete reports of their methods, data, and analytical procedures before other scientists will pay any attention to their findings. Some of their colleagues who are interested in the same topic will repeat the experiments, which will either confirm the original conclusions or cast doubt on them and lead to still further experimental efforts to see what the truth really is.

Scientific ethics is an important part of graduate training. If a researcher is found to have broken the cardinal rule of honesty, there are a variety of sanctions that may be applied. These sanctions include being prevented from being considered for federal grants, being fired, and even being prosecuted under civil or criminal statutes.

The Three-Term Contingency

The interactions between each action or response and its environmental context involve biologically mediated processes called **conditioning** or **learning**. The laws of conditioning describe exactly how the relationship between an individual's responses and the environmental events surrounding them affects his or her behavior in the future. It may be easiest to understand how learning works in terms of what is called the **three-term contingency**. In this context, a **contingency** refers to relationships between instances of behavior (responses) and their environmental antecedents and consequences. Figure 1.1 identifies the three terms that define the basic contingencies underlying all behavior. Environmental events that immediately precede responses are called **antecedent events** or stimuli, and those that follow responses are called **consequent events**. (These terms are often shortened to "antecedents"

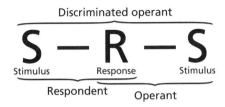

FIG. 1.1. Schematic representation of the three-term contingency.

and "consequences.") The contingencies involving these antecedent events, responses, and consequent events describe different relationships between a particular behavior or action and those features of the environment that precede or follow it. These relationships are termed **respondents, operants**, and **discriminated operants**.

Conditioning. The process of changing a behavior that involves interactions between responses and environmental events whose effects depend on the processes of reinforcement and punishment.

Learning. The relatively enduring changes in behavior that result from conditioning processes.

Contingency. A relationship between a class of responses and a class (or classes) of stimuli. Implies nothing about the nature of the relationship or its effects.

Three-term contingency. A set of functional relationships among distinct classes of antecedent stimuli, responses, and consequent stimuli that together constitute the model of how behavior is influenced by the environment.

Antecedent event. An environmental event that occurs immediately before a response. Used generically when it is not certain what function the event serves.

Consequent event. An environmental event that occurs immediately after a response. Used generically when it is not certain what function the event serves.

Respondent. A class of responses elicited by a particular unconditioned or conditioned antecedent stimulus.

Operant. A class of responses defined by a functional relation with a class of consequent events that immediately follow those responses.

Discriminated operant. A class of responses that are functionally related to classes of both antecedent and consequent stimuli.

The three-term contingency is a useful way of summarizing how behavior works because the biology of organisms, together with their unique life experiences, makes their behavior especially sensitive to certain kinds of environmental events. For example, humans are from birth especially sensitive to sweet-tasting substances, and their experiences with particular foods (e.g., cookies) can make such stimuli especially important. When a child's behavior such as standing on a chair to reach the kitchen counter where the cookies are kept leads to the consequence of eating the cookie, that behavior is more likely to occur again in the future. This instance of the three-term contingency is called **positive reinforcement**. If the same behavior resulted in a different kind of consequence such as falling off the chair or being scolded by a parent, the behavior might be less likely to occur again. This instance of the three-term contingency is called **positive punishment**. Of course, there are other kinds of contingencies as well.

> **Positive reinforcement.** A class of procedures involving the occurrence of a stimulus immediately following responding that results in an increase in some aspect of the response class over baseline levels.
>
> **Positive punishment.** A class of procedures involving the occurrence of a stimulus immediately following responding that results in a decrease in some aspect of the response class over baseline levels.

The relationship between instances of behavior and the antecedent side of the three-term contingency also influences behavior, although somewhat differently. If a certain behavior occurs when a particular environmental event is present and the behavior then produces a reinforcing consequence, that antecedent event comes to serve a sort of signaling function. The behavior (a discriminated operant) is then more likely to occur when similar antecedent events (called **discriminative stimuli**) are present than when they are not present. For instance, if you drive up to a store and see an "Open" sign on the door, you will usually get out of the car and go in because in the past such behavior has resulted in reinforcing consequences. Not surprisingly, you would be less likely to get out of the car and try to go in if such behavior has been followed by a punishing consequence (the door is locked) in the presence of a different antecedent (a "Closed" sign).

> **Discriminative stimuli.** Stimuli that have acquired the function of setting the occasion for a behavior to occur. A behavior is more likely to occur in the presence of a discriminative stimulus than in its absence. Abbreviated S^D.

Other antecedent stimuli have functions that depend less on the consequences of responding and more on an organism's biology. For example, when a stimulus such as a puff of air contacts our eye, we blink, and it is difficult to avoid doing so. Even innocuous events paired with a puff of air elicit the same kind of blinking response. This behavior is an example of a respondent. (See Catania, 2007, for a more detailed treatment of the three-term contingency and the resulting classes of behavior.)

The repertoire of each of us at any point in our lives is largely the result of our history of contingencies like these. What we do or do not do, our skills, our emotions, and the unique features of our individuality are largely a function of the laws of conditioning. As with other laws of nature, these relationships are at work even if we are unaware of what is going on, and no one is exempt from them, even for a moment.

Over the years, scientific study of the relationship between behavior and the environment represented by the three-term contingency has been very fruitful. Researchers have not only learned a great deal about the basic components of conditioning, but they have also learned how to apply these fundamental principles to human behavior, especially under everyday circumstances. As a result, a still developing but powerful technology for changing behavior has emerged. This technology, called **applied behavior analysis**, is now used in diverse areas, including mental retardation, autism, brain injury, education, business, medicine, and sports (Austin & Carr, 2000).

> **Applied behavior analysis.** A phrase that may refer to (a) the field of research that focuses on applying the findings of a basic science (the Experimental Analysis of Behavior) concerning fundamental processes of conditioning to address the need for changing behavior under everyday circumstances (b) the behavior change technology developed by applied researchers, or (c) the field encompassed by both applied research and delivery of the resulting technology.

SCIENCE AS THE BEHAVIOR OF SCIENTISTS

Scientific Behavior

The basic principles of conditioning or learning are relevant in a book on behavioral research methods because they are at the heart of how science works. The primary activities of scientists are figuring out what experiments to do, planning and conducting them, and interpreting and communicating their results. When scientists are doing these kinds of things, they are behaving. In fact, science is really no more than the behavior of scientists.

Although this may sound simple, the details can become complicated. We certainly do not know everything we might like to about the behavior of scientists. However, if we examine their activities in light of the three-term contingency, it can help to explain much of what goes on every day in the scientific workplace. This approach is also useful because it focuses on what researchers actually do and the environmental circumstances under which they do it. In other words, it helps us talk about scientific behavior in the same way we approach any behavior as a subject matter. We can try to identify the antecedent events that may prompt researchers to choose one course of action over another and the consequences that may reinforce some practices but not others.

This is a good perspective for a text on research methods because it helps to highlight the many choices that researchers face in conducting an experiment. Each choice about what to do and how to do it involves some antecedent circumstances and certain possible consequences. The alternative selected may lead to a reinforcing outcome or punishing outcome, which will then make similar decisions more likely or less likely in the future. Examining these scientific contingencies can help to show why some research practices are more effective than others under certain conditions. If we step back and examine the choices that researchers most often make in a certain discipline, we can identify the field's established methodological practices. The reason why those practices are preferred stems from their effectiveness for the individual researchers who choose them.

Examples of Methodological Choices

One of the first things a behavioral researcher must do is decide what behavior should be measured and how to measure it. For instance, as chapter 4 will show, there are different ways of defining a particular behavior. Some definitions are likely to produce more variability in the resulting data than others, and some may generate less variability. For instance, the behavior of cleaning a kitchen may be defined in terms of specific actions, such as putting dishes in the dishwasher, scrubbing the counters, and so forth. Alternatively, this behavior may be defined in terms of a certain outcome, such as clean dishes and counter, regardless of the actions involved (perhaps the dishes were washed by hand). As we will see, the degree of variability in the data is an important consequence of a researcher's methodological choices.

Another set of decisions will be required when choosing the particular features of a behavior that may need to be measured. For instance, measuring how often the behavior occurs will provide a different picture than measuring how long it lasts when it occurs. One of these pictures may be more useful than the other in revealing the effects of an intervention and answering the experimental question.

There are also a series of choices that must be made in designing procedures for observing and recording the target behavior. For example, the researcher must decide how often observation will take place and how long each session will last. Not surprisingly, the choices here can again have a big impact on what the investigator learns about the behavior. For example, measuring a participant's behavior only once before and once after an experimental treatment is certainly easier than measuring it repeatedly throughout both control and experimental conditions. However, the two kinds of data sets provide very different antecedents for the researcher's interpretive reactions.

Designing an experiment involves selecting experimental and control conditions and then arranging them in ways that show differences in responding between the two conditions. This aspect of research methods also faces the investigator with many choices. A key decision concerns how to compare data from control and experimental conditions.

One approach, which has a long tradition in psychology, is to divide a relatively large number of participants into two groups. The groups are treated the same except that one experiences the experimental condition and the other does not. The differences in the aggregate performance of each group are then analyzed using the rules of inferential statistics.

An alternative approach, which also has a long history, uses fewer participants but separately exposes each individual to a series of sessions under the control condition and a series of sessions under the experimental condition. Comparisons are then usually made using graphical techniques examining the performance of each participant.

These two approaches, which have many variations, are fundamentally different. As later chapters will show, they face the researcher with choices that lead to importantly different consequences for the nature of the data and for the kinds of interpretations that can be made.

Finally, once a study is completed and the data are available for analysis, figuring out what the data reveal about the experimental question provides still more choices. For instance: (a) Are all of the data fully appropriate for analysis, or should some data points be omitted because they represent the effects of extraneous factors such as illness? (b) What data analysis techniques are most appropriate? (c) If displaying the data graphically is planned, what kind of graphs should be used? (d) What type of scale should be used for the vertical axis? (e) What factors in the experimental procedures should be considered in interpreting the data? (f) Were there procedural problems that might make the data misleading?

CONTROL BY THE SUBJECT MATTER

This chapter has introduced three themes that continue throughout this volume:

1. The essence of science lies in the behavior of individual researchers.
2. This behavior results from the same kinds of environmental contingencies that determine all other behavior.

3. Viewing methodological choices in terms of their antecedents and consequences highlights important distinctions among alternatives and helps investigators to make sound decisions.

This perspective toward scientific behavior leads to the conclusion that experimentation is about control. Conducting an experiment requires the researcher to control the factors whose effects are under study (the **independent variable**). At the same time, the investigator must control all of the other factors that are not of interest but that might affect how clearly these effects are seen (**extraneous variables**). In other words, the investigator must manage not only the experimental circumstances to make sure that they operate as intended but the status of any extraneous factors whose influence might be confused with the effects of the independent variable. All the while, the investigator must manage procedures for accurately measuring the targeted behavior (the **dependent variable**) to see if it changes as the independent variable condition is systematically presented or terminated.

> **Independent variable.** Environmental event or events whose presence or absence is manipulated by the investigator in order to determine their effects on the dependent variable.
>
> **Extraneous variables.** Environmental events that are not of interest to the researcher but that may influence the participant's behavior in ways that obscure the effects of the independent variable.
>
> **Dependent variable.** In behavioral research, usually a response class. The objective is to see if changes in the dependent variable depend on manipulations of the independent variable.

Although it may seem that the researcher is doing all the controlling, the ideal outcome of these activities is that the researcher's behavior comes largely under the control of the subject matter. In other words, the data representing changes in the target behavior typically become a major influence on the researcher's decisions. Obtaining a clear picture of the effects of the independent on the dependent variable is a highly reinforcing consequence for a researcher, and good researchers work hard to pursue this outcome. For instance, an investigator might try to eliminate an extraneous factor such as distractions that might affect a participant's behavior in the hope that this action improves how clearly the data show the effects of the independent variable. A researcher might also work to improve how carefully staff members implement procedures in order to insure that an intervention operates exactly as intended.

As investigators attempt to produce a clear picture of the effects of experimental procedures on the target behavior, they use the accumulating data to evaluate their choices. The emerging data are often a good source of ideas about ways of improving the experiment. In sum, the subject matter (the behavior of participants) controls the behavior of a researcher by serving as feedback about how the experiment is designed and managed and by serving as a prompt for any needed improvements.

SCIENTIFIC METHOD

Scientific method may be described as a set of loose rules and traditions that have evolved over many years of experimental practice that bring the researcher's behavior under the control of the subject matter. This outcome is what makes these conventions effective in studying natural phenomena. These rules and traditions also keep behavioral scientists looking for better ways to see the effects of experimental interventions. Researchers often go to considerable trouble to improve the clarity of experimental findings because if the data are misleading in some way the consequences can be pretty serious. Investigators who recognize these kinds of problems may admit to themselves that the project failed to provide a sound answer to the experimental question. Investigators who fail to recognize serious methodological shortcomings will probably attempt to publish their results. If a journal accepts their submission, the findings may then mislead peers, who may be unable to identify the problems from a journal article.

> **Scientific method.** The established practices of scientific communities that have evolved over time because of their effectiveness in studying natural phenomena.

A field's scientific methods are important because the alternative to the researcher's behavior coming under the control of the subject matter is having other sources of control dominate decision-making. These other influences can lead to problematic choices and limit the effectiveness of a study.

When human behavior is the subject matter, for example, it can be especially difficult for investigators to be completely free of the many preconceptions about behavior that everyone learns from growing up in the culture. For instance, our language suggests that: (a) behavior is generally motivated and controlled by events going on in the mind, (b) emotions control subsequent actions, and (c) we can make choices that are free of outside influences. These prescientific convictions often lead to poor experimental questions and methodological decisions.

The objective of this text is to summarize what many researchers have learned about methods of studying behavior. One way in which this book differs from other books on research methods is by not offering a set of methodological rules that might give a misleading impression of simplicity. Doing science is not a matter of following specific rules like recipes in a cookbook. Cookbooks may work quite well when the recipe is well tested, but scientific discovery is more like creating the recipe in the first place. Getting nature to reveal secrets about behavior involves many decisions, judgments, and even guesses. Successfully playing the science game requires acknowledging this complexity and understanding how science really works. This book therefore describes methodological practices in terms of the scientist's behavior and the likely consequences of different courses of action that are available. Each research project requires a unique series of decisions, but their consequences must always lead to a clear picture of the effects of experimental conditions on the behavior of interest.

THE PRODUCTS OF SCIENCE

If science is largely the behavior of scientists, the results or consequences of scientific activities are the facts, empirical generalizations, and laws of nature that are discovered. In the case of behavior as a subject matter, these products are actually statements of contingencies that describe the relationship between behavior and other events. When researchers describe experimental findings in plain English, these statements summarize "if-then" relations. For example, a statement such as "if a person smokes cigarettes for many years, then his or her chances of developing heart disease, lung cancer, or emphysema will increase greatly" describes contingencies in nature. The value of science is that it allows scientists to identify and understand such contingencies with a high degree of accuracy. Their findings can then be used to guide the behavior of others who have not studied or experienced the contingencies.

Skinner (1974) described the role of scientific methods in the following way:

> By learning the laws of science, a person is able to behave effectively under the contingencies of an extraordinarily complex world. Science carries him beyond experience and beyond the defective sampling of nature inevitable in a single lifetime. It also brings him under the control of conditions which could play no part in shaping and maintaining his behavior. He may stop smoking because of a rule derived from a statistical study of the consequences, although the consequences themselves are too deferred to have any reinforcing effect. (p. 124)

RESEARCH METHODS AND SERVICE DELIVERY

Research versus Practice

As with fields such as medicine and engineering, the field of behavior analysis may be divided into two major endeavors: research and delivery of practical services. Some behavior analysts are employed in circumstances in which they are able to conduct research, and some portion of the research literature focuses on understanding relatively fundamental features of behavior. These

---

BOX 1.2

Rule-Governed versus Contingency-Shaped Behavior

The goal of science is to describe regularities in nature so that we may behave more effectively than would otherwise be the case. Scientific methods help researchers to figure out these regularities, which they express as rules. If what researchers learn is accurate and sufficiently detailed, these rules can lead others who have never experienced the contingencies to behave effectively.

The disadvantage of managing behavior with rules is that they are often less than fully accurate and complete. Furthermore, people may not follow the rules very well because their actions may be influenced by their experiences (contingencies). For instance, although the rule may be clear that smoking increases one's chance of certain diseases, the immediate consequences of smoking usually have the effect of making smoking more likely.

Behavior shaped by contingencies is usually very closely attuned to those contingencies, but shaping by contingencies requires each individual to experience them. This is not only less efficient than following a rule, but sometimes the consequences are quite costly in one way or another (as in developing heart disease from smoking).

The distinction between rule-governed and contingency-shaped behavior is relevant to research methods. As we have already pointed out, describing experimental methods as a set of rules to be blindly followed would not necessarily bring the researcher's behavior under very good control of what is going on with the subject matter. This rule-based approach tends to lead to behavior that is too strongly influenced by theory, the research literature, or factors other than the data from the experiment. In contrast, the approach taken in this book emphasizes the contingencies between the actions of the investigator and the characteristics of the resulting data. Such contingencies tend to shape sound decisions about designing and conducting an experiment, as well as good interpretations of the data, by encouraging close attention to the subject matter. This, in turn, tends to lead to more accurate and complete descriptions of nature—better rules.

---

studies are typically conducted under highly controlled conditions in laboratories, and they may use humans as well as nonhuman species as experimental participants. Much of the research literature, however, tends to apply basic research findings to develop ways of changing behavior for practical purposes. Applied studies are often conducted under fairly everyday circumstances and involve participants appropriate to the applied focus of the study (e.g., school children in a study of ways of teaching reading).

Most behavior analysts are employed not as either basic or applied researchers, however, but under circumstances that require them to provide behavior-change services to a wide variety of individuals. The focus of these services is to improve the lives of the individuals who are served, which is a very different kind of activity from conducting behavioral research (Johnston,

1996). Researchers try to identify empirical generalizations about the relationship between behavior and environment by arranging special conditions designed to answer experimental questions. In contrast, practitioners focus on changing an individual's behavior in targeted ways that solve problems in everyday living faced by the individual and others. Furthermore, practitioners do not typically work in situations where they can establish the degree of experimental control necessary for drawing accurate conclusions about the role of experimental variables.

Role of Research Methods in Practice

In spite of the different interests of researchers and practitioners, they share the same interest in using the best methods of studying behavior. In part, this is because when early applied researchers began studying how basic principles of operant conditioning might be used to develop practical procedures for changing behavior, they used the same research methods that worked so well in laboratory settings. As the applied research literature grew into a useful technology for changing behavior, practitioners continued using well-established methods for measuring changes in behavior and for evaluating the effects of intervention procedures. The result of this history is that today both laboratory researchers and practitioners approach their mutual interest in measuring behavior and assessing the effects of different conditions using much the same methods.

It might seem that giving scientific methods a key role in the practical delivery of behavioral services provides more sophistication than routine applications warrant. In fact, practitioners choose to hold themselves to these methodological standards, as reflected by the coursework requirements of the Behavior Analyst Certification Board (BACB[fi]) for training in this area (Shook, Johnston, & Mellichamp, 2004). The reason for this commitment is that changing an individual's behavior for practical purposes is at least as complex as answering research questions and is anything but routine. Not only is each situation that practitioners face unique, but behavioral treatment procedures are not yet so well developed that they always work as intended. In other words, even the best attempts of well-trained practitioners may at first fail to achieve clinical objectives and require some ongoing adjustments.

Practitioners acknowledge this risk by carefully measuring target behaviors and by evaluating the effects of different behavior-change procedures as a case proceeds. Along the way, the data may suggest revising the definition of the original target behavior or starting measurement of an additional behavior. It is not unusual for data to indicate that intervention procedures are not working exactly as planned. Adjustments to procedures or the substitution of new procedures create new phases of the project whose effectiveness must then be evaluated. Finally, even when an intervention is successful, the durability of the changes usually needs to be monitored for some time after the intervention is discontinued.

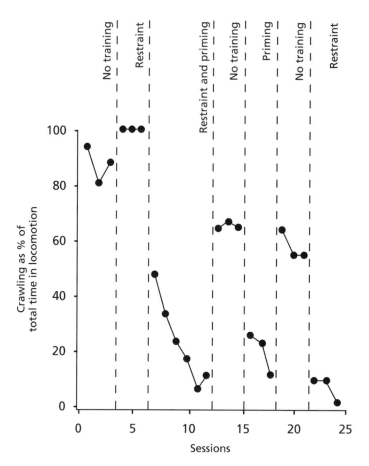

FIG. 1.2. Percentage of total time in locomotion spent crawling by a girl with profound mental retardation. Adapted from O'Brien, F., Azrin, N. H., & Bugle, C. (1972). Training profoundly retarded children to stop crawling. *Journal of Applied Behavior Analysis*, 5, 131–137, p. 134. Copyright 1972 by the Society for the Experimental Analysis of Behavior, Inc. Used by permission.

Figure 1.2 illustrates this kind of situation. The objective in this project was to reduce the amount of crawling by a young girl diagnosed with profound mental retardation in order to encourage her to move about by walking instead (O'Brien, Azrin, & Bugle, 1972). Three 10-minute training sessions were conducted each day and involved an adult located in one corner of a large room encouraging her to come to them. When she got close to the adult, whether by walking or crawling, she was praised and given food reinforcers.

The graph shows the percentage of time spent crawling (as opposed to walking) when she was moving across the room. During an initial baseline phase there was no training or intervention, and she moved mostly by crawling. The first intervention involved making crawling ineffective. They did this by holding her by the waist for 5 seconds each time she started crawling, which prevented her from making progress. Under this condition, she continued to try to get across the room by crawling, although the authors reported that she attempted crawling less often. In the third phase, they continued the restraint procedure but also prompted walking by raising her to a standing position. The data show that the percentage of time spent crawling instead of walking immediately decreased by about half and continued to decline to near zero. The authors next repeated the no-training baseline condition, but this time the child spent only about 60% of her time in motion crawling. When they then evaluated the effects of just priming walking by raising her to a standing position (without any restraint), the data show that crawling immediately decreased to relatively low levels. Following another no-training phase, they again tried the restraint procedure that made crawling ineffective, and the proportion of time spent crawling instead of walking decreased still further.

This example shows the value in a clinical project of measuring behavior carefully and evaluating the effects of each change in procedures. Of course, the authors could not know in advance the effects of each variation in training procedures. What they learned was that making crawling less effective (through the restraint procedure) worked best when it was combined with priming walking behavior rather than when it was used alone. They also learned that priming alone could be effective and that, after these training experiences, merely restraining crawling was much more effective than when it was first used. The availability of an ongoing picture of the child's locomotive behavior (crawling versus walking) allowed them to make a series of informed judgments about what procedural changes might be most effective and then to evaluate their predictions.

The approach to behavioral measurement and evaluation of a series of conditions represented in this example is fundamentally the same as that used by laboratory investigators whose interests are more narrowly scientific. Throughout this book, we will discuss methods for studying behavior in terms of the shared interests of researchers and practitioners.

CHAPTER SUMMARY

1. Scientists are behaving organisms. Their behavior is not special in any way and it is influenced by the same biological and environmental variables underlying the behavior of other species.

2. A behavioral contingency is a relationship between responses and the environmental events preceding and following them. The three-term contingency refers to antecedent and consequent contingencies that are involved in the processes of conditioning or learning. The repertoire of each individual is the result of a history of these contingencies.

3. The research literature studying these contingencies has explained how the basic processes of conditioning work. Applied research has generated

a widely used technology (applied behavior analysis) based on these conditioning processes.

4. It is useful to view the behavior of scientists in the context of conditioning processes because their behavior in designing and conducting experiments can best be understood by looking at the decisions that they must make and the consequences of these actions on the data that their study generates.

5. For example, different ways of defining a target behavior will lead to different kinds of data. Different features of a target behavior may show different effects of an intervention. Decisions about schedules of observation will yield different pictures of responding. Different ways of arranging comparisons between responding under control versus experimental conditions can lead to substantial differences in how data are analyzed.

6. There are three important themes throughout the book: (a) The essence of science lies in the behavior of individual researchers, (b) This behavior results from the same kinds of environmental contingencies that determine all other behavior, and (c) Viewing methodological choices in terms of their antecedents and consequences highlights important distinctions among alternatives and helps investigators to make sound decisions.

7. Conducting an experiment requires the researcher to control the factors whose effects are under study (the independent variable), as well as all of the other factors that are not of interest but might affect how clearly these effects are seen (extraneous variables). At the same time, the investigator must manage procedures for accurately measuring the targeted behavior (the dependent variable) to see if it changes as the independent variable condition is systematically presented or terminated. The researcher's behavior should come under the control of the subject matter (behavior).

8. Scientific method is no more than a loose set of rules and traditions that bring the researcher's behavior under the control of the subject matter, as opposed to prescientific, culturally based convictions.

9. The results of scientific activities are the facts, empirical generalizations, and laws of nature that are discovered. For behavioral science, these products are statements of contingencies that describe the relationship between behavior and other events. These findings guide the behavior of others who have not studied or experienced the contingencies.

10. Researchers try to identify empirical generalizations about the relationship between behavior and environment by arranging special conditions designed to answer experimental questions. In contrast, practitioners focus on changing an individual's behavior in targeted ways that solve problems in everyday living faced by the individual and others. In spite of these differences, both share the same interest in methods of studying or changing behavior. In order to accommodate the risk that interventions might not work as intended, practitioners routinely measure target behaviors and evaluate the effects of behavior-change procedures as a case proceeds.

TEXT STUDY GUIDE

1. The key to understanding how science really works lies in what two basic truths about scientists and their behavior?
2. What is a contingency?
3. Describe the three-term contingency. What are the three terms?
4. How is the three-term contingency a model for behavior?
5. What are three referents for the phrase "applied behavior analysis?"
6. Why is it useful to look at the activities of researchers in light of the three-term contingency?
7. Why is it important to consider the choices that a researcher faces in designing and conducting an experiment?
8. Describe two fundamentally different approaches to comparing the effects of experimental and control conditions.
9. Distinguish between independent and dependent variables.
10. What are extraneous variables?
11. What is probably a major reinforcer that controls how researchers choose to do experiments?
12. How is it that the researcher both controls and is controlled by the subject matter?
13. What is scientific method?
14. What is a key way in which this text is different from others on research methods?
15. What does it mean to describe the products of science as ". . . statements of contingencies that describe the relationship between behavior and other events?"
16. What is the difference between the primary focus of researchers and practitioners?
17. Describe the reasons why it is important for practitioners to use the same methods of measuring behavior and evaluating interventions as researchers?

BOX STUDY GUIDE

1. In what ways are scientists different from nonscientists?
2. What are the differences between behavior controlled by rules and behavior shaped by contingencies?

SUGGESTED READINGS

Austin, J. & Carr, J. E. (2000). *Handbook of applied behavior analysis.* Reno, NV: Context Press.

Catania, A. C. (2007). *Learning* (4th ed.). Cornwall-on-Hudson, NY: Sloan Publishing.

Johnston, J. M. (1996). Distinguishing between applied research and practice. *The Behavior Analyst, 19*, 35–47.

Johnston, J. M., & Pennypacker, H. S. (1993). The development of behavioral research methods: Contributions of B. F. Skinner. In J. M. Johnston & H. S. Pennypacker. *Readings for strategies and tactics of behavior* (pp. 8–17). Hillsdale, NJ: Lawrence Erlbaum Associates.

O'Brien, F., Azrin, N. H., & Bugle, C. (1972). Training profoundly retarded children to stop crawling. *Journal of Applied Behavior Analysis, 5*, 131–137.

Skinner, B. F. (1956). A case history of scientific method. *American Psychologist, 11*, 221–233.

DISCUSSION TOPICS

1. What are some common assumptions about how scientists are different from people working in other fields? If we look at them as no different from other individuals and focus on what they actually do, how does this change how we talk about them?

2. What kinds of consequences for a researcher's decisions in designing and conducting an experiment might be reinforcing, and what kinds might be punishing?

3. In pointing out that scientific methods help to bring the behavior of the investigator under the control of the subject matter, the chapter suggests that other sources of control would otherwise influence methodological decisions. What are some of these alternative influences? Why might their influence be problematic?

4. Select some well-known scientific findings and translate them into if–then contingencies. How do these contingencies save others from having to contact these contingencies personally?

EXERCISES

1. Select some instances of specific behaviors and identify the antecedent events and consequent events surrounding them. Make sure that the examples include both small or trivial responses as well as more obvious or important responses. In what ways are these responses affected by their relationship with antecedent and consequent events.

2. Select an experimental study from a scientific journal and identify the independent variable, the dependent variable, and possible extraneous variables. Does the study have more than one independent variable? What did the investigator(s) do to minimize the influence of extraneous factors?

CHAPTER TWO

Behavior as a Scientific Subject Matter

Science is not just concerned with "getting the facts ..." It leads to a new conception of the subject matter, a new way of thinking about that part of the world to which it has addressed itself.

—B. F. Skinner

THE EVOLUTION OF CONCEPTIONS OF BEHAVIOR

Prescientific

Curiosity about the behavior of living creatures is surely as old as the human species. In the absence of objective discoveries about the causes of behavior, people often simply invented explanations. These prescientific conceptions of behavior were chronicled in the literature of the time. The Greek playwrights wrote of their players' misfortunes as being the will of the Olympian gods. The characters of Shakespeare's plays behave in ways preordained by the existence of tragic flaws in their character. In the Victorian era of Sigmund Freud, moral authority was derived from theological doctrines concerning the nature of human conduct.

Not surprisingly, these invented explanations for human behavior were usually at least partly, if not entirely, wrong. Perhaps more seriously, their legacy is still with us. Prescientific explanations of human behavior were passed on from one generation to another and have long become engrained in our culture and language. As a result, they tended to discourage or at least conflict with early efforts to study behavior scientifically. In spite of scientific advances in other fields, this constraint continues today.

Social Scientific

The latter half of the 19th century marked both the origins of the social sciences and the beginning of attempts to measure behavior. These early efforts primarily focused on defining and quantifying intelligence and a wide array of traits, aptitudes, and cognitive qualities. These data were described and interpreted using newly developed statistical techniques that the young field of psychology embraced in the interest of promoting its scientific intentions. Instead of being the primary subject matter of the social sciences, however, behavior has remained largely a tool used to reveal hypothesized inner processes that are often remnants of prescientific inventions.

Natural Scientific

The emerging natural sciences provided a very different approach to the study of behavior. One of the most important early scientists who approached behavior as an objective subject matter was the Russian physiologist Ivan Pavlov. He insisted on direct measurement and controlled experimentation by systematically manipulating environmental variables. Although Pavlov was primarily interested in the interaction between the central nervous system and digestion, his approach paved the way for the study of behavior not as a means to hypothetical inner processes, but as a subject matter in its own right.

Although others such as John B. Watson played important roles in the early development of a natural science of behavior, it is generally agreed that

B. F. Skinner is the dominant figure in this history. In 1938, Skinner published *The Behavior of Organisms*, in which he described the emergence of this science:

> The investigation of behavior as a scientific datum in its own right came about through a reformation of psychic rather than neurological fictions. Historically, it required three interesting steps. . . . Darwin, insisting upon the continuity of mind, attributed mental faculties to some subhuman species. Lloyd Morgan, with his law of parsimony, dispensed with them in a reasonably successful attempt to account for characteristic animal behavior without them. Watson used the same technique to account for human behavior and to reestablish Darwin's desired continuity without hypothesizing mind anywhere. Thus was a science of behavior born, but under circumstances which can scarcely be said to have been auspicious. The science appeared in the form of a remodeled psychology with ill-concealed evidence of its earlier frame. It accepted an organization of data based upon ancient concepts which were not an essential part of its own structure. It inherited a language so infused with metaphor and implication that it was frequently impossible merely to talk about behavior without raising the ghosts of dead systems. Worst of all, it carried on the practice of seeking a solution for the problems of behavior elsewhere than in behavior itself. (p. 4)

Skinner called for the objective study of behavior for its own sake, rather than for what it might imply about inner processes. He pointed out that the laws of behavior do not depend on what we understand about its underlying biology. Indeed, these laws represent relationships that must eventually be explained by neurological science.

TOWARD A SCIENTIFICALLY USEFUL DEFINITION OF BEHAVIOR

The Nature of Scientific Definitions

In considering the characteristics of behavior that help us differentiate it from other phenomena, it is important to remember that the distinction is ours, not nature's. As scientists, we create distinctions among natural phenomena because these distinctions help us to ask good questions, carry out good experiments, and organize our answers. As we learn more about a particular piece of nature, we revise our conceptions in whatever ways seem appropriate.

In other words, in thinking about how we might define behavior, it is useful to remember that we are simply trying to identify and understand phenomena that share certain characteristics. Any definition is just our best guess at the time about the most useful way to organize our understanding of the world. The usefulness of a definition is often a better criterion for evaluating it than its correctness. After all, it can be sometimes difficult to assess whether a definition is correct because we cannot know what we have yet not discovered about a phenomenon.

BOX 2.1

Inner "Causes"

B. F. Skinner (1953, chapter 3) pointed out that in their early histories all sciences have looked for causes of action inside the things they studied. The problem is not that inner causes cannot be true but that they are likely to be difficult to observe and study. This difficulty may encourage us to be casual in assigning properties to inner causes because it will be difficult for someone to prove us wrong.

Skinner classified the most common inner "causes" of behavior into three categories. *Neural inner causes* use the nervous system as a convenient explanation without clear evidence of its actual role. Our colloquial language offers many such possibilities. We speak of a nervous breakdown or that our nerves are on edge, even though we have merely invented this notion for momentary convenience. Researchers in the social sciences often show the same tendency to rely on hypothetical neural causes, complete with technical terminology.

Psychic inner causes lack the physical dimensions of neural causes, instead referring features of behavior to a corresponding feature of the "mind" or an inner "personality." From this perspective, the inner man (sometimes called a homunculus) is seen as initiating the action; the outer man executes it. The psychic agents might be called processes, faculties, traits, wills, impulses, wishes, instincts, emotions, and so forth. The trap lies in the ease with which they can be given the properties necessary to account for the behavior of interest.

The most common inner causes are what Skinner calls *conceptual inner causes*, and they have neither neurological nor psychic dimensions. These include general qualities such as intelligence, abilities, talents, habits, and so on. However, explanations in these terms are not really causes but redundant descriptions of the same observed facts. If someone is often seen fighting, saying that he does so because he is aggressive, it does not explain why he often fights but only restates this fact in other terms.

Behavior as a Biological Phenomenon

Distinguishing Behavior from Biology. Even as we focus on the study of behavior as a subject matter in its own right, it is important to acknowledge that behavior is fundamentally a biological phenomenon. A science of behavior investigates the ways in which particular behaviors change as a result of interactions between an organism and its environmental circumstances. However, any such changes are also reflected as changes in the organism's biology. These biological processes are the subject matter of other scientific specialties, but they have important consequences for the study of behavior.

Although an organism's behavior is rooted in its biology, it has been useful for researchers to distinguish between them. Although we might like to assume that biological phenomena occur inside the skin and behavior is what happens outside the skin, this has long been recognized as an arbitrary and probably not very useful demarcation. It is true that we are most often interested in behavior that involves movement that others can easily see. However, some movements may be very small or very brief or even going on inside the skin. These characteristics do not mean that they should not be considered as behavior.

For example, Hefferline and Keenan (1963) showed operant control over invisibly small thumb-twitch responses that were measured in microvolts of muscle contraction. Should they be considered behavior? What about the movement of various valves inside the body or the beating of the heart? What about the time required for a movement to occur? Although the duration of most responses we are interested in can be measured in seconds or longer, some movements can occur in fractions of a second. Should they be considered instances of behavior?

The answers to these questions are neither obvious nor certain. The distinction between behavioral and biological events remains somewhat vague and often arbitrary. Perhaps the best we can do is acknowledge that scientific definitions of a phenomenon are limited by what we do not know and are therefore always works in progress. Fortunately, questions such as these do not arise very often. The movements that most researchers and practitioners comfortably call behavior are easily identified and measured by relatively simple, noninvasive methods—often based on no more than visual observation.

Intraorganism Phenomenon. Another implication of the biological basis for behavior is that it occurs only at the level of individual organisms. This may seem obvious, but it conflicts with some popular cultural preconceptions. For example, it means that references to **group behavior** are misleading. A group is not a biological organism and therefore cannot behave. When we talk about a group of individuals responding to some environmental event, it is the individuals in the group who are responding, not the group as a whole. This is true even when the individuals are responding in a coordinated way, such as "doing the wave" at a football game. The **intraorganism** nature of behavior does not imply that individuals might not behave differently in social environments, however. For instance, people might do things as part of a mob that they would not do if they were alone, but even in a mob that it is still individuals who are doing the behaving.

> **Group behavior.** The mathematical result of combining the data from multiple individuals who are related in some way (e.g., exposure to an experimental condition or applied intervention). Does not refer to a natural phenomenon distinct from the behavior of an individual organism.

> **Intraorganism.** A reference to the individual organism as a level of analysis (e.g., behavior is an intraorganism phenomenon in that it involves only relations between the individual organism and its environment).

It follows that if we wish to study the effects of some variable or intervention on behavior we must look for outcomes by examining the behavior of individuals. Even though an intervention in an applied setting may be implemented for all children in a classroom, for example, its effects are on the behavior of each individual child. This also means that if the individual responses are summarized in a group average, the combined data will obscure the real effects of the intervention. They can only be seen by looking at each child's data separately. This point will be discussed further in other chapters. Figure 12.3, for instance, shows how grouped data can hide individual differences in responding.

Movement and Environmental Interaction

Active Movement. Whatever our uncertainties about the boundaries between behavior and biology, it is easy to agree that behavior involves movement or action. As we have already noted, the movements of interest to researchers and practitioners are usually easily observable, at least in principle. The movement of interest may involve gross motor activity (an individual with mental retardation doing his laundry in a group home) or more subtle actions (a child sitting quietly at a desk in a school classroom).

One limitation we might wish to impose is that the actual movement associated with a behavior stems from the organism's biology rather than mere physics. That is, if the movement can be fully explained by the laws of physics—in other words, if it does not require a live organism—we would probably not wish to call it behavior. The **Dead Man's Test** (see Box 2.2) will help to explain this point. For example, although the action of "falling down stairs" involves movement, it does not pass the Dead Man's Test and would not be considered behavior. On the other hand, if you were to fall down the stairs, an observer would see you grab for the railing or try to protect your head. These actions mean that you passed the Dead Man's Test—at least for the moment!

> **Dead Man's Test.** An informal test of whether a particular event is a behavior. The test is that if a dead man can do it, it is not behavior. See Box 2.2.

Behavior as an Interface. This example suggests another consideration for how we define behavior. We know that an organism's behavior results not just from its biology but from the effects of its behavior on the environment.

BOX 2.2

The Dead Man's Test

Ogden Lindsley was a behavioral psychologist at the University of Kansas who devoted much of his career to helping teachers use behavioral principles in the classroom. He described this approach as *Precision Teaching* because of the central role it gives to precisely measuring children's behavior and graphing the data on a standardized graph. Among the many ideas he developed to help teachers learn this technology is the Dead Man's Test, which is a rule for making sure that what teachers target for measurement really is behavior. The rule is quite simple: *If a dead man can do it, it isn't behavior.*

This fact suggests that behavior is the biological result of the interaction between an organism and its environment. Another way to put it is that behavior is not a part of the organism; it is part of the interface between the organism and its environment.

One of the implications of this perspective is that it is not useful to think of behavior as a property or attribute of the organism. Behavior is not something that an organism possesses. A particular behavior is not stored somewhere waiting to be called forth. A behavior exists only when there is a certain interactive condition between an organism and its surroundings. This means that being hungry and being anxious are not behaviors because there is no interactive condition between some action and the environment. Hunger and anxiety are often referred to as "states" of the organism. They refer to real biological conditions, but there is no movement and environmental event that are actively related.

In a similar sense, independent conditions or changes in the environment do not define occurrences of behavior because no interaction is specified. For example, someone walking in the rain gets wet, but "getting wet" is not an instance of behavior. A child may receive tokens for correctly working math problems, but "receiving tokens" is not a behavior. Both examples fail the Dead Man's Test because there is no interactive movement.

Impact on Environment. There is still another implication of thinking about behavior in terms of movements that involve interaction with the environment. It is impossible for a behavior to occur that does not influence the environment in some way. We use some of these environmental effects to measure behavior. That is, when a researcher or practitioner measures the occurrence of individual responses, they are actually measuring some environmental effect of these responses. Often the impact of a response is easy to detect. For instance, a laboratory researcher measures a pigeon's key pecking by recording the displacement of the key. A practitioner measures an individual's progress in learning to make a change by counting the coins that a learner hands to the trainer on each trial following the trainer's prompt.

BOX 2.3

Is Thinking a Behavior?

If it seems obvious that behavior involves movement, what about the "activities" we usually talk about in behavioral terms but for which we can detect no movement? For instance, we often discuss thinking as a behavior (Skinner, 1953), but not even the thinking individual can detect any actual movement. This is a tough problem because we certainly do not want to deny that thinking is something that people do, but how does it qualify as behavior if there is no evident movement?

The solution to this problem goes back to our discussion of the nature of scientific definitions. Even though we cannot define thinking in terms of movements, it has proven useful to conceptualize it as behavior. This approach has the advantage of encouraging researchers and practitioners to approach thinking in the same way that they approach more obvious human activity. From this perspective, thinking is a behavior influenced by antecedent and consequent events, as described by the three-term contingency.

This approach is especially important because the culture has taught us to view thinking as controlled by the mind, a view that is incompatible with scientific investigation. Viewing thinking as behavior is consistent with the philosophy of science called radical behaviorism. This conceptual framework for a science of behavior acknowledges the importance of studying all real aspects of behavioral phenomena but denies scientific legitimacy to qualities that are only fictional (Baum, 2005).

As chapter 6 will discuss, in many applied settings one of the environmental impacts of a behavior is the effect it produces on the behavior of a trained observer. This is a perfectly acceptable approach to measurement as long as two conditions are met. First, the changes in the measuring "instrument" must not be the only evidence of the existence of the behavior. If there is truly no evidence that the behavior exists apart from the measurement process, it is probably not really a behavior. Second, it is important that all statements describing the behavior are in terms of the organism–environment interaction.

In order to understand these two requirements, consider the following examples. If it is said that a person "expects" to do well on a test, is "expecting" a behavior? What is the evidence for the existence of a behavior that we might call "expecting?" Because there is no evident movement involved, the usual evidence that might be offered is some kind of verbal report. This kind of evidence might come from the person's score on a questionnaire in which their responses to various items were combined into measures of "expectation." In this case, we would have to acknowledge that the only basis for talking about expecting as a behavior was the "expectation" score on the questionnaire. Of course, this score partly represents the behavior of the person who designed the instrument. It might be more honest to describe the behavior of the individual who responded to the questions as "filling out questionnaire" behavior. It is certainly not useful to call such behavior "expecting."

As another example, consider referring to the act of helping someone pick up a heavy object as "cooperativeness" or "being cooperative." This raises the question of whether cooperativeness is a behavior. If it is, what is the movement and what are its effects in the environment? If we answer this question by referring to the act of "picking up a box," it could be argued that "picking up a box" would be a more descriptive label than "being cooperative." Perhaps it is better to use "cooperating" as a colloquial label rather than a scientific term. After all, in everyday language, a wide variety of different behaviors under different circumstances might be described as "being cooperative." However, if all such instances were described with this single label it would be difficult to learn about the different behaviors actually involved in each circumstance. We avoid this problem when we relate particular types of actions to certain environmental circumstances.

Meaning of Environment. Finally, it is important to understand that in the study and management of behavior the term "environment" is defined in a specific yet comprehensive way. **Environment** refers to the full set of physical circumstances in which the organism exists. The term is comprehensive in that any facets of the physical world may be considered for their contribution to behavior. The term is specific in that for any particular behavior, the focus is usually on only those environmental events that are functionally related to individual responses. That is, the environmental events that are most important are those related to the behavior in the three-term contingency.

> **Environment.** The complex of physical circumstances in which the organism or referenced part of the organism exists. This includes any physical event or set of events that is not part of a behavior and may include other parts of the organism.

The relevant environment can even include the organism doing the behaving. In a general sense, biological events going on inside the skin are probably always related to behavior. For instance, if you go out for a run on a hot summer afternoon, some of the stimuli related to how far and how fast you run involve your physiology. You may be aware of some of these stimuli (increasing discomfort in your leg muscles), but others you may not be able to sense (various changes in your biochemistry). As another example, when you scratch an itch, the stimulation from your skin probably increases the effectiveness of relief from the itching as a negative reinforcer and makes the behavior of scratching more likely. Our bodies are an ongoing source of antecedent and consequent environmental events related to responding. This fact reminds us that the skin is not an especially important boundary in understanding behavior.

BOX 2.4

Traits and Colloquial Language

By actual count, there are thousands of terms in the English language referring to enduring or temporary traits of human behavior. In discussing the issues they raise for a science of behavior, B. F. Skinner (1953) provided an example of familiar traits using just those starting with the letter "h:"

> "There was a remarkable change in his behavior. Where he had been *happy-go-lucky*, he grew *hesitant* and *heavy-handed*. His natural *humility* gave way to a sustained *haughtiness*. Once the most *helpful* of men, he became *heedless* and *hard-hearted*. A sort of *histrionic horseplay* was all that remained of his fine sense of *humor*." (pp. 194–195)

In everyday language, we use traits as summary references to an individual's behavioral tendencies or characteristics. It would be awkward and time-consuming to describe the behavioral details of many different samples of a person's behavior, so we just summarize our observations. These summaries usually work fairly well for conversational purposes, but they fall well short of the precision of reference required by scientists.

A more serious problem lies in our tendency to use traits not just as summaries of behavior but as causes for the same behavior as well. We do this, for example, when explaining someone's sunny disposition by saying that it is because they are a happy person at heart. As Skinner has observed, there is only one set of behavioral facts involved (observations of the person smiling, laughing, etc.). If we are going to summarize those facts by describing the person in terms of a trait, then using the same facts to explain the trait contributes nothing to our understanding of why the person behaves in this manner. In order to understand the causes of this kind of behavior, we would have to know about the environmental factors in their history that made such behavior likely. The colloquial conception of behavior, however, assumes that traits are somehow inherent qualities in each individual's personality.

A WORKING DEFINITION OF BEHAVIOR

An Interim Guide

As we noted earlier, in drafting a definition of behavior we are guessing about the fundamental nature and extent of a natural phenomenon. It is necessarily a guess because we can never be certain about any characteristics and limits that may lie beyond our present understanding. Furthermore, a definition of behavior is only a bit of verbal behavior, and it certainly does not mean that the phenomenon exactly matches our assumptions. It is important to remember that our task as behavioral scientists is to discover through experimentation the dimensions of behavior and how they relate to other natural phenomena, and not try to force nature to fit our preconceptions.

This perspective suggests that any definition is only an interim guide to help researchers and practitioners do their jobs. The value of a definition of behavior lies in the extent to which it helps researchers to ask good experimental questions, design measurement procedures, and evaluate the impact of experimental variables. For practitioners, a definition of behavior is especially important in deciding how to define and measure target behaviors that are important in everyday life. As upcoming chapters will show, how we define behavior also directs us toward, or away from, certain methodological practices.

A Definition of Behavior

The following definition of behavior identifies the key features of behavior that are important for researchers and practitioners:

> *Behavior is that portion of an organism's interaction with its environment that involves movement of some part of the organism.*

Let us consider the parts of this definition in light of the issues discussed in the previous section. First, it makes clear that behavior is biological in nature by limiting it to organisms. So, for example, references to the "behavior" of the stock market clearly do not meet the requirements of this definition. Any implication that the aggregate effect of buying and selling stocks involves something more than the behavior of individual investors or fund managers misunderstands the nature of behavior as a biological phenomenon.

Second, the definition identifies behavior as an interaction between organism and environment. This focus avoids implying that behavior is a possession of the organism and highlights the requirement for an interactive condition. In other words, the definition identifies behavior as the result of an interactive condition between organism and environment. It is the interface between organism and environment.

Third, the definition specifies that behavior involves movement of some part of the organism. Movement is the most obvious aspect of behavior, of course, and is often the feature of behavior that is observed and recorded. (As we will see later, however, sometimes a behavior can also be defined in terms of its effects rather than the actual movements that produced those effects.) Reference to "some part of the organism" means that although the whole organism participates in behavior, we may sometimes be interested in actions involving only coordinated parts of the organism. For example, when a practitioner is teaching an individual who has had a traumatic brain injury to write her name, the focus will probably be on only certain movements of the fingers, hand, and arm.

Finally, it is important to understand that we intend this definition of behavior to do no more than circumscribe the limits of behavior as a natural phenomenon for the purpose of scientific study and delivery of behavioral services. It is certainly not an adequate guide for defining particular instances of behavior that a researcher or practitioner wishes to measure. Chapter 4 will address this need in detail.

SOME IMPLICATIONS

Inclusions and Exclusions

The task for any definition is distinguishing what belongs in the defined category from what does not. Although at first this definition of behavior might seem narrow, it is actually broadly inclusive. Any movement of an organism involving an interactive condition with the environment fits its basic requirements. This includes a truly infinite array of actions. In fact, making up a comprehensive list of behaviors would be impossible if only because we do not have enough different labels to accommodate all of the different behaviors we could identify.

If discussing the inclusiveness of the definition is almost pointless, perhaps examining its exclusions will help to clarify its usefulness. The definition denies behavioral status to all of the following:

1. Events that do not involve an organism.
2. Events that do not involve the physical environment.
3. Events that do not apparently involve movement.
4. Movements that do not involve an interactive condition between organism and environment.
5. Events for which the sole evidence is their effect on a measuring instrument.

In summarizing this list, these exclusions suggest that anything that does not involve a live organism interacting with the physical environment is probably not usefully called behavior. If this is a good definition for guiding scientific research and clinical practice, its requirements should exclude only events that are more usefully described in other ways.

Actually, calling them "events" may sometimes be too generous. For example, in considering whether cognitive "activities" meet the requirements of this definition, it may be important to ask whether the "event" in question involves the physical environment. If it is said that a person is "anticipating" a trip to the dentist, it is fair to ask if "anticipating" is a physical event. Failure to meet the terms of this definition certainly does not mean that cognitive "activities" do not occur but how are we to know if they do? How can we know what they are and how they are different from physiological events in the brain that are already described in terms of physical or chemical measures?

BOX 2.5

Theory, Concepts, and Observability

It is important to understand that the methodological problems faced by cognitive researchers are not that the focus of their interests seems to be unobservable. Many phenomena of scientific interest are not directly observable, but this has not proven to be a serious stumbling block in the development of the natural sciences. The problem, at least in part, is that their explanatory concepts are based on unobservables located inside the organism (Lee, 1981). To understand this problem, it is necessary to consider the nature of scientific theory.

Skinner (1961) identified three stages of theory building. The first stage involves identifying the basic data. This has proven a considerable challenge in psychology, although behavior analysts long ago decided that behavior would be a sufficient source. The second stage focuses on expressing relations among these data. This effort culminates in well-established laws or summaries of consistent relationships. The science of behavior has made considerable headway on this task. The third stage goes beyond observable relationships to unobservable concepts. For instance, Galileo studied the relationship between the position of a ball on an inclined plane and the elapsed time since its release, and developed the unobservable concept of acceleration. (He did not, however, attribute acceleration to a force inherent in the ball.) Skinner (1961) emphasized the importance of this stage by pointing out that terms like wants, faculties, attitudes, drives, ideas, interests, and capacities should be developed as proper scientific concepts at this level.

In other words, theories are built on concepts that refer to unobservable features of the observable subject matter. These unobservable concepts must not be simply invented, however. In order for a theory to work, it must emerge from a sound database describing functional relations in the subject matter. Ultimately, explanation in the natural sciences is made in terms of such theories (Lee, 1981).

Although researchers can now directly measure brain activity of some kind when a person is engaging in some task, it is risky to assume that these images reflect specific cognitive qualities or functions. Without such physical referents, researchers interested in studying cognitive phenomena face the most difficult of scientific challenges—studying events whose very existence is unclear.

Challenges like these result from the fact that psychology is burdened with cultural preconceptions about human nature. Not surprisingly, a definition of behavior based on sound scientific findings fails to accommodate many of these preconceptions. Some readers may even feel that the definition leaves no place for cherished human qualities. It may help to consider that these omissions are only a matter of the difference between how we have learned to talk about behavior in everyday life and what is really there.

For instance, when we speak of someone as having a particular attitude, we imply that attitudes really exist as physical things. The fallacy in this assumption can be uncovered by considering what prompts us to describe someone as having a certain attitude. In fact, it is observing this person doing something or emitting certain behaviors under certain conditions that encourages us to use the attitudinal terms we have been taught by our verbal community. At best, attitudes are only crude ways of summarizing many instances of behavior. They may be convenient for everyday conversation, but they are not useful for researchers because they lead to scientific dead ends.

The problem, then, is not that the definition of behavior leaves out real aspects of human nature but that the culture has "created" so many fictional qualities. It is only how we have learned to talk about behavior that implies that these qualities actually exist nonphysically "inside" us. In fact, when researchers study mental activity, they almost always measure either behavior or physiological events because that is all there is to measure. They must then infer some relationship between their measures of these physical phenomena and the mental "events" of interest. The resulting subject matter is therefore a collection of these kinds of culturally based assumptions. This sets psychology and the social sciences apart from sciences that investigate phenomena whose existence is the basis for, rather than the result of, experimental inquiry.

BOX 2.6

Parsimony

Even though it is not often spoken of, *parsimony* is one of the most respected attitudes of science. In a word, it means to be stingy. Scientists are parsimonious in their preference for exhausting simple and well-established explanations of phenomena before turning to complex and less-well-understood explanations. Scientists follow this strategy because they have learned over the years that it makes science more efficient. It helps to avoid wild goose chases and blind alleys, which are always a risk in scientific research. Instead of offering fanciful explanations of some event, scientists cautiously insist on trying to explain the event in terms of laws that they already understand fairly well because the odds of successful resolution are usually better than with more "far out" notions.

This approach urges us to explain the observable facts of behavior with reference to variables in the physical world, which the natural sciences understand pretty well, before inventing a nonphysical world of the psyche, which certainly goes beyond the laws of nature. We need to remember the principle of parsimony when we theorize about human qualities and their explanation.

Learning to talk about behavior, especially human behavior, without using familiar everyday terms is difficult at first. The correct terms seem awkward and insufficient, and something often seems left out. The richness with which we talk about behavior in ordinary language is clearly missing. After all, we have had a lifetime of informal "training" from our verbal community in how to talk about human behavior. It may be some consolation to realize that students new to other sciences such as biology, physics, and chemistry typically face the same challenges. Unfortunately, the colloquial language that works so well for poets contrasts with the need for a precise scientific vocabulary that is devoid of surplus meaning and limited to real events. With a scientific language that follows rather than leads discovery, behavioral researchers are uncovering the kind of richness and complexity that scientists long ago revealed in other natural phenomena.

Methodological Consequences

As the chapters in this book unfold, it will become clear that the primary importance of this definition of behavior lies in how it guides researchers and practitioners to work with this subject matter. Almost every facet of the methods described in this book is partly based on the implications of this definition. In fact, these methods have emerged from what science has already taught us about behavior. We know, for example, that behavior occurs only at the level of individuals, that it has effects on the environment and is in turn affected by the environment, that it is a continuous process, and that what has happened with a particular behavior in the past may continue to influence it in the present. Of course, these are only a few of the most basic facts about behavior. Over the years, the accumulating research literature has revealed a wealth of general principles and complex details (see, for example, Catania, 2007).

When we look to an evolving understanding of behavior for guidance about the best ways to study and manage it, a number of experimental practices seem important. For instance, in order to capture all of the fundamental qualities of behavior, we need to measure the behavior of each participant separately. Furthermore, we need to keep each individual's data separate as we analyze their performance. As we have already suggested, combining observations of different participants into group averages makes it difficult to see any differences in how interventions affected the behavior of each individual.

What we know about behavior also suggests that it is important to measure a target behavior a number of times under each phase of an experiment or a clinical intervention. Any behavior is influenced by its continuously evolving history, and the more recent the history, the greater its impact. This means that we can get a clear picture of any particular environmental condition only if we give each participant enough exposure to that condition to be sure that the effects we see on the target behavior are due primarily to that condition and not to prior experiences.

The following chapters will explain these and many other methodological practices that have proven to be highly effective for behavioral researchers and practitioners. The scientific "bottom line" is that nature's secrets will be revealed only when we ask the right questions in the right way. We cannot force nature to fit our preconceptions and methods. Those who work with

BOX 2.7

Pure versus Quasi-Behavioral Research

The ways in which investigators approach behavior as a scientific subject allow a distinction between pure behavioral research and quasi-behavioral research (Johnston & Pennypacker, 1993b). *Pure behavioral research* uses methodological practices that preserve the fundamental qualities of behavior in undisturbed and uncontaminated form. *Quasi-behavioral research* is based on data that originated with observations of behavior but whose methods prevent the data from representing its fundamental qualities fully and without distortion or contamination.

Another way of characterizing this distinction is between studies designed to learn about the effects of environmental variables on behavior versus studies that use behavioral data to learn about behavior in a more superficial or informal sense. Pure behavioral research requires identifying relationships at the level of the individual, whereas quasi-behavioral research may permit aggregating the data from different individuals.

For example, in a study analyzing the behavioral effects of a treatment procedure, interest may lie in understanding not just its main effects, but the reasons why those effects occur. Such corollary questions might concern the role of different components of the treatment procedure, whether participant characteristics are relevant to the effects, and the factors that will ensure that the treatment yields consistent effects. These interests would require measuring and analyzing the behavior of individual subjects, which is where the treatment's effects actually occur.

On the other hand, an investigator's interest might be more superficial, limited to a statistical description of the average outcomes of the treatment. In this case, collating data across participants might be quite permissible. However, this would prevent the investigator from finding a clear answer to more analytical questions that require understanding what is happening at the level of the individual participant. Using behavioral data to answer questions about aggregate outcomes can be quite legitimate. However, the investigator should not suggest that the grouped data represent the effects observed for each individual or argue that the study identified the reasons for the aggregate outcome.

Choosing one kind of behavioral interest over the other should be done at the outset based on the focus of the question. However, this distinction often unintentionally results from the experimenter's methodological decisions. A study aimed at discovering behavior–environment relationships can become quasi-behavioral by incorporating methodological practices that prevent a clear picture of the fundamental qualities of behavior.

The challenge lies in figuring out when each type of question about behavior is appropriate, as well as being willing to live within the interpretive constraints required by the way the experiment is conducted. This text focuses on pure behavioral research interests. In doing so, it highlights the weaknesses of some tactics (such as aggregating data across individuals) that might otherwise be acceptable in studies aimed at quasi-behavioral interests.

behavior must adapt the general principles of scientific method that have worked so well with other sciences and their technologies to suit the features of behavior.

CHAPTER SUMMARY

1. Prescientific conceptions of behavior were invented to explain what people did not understand. They have become part of the culture and tend to discourage scientific investigation and conflict with its results.

2. Social scientific approaches to studying and explaining behavior tend to be based on hypothesized inner processes (prescientific fictions) and to use inferential statistical techniques as a methodological framework.

3. The natural scientific approach to studying behavior involves direct measurement and controlled experimentation and focuses on studying behavior for its own sake, rather than as a way of "getting at" inner processes.

4. Behavior is a biological phenomenon, but the skin is not a useful dividing line between behavior and biology. The distinction is somewhat arbitrary and not often important.

5. The biological basis for behavior makes it clear that behavior occurs only at the level of individual organisms. This means that there is no such phenomenon as group behavior because groups are not organisms. When people behave in a way influenced by others, each is still behaving individually. Group data cannot reveal behavioral effects.

6. Behavior involves movement, though it can be subtle. The Dead Man's Test is an easy way to determine if movement is involved in a definition of a behavior.

7. Behavior results from interactions between the organism and its environment and is therefore not a part of or possessed by the organism. This means that "states" of the organism, even real biological conditions, are not behavior, and neither are independent conditions or changes in the environment behavior.

8. Behavior must have some impact on the environment, however small in some cases. This effect is often what is measured in research, although such data must not be the only evidence that the behavior exists.

9. Environment refers to the physical circumstances of the organism, including its own body.

10. Following from these considerations, behavior is defined as that portion of an organism's interaction with its environment that involves movement of some part of the organism. This definition excludes events that do not involve an organism, events that do not involve the physical environment, events that do not apparently involve movement, movements that do not involve an interactive condition between organism and environment, and

events for which the sole evidence is their effect on a measuring instrument.

11. The definition of behavior guides methodological decisions made by researchers and practitioners in ways detailed in subsequent chapters. Research will only be effective to the extent that we adapt our experimental methods to the nature of this subject matter.

TEXT STUDY GUIDE

1. The authors pointed out that the natural science approach to behavior involved accepting behavior as a subject matter in its own right. What does this mean?

2. What function does a scientific definition of a phenomenon serve?

3. Why is the skin not a good basis for distinguishing between biology and behavior?

4. What does it mean to say that behavior is an intraorganism phenomenon?

5. What is group behavior?

6. What is the Dead Man's Test?

7. What are some examples of "behaviors" that do not pass the Dead Man's Test?

8. "Behavior is the biological result of the interaction between an organism and its environment." Why does this suggest that behavior is not a property, attribute, or possession of the organism?

9. Why is it that real or hypothetical states cannot be behavior?

10. Why is "waiting for someone" not a behavior?

11. Can you think of an example of a behavior that does not affect the environment in some way? If you can, are you sure that it meets the requirements of the definition of behavior?

12. What would be the problem if the only evidence for the existence of a supposed behavior was from the measurement process?

13. What does it mean to say that there must be some independent evidence of the existence of a behavior?

14. Why is "aggression" or "being aggressive" not usefully referred to as a behavior?

15. Explain how an individual can be part of the environment for his or her own behavior.

16. What are three key implications of the definition of behavior?

17. Why could researchers not develop a comprehensive catalog of all human behaviors?

18. What is a good one-sentence summary of the exclusions implied by the definition of behavior?

19. Describe the influence of cultural language on how we talk about and explain behavior.

20. What are the problems for a science of behavior with hypothesizing mental qualities?

BOX STUDY GUIDE

1. What is wrong with referring to "inner causes" in attempting to explain behavior?

2. Define and provide examples of neural, psychic, and conceptual inner causes.

3. What is the Dead Man's Test?

4. Explain the reasons why it is useful to conceptualize thinking as a behavior, even though there is no obvious movement.

5. Describe two reasons why traits are not useful concepts for a science of behavior.

6. What are the three stages of theory building that Skinner described?

7. How does the approach to explaining unobservable concepts taken by the natural sciences differ from that often found in cognitive psychology?

8. Describe the scientific attitude of parsimony.

9. How is the scientific attitude of parsimony relevant to how behavioral scientists approach a definition of behavior?

10. Distinguish between pure and quasi-behavioral research.

11. What are the limitations of quasi-behavioral research?

SUGGESTED READINGS

Baum, W. M. (2005). *Understanding behaviorism* (2nd ed.). Malden, MS: Blackwell Publishing.

Hefferline, R. F., & Keenan, B. (1963). Amplitude-induction gradient of a small-scale (covert) operant. *Journal of the Experimental Analysis of Behavior, 6,* 307–315.

Moore, J. (2008). *Conceptual foundations of radical behaviorism.* Cornwall-on-Hudson, NY: Sloan Publishing. [Chapter 4: Behavior as a subject matter in its own right]

DISCUSSION TOPICS

1. Consider phenomena at the boundary between behavior and biology, such as heart beating, burping, etc. Discuss the pros and cons of considering these as behavioral or biological events.

2. Discuss how to study the actual behaviors involved in what might generally be talked about as group phenomena, such as a conversation between two people, three friends loading a sofa on a pickup truck, or a riot.

3. Discuss the list of exclusions resulting from the definition of behavior. Is there anything else the definition seems to exclude? If so, consider why these exclusions might not actually be behavioral events.

EXERCISES

1. Come up with examples of what might usually be referred to as behavior but would not pass the Dead Man's Test.

2. Choose some examples of everyday behaviors that we do not pay much attention to and figure out their specific effects on the environment.

Asking Experimental Questions

There are doubtless many men whose curiosity about nature is less than their curiosity about the accuracy of their guesses, but it may be noted that science does in fact progress without the aid of this kind of explanatory prophecy.

—B. F. Skinner

THE NATURE OF EXPERIMENTAL QUESTIONS

Questions as Verbal Behavior

Before an investigator can actually begin a study, he or she must have some experimental question that can guide methodological decisions and interpretations. Developing such questions is a task that may seem difficult at first, but the more you know about a particular topic of interest, the easier it is to come up with a variety of questions. The real challenge, however, is not just finding a question but figuring out the best question for the topic under investigation.

Asking good questions is a challenge not only for researchers. When practitioners need to change an individual's behavior, there are a number of questions they must answer. These questions come from assessing the nature of behavioral deficits or excesses and designing interventions intended to produce specific behavioral outcomes. For example, assessment procedures usually involve collecting behavioral data under specific conditions in order to determine the nature of the target behavior and the variables influencing it. Sometimes these assessment procedures are explicitly experimental in style (Iwata, Vollmer, & Zarcone, 1990).

Furthermore, treatment programs aimed at changing a target behavior often take the form of informal experiments. Most interventions involve a series of phases in which specific environmental variables are manipulated in order to produce particular changes in a target behavior. Ongoing measurement allows practitioners to evaluate the effects of each adjustment of intervention procedures. (This is illustrated in chapter 1 by the project focusing on increasing walking and decreasing crawling with a girl diagnosed with mental retardation.) Sometimes these adjustments are planned, but when expected outcomes are not obtained, the clinician must figure out what changes may be more effective. At this point, the practitioner is asking the same kind of questions that researchers might entertain (What are the effects of this condition?).

Whether developed by a researcher or a practitioner, perhaps the most important fact about experimental questions is that they are verbal behavior. This means that investigators do not "create" experimental questions any more than they "create" other behavior such as eating, driving a car, or watching a baseball game. Furthermore, composing research questions is not the only behavior of interest. This behavior is the result of an extended process involving the reading of experimental and clinical literature, talking with colleagues, and writing and thinking about the topic of interest. Being aware of the behavioral status of experimental questions helps us to consider both the factors that influence question-asking behavior and how these questions affect the way we design, conduct, and interpret experiments.

Sources of Control

Graduate Training. Although it may often be overlooked, graduate training is certainly one of the most powerful influences on question-asking behavior. It is in graduate school that we are metaphorically conceived as scientists or practitioners. Through the contributions of our professors, we gestate as fetal behavioral scientists and practitioners. We are finally thrust out of the ivy-covered womb wearing only a scanty thesis or dissertation, still very much a neonate in a field that is itself still relatively young.

We come to graduate school knowing relatively little about this field and leave with an extensive professional repertoire. Along the way, we learn to restrict much of our culturally learned repertoire about behavior to everyday situations. A specialized, scientific verbal repertoire about behavior gradually replaces this colloquial repertoire in a growing range of professional circumstances.

This academic experience also creates a variety of powerful professional reinforcers that influence our behavior throughout our careers. As a result, for some, laboratory research may be more reinforcing than clinical practice. Working with individuals diagnosed with mental retardation who live in group homes may be more enjoyable than working with children with autism spectrum disorders in school settings. Others may prefer working as supervisors or managers in business environments. Certain issues in the research literature are likely to be much more interesting than others. These preferences often stay with us throughout our careers and lead us in one direction or another as researchers or practitioners.

Experimental Literature. One of the effects of graduate school is to make the research literature of the field a powerful influence over our professional activities, especially on how we develop experimental questions. Of course, any single individual can be familiar with only some areas of the field's literature. Although this unavoidable specialization is a blessed relief to the overachievers among us, it also means that we might not be aware of studies that could be relevant to our interests.

The primary literature concerning a topic should guide the development of research questions. That is, if an investigator is interested in learning more about stimulus equivalence (Sidman, 1994), for example, it is natural that the existing literature on this topic would be the best place to look for guidance about what has already been accomplished and what issues need attention.

However, it is also important to examine broader areas of literature that might suggest useful ways of approaching the issue of interest. Some areas of literature might represent conceptual perspectives and methodological practices that are not well suited to the study of behavioral phenomena. However, behavioral researchers can often find ideas in such literature that merit improved experimental attention. Deguchi (1984), for example, reviewed the literature on observational learning and provided interpretations of this distinctively cognitive literature that suggested interesting opportunities for behavioral researchers.

Finally, familiarity with the field's literature contributes to a researcher's overall perspective about its general directions and needs. This sense of where the field is going and where it needs to go are important influences on how a researcher reacts to particular studies in a literature. A newly published experiment does not lead everyone in the same direction, and some directions will probably be more productive than others. The best experimental questions lead to answers that are not only useful for a specific topic but serve the larger interests of the field.

Observing Behavior. Relying too heavily on the archival literature as a source of experimental questions carries its risks. Questions that emerge from published studies naturally tend to pursue the general directions already established in the literature. This is not necessarily bad, but it can lead to the questions gradually becoming more about the literature than about the phenomenon of interest. To the extent that an area of research does not probe all of the interesting possibilities, it is less likely that new questions will move into uncharted areas. This was one of the complaints made by Zeiler (1984) concerning the state of research on schedules of reinforcement.

It is a matter of balance. How researchers develop questions should be influenced not only by the existing literature but by our experiences with the subject matter itself. Behavior is a phenomenon that is always present in accessible and relevant forms. The well-trained behavioral scientist is skilled in observing behavior in any settings. Even observations from everyday life can lead to fruitful research directions. This finding has a long tradition in other sciences, and in his autobiographical volumes B. F. Skinner (1976, 1979, 1983) revealed that his contributions to the study of behavior often had such origins. Many examples of his lifelong observations of behavior in daily life are captured in a sampling of entries from his notebooks (Epstein, 1980).

Existing Resources. It is understandable that researchers tend to develop experimental questions that fit the resources to which they have access. If an investigator is affiliated with an early intervention program for children with autism, it is unlikely that he or she would consider questions that required a laboratory setting and rats as subjects. Budgetary or personnel limitations have a similar constraining effect on scientific curiosities. Of course, this argument can be turned around. Existing resources encourage investigators to search for sound questions that can make good use of participants, settings, and other experimental necessities that are already available.

Whether existing resources facilitate or constrain the kinds of questions asked by each investigator, the real issue is how well the resulting question suits the needs of the literature on a topic. If investigators tend to frame questions based on access to a particular kind of setting or type of participant, could this priority make it less likely that the literature on a topic will grow in needed directions? This possibility suggests that it may be important to balance

BOX 3.1

Research Styles

Scientific research has little in common with the fashion industry, but there are different styles of investigation. Instead of changing seasonally, these styles can be observed year after year in all scientific disciplines. The style of a research project refers to the function that it serves for the experimenter and the effect that it has on the field. A study's style is largely determined by its question and the question's impact on how the researcher designs, conducts, and interprets the experiment.

These research styles sometimes come in complementary pairs. For instance, a **thematic research** style can be contrasted with an **independent research** style (see Box 3.2). A thematic study is designed to fit into a predetermined position in a larger research program or area of literature, whereas an independent experiment is not conceived of in the context of any ongoing program or research area. These differences have important consequences for the field (see Box 3.2).

Another contrasting pair of research styles may be labeled **demonstration research** versus **explanatory research**. Demonstration research focuses on showing that a certain result is possible, which can be a very important achievement. In contrast, explanatory research strives for an understanding of how and why certain relationships work. Although they can be valuable, demonstration studies leave important questions unanswered because they fail to follow up and show why their results occurred. This is why it is important that any area of literature have many explanatory studies for each demonstration study.

Pilot and **in-house research** styles often involve methodological short cuts. Pilot research is conducted as a preliminary effort to learn things that will guide a more substantial experimental project. The risk is that the preparatory nature of the effort will justify weak or sloppy methods, which will be an unsound basis for making decisions about how to conduct the planned research project. Research that is only designed for local or in-house use carries the same risk. Sidman (1960) offered a simple rule for avoiding such problems: If the methods are sound, then conclusions are justified; if not, then conclusions may be inappropriate.

A research style that raises a similar concern about what the outcomes mean results from a researcher using experiments to advocate for a particular result. **Advocacy research** may involve decisions about what to do and how to do it that are biased toward the investigator's interests in getting certain results (see Box 3.3). Such studies can often be identified by examining the focus of the question and the related methodological decisions. These choices may facilitate a certain result instead of evaluating the impact of experimental conditions in a neutral manner. The risk is that the findings may differ from those that would have been obtained from a less biased approach.

Finally, although these research styles represent important aspects of how scientists approach their work, these distinctions are not "official" in any way, and you can look for other styles as you learn more about research literatures. Each of these research styles will be discussed further as they appear in different chapters.

the influence of existing resources with consideration of the larger needs of
the literature in the area of interest. The published studies on a topic can guide
the development of new experimental questions by revealing uncertainties
that need to be resolved, weaknesses in experiments that should be overcome,
issues that have not yet been addressed, and where research interests are going
over time. The importance of using the literature as a touchstone in developing
experimental questions suggests that questions that *can* be pursued are not
necessarily those that most *need* to be pursued. The goal is that each research
project be as useful as possible, not just for the investigator but for the larger
scientific community.

Experimental Contingencies. For many investigators, experimental
questions flow from an ongoing program of research. In one way or another,
each study may provide the foundation for the next. One study often yields
findings that suggest a new question. Sometimes this next question might have
been anticipated from the outset, but it is common for the emerging data to
point toward the next project. (If researchers could accurately predict their
results there would be little reason to do experiments.) It may also be the case
that the results of a study are unclear or confusing. For example, it may be that
some participants reacted to a condition in one way and others responded in
a different way. This kind of result begs for resolution, usually by trying to
determine what factors underlie the different outcomes. Finally, conducting a
study may reveal problems with measurement procedures or how control and
experimental conditions were designed or implemented. These problems may
need to be corrected by conducting an improved study.

These outcomes are consequences for the investigator's behavior in
planning and conducting the experiment. Such contingencies are a valuable
influence on asking questions because they encourage thematic research
efforts. In contrast to experiments conceived independently of other studies,
experiments conducted in a thematic research style fit systematically into
the literature on a topic and are designed to serve particular functions for
that literature. Although experiments developed more independently of the
literature may be quite sound in every respect, studies designed to play a
specific role in relation to past and future research projects are likely to be
especially valuable for the field (see Box 3.1).

Extra-Experimental Contingencies. Another set of contingencies may
have somewhat different effects. These contingencies might be described as
extra-experimental because they do not directly concern the details of the
experiment or its role in the literature. Instead, these contingencies involve the
nonscientific consequences of a study's results. These include professional
reputation, grants, patents, consulting contracts, books, tenure and promotion,
access to a setting and population, and so forth.

When these issues intrude on the process of developing experimental
questions, the resulting findings may not always be in the best interests of the
field. They can lead to questions that serve personal interests more than the

---

BOX 3.2

Thematic versus Independent Research Styles

Researchers who design experiments that are related to other studies in specific ways are using a **thematic research** style. Any experimental question can lead to thematic research. The key is that the study is part of a coherent program or aims at filling in gaps in the literature. With this approach, the resulting picture is likely to be complete and easily interpretable. The value of thematic research lies in the integration of the resulting data. Thematic findings are likely to have collectively greater utility than the results from the same number of independent experiments addressing the same topic because they were designed to fit together, like pieces of a jigsaw puzzle.

An **independent research** style results from a researcher conceiving of a study independently of any coordinated research program or even the existing literature. In other words, such studies are not designed to precede or follow other studies in a predetermined way. They often originate from opportunistic situations having to do with the availability of subjects or a setting. Experiments conducted in an independent style may be perfectly worthy studies in every way, and their results may be quite useful. Sometimes their importance may only become clear at a later point in a literature's development. This style becomes a problem, however, when it tends to dominate a literature or field. It can lead to a lack of cohesiveness among studies and contribute to a lack of direction in the literature.

---

needs of the literature. More extreme examples of this influence can involve biased interpretations or even fudging the data in some way, although this outcome is rare.

Developing and Phrasing Questions

A Strategic Approach. It is not difficult to come up with experimental questions. Even modest familiarity with an area of literature will suggest possibilities. At times it almost seems as easy as starting a sentence with "Which," "Why," "What," or "When" and ending it with a question mark. Even such casual questions might be able to generate a workable experiment.

The challenge for investigators is more demanding than this. Their objective is to develop a question whose subsequent experiment will generate data that are more revealing and useful than might be produced by any other question. What this objective implies is that for any area of literature some questions are simply better than others. The best question for a topic results from a process of comparing and refining possible questions in the context of the literature. Eventually, one question will seem to be better than the rest, at least to a particular investigator.

BOX 3.3

Advocacy Research

When an experiment's question, procedures, and write up suggest that the investigator's primary goal was to generate support for a predetermined conclusion, it can be called **advocacy research**. Because an investigator has preconceptions about the topic of a study and an interest in how the data turn out, does not mean that the experimental procedures and interpretations will be inappropriately biased. However, when the extra-experimental contingencies are powerful, there is naturally a good chance that the way an experiment will be conceived, conducted, and interpreted will be biased in favor of the preferred outcome, even if the researcher is unaware of this impact.

The ways in which a study can be improperly prejudiced are endless, ranging from asking a question that looks only for a desired outcome, to making measurement and design decisions that facilitate preferred results and discourage contrary data. Sometimes the most obvious evidence of an advocacy posture is the tone of the published report.

We all have our prejudices, and it is the rare scientist who can scrupulously ignore all of them. But when the influence of such partialities begins to interfere with conducting a fair experiment, the result can be promoting results that are less than fully true or do not hold up well when others use them. Under these conditions, the researcher has taken on the role of an advocate who defends a cause, not a scientist who searches for understanding.

Along the way, perfectly sound questions may be bypassed in favor of one that is a bit better. This approach certainly does not mean that these good questions should never be dignified by an experiment. The researcher may find some candidate questions worthy of experimental attention at a later point. Different investigators may believe some of these other questions to be the best from their perspective. Each researcher that takes this approach to developing questions will certainly not decide on the same "best" question.

The objective of figuring out the best question for a particular topic is inevitably a productive and profitable activity. Carefully sifting through existing studies, considering different research issues, and comparing one question to another can only lead to more useful experiments and research literatures. Even though different investigators will arrive at different choices, the field will surely gain from such efforts. Without this kind of investment in developing experimental questions, there is a greater risk that a field's literature will be less useful than it could be. This can be an expensive risk. Any field's scientific resources are finite, and studies that fail to make valuable contributions take the place of those that might have generated more valuable findings.

Criteria. What makes one question better than another? This is a difficult challenge. Great questions tend to be those that go to the heart of an issue and lead to experimental findings that help to resolve the issue. Great questions address gaps in existing knowledge so that their results help to complete a picture. Great questions overcome weaknesses in other studies, correct misunderstandings, or clarify what was previously unclear. Great questions show new possibilities or identify new directions that turn out to be valuable. Perhaps we could summarize these criteria by stating that, above all, great questions lead to results that are importantly useful to other researchers or to practitioners.

What does it take to generate such questions? Certainly the researcher must be thoroughly familiar with the relevant literature. The focus, methods, and findings of published studies should be considered carefully in order to see if there are weaknesses or omissions that might need to be addressed. The relationship among studies should be assessed to determine what is clearly known, what is unclear, and what is only suspected to be true.

Beyond this general advice, it is hard to say what criteria might assure that one question will be better than another. Nevertheless, scientists routinely confront this challenge themselves, as well as make their own assessments of the questions posed by their colleagues. In fact, the soundness of the experimental question is one of the standards that peer reviewers use in deciding whether to fund a research proposal or recommend that an experimental report be accepted for publication in a journal.

Wording. We began this chapter by pointing out that experimental questions are the verbal behavior of investigators. Let us look at this verbal behavior more closely. It turns out that committing a specific question to paper is a revealing and educational task. Sometimes what is revealed is that there really is no question as such. That is, the real interest may lie more in demonstrating an outcome that is already known or at least strongly suspected than in learning something new. Demonstration studies certainly have their place in science, but their focus is often more in the form of a prediction ("this will happen when you do that") than a question. For example, in 1949 Paul Fuller, a graduate student at Indiana University, showed that he could systematically increase and decrease a simple motor response by a profoundly retarded individual (Fuller, 1949). This early demonstration of operant conditioning applied to human behavior was important because it showed that profoundly retarded individuals could indeed learn, a conviction not widely held at the time. However, Fuller's demonstration did not explain the variables responsible for his results (although they are now well understood).

Another observation is that questions are sometimes not actually asking about behavior. They may instead focus on a theoretical issue or a method of controlling behavior. It is common in the applied literature for studies to assess whether a certain procedure will change behavior in particular ways. Although such questions clearly involve behavior, their primary focus tends to lie with procedures. This emphasis is not improper in any way, but such questions may reveal less about behavior than questions that directly ask about behavior. For example, a study by Fisher, Piazza, Bowman, Hagopian, Owens, and Slevin

(1992) compared two approaches for identifying reinforcers for individuals with severe and profound mental retardation. Although their results were clear and valuable, the outcomes revealed more about the procedures being compared than the behavior of individuals with significant disabilities.

These examples suggest that it is important to recognize the subtle themes implied by how questions are phrased. The real interest of the investigator

---

BOX 3.4

Experimental Questions versus Hypotheses

Although this chapter is about experimental questions, you may be surprised that we hardly mention hypotheses. In a way, a hypothesis is the opposite of an experimental question. Instead of asking a question, a **hypothesis** states a conjecture or prediction about the outcome of an experiment, which is a fancy way of referring to an educated guess. In this sense, all researchers have hypotheses or make speculations about the outcomes of their experiments. If an investigator had absolutely no suspicions about how a study might turn out, he or she could probably be accused of not knowing the relevant literature very well. Furthermore, even though scientists are supposed to be fairly neutral or at least open to any and all results, it is the rare investigator who does not have some preference for one outcome over another.

Any such speculation can be dressed up and called a hypothesis as long as you understand the risks of doing so. Because even the best investigators do not approach their studies in a completely neutral manner, there is a real possibility that any biases will have an impact on how experiments are designed, conducted, and interpreted. When the investigator replaces the experimental question with a public commitment in the form of a hypothesis, the prediction only increases this risk. Having forecast the experiment's outcome, it is understandably tempting to design and conduct the study in a way that confirms the prediction. This certainly does not mean that researchers who state formal hypotheses intentionally bias their experimental decisions, but there are many ways of increasing the chances of getting the "right" results that have become an accepted part of this tradition. One such tactic is to increase the number of participants in each group to help "reach" statistical significance.

Actually, researchers do not need to state hypotheses if they are asking questions about nature. When the experimental question simply asks about the relation between independent and dependent variables, there is no scientific reason to make a prediction about what will be learned from the data. Whatever is learned will describe something about that relation that was presumably not known before. Whether it matches anyone's expectations has nothing to do with its truth or importance (Sidman, 1960). It is only when the question is about a formal theory or when statistical procedures will be the basis for inferences that a formal hypothesis becomes part of the exercise (for reasons having to do with experimental logic). Otherwise, heed B. F. Skinner's warning quoted at the beginning of this chapter. Ask yourself whether you are more interested in learning about nature or the accuracy of your guesses.

needs to be plainly stated so that no one is likely to be misled about the objectives of a study. For the researcher, this clarity helps to guide the decisions that transform a question into an experiment. It also helps those who read the published study to evaluate the investigator's methodological choices in light of the conclusions that the study offers.

Even when the focus of a question is clear, there are still issues about how it is phrased. Consider the following examples:

1. Will a fixed-interval schedule of positive reinforcement generate positively accelerating patterns of responding (scalloping) in verbal human subjects if they are instructed about the schedule contingency?
2. What are the relations between responding by verbal human subjects under a fixed-interval schedule of positive reinforcement and contingency instructions?

At first glance, both questions may appear to pose the same query, and in a general sense they do. However, the differences between how these questions are phrased suggest that their authors may well set up their experiments somewhat differently. If so, there is a good chance that one experiment might be more fruitful than the other. The first question appears to be fairly narrow in its focus. It asks if giving participants instructions about a fixed-interval schedule will produce a certain pattern of responding. The answer will likely be equally narrow: yes or no. When questions are asked in a way that allows them to be answered in such a simple and specific manner, it can be important to see how the investigator's limited curiosity affected the construction and interpretation of the experiment. Such questions suggest that the researcher is more interested in one outcome than the other. This is hardly improper, but it could encourage designing the experiment in ways that make the desired results more likely than might be the case had a somewhat different preparation been used. Sometimes this subtle bias is evident in how the investigator approaches data analysis.

In contrast, the second question is open-ended in that it does not imply a specific outcome. It simply asks what will happen to fixed-interval performance when contingency instructions are given, which might suggest that the researcher is interested in whatever results might be obtained. This possibility is further implied by the fact that "relations" is plural, suggesting that the results could be complex: not simply yes or no. An experimenter that phrased the question in this way might design procedures that probe for the fullest possible description of these relations.

In general, it seems wise to phrase questions in ways that do not anticipate experimental results. "What are the relations between . . ." is a pretty good representation of this neutral posture. When a question's wording leans toward a particular outcome, this bias, even if innocent, may show up in how the experiment is designed, conducted, and interpreted.

BOX 3.5

The Null Hypothesis Game

For historical reasons that are beyond the scope of this book, a tradition has evolved in psychology and the social sciences (in marked contrast to the natural sciences) that has a rigid influence on how experimental interests are conceived and phrased. When inferential statistics will be used to interpret experimental data, the investigator must usually identify both a null hypothesis and an alternative hypothesis. The **null hypothesis** is a routine statement that there is no difference between the performance of the experimental group and the control group. The **alternative hypothesis** states that there is a difference and that it is due to the only thing that distinguished the two groups: exposure to the independent variable.

If a statistical test of the data shows that there is indeed no substantial difference, then the null hypothesis must be accepted, and the investigator can only argue that there would have been a difference if things had been different. If the test shows that there is a difference, the investigator happily rejects the null hypothesis and turns to the alternative hypothesis as the best explanation of the difference between the groups (given a small likelihood that the difference occurred by chance).

There are a number of problems with this approach to asking experimental questions that will be examined in other chapters. However, in the present context, you should understand that it restricts the type of question asked to the general form, "Is there a difference (between experimental and control groups)?" The sole permissible answers are inevitably "Yes" or "No," which is both inefficient and a distortion of customary scientific curiosity. The tradition of statistical hypothesis testing requires researchers to play science by the rules of the Twenty Questions Game, in which queries must be phrased in ways that can be answered by yes or no.

In fact, if we look closely enough, there will almost always be a difference. What we really want to know, however, is the nature of the difference and the reasons for it. Instead, this approach encourages the researcher to focus experiments on detecting a particular predicted difference rather than on capturing any features of the relationship between independent and dependent variables. Worse still, this wording encourages researchers to design and conduct the experiment in whatever ways are necessary to get an affirmative conclusion, regardless of its truth in nature.

THE FUNCTIONS OF EXPERIMENTAL QUESTIONS

Guiding Experimental Procedures

Strategy. A good experimental question about behavior is a carefully worded expression of the investigator's best judgments about the direction and focus of his or her interests. As such, it should serve as a guide for the many decisions the researcher must make in order to create and manage an experiment that will satisfy those interests. The question may suggest obvious or subtle choices from one topic to another, but almost every methodological decision can be usefully related to the experimental question.

The reason for making sure that the question serves as a touchstone for these decisions is that we expect the experimental procedures to yield data that answer the question. When the design and conduct of an experiment fail to properly reflect the interests of the question, there is a risk that the results will not provide a clear answer. The problem arises when the investigator fails to recognize this risk and proceeds to answer the question based on procedures and data that do not fully suit the question. In this situation, the conclusions may not be entirely correct and therefore may not hold up when others use them.

Consider, for example, an experimental question that asks about the effectiveness of procedures for training students to use good study skills. If the investigator chooses to measure only test performance to assess the possible effects of training in particular study skills, the data may not clearly answer the question. Although we might expect changes in study skills to result in changes in test performance, these test scores may not clearly reveal the effects of the training procedures. One reason for this limitation is that test scores will not provide evidence that the trained study skills were actually used as designed. Test performance is also likely to reflect the influence of factors other than study practices, such as pre-existing knowledge of the material and test-taking skills. Keep in mind that the question was about the effectiveness of procedures for training students to study in particular ways, not the effects of certain study practices on test performance. With this focus, a decision to measure the effects of study skill training procedures using only test performance would not generate data that directly reflected the impact of these training procedures and nothing else. Although measures of test performance might partly represent the effects of the training procedures, they would also reflect the influence of other factors and thereby limit the accuracy and generality of conclusions.

Selecting Participants. One of the first challenges that a researcher faces is selecting participants whose behavior will serve as the dependent variable in the experiment. The criteria for choosing some individuals over others emerge from examining the needs of the experimental question. The question should suggest certain participant characteristics that will help to reveal how their behavior is affected by experimental variables, as well as other features that might interfere with seeing these effects.

For many experimental questions, the need for specific participant characteristics is obvious. Species, gender, age, history, and repertoire are almost always important considerations. The focus of the question, the nature of experimental conditions, and the planned setting will usually dictate some of these criteria. For instance, a study investigating procedures for obtaining compliance with exercise regimens for arthritis patients will presumably

BOX 3.6

The Hypothetico-Deductive Method

Perhaps the most elaborate way of asking experimental questions is the **hypothetico-deductive method**. In this approach, the experimenter's reasoning is from a set of general postulates or axioms to a series of specific theorems that can then be verified by experiment. Each verification not only confirms the empirical relation suggested by the theorem, but substantiates the validity of the postulate set as well. The rules by which the experimenter deduces relations from the postulates or established theorems are quite formal and generate relatively specific predictions.

To the extent that experimental outcomes verify the predictions, the experimenter may increase confidence in the validity of the postulates. However, if the experiment fails to support a logically valid prediction from a postulate, then one or more of the postulates have been falsified. The appropriate action is then to revise the postulate set until the obtained results can be predicted and to confirm the new prediction by repeating the experiment. In this manner, the entire enterprise is supposedly self-correcting (Salmon, 1966).

One of the problems with this strongly deductive mode of inquiry is that it often leads to a more restricted form of question than when the experimenter approaches the topic inductively. Experimental hypotheses take the general form, "When x occurs, y will occur." When y fails to occur, little attention may be paid to what happened instead (see Box 3.5).

Another difficulty of this approach is that it requires precise measurement and a clear correspondence between the formal elements in the theoretical structure and the empirical elements involved in the experimental procedures. The method worked for Newton in the 17th century when he arrived at the basic laws of motion in physics, but it did not work in 20th century psychology. These requirements had not been met when Hull (1940, 1943) launched the first major effort to apply the hypothetico-deductive method to the study of behavior. The coordinating definitions relating abstract concepts in the formal system (habit strength, for instance) to experimental operations in the laboratory were simply too vague, so that the data did not constitute an unequivocal test of the hypotheses (Koch, 1954).

---

require not only individuals with this disorder but even a particular type of arthritis or a certain level of severity. An experiment investigating error correction procedures associated with teaching skills to individuals with mental retardation will probably not only require such individuals but they may also need to share a certain level of functioning and prerequisite skills so that they are suitable for the training procedure that will provide the context for different error correction procedures.

Aside from personal features, each experimental question will require participants who can contact experimental conditions in a certain manner. Even simple availability can be an issue. For instance, a laboratory study designed to measure the effects of psychotropic drugs on the behavior of individuals with diagnoses of schizophrenia might require a decision to use persons residing in a facility of some sort rather than individuals living on their own or with their families. Those living with family might be less likely to consistently attend daily testing sessions.

It is also important to select participants whose repertoires include the behavioral characteristics needed to serve as the dependent variable. By directing selection of treatment and control conditions, the question may suggest how participants will need to behave in order to react meaningfully to these conditions. For example, a study of how the stimuli used in a matching-to-sample procedure affect discrimination learning in young children would probably require that the children share a certain level of development in their verbal repertoire, as well as being able to respond to match-to-sample tasks using a touch screen.

TABLE 3.1
Considerations in selecting participant characteristics

• Species	• Accessibility
• Gender	• Repertoire
• Age	• Environmental history

Choosing a Response Class. The experimental question is also important in determining the characteristics of the behavior or response class that the investigator chooses as the dependent variable. (Chapter 4 will address this topic in detail.) In some studies, particularly those guided by applied interests, the target behavior may be largely specified by the focus of the question. If the experiment is to examine procedures for reducing self-injurious behavior, for instance, the researcher will only have to determine whether there are any particular features of such behavior that might be important to include. In other studies, often those conducted under laboratory conditions, the selection of a response class may be fairly open.

The general task is to figure out the features that a response class should, or should not, exhibit. With such a list, the researcher is then ready either to identify a behavior already in the participant's repertoire with these characteristics or to determine how to create the desired behavior by arranging pretraining or experimental conditions. There are a number of key features that might be of interest.

For instance, the procedures making up the control and treatment conditions will require participants to behave in particular ways. In a project focusing on procedures for training new skills using individuals with mental retardation, for example, certain prerequisite skills such as making eye contact on command, sitting at a table, and perhaps following basic instructions will

BOX 3.7

Ethical Considerations in Behavioral Research

The days are long past when behavioral researchers could design and conduct a study with concern only for methodological niceties. Today behavioral scientists using any vertebrate species in their studies must comply with a complex array of detailed regulations and guidelines. By design, these policies have a pervasive and often intrusive impact on the kinds of questions that may be asked and how they may be pursued with experimental procedures. In fact, their influence usually touches most features of a study, including the characteristics of participants, how they are acquired or recruited, the circumstances under which their participation may continue throughout the project, the procedures and conditions to which they may be exposed, and how they must be treated when the study is completed.

Research ethics are about cultural values. There are different ways of defining cultures and cultural values, but it is at least clear that there are widely varying views about science and how it should be used and conducted. For example, although some revere science and have high hopes for its accomplishments, others question what science can learn and therefore the value of scientific knowledge. Most people are comfortable with humans using other animal species for food, products, and entertainment, but we may also know people who avoid eating meat, refuse to buy leather clothing, and view the animal acts at the circus as mistreatment. And when it comes to research, a sometimes vocal community believes it is immoral to use animals as subjects, especially when it involves any form of discomfort. Others are willing to use animals as subjects as long as the research can be justified in terms of its potential benefits for society.

The practical challenge is how to resolve these differences among various cultural convictions and interests. The laws and regulations governing behavioral research today are the result not only of governmental commissions, panels, bureaucratic procedures, and legislative actions, but also of public debate, citizen protests, and even terrorist activity against universities and individual scientists. Furthermore, these laws and regulations are not static. Cultures and cultural values change, and practices that were once acceptable may later become objectionable. For example, it was once common to design research procedures that involved deceiving human participants about not only the reasons for the procedures they would experience but what these procedures actually involved. Today the requirements for informing participants about the conditions they will experience and getting their consent greatly limit this kind of deception. The transitional nature of cultural values and regulations is particularly clear in animal research. For instance, society's interest in continuing to reduce or limit the use of animals in research is built into animal welfare policies and regulations.

In sum, compliance with research regulations demands careful study of the rules that apply to human or nonhuman species, consultation with regulatory bodies about the details of a proposed project, submitting required paperwork, obtaining necessary approvals, and conforming to the protocols that have been approved.

likely be necessary. Other behaviors will be required by the nature of the procedures making up the control and experimental conditions. At least one of these behaviors is likely to be used to measure the effects of experimental conditions. If the task in the skills training project involves packaging items, making change, or setting a table, for instance, the target behavior will necessarily involve certain forms of such behaviors.

Perhaps the most important role for any behavior that will serve as the dependent variable is to be sensitive to the independent variable. Sensitivity does not mean that the candidate response class must already be known to be strongly affected by the treatment condition. If this were true, there might be little reason to conduct an experiment. In this context, sensitivity means that, whatever the nature of the relationship between a treatment condition and the behavior, the behavior will change in ways that reflect that relationship. An appropriately sensitive target behavior would require, for example, that it be able to vary over an adequate range of values. This would not be possible if the chosen behavior occurred very infrequently (or very often) because then it might be difficult to detect decreases (or increases).

One of the most common constraints on the sensitivity of a behavior comes from powerful extraneous variables, which are often not under the researcher's control. If measures of participant behavior reflect not just the impact of carefully controlled experimental conditions but the effects of factors that are not of interest, it will be difficult to draw conclusions about the effects of treatment conditions alone.

This is a common problem in laboratory research using college students as participants, for example. If the researcher is trying to study the behavioral effects of reinforcement schedules, it is well established that individuals with good verbal repertoires are likely to talk to themselves during sessions about what they think is going on. This self-instructional behavior often influences responding and prevents seeing the effects that particular schedules might have in the absence of this extraneous influence (Catania, 2007).

Selecting response classes that are not overly susceptible to extraneous factors is a frequent challenge in applied studies because nonlaboratory settings typically involve many powerful influences that are not the focus of the experiment. Although one of the reasons for choosing applied research settings is to assess interventions under real-world conditions, if extraneous factors are too powerful then their effects can make it difficult to see the effects of treatment variables. (Later chapters will consider extraneous variables in greater detail.)

Another characteristic of a response class that can have a big impact on what the data reveal is its dimensional quantities. (Chapter 5 will address this topic fully.) The dimensional quantities associated with behavior include the number of responses (count), their duration, and the frequency of responding (how often the behavior occurs), among others. Each quantity reflects a different aspect of a behavior, much as describing an object in terms of its weight, volume, or color reveals different characteristics. The experimental question, together with the nature of the experimental and control conditions, may suggest that some aspects of the behavior will be more useful than others in reflecting the effects of experimental conditions. For instance, if a treatment procedure is likely to produce important variations in the duration of responding, it may be necessary to choose a response class that can vary in this feature, such as watching television. On the other hand, if the experiment is to use a discrete trial procedure, in which the participant must wait for the investigator to start each trial, measuring the participant's behavior in terms of frequency of responding is likely to be misleading. In such a procedure, the pace of the participant's responding will partly depend on the behavior of the investigator and therefore it will not clearly represent only the impact of the treatment condition.

Finally, because the target behavior will serve as the dependent variable, it is important that it can be accurately measured. This means that the selected feature of each instance must be observed and recorded. This is usually not difficult in more controlled research settings, but it can be challenging in some field settings, especially when human observers are used. Chapter 6 will consider these issues.

TABLE 3.2
Considerations in choosing a response class

• Compatibility with procedures	• Dimensional quantities
• Sensitivity to independent variable	• Measurability
• Influence by extraneous variables	

Designing Measurement Procedures. Many of the considerations involved in setting up measurement procedures are fundamental and do not vary much from one experiment to another. For instance, obtaining accurate measures of responding is always important. However, the issue of how long and how often periods of measurement should occur partly depends on what the question needs to learn about how the treatment condition influences responding. Sometimes relatively brief daily sessions may provide adequate information, but under other circumstances measurement may need to continue for extended periods.

Consider an investigation of the effects of diet on hyperactivity in young children. An experiment might compare the effects of a therapeutic diet versus a typical diet, with each type of diet being followed for a few weeks at a time in turn. In this situation, it may be necessary to obtain samples of behavior throughout each day in varied settings, probably involving parents, teachers, and others as observers. In contrast, a different experiment on this topic might ask about the effects of a particular food by preparing a series of dietary challenges. Under this procedure, the effect of consuming the food in question would last only a few hours, and measurement would therefore need to occur continuously throughout this period following each challenge in order to capture any effects.

Selecting Independent Variables. The independent variable (also called the treatment condition or intervention) is the centerpiece of experimental procedures, and the experimental question's most important role is guiding its selection. The question is only the researcher's verbal behavior and is not worth much until it leads to experimental action. The independent variables that are embedded in experimental procedures are the means by which we translate the question into environmental features that the participants will experience. The correspondence between the question and its treatment conditions must therefore be very close in order for the data to clearly answer the question.

Unfortunately, there are no simple rules for how the experimental question should lead to selecting independent variables. One way to approach the problem, however, is to ask what kind of data will be required to answer the question. That is, given the question, imagine the ideal kind of data that would unambiguously answer it. With this guide, then consider what particular features of a treatment condition might generate such data.

For instance, what if a question asks about the effects of quantity of food consumed on the behavior of ruminating after meals in individuals diagnosed as severely or profoundly mentally retarded (Rast, Johnston, Drum, & Conrin, 1981)? If we ask what kind of data would answer this question, we might find that we would need to be able to compare the effects of eating different amounts of food on ruminating behavior. Although we could certainly select three or four different amounts of food for comparison, if there is no evidence from prior studies about whether food quantity has any effects on ruminating at all, it might be sufficient for an initial study just to see if such a relationship exists.

In this case, then, it would be important to be able to compare frequencies of ruminating under a typical diet with frequencies under a diet that showed a clear impact on ruminating. A typical diet might mean single portions of foods that would normally be served to individuals residing in a developmental center. It would not be permissible to serve less food than this, so in order to assess the effects of food quantity the comparison condition would need to involve larger amounts of food. Because we would not know how big a difference in food quantity might be required to see an effect on frequencies of ruminating, we would want to choose a sufficiently large amount of food to capture any effect, if there was such a relationship. Assuming no associated health risks, we could encourage participants to eat until they were satiated (defined as refusing additional food).

In sum, a question focusing on the effects of food quantity on ruminating might be well served with an independent variable defined as satiation quantities of foods that were in all other respects the same as food consumed under control conditions involving single-portion quantities. Developing the full details of both control and experimental conditions would require further decisions about how the food was presented and consumed, how satiation was defined in terms of participant behavior, and so forth.

Selecting an experiment's independent variable immediately defines all other variables as extraneous to experimental interests. In a way, the unfortunate function of extraneous variables is to supply alternative explanations for what might otherwise appear to be the effects of the treatment condition. Sometimes these extraneous factors come attached to the independent variable. For example, it would unavoidably take longer to eat a satiation meal than a single-portion meal, and it is possible that the extra time has its own effects on ruminating, unrelated to how much food is consumed. Extraneous factors can also accompany features of control conditions, the general experimental setting, the behavior serving as the dependent variable, or other characteristics of participants. In fact, extraneous variables can intrude on the effects of treatment conditions in endless ways, and they are a major challenge to drawing clear and sound conclusions about the contribution of the independent variable alone. Discussion of extraneous variables will occur throughout this book.

Creating Experimental Comparisons. Designing an experiment involves arranging control and treatment conditions in ways that create meaningful comparisons of responding under each type of condition. These two conditions are usually designed to be the same except for the presence of the independent variable in the treatment condition. If responding is found to be consistently different under control and treatment conditions, the investigator reasons that these differences are likely to be due to the only thing that differed between them—the independent variable. Such a conclusion should help to answer the experimental question. By guiding the selection of the independent variable and its complementary control conditions, the question indirectly suggests such meaningful comparisons.

In order to create meaningful comparisons between responding under control versus treatment conditions, at least two requirements must be met. First, each participant must be exposed to both control and treatment conditions. Second, the data for each participant must be measured and analyzed separately. Together with some other features that will be discussed in later chapters, this approach is called a within-subject (participant) design. "Within-subject" refers to the fact that comparisons are made using data obtained from individual participants who experienced both control and treatment conditions at different points. That is, the key comparisons are made using data from or "within" each participant. It also implies that these comparisons are made separately for each participant. This approach contrasts with between-group designs, in which each participant is assigned to either the control condition or the treatment condition (but not both), and the grouped data from control participants are compared with the grouped data from treatment participants.

Given a commitment to a within-subject design, which as we will see is necessary to answer certain kinds of questions about behavior, the remaining decisions concern how to arrange the sequence and timing of control and treatment conditions throughout the course of the study. The experimental question is unlikely to suggest particular arrangements, but it is important to keep in mind exactly what comparisons will be needed to answer the question. As later chapters will show, there are a number of factors that must be considered in determining how control and treatment conditions are arranged over time.

Data Analysis

The data in a study result from measuring the behavior serving as the dependent variable as each participant experiences control conditions and treatment conditions. Given the role of the experimental question in selecting independent and dependent variables, it should be expected that the question should also influence how the investigator analyzes the data.

Analyzing the data using different techniques serves three objectives: (a) modifying the initial decisions about how the experiment will be conducted as the study proceeds; (b) identifying and describing data that may answer the question; and (c) discovering relationships in the data that were not anticipated and that may be interesting. The first two objectives should be guided by the experimental question, which tells the investigator what to look for. The third objective must not be ignored in trying to answer the original question, however. It is important that the question not limit the researcher's general

---

BOX 3.8

Serendipity

The term **serendipity** comes from an old Persian fairy tale, titled *The Three Princes of Serendip*. The princes had a faculty of finding valuable or agreeable things they were not looking for. In science, serendipitous discoveries are actually fairly common. This should not be surprising, however, because the openly inquisitive nature of science encourages researchers to be on the lookout for features of their data that might be unexpected. Such unanticipated discoveries are sufficiently frequent that most researchers can point to examples in their own careers. Although serendipitous findings are not typically so important or unusual that they resolve major problems or redirect entire fields of study, they can be very useful in the context of specific areas of research.

Behavioral investigators can increase the chances of making important serendipitous discoveries by the way they do research. Using experimental methods that capture the essential qualities of behavior and making sure that the data are free of contaminating and misleading influences are essential steps. However, the researcher's attitude toward the experimental process is no less important. Investigators who approach experiments as opportunities to learn whatever their experimental procedures might reveal should be expected to make serendipitous observations more often than those who see experiments as occasions for showing things they already assume are true.

TABLE 3.3
Objectives of data analysis procedures

- Modifying initial decisions as the experiment proceeds
- Identifying and describing data that answer the question
- Discovering unanticipated relationships

---

curiosity. It is this open search for any potentially interesting findings that leads to serendipitous discoveries, which are neither rare nor trivial in science.

Guiding Experimental Inferences

All of the functions of the experimental question involved in designing and conducting a study support the final step in the process—drawing conclusions that may answer the question. These conclusions are inevitably important to the researcher, who has gone to a lot of trouble to get to this point. This motivation to find particular results is understandable but risky. Although it is appropriate that the data should exert substantial influence on the researcher's interpretive reactions, the conditions under which the data were obtained must be given a major role as well.

It is easy to appreciate this caution in the case of measurement procedures. For instance, without considering the different components of measurement operations that changed behavioral facts (what actually happened) into behavioral data (the quantitative picture of what happened), it is impossible to know exactly what each data point represents. The same issue exists for response class definitions, independent variable conditions, how extraneous variables were controlled, and so forth. In other words, as we will see in chapter 13, the task of interpreting the data is really a much broader challenge of interpreting the entire experiment.

Guiding the Science and the Culture

You can tell a lot about a science from its experimental questions. They reveal where the science has been and where it is going. Experimental questions are more than merely revealing, however. Because of their influence on research methods, and the impact of methods on discovery, they guide the style and direction of a science's development.

This suggests that, in addition to the particular influences already discussed, when we develop our experimental questions we should consider their impact on the development of the science. This requires some awareness of where the field is at any point and where it needs to go. Are the questions that are already established in the literature good for the science's development? Are there more profitable directions in which to invest the field's resources? Are there unexplored areas that should be pursued? Are there particular themes that should be avoided? What effects might each single experiment have on the field as a whole?

Finally, scientists may also examine experimental questions for their larger impact on society. This is not an uncommon consideration in science. After all, researchers are part of the culture and are influenced by their membership in society. In addition, federal, corporate, and foundation funding sources encourage researchers to be aware of the relation between experimental questions and their potential impact on everyday life. Science has, for many years now, been an indispensable part of daily life. We need it just to survive the complexities and problems that it has, in part, allowed us to create. The culture has only recently begun to appreciate the need for scientific explanations of human behavior so that effective technologies can be developed. As the mature science of behavior shoulders its share of this burden, we must compose our experimental questions with the care that is appropriate to their consequences for the culture.

CHAPTER SUMMARY

1. For both researchers and practitioners, the challenge in developing an experimental question is determining what the best question to ask is. The development of these questions, like other behaviors, has multiple sources of control.

2. Researchers often rely on the primary literature to guide the development of research questions. It is important, however, to examine broader areas of literature and our own experiences with the subject matter in order to identify where it is that the field must go to continually produce experimental questions that will be useful to the specific topic and the overall interests of the discipline.

3. While existing resources usually facilitate or constrain the type of questions asked by each investigator, it is important to recognize that questions that can be easily pursued are not always the questions that should be pursued.

4. The best question for a topic results from a process of comparing and refining possible questions in the context of the literature, and in general should be phrased in ways that do not anticipate experimental results.

5. The experimental question should serve as a guide in selecting participants with specific characteristics that will help to reveal how their behavior is affected by the independent variable, as well as any extraneous variables that might interfere with seeing these effects.

6. When selecting a response class to serve as the dependent variable, the investigator must choose a behavior that will be sensitive to the independent variable. Researchers must also be sure that their dependent variable(s) can be accurately measured and will not be overly susceptible to extraneous factors.

7. The experimental question's most important role is guiding the selection of the independent variable(s). To accomplish this task, the investigator must determine what kind of data will be required to answer the question.

8. In order to create meaningful comparisons between responding under control versus treatment conditions, each participant must be exposed to both conditions, and the data must be measured and analyzed separately.

9. The analysis of the data allows the investigator to modify the experimental design as the study proceeds and to identify and describe the data that may answer the experimental question. Data analysis also allows the investigator to discover relationships in the data that were not anticipated but are of interest, even if it was not part of the original experimental question.

10. Experimental questions are informative not only because they address a particular need in the field, but because they can reveal how a science has developed and identify where it is going.

TEXT STUDY GUIDE

1. Why is it important to acknowledge that experimental questions are verbal behavior?

2. What does reinforcement have to do with how graduate training affects our professional interests?

3. How can studies outside of the primary literature of interest be useful to researchers?

4. What is the risk of using only the research literature as a basis for experimental questions?

5. How can one protect against existing resources having an undesirable influence on the focus of experimental questions?

6. What are experimental contingencies, and how do they influence the way we might ask questions?

7. What are extra-experimental contingencies?

8. How do you think your personal history might influence the style of experimental questions you would ask?

9. What is it useful to focus on when developing the best experimental question for a topic?

10. Why is it valuable to actually write out questions under consideration?

11. Why might it be wise to phrase questions so that they do not anticipate or forecast results?

12. What is the overall strategy for how questions should guide the development of experimental procedures?

13. How can the question guide the selection of participants?

14. What are some of the considerations in choosing a response class that might stem from the experimental question?

15. According to the authors, what feature of measurement procedures depends on what the question is asking?

16. What tactic do the authors recommend for figuring out how the question might guide the selection of independent variables?

17. What are two, key requirements for creating meaningful comparisons between the effects of control and experimental conditions?

18. What are three objectives that the data analysis should meet?

BOX STUDY GUIDE

1. What are research styles?

2. Contrast thematic versus independent research styles.

3. How are explanatory and demonstration styles of research different?

4. How might you recognize research that advocated a particular outcome?

5. What is a hypothesis? What are the risks of using hypotheses to guide experimentation?

6. What is a null hypothesis? What are possible problems with this approach to asking questions?

7. Describe the hypothetico-deductive method.

8. What is the scientific attitude of serendipity?

9. How can researchers maximize their chances of making serendipitous discoveries?

SUGGESTED READINGS

Deguchi, H. (1984). Observational learning from a radical-behavioristic viewpoint. *The Behavior Analyst*, 7, 83–95.

Epstein, R. (1980). *Notebooks, B. F. Skinner*. Englewood Cliffs, NJ: Prentice-Hall.

Rast, J., Johnston, J. M., Drum, C., & Conrin, J. (1981). The relation of food quantity to rumination behavior. *Journal of Applied Behavior Analysis*, *14*, 121–130.

DISCUSSION TOPICS

1. Select some observation about everyday behavior that you have made recently and consider the experimental questions that it might generate.

2. Select a specific research issue that can generate different experimental questions. Ask small groups of students to each develop one question addressing this issue. Discuss the pros and cons of the resulting questions.

EXERCISES

1. Select a research article from a journal and figure out the experimental question. Evaluate different ways of phrasing the question.

2. Using this research article, evaluate how the question might have guided the investigator's decisions about some of the study's methodological features, including participant characteristics, target behavior, measurement procedures, and independent variable.

PART TWO

MEASUREMENT

Selecting and Defining Response Classes

> *The analysis of behavior is not an arbitrary act of subdividing, and we cannot define the concepts of stimulus and response quite as simply as "parts of the behavior and environment" without taking account of the natural lines of fracture along which behavior and environment actually break.*
>
> —B. F. Skinner

STRATEGIES OF SELECTING AND DEFINING RESPONSE CLASSES

The Unit of Analysis

In chapter 2, we considered the general characteristics of behavior as a natural phenomenon. The proposed definition of behavior identified its key features that are important to researchers and practitioners. In any single experiment, however, we do not study behavior in general. We approach each experimental question by studying only a small piece of each participant's entire repertoire. The decision that investigators face in each study concerns what specific examples of behavior will suit the needs of the experiment and how to go about distinguishing those instances of behavior from the rest of a participant's repertoire.

As in other sciences, that part of the phenomenon serving as a basis for experimental study is called the **unit of analysis**. Any phenomenon may have different units of analyses, depending on the researcher's interests. The cell, for example, is an important unit of analysis in the study of biological systems, even though cells are composed of even smaller components that can also serve as units of analysis (Zeiler, 1984).

> **Unit of analysis.** A constituent part of a whole phenomenon that serves as a basis for experimental study. In the study of behavior, the unit of analysis is the response class.

BOX 4.1

Units of Analysis versus Units of Measurement

Because units of analysis and units of measurement share a reference to units, it is easy to confuse them. As defined in this chapter, a **unit of analysis** is that part of a larger phenomenon that serves as a basis for study. The atom, the cell, and the response class are units of analysis. In contrast, a **unit of measurement** refers to a specific amount of some dimension of the thing being measured. For example, the meter is a unit of measurement for measuring length, just as the kilogram serves the same function for measuring weight. A unit of measurement is therefore a particular amount by which we quantify dimensions such as weight and length. A unit of measurement tells how much of a dimension was observed.

You can keep these two types of units straight by remembering that a unit of measurement describes how much of some dimension of a unit of analysis is observed. For example, an observer might report that a school child sat at her desk for a duration of 37 minutes. The unit of analysis is the response class of "sitting at desk." The unit of measurement is the minute, in this case used to describe how much duration was observed.

The scientific study of behavior was initially hindered by the lack of a clear understanding of an appropriate unit of analysis. Early researchers tended to define classes of environmental stimuli and classes of responses in purely physical terms and independently of any relationship between environment and behavior. One of B. F. Skinner's earliest and most important contributions was to propose a different approach (Skinner, 1935). He argued that stimuli and responses should be defined not just in terms of their physical structure or form but in terms of their function or relationship with each other.

Instead of defining the response class of "making a bed" in terms of specific movements, for example, Skinner's position was that the behavior should be defined in terms of any movements that produced beds that were "made up"— in other words, the responses necessary to make beds form a class defined by their shared effects (beds that are made up). These stimulus consequences also function as a class of stimuli because they presumably serve as reinforcers for making beds. This approach to defining response and stimulus classes is important because it accommodates the way behavior and environment actually work together.

Natural Response Classes

The challenge for both researchers and practitioners is to define target behaviors in ways that closely approximate to the way individual **responses** come together as classes in nature. The reason for this objective is to avoid defining response classes that include a mixture of responses that do not share the same ties with the environment and that may therefore vary in different ways. As we will see, this problem can sometimes limit the clarity and usefulness of conclusions.

As the example of making beds illustrates, the relationship between responses and their surrounding environmental stimuli organizes the infinite number of individual responses in a person's repertoire into natural groupings called **response classes**. We recognize these groupings when we distinguish one behavior from another in daily discourse. These response classes are the units of analysis for the science of behavior. There are three general types of response classes: respondent, operant, and discriminated operant.

> **Response.** A single instance of a response class.
>
> **Response class.** A collection of individual responses that have common sources of influence in the environment. Also called a behavior.

In the case of respondent behavior, specific environmental events consistently elicit specific responses. Classes of such stimulus–response relations are called **reflexes**. If the eliciting stimulus is able to produce a response without having been paired with stimuli, the relationship is termed an **unconditioned**

BOX 4.2

Behavior, Response Classes, and Responses

It is tempting to use these three terms interchangeably, but to a well-trained behavioral researcher or practitioner they have distinct referents. We have already defined the term *behavior* when used in the general manner described in chapter 2. However, when reference is made to *a behavior*, the term specifies a single class of responses, such as reading, dressing, walking, and so forth. (Branch and Vollmer, 2004, argue that there are some technical problems with this usage, although it is widespread in the applied community.) Therefore, another way of referring to a particular behavior is as a response class. As chapter 4 explains, a *response class* is a grouping of individual responses that share those commonalities included in the definition of the class. *Responses*, then, are the individual instances of behavior that make up each class.

Given these distinctions, it would be incorrect to say that "Betty did 15 behaviors today" if what is meant is that she emitted 15 instances (responses) of a particular target behavior or response class. Similarly, saying that the study focused on three responses would be misleading if what was meant was that three response classes served as target behaviors.

---

reflex. If a history of pairings with other stimuli is involved, it is designated a **conditioned reflex**. The process of creating conditioned reflexes is called **respondent, classical**, or **Pavlovian conditioning**.

> **Reflex.** A class of stimulus–response relationships in which certain environmental events consistently elicit specific responses.
>
> **Unconditioned reflex.** A reflex in which the class of eliciting stimuli serve this function without a history of being paired with unconditioned stimuli.
>
> **Conditioned reflex.** A reflex in which the class of eliciting stimuli have acquired this function because of a history of being paired with unconditioned stimuli.
>
> **Respondent.** The class of responses elicited by particular unconditioned or conditioned antecedent stimuli.
>
> **Respondent conditioning.** The processes involved in creating conditioned reflexes from unconditioned reflexes. Also called *classical conditioning* or *Pavlovian conditioning*.

The biological processes that create unconditioned and conditioned reflexes define those responses that are elicited by certain stimuli as belonging to the same class, which is called a **respondent**. The shared ability to elicit a particular respondent class also defines those individual stimuli as a class as well. Those responses elicited by the stimuli constitute a class because the likelihood of their occurrence depends on whether the stimuli are presented. For Pavlov's dogs, then, the stimuli comprising each presentation of meat powder functioned as a class of events because they all elicited salivation responses, and their effects on salivation made those responses a class as well.

A second kind of relationship exists when responding is followed by certain kinds of changes in the environment, with the result that similar responses are more likely to occur in the future. This relationship, which is ultimately rooted in the organism's biology, is called **positive reinforcement** or **negative reinforcement**, depending on the nature of the environmental changes. Each class of responses sharing a particular effect on the environment is termed an **operant**, and the processes involved in changing such behavior are called **operant conditioning**. The stimulus changes that are produced by operant responses and that have a common reinforcing effect also constitute classes called **positive** or **negative reinforcers**. The same organization of individual responses and stimuli into classes also holds for shared relationships that make responses less likely to occur. In these cases, we talk about **positive** and **negative punishment** and **positive** and **negative punishers**.

> **Positive reinforcement.** A class of procedures involving the occurrence of a stimulus immediately following responding that results in an increase in some aspect of the response class over baseline levels.
>
> **Negative reinforcement.** A procedure involving the termination of a stimulus immediately following responding that results in an increase in some aspect of the response class over baseline levels.
>
> **Operant.** A class of responses defined by a functional relation with a particular class of environmental stimuli that immediately follow these responses.
>
> **Operant conditioning.** The processes involved in changing operant behavior based on its environmental consequences.
>
> **Positive reinforcers.** A class of stimuli that occur immediately following responding, resulting in an increase in some aspect of the response class over baseline levels.
>
> **Negative reinforcers.** A class of stimuli that are terminated immediately following responding, resulting in an increase in some aspect of the response class over baseline levels.
>
> **Positive punishment.** A class of procedures involving the occurrence of a stimulus immediately following responding that results in a decrease in some aspect of the response class over baseline levels.

> **Negative punishment.** A procedure involving the termination of a stimulus immediately following responding that results in a decrease in some aspect of the response class over baseline levels.
>
> **Positive punishers.** A class of stimuli that occur immediately following responding, resulting in a decrease in some aspect of the response class over baseline levels.
>
> **Negative punishers.** A class of stimuli that are terminated immediately following responding, resulting in a decrease in some aspect of the response class over baseline levels.

A third classification of behavior-environment interactions is based on relations between responses and both the stimuli that precede and that follow them. When these stimuli regularly precede responding that is followed by reinforcement, these stimuli tend to acquire the function of making such responding more likely to occur in their presence than in their absence, when reinforcement is unlikely. These stimuli are called **discriminative stimuli**, and their relations with responses create another class called a **discriminated operant**.

> **Discriminative stimuli.** Stimuli that have acquired the function of setting the occasion for a behavior to occur. A behavior is more likely to occur in the presence of a discriminative stimulus than in its absence. Abbreviated S^D.
>
> **Discriminated operant.** A class of responses that are functionally related to classes of both antecedent and consequent stimuli.

These three sets of relations between behavior and environment are diagrammed in Fig. 1.1 (see Catania, 2007, for a more detailed treatment of these classes of behavior). These three fundamental units of analysis have been described by Zeiler (1984) as ". . . the smallest entities that display the full characteristics of adaptive behavior" (p. 4). He continues:

To pursue the analogy to cells, behavioral units are the smallest bit of integrated behavior, just as cells are the smallest living structure. They can be observed with appropriate methodology, just as cells can be seen with a microscope. They have components; cells do as well. Indeed, experimental analysis of these components can serve as a primary focus of behavioral research, just as intracellular study can be a major emphasis in contemporary biology. Whether or not component analysis . . . proves to have an impact equivalent to that of molecular biology and subatomic physics, at least the parent units of the various sciences are parallel. (pp. 4-5)

Another point to emphasize about these three types of response classes is that they are not defined on logical grounds. Each represents a functional or working relationship in nature. The everyday behavior of opening doors is a good example of these practical relations.

The responses in our repertoire that produce open doors come together in a coordinated way in the presence of doors. Their outcome of opening doors is usually a reinforcing change in the environment that makes those responses occur specifically in contact with doors under conditions that make their opening reinforcing. It is no accident that we do not walk up to blank walls and behave in the same way that we do in front of doors. Although all of the pieces of the behavior required to open doors are in our repertoire, it is our experience with such responses and their consequences that pulls them together into an organized and functional form only under these relatively specific conditions.

Functional versus Topographical Response Classes

In spite of the endless variety of behaviors in an organism's repertoire, there are only two basic ways of defining a response class. Researchers or practitioners can define a response class in terms of the functional relations between particular features of the environment and particular aspects of behavior, or they can designate a class in terms of its form or topography.

It is termed a **functional response class definition** if the behavior is defined as including only those responses whose occurrence depends on (is a function of) particular classes of stimuli that precede or follow responses. This means that the form or topography of the responses in a functionally defined class may vary considerably. Continuing the previous example, we often engage in some very different actions (pushing, pulling, twisting, and sliding, for instance) that nevertheless result in open doors. As we have already seen, respondents, operants, and discriminated operants are the three general types of functional response classes that are possible (see Fig. 1.1).

The alternative approach to defining a response class is to specify particular requirements of form or topography for membership in the class. This is called a **topographical response class definition** because it requires deciding on the three-dimensional form that each response must have to fall in the class. For example, a topographical definition of door-opening behavior might specify that responses must involve twisting a doorknob with the right hand and pushing the door open at least 12 inches. It is quite possible, however, that not all of the responses that meet such a definition will serve the same function. In the case of the door-opening example, it might be that opening a door only 12 inches sometimes does not result in a reinforcing consequence. Similarly, other responses may occur, such as using the left hand, that produce the same outcome but do not satisfy the definition.

Functional response class definition. A definition of a response class based on the functional relations between its responses and classes of antecedent and consequent environmental events.

Topographical response class definition. A definition of a response class based on the form of responses in three-dimensional space.

If we applied these two types of definitions to roughly the same behavior, they would probably result in somewhat different rules for which responses would fall into each of the two types of classes. After all, each type of definition specifically ignores the criteria of the other. A functional definition means that responses may be included even though they may look quite different from others, and a topographical definition includes responses that may not share the same functional relations with environmental events even though they share the same form.

As an example of what these differences might mean, let us suppose we are studying self-injurious behavior in individuals diagnosed as mentally retarded who live in a developmental center. Our task is to define and measure such behavior as part of an effort to treat this problem behavior. A functional definition would focus on determining the antecedent and consequent stimuli related to the self-injurious behavior. For instance, if Mariel often hits her head with her hands, we might look for the stimuli that serve as important consequences for such responses because different responses that involve touching her head may serve different functions. Some responses may leave a red mark or make a sound, both of which will generate certain tactile consequences as well as possible attention from care-givers. Other responses may involve scratching an itch, playing with her hair, or putting on a hat, which presumably involve different consequences. We would want our definition to capture only those responses that produced environmental effects (tissue damage) related to the self-injurious character of the behavior. In this example, these effects may also include attention (a possible reinforcer), which may be paired with tactile consequences. That is, staff members are likely to intervene only when Mariel hits her head hard enough to be heard or leave a mark and are not likely to react when she touches her head in other ways.

In contrast, a topographical definition would specify the physical details that each response must show in order to be measured. The criteria would include exactly what constituted a "head hit," such as what area of the head was hit, how hard the blow was, whether it involved her hand or an object, and so forth. A purely topographical definition would not include criteria related to the consequences of the responses, such as whether they left a mark or made a sound. This means that we would have to be careful to craft the definition so that we did not include other ways of touching her head that did not involve risk of injury (combing her hair, for instance).

Although topographical definitions have their place for both researchers and practitioners, functional definitions are always important. Functionally defined classes include responses that share influence by the same kinds of antecedent and consequent events. It is these influences that pull the included responses together into a naturally occurring class, rather than one contrived by a definition. In fact, an organism's repertoire is organized into functional response classes because of environmental influences. Because the events occurring immediately before and after responses are powerful influences on when and how often responses occur, it is useful for researchers and practitioners to accommodate these forces in identifying target behaviors. The alternative approach (topographical definitions) ignores these influences, although they will still be present.

It is especially important to use functional definitions in applied projects when the target behavior already exists in the participant's repertoire. In this situation, the question is often whether a particular intervention will change the behavior, whether for research or practical purposes. It is important that the responses that are measured include all responses that belong in the existing (natural) class and none that do not belong. If the definition fails to cover all responses in the existing class or includes responses that do not belong in this class, the data are likely to be more variable than necessary and may not show dependable intervention effects.

Selection Objectives

Given these strategic interests, what are the objectives that should guide how researchers and practitioners select response classes? First, as chapter 3 points out, it is paramount that the target behavior suit the needs of the experimental question. Experimental questions typically ask about how features of the environment influence behavior. The characteristics of the target behavior included in its definition therefore provide one set of limits on what the data will reveal.

For instance, if an experimental question asks about the behavioral effects of a certain psychotropic drug with children, the investigator must be confident that the target behavior will reveal the effects of interest, if there are any. There might be a number of choices, including performing selected learning tasks in the classroom, engaging in disruptive behavior during recess, and so forth. If it was possible to select a number of different response classes, it would likely be found that they differ in how clearly they show changes between drug and no-drug conditions. Of course, this luxury is not often available, so making sure the behavior suits the question requires careful consideration.

Second, the characteristics of the selected response class must also suit the general needs of the experiment. As a later discussion will show, for instance, if in a field study the behavior occurs very infrequently, it might inadequately reflect the influence of experimental variables because it does not contact them very often. Another kind of problem that would limit the sensitivity of the response class is excessive influence by extraneous factors. This might be the

---

BOX 4.3

Another Kind of Response Class?

In addition to the three types of response classes resulting from behavior–environment interactions (respondents, operants, and discriminated operants) already described, we can add a fourth type of relationship. In 1961, Falk described an interesting phenomenon observed with rats exposed to a concurrent schedule of food reinforcement for lever pressing. The free availability of water throughout sessions, although not required by the food reinforcement schedule, led to a pattern of excessive water drinking called *polydipsia* that was shown to be a function of the schedule of food reinforcement.

Since then, researchers have shown that the intermittent delivery of food or other reinforcers can induce various kinds of excessive behavior, including aggressive behavior, pica, wheel running, hyperactivity, eating, smoking, alcohol consumption, repetitive motor behavior, drug taking, and chronic dependence (see Falk, 1981, for a review of this literature). Such behaviors are evoked by, or adjunctive to, the relationship between behavior and environment represented in a schedule involving some other behavior (such as lever pressing with polydipsic rats) and have therefore been called adjunctive behavior (Falk, 1971) or evoked behavior (Thompson & Lubinski, 1986).

---

case if an academic target behavior for a school child was heavily influenced by peers, which therefore interfered with seeing the effects of an instructional intervention. Still another example involves a study's experimental design. For instance, if the design alternates control and treatment conditions every other day, it will be critical that the selected behavior change rapidly in order to reflect any differences in the effects of each condition.

Third, how a response class is defined may have some consequences for measurement procedures. A response class that accommodates other criteria may provide observational challenges, for example. Although an automated approach to observation and recording is often feasible under laboratory or relatively controlled conditions, in applied settings human observers are often required. The target behavior must be accessible to them for adequate periods of time, which usually requires good visual contact. Furthermore, as upcoming chapters will show, the response class definition must help observers to distinguish between those responses that are supposed to be measured and the rest of the participant's ongoing behavior.

TABLE 4.1
Objectives of selecting response classes

- Suit the needs of the experimental question
- Suit the general needs of the experiment
- Suit the requirements for measurement

Finally, it is worth noting that practitioners may be in a different situation than researchers when it comes to selecting response classes. Practitioners might point out that they may not have a choice about what response classes must be measured in order to track the effects of interventions. When the objective is to modify behavior for practical purposes, it is often the case that the presenting circumstances require that certain target behaviors be measured. If the challenge is to teach verbal skills to a child with autism or to improve math skills in a sixth grader, for example, these interests will limit the practitioner's options in selecting response classes. Nevertheless, some of the issues discussed above are just as important for practitioners as for researchers. In fact, practitioners will usually have some choice about exactly how required target behaviors are defined. Furthermore, it is always important that the target behavior be easy to measure and clearly reflect the influence of the intervention procedures.

TACTICS OF SELECTING AND DEFINING RESPONSE CLASSES

Developing Functional Response Class Definitions

The first step in developing a functional definition is to consider the everyday context of the behavior of interest. For example, if we intend to study the behavior of stealing with adolescent boys assigned by the courts to a secure residential facility, we can start off by narrowing our focus to behavior that leads to possessing something that belongs to someone else without first getting permission.

Next, we might speculate on the events that could precede and follow acts of stealing. We could test our guesses about how to define stealing by informally observing this kind of behavior in the facility. In doing this, we are using both our personal and professional histories as a kind of crude screening device to see what we might learn about functional relations between the environment and this kind of behavior. For instance, what we usually call stealing are responses that involve taking or possessing things belonging to other people under antecedent conditions that fail to include the owner's approval. In fact, the owner is usually either absent or the item is taken by force. Furthermore, possession of the stolen item is likely to be strongly reinforcing.

If our informal assessment of this starting point seems sound, we may be ready to try out possible definitions and see how they work. Trying out a definition means writing it down, using it to guide measurement activities, and evaluating what is recorded. In this case, let us suppose that we begin with a definition that specifies responses that produce the consequence of possessing something belonging to someone else.

As staff members observe and record this behavior, it will probably be called to our attention that the definition includes responses that were preceded by the owner of the "stolen" object having granted permission for its use. This antecedent distinction is probably an important basis for differentiating between stealing something and merely using it, so we might modify our definition accordingly. Unfortunately, it is likely to be difficult to know if prior permission was given before a boy is observed possessing an item belonging to someone else. One solution is to ease the definitional task by modifying the research environment. We might institute a policy that no boy may possess or use something belonging to others without first getting a staff member to witness the owner's permission and then sign a "borrowing card" that the borrower must keep until the item is returned. The card will be a permanent product of this interchange that will allow staff to distinguish between stealing and legitimate borrowing.

We can now revise our definition to include responses that involve possessing something belonging to someone else that occur in the absence of the owner, as evidenced by the lack of a borrowing card. As we continue measurement trying out this revised definition, we may see the need for further changes. For example, staff members may report that they are recording both responses that involve surreptitious taking and taking by force or threat of force. This distinction certainly reflects different antecedent conditions, not to mention different legal consequences. We might want to view this distinction as reflecting two different response classes. Although we could lump them together in our research project, they involve different circumstances and might be affected differently by treatment conditions. Lumping them together might increase the variability in our data and make it more difficult to see the effects of these conditions clearly. In order to avoid this risk, we could add to our definition a proviso that the owner must not have been present when the item was taken.

This example should make clear that developing a functional response class definition is not just a literary exercise. Neither does it necessarily require a lengthy trial-and-error process, however. It is often easy to develop a sound functional definition by simply observing the behavior of interest under normal environmental conditions and making reasonable assumptions about the antecedent and consequent events to which responses are related. The key is that definitional criteria should result in a class of responses that share the same relations with surrounding environmental events.

Developing Topographical Response Class Definitions

Because topographical definitions specifically avoid considering functional relations between target responses and the surrounding environment, they are comparatively easy to develop. The experimenter should begin by identifying the reason for defining the behavior in terms of the form of individual responses. For instance, if a researcher is working with physical therapists to develop more effective rehabilitation methods for patients with a certain type of injury, it may make sense to define specific therapeutic exercises strictly in terms of their form. A definition might specify bending an arm in a certain way or reaching a certain distance. Although eventually these movements may need to accomplish practical functions, it is understandable if the therapist's focus is initially limited to form alone. As a different example, an investigator might be interested in studying the form of responses on a particular task with employees in a manufacturing facility. It may already be known that certain topography of responding is related to rapid production, low frequency of errors, proper use of equipment, or safety.

Developing a topographical definition involves carefully describing the limits of form that responses must show in order to be measured. The written definition should involve rules for observers that tell them which responses meet those limits and which fall outside the class. Response class definitions involved in teaching skills to individuals with developmental disabilities often focus on the form of responses because target behaviors must be built or formed in a deliberate manner. For example, if a trainer is teaching individuals with mental retardation some basic cooking skills, such as how to make Jell-O^{fi}, the definition of this behavior will require specifying the form of each component of this complex skill, as well as their sequence. Of course, this topographical focus is based on a prior understanding that these responses must take a certain form in order to serve the function of making Jell-O^{fi} that can then be eaten.

Combining Functional and Topographical Elements

If you were unaware of the distinction between function and topographical response class definitions, the definitions you developed based on your general experience would often include both functional and topographical elements. We have already seen that both approaches have their place, which depends in each case on the nature of the behavior of interest, the circumstances or objectives of the project, and the needs of researchers or practitioners. Combining functional and topographical elements in a definition can work well as long as there are good reasons for including both kinds of features. Although the distinction between these types of definitions is important, if functional and topographical definitions were developed for the same behavioral interest, any differences in the resulting response classes would not always be significant.

It may help to recall that the underlying reason for defining any behavior is to distinguish targeted responses from those that might seem similar but that are actually different in some important way. The responses that meet the definitional criteria will constitute the data describing what happened under control and treatment conditions. The key is that these data reflect the effects of such conditions on a behavior that is a meaningful basis for drawing conclusions about what happened when the treatment condition was initiated or withdrawn. Defining the target behavior in a particular way is based on the conviction that other definitions of the behavior would lead to data that would not be as meaningful for some reason. Perhaps the most important step in developing a response class definition is carefully thinking through the reasons for defining the behavior one way versus another.

BOX 4.4

Parent: "What Did You Do Today?" Child: "Nothing"

As parents have always suspected, because behavior is one of the characteristics of living as opposed to dead organisms, someone cannot ever be "not doing anything." A person can, however, not do a particular thing at a certain time. When that particular behavior is of experimental or practical interest, it is occasionally tempting to talk about "not doing _____." Of course, when the person is "not doing _____," he or she is actually doing something else.

Defining a response class in this negative form is difficult, to say the least. For instance, how will the observer know when to record each nonresponse, given that the individual will be "not doing _____" most of the time? One solution is to define a specific class of environmental events that function as an occasion or opportunity for the behavior of interest and then count those occasions on which responses do not occur. There are problems with this approach, however. The events that seem to serve as opportunities must first be empirically determined to actually have this discriminative function. Second, these events must not also set the occasion for other behaviors that might interfere with the target behavior. Third, interventions are likely to change these discriminative relations. Because measurement of the nonbehavior is tied to these opportunities, this would require changing the definition, perhaps repeatedly. These changes will make it difficult to know what the data actually represent.

In clinical interventions, it will also be difficult to arrange contingencies involving such nonbehaviors. When a defining opportunity occurs and a response is not emitted, what should a consequence be contingent on? It cannot follow the behavior of interest because it did not occur. A consequence must follow whatever behavior did occur, and it might be these behaviors that change as a result, rather than the nonbehavior.

The message is this: If you are interested in studying a nonbehavior, keep thinking about the situation until you figure out another way to define your interests. For example, if you are concerned about "not getting out of bed in the morning," it would be better to define the behavior of "getting out of bed" and measure its latency from when the alarm clock goes off.

Variations and Refinements

Added Temporal Dimensions. It is impossible to define a response class solely in terms of a temporal dimension. However, it may sometimes be useful to add a temporal requirement to a functional or topographical definition. This means that responses that satisfy the basic definition but fail to meet the temporal requirement would not be recorded. There are three basic ways of doing this.

First, you can specify the amount of time that can or must occur between successive responses. This requirement might be imposed when the frequency or pacing of responses is of special interest. In sculling, for example, the response time between pulling oars, regulated by the rhythmic chanting of the coxswain, is a major determinant of the boat's speed.

Second, you can add a requirement for the latency between particular events and target responses. A response might be counted only if there is some minimum or maximum latency between an event and the response. This option might be exercised when a safety engineer is concerned about how quickly employees initiate corrective action following a signal of an unsafe condition.

Third, you can add a requirement for the time required to complete a response. This requirement would add a minimum or maximum duration to the definition of the response class. For instance, the time it takes a surgeon to tie off a bleeding artery during an operation is obviously important.

TABLE 4.2
Adding temporal dimensions to response class definitions

Temporal dimension	Example
• Interresponse time	Pacing of rowing responses
• Event response latency	Response to emergency alarm
• Duration	Tying a bleeding artery

Response Products. Changes in the environment produced by responding are often transient. If you say "Hello" as you pass a colleague in the hallway and she answers by saying "Hi," there is no trace of your behavior once she walks on. However, it is not uncommon for some effects of a behavior to leave some relatively durable change in the environment. Changes that last for at least a while are called **response products**. These products are sometimes tangible, such as a composition that results from writing behavior or the litter in a city park that is a consequence of use by citizens. They may also be intangible, such as a light left on in a room indicating that someone was there.

Response products. The tangible or intangible environmental effects of responding that are more than transitory in duration.

Defining a response class in terms of its environmental products is a special version of a functional definition. What is observed is one of the effects or functions of responding, rather than the responses themselves. Response product definitions can be especially useful when real time observation would be difficult. This might be the case when the target behavior occurs infrequently over extended periods of time. The National Park Service uses this approach when it estimates usage of a remote hiking trail with a logbook at the trailhead that hikers are asked to sign when they start out. It may also sometimes be easier to define a behavior in terms of its products so that it is not necessary to maintain real time observation procedures. This might be the case in a manufacturing facility, for example, where each employee's work results in completed steps in a manufacturing process.

The physical products of responding can be a useful way of specifying a response class, but there are three possible problems that can complicate interpreting the resulting data. First, the owner of two puppies who comes home to find a single pile of excrement on the living room rug will recognize the problem of *determining ownership* of the defecation response that created it. A park ranger may likewise question the existence of a group of hikers that included George Washington, Mick Jagger, and Marilyn Monroe.

A second challenge in drawing conclusions from response product data may be illustrated by attempting to measure the number of people using a city park by counting pieces of litter. Because there is no direct observation while the behavior is occurring, *assuming one-to-one correspondence* between response products and actual responses can be unwise in some cases. It is possible, for example, that most of the litter may have been left by only a minority of the park's users.

A third possible limitation of this definitional approach arises from the investigator's *lack of contact with the actual topographical variations* that make up the response class. Observing the response product may often tell little about the form of the different responses involved. Sometimes variations in the form of responses may be unimportant, of course, particularly in situations in which topography may be narrowly constrained by the situation. For example, the form of a worker's behavior may be dictated by the equipment being used. However, subtle variations in the form of responses can sometimes determine their effectiveness. This is often true of athletic behavior, such as swinging a golf club. Researchers and practitioners may learn useful things from seeing these variations. A researcher studying manufacturing productivity, for instance, may find it valuable to observe responding as it is happening in order to see differences from one response to another that might affect productivity or safety.

TABLE 4.3
Risks in interpreting response product data

Interpretive risk	Example
• Determining authorship	Puppy mess
• Assuring 1:1 correspondence	Litter in a park
• Lack of contact with topography	Golf swing

Group Definitions. Thus far, we have considered ways of defining response classes for individuals. This is appropriate because behavior is a phenomenon that occurs only between individuals and their environments (see chapter 2). There may be times, however, when scientific interest lies in the behavior of individuals only as it contributes to a collective performance of a group. It is the collective behavior of individuals who behave in a related way that we might call **group behavior**.

> **Group behavior.** A mathematical result of combining behavioral data from multiple individuals whose behavior is related in some way. Does not refer to a natural phenomenon distinct from the behavior of individual organisms.

As we have already suggested, this phrase is easily misunderstood. Although we often refer to the "behavior" of groups ("the class was making too much noise when the teacher was out of the room"), groups do not behave. Behavior is a biological function of organisms, and a group is not an organism. It is certainly true that individuals often behave differently when they are with others than when they are alone, but their behavior in social environments is still just individual behavior. There is no new, fundamentally different phenomenon that emerges when individuals behave in social situations. The differences in a person's behavior under social versus solitary conditions are due to the different contingencies often operating in social environments.

When there is a legitimate interest in the collective output of the behavior of multiple individuals, there are three basic ways they can contribute to some "group" outcome. First, the behavior of different individuals may make collective and equivalent contributions to some result through their interactions. For example, the noise made by a class of second graders could serve as the dependent variable in a study of class management procedures. If a recording device is used to make a record of sound levels in the classroom, the noise-making behavior of any or all of the children will contribute in an equivalent way to the collective effect. Furthermore, this functional definition of the group's "responding" takes into account the possibility that each child's behavior may be influenced by the behavior of others.

Second, interest may center on an arbitrarily defined collection of individuals who do not interact in ways that might usually define a group but who may all respond in the same way in the same setting. Customers who make purchases in a store illustrate this point. Using sales receipts, we could identify purchasing responses by all of the people who buy something, even though they do not interact.

Third, the behavior of individuals may contribute to some collective outcome, although their behavioral contributions may differ and the individuals may or may not interact. This would be the case in many work scenarios, for example, in which some product such as automobiles results from the varied efforts of different workers.

TABLE 4.4
Types of group response class definitions

Type of group contribution	Example
• Collective, equivalent, interactive	Measuring effects of noise-making behavior
• Collective, equivalent, noninteractive	Measuring store purchases of shoppers
• Collective, nonequivalent	Measuring work products

These ways of measuring the collective behavioral contributions of individuals may sometimes be useful. However, it is important to realize how these definitions of "group behavior" restrict interpretations of the resulting data. Although such data in some way take into account the behavior of different individuals, their different contributions to the collective outcome are usually not separately recorded. Measures of behavior are typically expressed only in some aggregate form. This constraint means that we cannot make statements about the effects of treatment conditions on the behavior of individuals.

For instance, if a teacher's implementation of a classroom management plan is followed by a decrease in sound-level data from that second grade class, we only know that the sum of all noise-making responses decreased. We do not know whether this decrease occurred for each child or only some. In other words, we do not know from the data how the effect on the group "response" was produced. Even though the data include intervention effects on the behavior of at least some of the children, we do not have any evidence about those effects for individual children. Because this is the level at which the effects occurred, this means that we do not actually know the effect of the intervention on behavior. This might seem contrary to common sense, but remember that behavior exists only at the level of the individual.

As we will learn in later chapters, this is a significant limitation that applies whenever the data from different individuals are grouped by any method of defining, collecting, displaying, or analyzing behavioral data. Drawing conclusions based on any type of grouped data must be limited to statements about the effects of treatment conditions only as aggregate outcomes. As a result, how well these statements will hold for individuals will be less clear than if the data showed the effects for each individual.

In the example of the second grade class, individual data might have shown that although a majority of the children got quieter when the intervention was initiated, a number of them made as much or more noise. With only grouped data, we might conclude that the aggregate effect of the intervention was to produce a decrease in noise-making behavior. Individual data would allow us to describe two kinds of effects (less noise-making behavior versus no change or an increase). Such data might encourage researchers to conduct further studies to determine what factors predict the two different outcomes, which would then allow teachers to know whether the intervention is appropriate in different situations.

Is it always important to be able to identify the effects of interventions on the behavior of each individual?—not necessarily, but more often than you might think. If the research objective is to learn something about behavior, the answer is almost always "yes." If a company hired you to do a study of why worker performance in a section of a plant has deteriorated, a group definition of the target behavior will probably not be sufficient. As you implement changes and look at their effects on performance, you may need to know what those effects are for each worker. For example, if you compare the effects of two different types of equipment on performance, you would want to know if the effects depended on whether workers were right or left handed or wore glasses. Grouping the data across workers would usually hide such variations.

On the other hand, if you truly only need to measure behavior in aggregate form, you might be able to get away with a group definition of target behavior. For example, if you address a factory's absenteeism problem by implementing a well-established program for dealing with such problems, it might be sufficient to show an improvement in aggregate data. If things did not turn out as planned, however, you might need to learn why. This would probably require looking at individual patterns of absenteeism.

BOX 4.5

Operational Definitions and Behavioral Measurement

In 1927, a Harvard physicist named Bridgeman published a landmark book, *The Logic of Modern Physics*, in which he proposed that what we mean by any concept is synonymous with the operations by which it is measured. Psychology was particularly taken with the idea that its challenges with defining psychological concepts could be resolved by using operational definitions. Anxiety, for example, would be defined not in terms of hypothetical internal processes but as the outcome of particular experimental and measurement procedures. Unfortunately, it did not improve the understanding of concepts such as anxiety for each researcher to report that the term referred to the outcome of measurement operations in his or her experiment. Although these operations might be clear in each case, anxiety was still defined differently from one researcher to another.

Behavioral scientists approached the notion of operationism very differently (see Kantor, 1945; Skinner, 1945). For them, because scientists are behaving organisms (just like their experimental participants), the terms that scientists "use" must be understood as no more than instances of behavior. A researcher's words are not symbolic objects that substitute for physical events. They are simply verbal responses that he or she has learned to emit under certain conditions. Therefore, the meaning of a term or concept (a verbal response) lies in the factors that influence its use (emission). For behavior analysts, operationism focuses on assessing how participant responses and experimental factors influence the verbal behavior of the researcher (see Moore, 1975, for discussion of this topic). From this perspective, what terms mean are not defined by other words but by the factors that lead researchers to "use" them.

For behavioral researchers and practitioners, then, **operational definitions** are not another way of defining a response class. They are not a third alternative to functional and topographical definitions or a general approach common to both. Because we do not define a behavior in terms of hypothetical, internal processes, there is no need to search for clarity or agreement by trying to define a behavior in terms of our measurement operations. Although measuring a behavior always involves some procedures (or operations) by which we implement a definition, it is incorrect to describe these procedures as operational definitions.

In sum, the decision to define response classes in terms of the collected behavioral contributions of individuals depends on the kinds of conclusions desired. If the goal is to understand behavior–environment interactions, target behaviors must be defined, measured, and analyzed for individuals. This approach is also preferable when the goal is to apply established procedures to achieve a practical outcome, even if the interventions involve multiple consumers. (Analysis of the effects for each individual can also be supplemented with grouped summaries of individual data.) In some instances, however, it may be sufficient to define target behaviors in terms of some kind of combination of the behavior of different individuals. This choice should be based on reasoning that the nature of the behavioral interest and the objectives of the project justify the limited conclusions that will be available.

Selecting a Response Class

Specificity. Defining a response class involves developing a rule for separating selected responses from the rest of an individual's repertoire. As we have seen, the major features of the target behavior will be determined by the focus of the question, the characteristics of participants, the opportunities for measurement, and the needs of experimental or treatment conditions. In accommodating these interests, the researcher or practitioner has the opportunity to choose the breadth or specificity of the response class.

The "size" of the response class can be important. If too small a piece of behavior is targeted by the definition, it may lack adequate relevance for the study. For example, making spelling errors may not adequately represent certain qualities of more complex behaviors in everyday life, such as completing writing assignments. On the other hand, selecting too large a piece of behavior may prevent the discovery of important sources of variability. For instance, if a consultant is studying an employee's work performance, defining a response class as "completing assigned projects" may make it difficult to learn that poor performance is due to problems with smaller response classes within the larger class, such as gathering needed materials, coordinating with coworkers, or writing the final report.

Aside from defining a response class with a meaningful level of specificity, the frequency with which responding occurs can also be important. If the behavior of interest occurs very often or very infrequently, it may require adjusting the specificity or size of the response class. Consider the example of a child in an alternative classroom who often gets into fights with peers. Although such aggressive behavior may occur only once or twice each week, the behavior of hitting others may occur so rapidly in a fight that it is difficult for observers to count them accurately.

One solution is to define bouts of hitting responses as an **episode** of responding. It may even be that such episodes constitute functional classes themselves (such as fighting, which might include the different response classes of hitting, kicking, and cursing). The use of episodes as a way of measuring a response class requires rules defining the onset and offset of each episode. Although it may be clear when fighting is occurring, it must also be clear when each episode starts and ends. The risk with this approach is that changes in the number of episodes may mask what is happening with the smaller response classes subsumed by the definition of the episode. For example, a decrease in the number of fighting episodes each day may hide the fact that the number of cursing responses per episode is increasing.

> **Episode.** A relatively brief period of responding defined by the relatively frequent occurrence of one or more specific response classes and which is distinguished from other such bouts by relatively extended periods in which the target responses do not occur.

A different problem can occur when the behavior of interest happens very infrequently. One such example might involve customers who make purchases in the stores of a shopping mall. An individual customer may purchase items only occasionally (two or three times per month). This is so low a response frequency that it would be difficult to detect decreases in responding. A tactic that can address this problem is to look for subclasses that compose the larger class of purchasing behavior that might occur with a more useful frequency. These might include going into different stores, handling merchandise, or asking questions of sales persons. These behaviors may occur much more often than actual purchasing and may be better able to serve research interests.

This approach can be particularly useful in addressing problem behaviors that are serious in their consequences but occur too infrequently to be a suitable target for interventions. For example, an individual with mental retardation living in a group home may break a window with his fist only a couple of times a year, though with obvious medical risks. However, precursor behaviors involving getting upset or destroying property may constitute part of a larger response class that includes breaking windows. This larger class may occur much more often and therefore make a suitable target for intervention.

Sensitivity. Finally, one of the most important considerations in selecting a target behavior lies in its potential to be influenced by treatment variables. In both experimental and practical scenarios, it is important that the behavioral features of interest are free to vary so that any effects of interventions can be detected. One kind of limit to this sensitivity occurs when the behavior being measured has lower or upper limits on variability for some reason. Under such circumstances, measures of responding may not reveal the effects of interventions that would otherwise be found.

For instance, in a social skills training program, the behavior of initiating conversations is clearly limited by the number of possible daily contacts. If a participant is already initiating conversations at almost every available opportunity, it might be difficult for a treatment program to produce an increase in responding.

A similar limitation may occur for different reasons when the target behavior occurs very infrequently. If a behavior does not occur very much at all, it may receive so little exposure to a treatment condition that it does not show any effects, even though effects might be clear if there were greater contact with the condition.

Perhaps the most common risk to the sensitivity of the response class is when it is so heavily influenced by extraneous factors that it is not very susceptible to the impact of a treatment condition. This pre-emptive control by extraneous variables can result from a single, powerful source or from a collection of weaker influences. It is not unusual in educational settings, for example, for academic behavior to be so heavily influenced by social factors associated with peers and teachers that the impact of teaching procedures that would otherwise be effective is difficult to document.

TABLE 4.5
Limitations on sensitivity

Type of limitation	Problem	Example
• Upper limit on variability	Increases in responding may not be seen	Limited opportunity for behavior to occur
• Lower limit on variability	Inadequate contact with treatment conditions	Behavior occurs very infrequently
• Excessive extraneous influences	Treatment effects not found	Behavior heavily influenced by nontreatment factors

Although it is easy to recognize these limitations on the sensitivity of the target behavior in principle, it is usually more difficult to identify these risks in practice. The impact of extraneous factors will not necessarily show up in the data, which is a bit late to be addressing this problem anyway. The only recourse is for researchers and practitioners to consider the susceptibility to significant extraneous factors when they are considering possible target behaviors.

Defining a Response Class

Assuming that the general nature of the target behavior is already clear, let us summarize the steps in developing a response class definition. First, consider the characteristics of the behavior. What are its functional relations with environmental events? What are its topographical features? How might it be affected by experimental variables? What observational challenges is it likely to involve?

Second, decide whether the definition will be functional or topographical or if both kinds of elements should be taken into account. In this decision, consider the differences in the defined response class (and the data) that would result from one approach versus another. How important might these differences be?

Third, write out a draft definition that includes all of the features and criteria you think will be necessary. Compose the definition like a lawyer writing a contract. Make sure that every required detail needed is present and that nothing unnecessary is included. The definition should be a plain statement that specifies for each candidate response whether it should be recorded or ignored. If measurement will be conducted by observers, the definition should be seen as a rule telling them what to observe and record. It should not include any reference to the reason why the behavior is being measured, the performance criteria related to the intervention, or the outcomes that might be anticipated.

Fourth, try out the draft definition by making some informal but careful observations. Use this experience to modify the definition in whatever ways seem appropriate. Continue collecting data using the now improved definition. Evaluate the effects of any modifications by comparing the data to data obtained under earlier versions. What do the data tell you about your definition?

Fifth, once you are satisfied with the definition, determine how it will guide measurement procedures. If observation will be conducted automatically, insure that the equipment performs in exactly the way required by the definition. If observers will be used to collect data, how might the definition suggest that they will need to be trained and monitored (see chapters 6 and 7)? Collect the evidence you feel you need in order to convince yourself and others that the definition you have written down is the same one being used to collect data.

Sixth, start the experiment or intervention using your measurement system. As you gain continuing experience with the definition, be ready to modify it if the target behavior changes significantly in its functions or form. Although this may require throwing out the data collected to that point, it may be worth it to avoid burdening the data with serious limitations.

In sum, developing a response class definition is not difficult, but it takes thoughtful consideration of the behavior you want to get a picture of and what definitional criteria will best guide measurement procedures. Beyond the intellectual effort, it involves putting draft definitions to the test by using them to generate some data, learning from the experience, and trying again. Coming

TABLE 4.6
Steps in defining a response class

- Consider the characteristics of the behavior
- Decide on the type of definition needed
- Compose a written draft definition
- Try out the draft definition by using it to measure responding. Modify as necessary and try out the modifications
- Determine how the definition will guide measurement procedures
- Start the experiment or intervention but be ready to modify the definition further if necessary

---

up with the right definition is not a mundane exercise. After all, it specifies the dependent variable in research or practical interventions, which will be the basis for conclusions about treatment effects.

Labeling Response Classes

One of the biggest challenges in defining a response class has to do with how others will interpret your research or clinical findings. Whatever its detailed features, each definition is usually described with a brief label that serves the everyday communication functions as other labels for objects and events. Unfortunately, any summary label may be interpreted differently by different readers. "Disruptive behavior," for example, could certainly mean different things to different people, regardless of how a response class was defined in a particular study. One teacher might consider talking in class as disruptive, whereas another teaching a different kind of class might consider talking among students perfectly acceptable.

Other sciences minimize this problem by using a technical vocabulary in place of colloquial terms. Instead of referring to "vultures," for instance, ornithologists refer to a specific grouping of birds, such as the families Aegypiidae and Cathartidae, or even to a specific genus and species. Among ornithologists, these technical labels have very narrow definitions and there is little chance of misunderstanding what kinds of birds are being referenced.

The science of behavior has no such taxonomic vocabulary of behavior, nor is it even possible to come up with a technical label for every possible behavior. This limitation stems from the fact that each response class is unique from one person to another. Furthermore, because behavior continuously adapts to changing environmental circumstances, any response class is always changing for each person, even if in subtle ways. Together, these characteristics mean that there is probably an infinite number of response classes in an organism's behavior, let alone across all members of a species.

When a researcher attaches a shorthand label to a carefully defined response class in a study, anyone reading the published study can be pretty clear about what the label refers to. However, when other researchers use the same label in their projects, it will refer to somewhat different definitions from one study to another. Nevertheless, such labels are often used to refer to an entire area of research literature (for example, self-injurious behavior).

These unavoidable variations in how particular labels are used raise an important question: If a researcher publishes a study investigating cooperative play behavior in preschool children, how can other researchers or practitioners know if those results will also be found if they use the same procedures in their situation? More broadly, in an area of literature defined by a certain behavioral label (self-injurious behavior, for instance), how well do the different studies using somewhat different definitions fit together to provide a coherent picture of what we know? There is no easy answer to this kind of question, of course. Each chapter of the book identifies some factors that bear on the answer to this question, and chapter 13 will address the issue of generality in detail. However, the label we attach to particular response class definitions used in each experiment or practical intervention can make a difference in how we interpret their results.

What, then, can researchers and practitioners do to communicate clearly about the kind of behavior under study? First, clearly stating the definitions of each target response class will probably help more than anything else. It will often help if the behavior is also defined functionally so that all responses in the class share common relations with the environment. Second, when deciding what to call target behaviors, it can help to be aware of how others may interpret or use the label. Calling a response class "hitting others" is less likely to be misinterpreted than the more general label "aggression." Similarly, "writing reports" or "calling clients" is probably a better label than "working." Third, choosing labels that clarify the relation of the movement to the environment may also encourage narrow interpretations. For example, the term "playing" covers an endless variety of behavior–environment possibilities. In contrast, "playing with blocks" or "playing house with peers" narrows down the possible interpretations.

Although these suggestions may aid communication about behavior among researchers and practitioners, there is no real solution to this challenge. The nature of behavior guarantees endless variety in its forms and relations with the environment, and everyday language cannot meet the requirements for scientific specificity. Nevertheless, it is our task as researchers and practitioners to translate our investigations into everyday language. As we come to better understand the factors that determine the generality of research findings, we will be better prepared to refine the way we describe response classes.

CHAPTER SUMMARY

1. Researchers and practitioners have shifted from defining stimuli and responses in purely physical terms, to including a description about their function and relationship with each other.

2. There are three general types of response classes. In respondent behavior, specific environmental stimuli consistently elicit specific responses called reflexes. During operant behaviors, responding is followed by a change in the environment that results in similar responses becoming more likely to occur in the future (reinforcement) or less likely (punishment). The third classification of behavior–environment interactions is based on stimuli that regularly precede operant behaviors that are followed by reinforcement, and acquire the function of making these responses more likely to occur in their presence than in their absence.

3. Functional response class definitions include only those responses whose occurrence is dependent upon a specific class of stimuli that either precede or follow the response. In contrast, topographical response class definitions may include responses that do not share the same functional

relations with environmental stimuli, even though they are topographically the same.

4. When conducting applied studies, it is important to use functional definitions that cover all of the responses that belong in the existing class and avoid including responses that do not belong in that particular class. If the definition is not accurate, the data are likely to show more variability than would be necessary and may not show dependable intervention effects.

5. The first step in developing a functional definition is to consider the everyday context of the target behavior, including possible antecedents and consequences. Following this assessment, the investigator can write a preliminary definition and use it to guide measurement activities and evaluate what is recorded.

6. The first step in developing a topographical definition is to identify why it is necessary to define the behavior in terms of the form that each individual response takes. The experimenter should then carefully describe the limits of form that responses must show in order to be measured.

7. Response class definitions may include temporal requirements. Requirements may be added that address: (a) the time between the presentation of a stimulus and the occurrence of the target behavior; (b) the time required to complete a response; or (c) the amount of time that must occur between successive responses.

8. Response product definitions may be useful when real time observation may not be feasible. However, these definitions are limited due to the fact that: (a) one may not always be able to determine who produced the product; (b) you cannot assume that there is a 1:1 correspondence between the response product and the occurrence of the target behavior; and (c) the response product may not tell the researcher anything about the topography of the response.

9. Recall that behavior exists only at the level of the individual. When speaking about group behavior and drawing conclusions based on any type of grouped data, our conclusions must be limited only to statements about the effects of treatment conditions as an aggregate outcome.

10. When selecting a response class, the researcher must be sure that the class is neither too small (may not be relevant to the study) nor too large (may inhibit the identification of important sources of variability). Researchers must also consider how frequently the target behavior occurs in deciding what behaviors to include in the response class.

11. One of the most important considerations in selecting a target behavior lies in its potential to be influenced by the independent variable(s). It is important that the target behavior not be too restricted, otherwise it will not be able to display all of the effects that the intervention may produce. Additionally, the investigator must make sure that the response class is not so heavily influenced by extraneous factors that it is not very susceptible to the impact of the treatment condition.

12. When labeling response classes, researchers and practitioners must be sure to communicate clearly what the behavior is. This may be accomplished by clearly stating the definition of each target response, being aware of how others may interpret or use the label that you have selected, and using behavior-specific labels when possible.

TEXT STUDY GUIDE

1. What is a unit of analysis?
2. What is a response class?
3. Explain the three types of response classes associated with environment–behavior relationships: respondents, operants, and discriminated operants.
4. Distinguish between functional and topographical response class definitions.
5. List three objectives that should guide the selection of target response classes.
6. How do you go about developing a functional response definition? What should be common to all defined responses?
7. What is required to develop a topographical response class definition?
8. Describe three ways of adding a temporal requirement to a behavioral definition.
9. Explain each of the following issues associated with defining a behavior in terms of its products: (a) determining authorship; (b) assuring a one-to-one correspondence between responses and products; (c) lack of contact with topographical variations.
10. Defend the statement that there is no such phenomenon as group behavior.
11. What are three ways of defining a response class that involves the behavior of different individuals in some combined form?
12. What are the interpretive restrictions required by using group response class definitions?
13. Explain the problems that can result from a response class being too large or too small.
14. What is meant by the "sensitivity" of a response class?
15. List the steps in defining a response class.
16. Describe the problems with attaching everyday labels to response classes.

BOX STUDY GUIDE

1. Distinguish between units of analysis and units of measurement.

2. Explain the proper use of the following terms: behavior, response class, and responses.

3. What is adjunctive behavior?

4. Explain the complications of defining a nonbehavior.

5. Why are operational definitions not necessary when studying behavior that can be directly measured?

SUGGESTED READINGS

Falk, J. (1981). The environmental generation of excessive behavior. In S. J. Mule (Ed.), *Behavior in excess: An examination of the volitional disorders* (pp. 313–337). New York: Free Press.

Moore, J. (2008). *Conceptual foundations of radical behaviorism*. Cornwall-on-Hudson, NY: Sloan Publishing. [Chapter 5: Categories of behavior]

Skinner, B. F. (1945). Operational analysis of psychological terms. *Psychological Review, 52*, 270–281.

DISCUSSION TOPICS

1. Select some everyday references to behavior and discuss how to translate them into specific response classes.

2. Start with a general description of a behavior and then discuss how to come up with a functional versus topographical definition.

3. Discuss examples of definitions of behavior involving groups of individuals in terms of how they would limit conclusions about behavior.

4. Using some response classes defined in journal articles, discuss the implications of different kinds of summary labels that might be used.

EXERCISES

1. Without prior discussion, ask each student to write a definition for a generally described behavior. Then analyze the differences among the definitions, focusing on how these differences would generate differences in observations and the resulting data.

2. Identify some examples of when it might be useful to add temporal requirements to a response class definition.

3. Develop some response class definitions in terms of response products. Identify, for each, whether any of the three problems described in the chapter might apply.

CHAPTER FIVE

Dimensional Quantities and Units of Measurement

The need for quantification in the study of behavior is fairly widely understood, but it has frequently led to a sort of opportunism. The experimenter takes his measures where he can find them and is satisfied if they are quantitative even if they are trivial or irrelevant.

—B. F. Skinner

INTRODUCTION

Functions of Measurement

Thus far, we have considered the nature of behavior as a scientific subject matter (chapter 2) and how to select and define particular instances of behavior for investigation or practical intervention (chapter 4). We now turn to the next step in measuring behavior. We have to decide what features of the

97

target behavior we might be interested in and how to describe what is observed.

Measurement involves assigning numbers and units to particular features of objects or events, and it is one of the foundations of scientific method. Measurement allows us to accomplish three functions: description, comparison, and prediction.

We are so familiar with measurement in everyday life (e.g., weighing ourselves on a scale) that we may not appreciate the formalities involved.

Description involves attaching a number to an event to distinguish it from other events. For instance, you might describe your weight with the number 68, which would permit you to notice that it is different from yesterday's weight of 69. Of course, this should seem a bit odd because we are accustomed to attaching some unit of measurement to an observation so that we can be clear about what dimension of an event we are describing. In this case the unit would be the kilogram, which, because it is a unit that describes some amount of weight, also tells us that weight is the dimension being referenced. So, you would report your weight as 68 or 69 kilograms, and this description would be interpreted the same way all over the world. (By the way, we used the kilogram instead of the pound in this example because all scientists use the metric system of units.)

Comparison involves using descriptions of multiple individual events to identify differences or similarities among them. Of course, comparisons are most useful if the descriptions being compared specify a unit of measurement. This makes the comparison valid for a particular dimension. In our example of weight, comparing 68 kilograms to 69 kilograms allows us to observe that the events differ by 1 kilogram.

Prediction requires repeated descriptions of events made over time. As changes in a series of measures are observed, a statement relating these changes to the passage of time can be used to predict the outcome of future measurements. If, for instance, we knew that your weight was 68 kilograms at the beginning of January, 69 kilograms at the beginning of February, and 70 kilograms at the beginning of March, we might predict that it would be 71 kilograms at the beginning of April.

> **Description.** Attaching a number to an event to distinguish it from other events.
>
> **Comparison.** Using descriptions of multiple individual events to identify differences among them.
>
> **Prediction.** Making repeated descriptions of an event taken over time in order to predict the outcome of a future measurement.

Dimensional Measurement

When we attach a number to a particular dimension representing how much of that dimension was observed it is called **dimensional measurement**. Measuring events in terms of specific dimensions requires distinguishing among properties, dimensional quantities, and units of measurement. A **property** is a fundamental quality of a phenomenon. For instance, an object moving in space has the property of motion. A **dimensional quantity** (often just called a quantity) is a quantifiable aspect of a property. The property of motion can be measured in terms of the dimensional quantities of velocity and acceleration, for example, among others. Finally, we cannot measure dimensional quantities without specifying exactly how much of the dimension was observed, and this is the function served by **units of measurement**.

> **Dimensional measurement.** An approach to measurement that involves attaching a number representing the observed extent of a dimensional quantity to an appropriate unit of measurement.
>
> **Property.** A fundamental quality of a natural phenomenon. See *Dimensional quantity*.
>
> **Dimensional quantity.** A quantifiable dimension of a property of a natural phenomenon. Also referred to as a *quantity*.
>
> **Unit of measurement.** A determinate amount of a dimensional quantity of the phenomenon being measured.

We have already suggested that in order to be scientifically useful a unit of measurement must refer to a fixed amount of a dimensional quantity. It is important to add the requirement that these units be defined independently of what is being measured and that their definition be standard within and across scientific disciplines.

The reason why a description such as "68 kilograms" is unambiguous is that a kilogram is defined in terms of the mass of a platinum–iridium cylinder kept at the International Bureau of Weights and Measures near Paris. If different researchers had different ways of defining a kilogram, or if this unit of measurement could vary from one application to another, such descriptions of weight would lead to confusion. Units of measurement that are defined in a fixed or unvarying manner independently of the event being measured are called **absolute units**. When these absolute units are accepted and used in the same way by all scientists, they may also be described as standard. All of the natural sciences long ago accepted the need for absolute and standard units of measurement.

> **Absolute unit.** A unit of measurement whose value is defined in a fixed or unvarying manner independently of the phenomenon being measured.

PROPERTIES, DIMENSIONAL QUANTITIES, AND UNITS

Features of Individual Responses

First, let us look at dimensional quantities that may be used to describe individual responses. We can start by noting that behavior shares some of the properties and dimensional quantities of other natural phenomena. For example, interactions between organisms and their environments occur in time, and we can therefore locate responses in time. One property of behavior is therefore its **temporal locus**. This property is reflected by the dimensional quantity of **latency**. Figure 5.1 shows one type of latency called an **event-response latency**. This quantity describes how much time elapses following an environmental event before a response occurs. For example, we might be interested in how quickly an employee returns phone calls from clients. We cannot only record the event-response latency of individual responses but we can also sum them across all responses in a session or even calculate an average latency.

FIG. 5.1.   Schematic representation of event-response latencies.

Temporal locus. A property of any phenomenon that occurs in time. Described in terms of the dimensional quantity of latency.

Latency. A dimensional quantity that refers to the time between two events. In the study of behavior, the second event is usually a response and the first event may be an response or an environment event.

Event-response latency. In the study of behavior, a type of latency representing the time between an environmental event and a response.

The units of measurement that specify exactly how much latency is observed are the units of time with which we are already familiar. The basic unit of time is the second, which is defined with reference to the vibration frequency of the cesium atom of atomic mass 133. The second and its multiples (minutes, hours, days, etc.) are absolute and standard descriptors of temporal features of behavior.

A second temporal property of behavior is **temporal extent**, and **duration** is a quantifiable dimension of this property. The duration of a response is defined as the time from its onset to its termination. Figure 5.2 shows a diagram representing the durations of two responses. The response class definition

FIG. 5.2. Schematic representation of the duration of two responses.

should make it possible to determine when target responses are or are not occurring. With this capability, it is possible to measure when each response starts and stops and therefore determine the time that each response takes from beginning to end. In Figure 5.1, observation would show the duration of r_1 and r_2, and we could add these durations together to obtain the total duration of this behavior during this "session." As with latencies, the units of measurement for duration are the units of time.

> **Temporal extent.** A property of any phenomenon that occurs in time. Described in terms of the dimensional quantity of duration.
>
> **Duration.** A dimensional quantity that refers to the elapsed time between the beginning and ending of an event, such as a single response.

A third property of behavior may seem less obvious than temporal locus and temporal extent, but it is no less important. For any class of responses, individual responses can occur repeatedly, which suggests the property of **repeatability**. The dimensional quantity reflecting the recurrence of an event is called **countability** (or just "count"). We describe how much countability is observed in terms of the **cycle**. The cycle is the unit of measurement used in the natural sciences that specifies one instance of whatever is being observed. This is not a term that is widely used in behavioral research and practice, however. For example, it would be common to report that a participant emitted 32 responses during a session. The more technically correct reference of 32 cycles of the response class maintains the distinction between the unit of analysis (the response class) and the unit of measurement (cycles). Technicalities aside, the more common reference is acceptable.

> **Repeatability.** A property of events that can recur. In the study of behavior, a property of a class of functionally equivalent responses. Described in terms of the dimensional quantity of countability.
>
> **Countability.** A dimensional quantity reflecting the property of repeatability that refers to the occurrence of the event being measured and is measured in terms of cycles.
>
> **Cycle.** A unit of measurement for the dimensional quantity of countability.

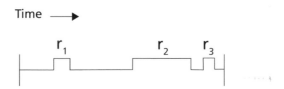

FIG. 5.3.   Schematic representation of the countability of three responses.

Figure 5.3 diagrams the countability of three responses. Even though the figure suggests some temporal information (e.g., we can see that r_2 has a longer duration than the other two responses), if we were measuring only countability for this "session" all we would know would be "three cycles." We would not know anything about their durations or how much time elapsed between responses, for instance. Nevertheless, what we would make of the fact that three responses occurred might partly depend on temporal information.

This shortcoming highlights the fact that although each of these three dimensional quantities tells us something important about behavior, each fails to describe other aspects of responding that might also be important. For example, if we knew that a child solved 75 problems correctly, we would also probably like to know how long it took. Similarly, if all we knew was the total duration of all responses during a session, we would probably want to know how many cycles or responses contributed to the total duration. In our example, although it might be useful to know that a child spent 30 minutes working on math problems, it would be even more informative to also know that she solved 75 problems correctly during that time.

Features of Multiple Responses

Countability, duration, and event-response latency are quantities that can be used to describe aspects of a single response. However, researchers and practitioners usually observe a particular behavior throughout a session, during which time multiple responses from that class are likely to occur. When this is the case, some additional dimensional quantities become available to describe responding.

For example, a second type of latency that is characteristic of repeated responses is **interresponse time (IRT)**. Interresponse time refers to the time elapsing between two successive responses. The IRT for a response is measured from the end of the previous response, so in Figure 5.4 the interresponse time for r_2 is l_1. The unit of measurement for IRT is **time per cycle**. Interresponse time can be an important aspect of responding, especially when

> **Interresponse time (IRT).** A dimensional quantity refering to the time elapsing between two successive responses.
>
> **Time per cycle.** The unit of measurement for interresponse time.

FIG. 5.4. Schematic representation of interresponse latencies.

interest lies in the pace of responding. Many skills require short IRTs to be effective. For instance, the IRTs associated with reading words must be fairly short in order for the skill to be useful. Long IRTs between reading words may suggest that other behavior, such as struggling to decode a word, is getting in the way.

One of the most broadly useful quantities that describes a response class is **frequency** of responding. Frequency reflects the properties of both repeatability and temporal locus. In the study of behavior, measures of frequency generally take the form of a ratio of the number of cycles of a behavior (responses) occurring over some period of time. Skinner (1938) regarded this quantity as the fundamental datum in the study of operant behavior, and it has proven to be a very useful feature. The unit of measurement for frequency is **cycles per unit time**, most often cycles per minute. This is a compound unit because it references two quantities (countability and latency).

> **Cycles per unit time.** The unit of measurement for the dimensional quantity of frequency. In the study of behavior, minutes is most often the time unit used (e.g., 1.5 cycles per minute).

There are two ways in which behavioral researchers and practitioners calculate frequencies of responding. The total count of responses is divided by either the total amount of time when responses were not occurring (i.e., the total IRT) or the total time when the behavior was observed. In the first instance, dividing count by the total IRT requires measuring the IRT of each response and summing for all responses. Alternatively, total IRT can be calculated by subtracting total duration from total session time. Either way, this is often easy to do in laboratory settings, where computers can be programmed to determine the exact time between responses. This can also be done under field conditions when human observers record responses on a computer. When data are collected manually, however, measuring IRT or duration can be more difficult, although it is certainly possible. The second approach only requires determining the total time of observation, which is usually much easier.

Aside from the effort involved in these two approaches to calculating frequency, it can be important to distinguish between the somewhat different pictures they might provide. It helps to remember that when we look at frequencies of responding, we are looking at how often a behavior occurred, with the assumption that it was possible to respond in the first place.

Let us examine this assumption more closely. Imagine, for example, that we are looking at frequencies of self-injurious behavior in an individual with profound mental retardation during 1-hour sessions under treatment and non-treatment conditions. Let us further assume that the behavior can occur at any time during nontreatment sessions but can occur only some of the time in treatment sessions because physical restraints are sometimes used to prevent serious injury. If frequencies are calculated by dividing the number of cycles (responses) by the 60-minute length of observation sessions, it might be difficult to make a fair comparison between the data from nontreatment and treatment phases. The problem is that if the individual was restrained for a significant portion of some treatment sessions, the frequency values might be lower just because there was less opportunity for the behavior to occur. In these cases, the lower frequencies would be misleading when compared to the frequencies obtained in the nontreatment condition when responding was possible throughout the full 60-minute sessions. Of course, the solution is to divide the total number of self-injurious responses by the number of minutes out of the hour during which the individual actually had the opportunity to respond. (Box 5.2 provides an example of this issue using quantitative values.)

BOX 5.1

Frequency versus Rate

We use **frequency** rather than *rate* to refer to a ratio of count divided by time. In the natural sciences, frequency usually refers to cyclic features of natural phenomena such as sound and light. Dictionary entries are consistent with this approach, defining frequency as the number of times something happens during a period of time. To confuse matters, however, it is used in descriptive statistics to refer to count, as in a frequency distribution (for example, the relative frequency of men versus women in the medical profession). It is easy to make the distinction between frequency as a ratio and frequency as count, however.

The problem with rate is that it has a greater number of meanings, none of which exactly suit our purpose. A common meaning is speed, as in miles per hour, which is a measure of count (number of miles) over time (hours). The numerator is not a recurring process, however, but a unit of distance. This meaning of rate (velocity) is not relevant to our need to describe the "oftenness" of a target behavior in terms of responses (cycles) per minute. Other meanings of rate are more colloquial and equally unhelpful. References to the rate for a double room, the interest rate on a loan, or how you would rate the service in a restaurant do not suggest ratios of count and time.

In sum, scientific terminology is driven by the need to be precise and clear, and frequency does a better job of meeting this standard than rate. Nevertheless, references to rate as count divided by time remain common in behavioral research. This means that you will need to be careful as both speaker and as listener or reader when considering ratios of count and time.

This example makes clear that when we look at a series of values describing the frequency of a certain behavior it can be important for them to reflect how often the behavior occurred *given that it was possible to respond*. This point is important because of the fact that all of the time during a session that the target behavior is occurring is the time during which there is no opportunity to respond. In other words, a behavior cannot usually occur when it is already occurring. For responses that are typically only momentary in duration (self-injurious behavior in the form of head hitting, for example), this limitation may not matter much. For responses that are often relatively extended in duration, this can greatly restrict how much time is available for additional responses to occur. For example, if the self-injurious behavior took the form of hand mouthing, each response could go on for some time, with the result that the amount of time available for additional hand-mouthing responses to occur during a session would be significantly less than the full observation period.

BOX 5.2

A Tale of Two Frequencies

In order to show the differences that can result from these two ways of calculating frequencies, imagine a study in which responding was measured during 20-minute sessions. Let us suppose that in the first session there were four responses and that their total duration was 16 minutes. If we calculated frequency by dividing the four responses by the total session time, the frequency would be 0.2 response per minute (4 responses divided by 20 minutes). If we calculated frequency using the total IRT, however, the frequency would be 1.0 response per minute (4 responses divided by 4 minutes).

Now, suppose that in a second session four responses also occurred but their total duration was only 8 minutes. If we calculated frequency by dividing the total count by total session time, the frequency would still be 0.2 response per minute (4 responses divided by 20 minutes). If the frequency for this second session was calculated by dividing the number of responses by the total IRT, however, the result would be 0.33 response per minute (4 responses divided by 12 minutes).

In other words, if we compared response frequencies in these two sessions, depending on which frequency calculation we used we would either find that the frequencies were the same (0.2 response per minute) or were different (1 response per minute versus 0.33 response per minute). The question is: Which calculation would provide us with the most useful information? Even though the same number of responses occurred in each 20-minute session, the "total session time" approach that gives us the same frequencies for both sessions would be misleading if we knew that the time available to respond was different in the two sessions. What we usually expect frequency to tell us is how often responding occurred, given that responding was possible in the first place.

One solution to this problem is to measure duration instead of frequency when the duration of responses can vary significantly. If frequency is being calculated, however, it may be necessary to divide the number of responses in a session by the amount of time when responses were not occurring—that is, to subtract total duration from total session time before dividing. Technically, then, even when responses are very brief, the ideal approach to calculating frequency is to divide total count by total IRT. This becomes especially important when response durations can be relatively long, however, which is not uncommon in applied settings. When response durations are consistently brief, there is probably little error involved in dividing total count by total session time.

TABLE 5.1
Methods of calculating frequency

Method	Application
• Total count/total IRT	Variable and/or long response durations
• Total count/total observation time	Consistently brief response durations

Let us now turn to a dimensional quantity that is closely related to frequency—**celeration**. Frequency of responding represents the number of responses divided by time. To calculate celeration, you then divide frequency by time. In other words, frequency reflects change in responding over time, but celeration represents change in frequency over time. We are familiar with this distinction when we are driving a car. If you are driving down the road at a more or less constant speed, your frequency would be described as, for example, 45 miles per hour. This represents the number of miles you would travel if you maintained that speed for one hour. If you started accelerating from 45 mph to 65 mph, the pace at which your frequency increased from moment to moment would be a measure of your acceleration. This is what you feel in a powerful car that seems to push you back against the seat.

> **Celeration.** A dimensional quantity that describes change in the frequency of responding over time.

Of course, we could talk about deceleration in the same way, and we feel it when putting on the brakes hard and are pressed against our seat belts. The term "celeration" drops the prefixes and becomes a general reference to a change in frequency over time. The unit of measurement is **cycles per unit time per unit time** (cycles per unit time squared).

> **Cycles per unit time per unit time.** The unit of measurement for celeration.

TABLE 5.2
Properties, dimensional quantities, and units of behavioral measurement

Property	Dimensional quantity	Units
• Temporal locus	Latency	Time units
• Temporal extent	Duration	Time units
• Repeatability	Countability	Cycles
• Temporal locus and repeatability	Rate	Cycles per unit time
• Temporal locus and repeatability	Celeration	Cycles per unit time per unit time
• Temporal locus and repeatability	IRT	Time per cycle

Finally, the dimensional quantities discussed thus far (see Table 5.2) are those most commonly used to describe behavior. There are many other aspects of behavior that may be relevant under some conditions, however. For example, chapter 4 indicated that the fact that behavior involves movement means that the topography or form of responses is sometimes an important feature. If a researcher or physical therapist is measuring the outcomes of rehabilitation

---

BOX 5.3

How Many Dimensional Quantities Are There?

The quantities reviewed in this chapter are only some of those that can describe aspects of behavior. What are some of the others and how many are there? The number of quantities that might reveal something about behavior are limited only by the nature of the data and the researcher's imagination about what features might be interesting. The literature of dimensional analysis describes hundreds of quantities that have been developed for studying physical phenomena (e.g., Barenblatt, 1987; Chertov, 1864; Ipsen, 1960).

Quantities useful in studying behavior may be created simply by specifying some mathematical way of describing a particular aspect of behavior. One quantity that has been used to describe the distribution of responding over intervals of time is called **quarter-life**. This measures the time required to emit 25% of the responses that occur during an interval (typically, under a fixed-interval schedule of reinforcement). Quarter-life provides a way of quantifying the curvature of a cumulative record of responding throughout an interval. Another quantity that was created to describe certain aspects of responding is **IRTs per opportunity**. This is a measure of the likelihood of occurrence of specific IRT values that accounts for the mutual exclusivity of all shorter IRTs in each instance of a given IRT range.

There is a limitation to the fun of developing novel quantities. Just because one can summarize some aspect of behavior with a calculated quantity does not mean that anything important or useful has been described. The usefulness of any quantity must be demonstrated through future research.

exercises for injured patients, for instance, it might be important to measure quantities such as the arc through which a patient moves an arm or leg or the speed (velocity) with which a movement is made.

TACTICAL ISSUES

Limitations of Ratios

Loss of Component Information. Ratios are valuable ways of looking at data, but they have two features that can sometimes be limiting. First, when we combine two dimensional quantities (such as total count divided by total IRT) in a ratio, we necessarily lose sight of the component values. This fact provides both an advantage and a disadvantage. The reason for calculating a ratio is to see the relationship between the two quantities more easily. The other side of the coin, however, is that you cannot then see the different count and time values that contributed to the frequencies.

Figure 5.5 illustrates this situation. Try covering up the bottom panel and first looking at the ratio values in the top panel. Describe the patterns of responding you see. When is responding stable or changing? Now, uncover the bottom panel. The ratios in the top panel were calculated by dividing the Q1 data set (the solid triangles) by the Q2 data set (the solid squares). Suppose that the Q1 values represent total counts over a series of sessions and the Q2 values represent time values, which would make the data in the top panel represent response frequencies. By comparing the three data sets, we can see that the frequency values do not reflect what is happening with either count or time values. For example, during sessions 9–19 the response frequency looks relatively stable, but you can see that the count and time data are both increasing during this period. The last dozen frequency values are also relatively stable, but in this case the component count and time data are both decreasing.

The fact that calculating ratios hides their contributing values is neither inherently good nor bad. It just means we need to take this limitation into account when we interpret the ratio values. For instance, we may need to look at the component values to see whether the ratios are changing because of changes in one or the other (or both) contributing measures. Again, assuming that the top panel shows frequencies of responding, it could be that frequencies are changing not because count measures are changing but because of changes in time measures.

Finally, when dealing with ratio data we should be careful to limit our description of what the data represent. For example, instead of describing frequency data by referring to "responding" changing in one way or another, we should qualify our reference by referring to changes in "frequency of responding." As the data in Figure 5.5 show, the way in which frequencies are changing does not correctly describe how counts are changing. Of course, this is a point that applies to any descriptions of responding in which we have

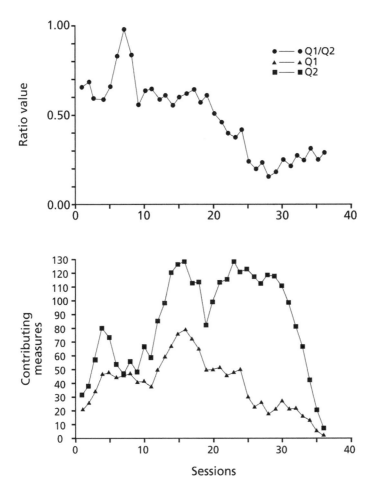

FIG. 5.5. Data illustrating how ratio values (top panel) can misrepresent their contributing component values (bottom panel).

data for only one dimensional quantity and do not therefore know what other quantities might reveal.

Dimensionless Quantities. When we divide total count by some measure of time such as minutes, the result retains the contributing units of measurement and is properly described as responses (cycles) per minute. If we are dividing two of the same kinds of quantities (e.g., duration of talking divided by duration of eating during a meal), the time units cancel and we are left with what is called a **dimensionless quantity**. Dimensionless quantities lack a

Dimensionless quantity. A unitless or scalar number that results from calculations whose components share the same dimensional quantities.

dimensional referent. In some scientific usages (e.g., describing variability in a set of measures) this can be an advantage. In other cases it can be a problem. For instance, a particularly common dimensionless quantity results from dividing two counts and multiplying the result by 100 to get a percentage. If we divided the number of items answered correctly by the number of items attempted and then multiplied by 100, for example, we would call the result "percent correct." Although this kind of calculation is often useful, keep in mind that percent correct is not a dimensional quantity. It is also important to remember that, as with other ratio-based calculations, it prevents one from seeing the component values.

BOX 5.4

Is Probability a Dimensional Quantity?

The concept of probability has a long history in science, and philosophers and mathematicians have been arguing about its meaning since the 17th century (Durbin, 1968). The three most common approaches include: (a) the *classical* or *a priori* definition, which defines probability as the ratio of favorable to total, equally possible cases; (b) the *frequency* or *a posteriori* interpretation, which defines probability in terms of the limit of the relative frequency of the occurrence of an attribute in an infinite sequence of events; and (c) the *subjective* interpretation, which says that probability is simply a measure of degree of belief (Salmon, 1966).

To further complicate matters, scientists seem to use the term in rather informal and varied ways. A survey of behavior analysts, for example, showed that all of the above usages were common, and almost a quarter of the respondents had still other meanings. Interestingly, more than 25% questioned the usefulness of the concept (Johnson & Morris, 1987), which seems to serve more colloquial than technical functions in the language of science. In sum, however, the term as used does not refer to a quantifiable dimension of behavior or any other phenomenon (Johnston & Pennypacker, 1993b, Reading 5).

Selecting Dimensional Quantities

How does a researcher or practitioner know which of the common quantities describing some aspect of behavior should be measured in a project? The short answer is that there is no way to be sure in advance which quantities will reveal important information about the target behavior. Furthermore, it is often impractical to try to measure all the usual suspects.

The solution to this dilemma lies in thinking through the factors that might guide the decision about which quantity, or quantities, to measure. First, the experimental question may suggest specific quantities. For example, it may ask how some variable affects the distribution of IRTs or the duration of a behavior.

Second, the research literature may be equally specific. Other researchers who have studied the same issue will have used certain quantities and generated evidence regarding their usefulness. It often makes sense to follow the lead of other investigators.

Third, the target behavior itself is likely to show obvious features that may require measurement. For example, if a practitioner is interested in seeing how outdoor recreational activities for a consumer in a group home are affected by a change in the daily schedule, duration of playing basketball would probably provide a more meaningful picture than counting the number of shots made.

Fourth, in most applied work the objectives of a study or intervention make certain quantities important. For example, if the focus of an intervention in a classroom setting with a student is to reduce off-task behavior, it will probably be important to measure the total duration of such activities in a class. Even though the actual intervention may target improving academic performance, being able to see what is happening with off-task behavior will still be important.

Fifth, the nature of experimental or intervention procedures can direct the choice of dimensional quantities. The question in each case concerns how an intervention procedure is likely to affect responding. Sometimes a procedure may directly involve a particular quantity, which will therefore be important to measure. For example, if reinforcers are earned by responding for long periods of time, then duration will likely be affected by the procedure. On the other hand, a procedure may suggest avoiding a certain quantity. As we already noted, if a discrete-trials procedure is used to teach a child with autism a skill, it would likely mean that measuring the frequency of responding would be unwise because the pace of responding would partly reflect the behavior of the trainer, not the child.

In sum, although there are no firm rules for selecting dimensional quantities for measurement, it is not usually difficult to figure out why some quantities would be more meaningful or useful than others for each target behavior. In this selection process, it is important to remember that the goal is to measure all quantities that will reveal data that help to answer the question. Another way of saying this is that the conclusions that can be drawn from the data are necessarily limited by the quantities that were measured. This is why we must limit our descriptions of responding to the quantities that were measured. It is not appropriate to make general statements such as "responding increased

TABLE 5.3
Factors that guide the selection of dimensional quantities

- Experimental question
- Research literature
- Target behavior
- Objectives of study
- Intervention procedures

---

under the treatment condition" because it implies that the statement is true for all quantities. Of course, we would not know how quantities that were not measured changed under the treatment condition.

CHAPTER SUMMARY

1. Measurement involves assigning numbers and units to particular features of objects or events. Through measurement, we are able to accomplish three functions: description, comparison, and prediction.

2. In order to be scientifically useful, a unit of measurement must have a standard definition within and across scientific disciplines. Additionally, the unit of measurement must refer to a fixed amount of a dimensional quantity.

3. Since the interaction of the environment and behavior occurs in time, an individual's behavior has several temporal properties that can be examined. Temporal locus is reflected by the dimensional quantity of latency, which measures the amount of time that passes between the onset of an environmental event and the occurrence of the target behavior (event-response latency).

4. We may also assess temporal extent, which is expressed quantifiably as duration. Duration of a response is defined as the amount of time from its onset to its termination. A third temporal property is repeatability, which is measured using the dimensional quantity of count.

5. One of the most useful quantities that describes a response class is the frequency of responding. Frequency is extremely useful because it reflects the properties of both repeatability (count) and temporal locus (latency).

6. Frequencies of responding are calculated in one of two ways. The first divides the total count of responses by the total interresponse time. Although more difficult to measure in applied settings, this approach is useful for behaviors that are often relatively extended in duration, as this can greatly restrict how much time is available for additional responses to occur.

7. The second approach to calculating frequencies of responding requires the investigator to divide the total number of responses by the total amount of time spent observing the behavior.

8. Ratios are valuable and common ways of looking at data, but they can limit our interpretations. When we combine two dimensional quantities (e.g., count divided by duration), we lose the ability to examine the component values. In order to interpret any changes in our ratio value, we must examine both contributing measures in order to determine why the change has occurred.

9. Dimensionless quantities (e.g., percentages) are similar to ratios. Although they are helpful, we must remember that they prevent us from

seeing the component values and this will necessarily limit our interpretations.

10. When selecting dimensional quantities to measure, our goal is to measure all the quantities that will reveal data that help us to answer the experimental question. Selection of these measures should be guided by the experimental question, research literature, target behavior, and intervention procedure(s).

TEXT STUDY GUIDE

1. Describe the three functions of measurement.
2. What is dimensional measurement?
3. Distinguish between a property, a dimensional quantity, and a unit of measurement.
4. What are absolute units of measurement?
5. Distinguish between event-response latency and interresponse time.
6. What is the unit of measurement for countability?
7. Define IRT. What is its unit of measurement?
8. Define frequency. What is its unit of measurement?
9. Distinguish between two ways of calculating frequency. Explain why response duration can make a difference in which approach is most useful.
10. Define celeration. What is its unit of measurement?
11. How is celeration related to frequency?
12. How do ratios limit the information about responding that can be easily seen?
13. What is a dimensionless quantity?
14. List the factors that might guide the selection of dimensional quantities for measurement.

BOX STUDY GUIDE

1. Why are rate and frequency likely to be confused?
2. How many dimensional quantities are there that characterize behavior?
3. Define quarter-life.
4. Define IRTs per opportunity.
5. Is probability a dimensional quantity?

SUGGESTED READINGS

Barenblatt, G. I. (1987). *Dimensional analysis*. New York: Gordon & Breach.

Johnson, L. M., & Morris, E. K. (1987). When speaking of probability in behavior analysis. *Behaviorism, 15*, 107–129.

Johnston, J. M., & Pennypacker, H. S. (1993). *Readings for Strategies and tactics of behavioral research*. Hillsdale, NJ: Lawrence Erlbaum Associates. [Reading 3: Traditions of behavioral measurement]

Johnston, J. M., & Pennypacker, H. S. (1993). *Readings for Strategies and tactics of behavioral research*. Hillsdale, NJ: Lawrence Erlbaum Associates. [Reading 4: Describing behavior with rations of count and time]

Johnston, J. M., & Pennypacker, H. S. (1993). *Readings for Strategies and tactics of behavioral research*. Hillsdale, NJ: Lawrence Erlbaum Associates. [Reading 5: Probability as a scientific concept]

DISCUSSION TOPICS

1. Discuss examples in which particular dimensional quantities would be more appropriate than others.

2. Discuss situations in which it might be important to calculate frequency by dividing total count by total IRT.

EXERCISES

1. Find examples in the research literature in which more than one dimensional quantity was measured for a particular target behavior. How do the data from each quantity provide different information about the effects of the treatment condition?

2. Start with a data set that includes both number of responses and number of opportunities to respond, measured across multiple sessions. Divide the former by the latter and multiply by 100 to calculate the percent of responses. Plot these values on a graph across sessions and describe the data. Then plot the number of responses and the number of opportunities separately and contrast these two functions with the percent function.

Observing and Recording

Observers, then, must be photographers of phenomena; their observations must accurately represent nature. We must observe without any preconceived idea; the observer's mind must be passive, that is, must hold its peace; it listens to nature and writes at nature's dictation.

—Claude Bernard

STRATEGIC ISSUES

Goal of Observation

We are now ready to address ways of observing target behaviors and recording the results. Although we may not often think about it in formal terms, behavioral measurement involves the following steps: (a) identifying those responses meeting the requirements of the response class definition; (b) determining the amount of the selected dimensional quantity for each response; and (c) making some kind of record of this amount in terms of the appropriate unit of measurement.

Behavioral measurement is also a way of systematically ignoring (at least for the purposes of formal measurement) those aspects of the participant's behavior that are not targeted for study. In other words, observing and recording filters everything going on with a participant's behavior during a session through a set of measurement procedures. This filtering process leaves behind everything the researcher or practitioner has decided is not important enough to measure in favor of a record of only the kind of information desired. This record is actually nothing more than a series of numbers and units of measurement. In sum, it is through observing and recording that facts get transformed into data.

TABLE 6.1
Components of behavioral measurement

- Identify those responses meeting the requirements of the response class definition
- Determine the amount of the selected dimensional quantity for each response
- Make some kind of record of this amount in terms of the appropriate unit of measurement

The overarching goal of behavioral measurement is to produce data that will guide correct and meaningful interpretations by the researcher or practitioner. In order to accomplish this, the record of participant's target behavior must be both complete and accurate. As data are analyzed, investigators may transform them into tables, graphs, or statistical outcomes (see chapter 12). As they manipulate the data in these ways, they try to produce stimuli that encourage both themselves and others to make the right kinds of interpretations.

These interpretations need not wait until the study is over. As we will see in upcoming chapters, behavioral researchers and practitioners study the data as they gradually accumulate throughout each phase and from one condition to another. What the data reveal is often useful in guiding the investigator's ongoing decisions about how to manage the study. For example, the accumulating data may indicate that the definition of the target behavior needs to be revised or that observers need to be given more training. If such problems were not addressed, the credibility of the entire project might suffer. As we will see in upcoming chapters, these are only a few of the ways in which data guide the management of a study.

Direct versus Indirect Measurement

When what you are measuring is exactly the same as what you are drawing conclusions about it is called **direct measurement**. In contrast, it is called **indirect measurement** when what you actually measure is in some way different from what you are drawing conclusions about.

> **Direct measurement.** Measurement practices in which the events measured are the same as those about which conclusions will be drawn.
>
> **Indirect measurement.** Measurement practices in which the events measured are not the same as those about which conclusions will be drawn.

For example, let us suppose that a researcher is interested in comparing the performance of employees in a manufacturing plant working under an old lighting system versus a new lighting system. If the researcher measures selected work behaviors under the old lighting system and then under the new lighting system in order to draw conclusions about the relative effects of the two lighting systems on job performance, it would be considered direct measurement.

In contrast, if the researcher instead asked employees to complete a questionnaire about how they thought their performance was affected by the change in lighting systems, it would be called indirect measurement. What makes measurement indirect in this case is that what is being measured (completing a questionnaire) is not the same as what conclusions will be about (actual work performance). There are a variety of reasons why the questionnaire data might not provide a good picture of actual work performance (perhaps the employees would want management to think that their work had improved because of the new lighting).

Scientists always prefer direct measurement over indirect measurement. The reason is that indirect measurement requires the investigator to make assumptions about the relationship between the indirect measures themselves (the questionnaire data) and what they are supposed to represent (actual job performance). When there is good evidence that such assumptions are warranted, indirect measurement can be acceptable. For example, the researcher could do a separate study showing that the data from this questionnaire closely correspond to measures of actual work performance.

However, researchers may be tempted to use indirect measurement when there is no apparent way to check the correspondence between the indirect measures and the events they are supposed to reflect. Social scientists often fall into this trap by defining their interests in terms of mental rather than physical processes. If a researcher is interested in ego-strength, for instance, it is likely that answers to some kind of questionnaire will be used as an indirect measure. Because there is no direct evidence that ego-strength is even a physical phenomenon, there is no way to assess what the questionnaire scores actually represent.

Automatic versus Human Observation

In designing, observing, and recording procedures, researchers and practitioners must first decide how observation will be accomplished. There are two basic choices. Target responses may be detected automatically or human observers may be employed.

In laboratory research, it is routine to use equipment to detect and record responses. When research interests require laboratory settings, target behaviors are typically defined in terms of some interaction with equipment. For instance, the target response may be pushing a lever, pressing a panel, striking a key on a keyboard, or touching a computer screen. Laboratory settings make it relatively easy to use computers to detect and record such responses. Depending on the nature of target responses, this approach is increasingly used in applied settings as well. A child's academic work in the classroom may be measured by a computer, for example.

In field settings, whether for research or service delivery, it is typical to train human observers to detect and record target behaviors. This approach usually results from the fact that field settings tend to be used when target behaviors are selected more for their relevance to daily life than for their scientific convenience. Although it is sometimes feasible to measure everyday behavior automatically, it would often require some investment in time and money to create this option.

The choice of automatic versus human observation involves more than the issue of feasibility, however. We might also ask which approach is more likely to provide accurate observations. Are there any general advantages in using equipment versus human observers? In answering this question, remember that the essential challenge of observation is to detect target responses accurately. Accurate data result from detecting and recording every response that fits the definition—no more and no less. In other words, the only influence on what is recorded should be the target responses themselves.

Especially in field settings, however, measurement must go on while all kinds of other things are happening in the environment. These other goings on can affect the performance of observers. For example, the behavior of individuals in the setting who are not themselves participants (care-givers in a group home or teachers in a classroom) is often important but can be distracting. Intervention procedures can have a substantial impact on how observers watch participants. Although such factors can involve important features of a study, they should not influence whether target responses are detected.

Under such "messy" conditions, automatic observation may have an advantage over human observers. Equipment generally has the characteristic

---

BOX 6.1

How Do You Measure Slouching?

Sometimes it may take some thought to figure out how automatic observation can work in a particular situation. If you want to measure slouching, for example, it might not be obvious how this behavior, which can occur in any circumstances at any time, could be detected automatically. Not only did a group of researchers figure out how to do it, but they used what we would today describe as crude 1960s technology. Azrin, Rubin, O'Brien, Ayllon, and Roll (1968) were interested in developing a means for controlling the body posture of typical participants in their natural environment. Instead of employing platoons of trained observers under varied observational conditions, they chose to develop a simple apparatus that continuously detected the key features of postural behavior under almost all daily circumstances.

   The apparatus defined slouching as an increased distance between two points on the back. This was detected with a snap-action switch taped onto the participant's back at a specific position. The switch was attached to an elastic cord so that rounding of the back caused the switch contacts to close. In order to eliminate switch closures due to normal activities, a mercury tilt switch was adopted that blocked the posture switch output when the torso was tilted forward more than 10°. The definition of slouching required an uninterrupted switch closure for at least 3 seconds. The cumulative duration of slouching was recorded by a miniature elapsed time meter. Calibration showed that measurement error was only about 30 seconds at the 4-hour time range used for most participants. In addition, the apparatus contained a small speaker and a transistor circuit that could sound a 500-hertz tone at 55 decibels when programmed by the experimenter, which played a role in modifying the behavior. All of the apparatus was worn under regular clothing. Of course, today's engineering technology could provide a smaller, simpler, and more sophisticated device.

---

of doing what it is designed to do and nothing else. As long as it operates as designed, for example, the apparatus described in Box 6.1 designed to measure slouching does its job consistently and without influence by other factors. In contrast, faced with the challenge of doing the same thing in exactly the same way over and over, human observers are, to put it gracefully, human. They get bored, pay attention to the wrong things, violate definitional rules, become confused, make idiosyncratic judgments, fail to show up, and so forth. In other words, for tasks where we need a high degree of consistency, human beings may come in second to "dumb" machines.

   On the other hand, human observers are very good at doing something that it is difficult to design equipment to do. Most machines are unresponsive to events that fall outside of their design parameters, but humans can be trained to be quite sensitive to novel or emergent features of a situation. These contrasts suggest that there may be complementary roles for equipment and human observers. Automatic observation may be most effective in detecting and recording target behaviors. Human observers may be ideal for providing supplementary monitoring to insure that equipment is working properly and to watch for events during sessions that might be important in managing the study. For example, it is often necessary to monitor the status of control and intervention conditions to make sure that they are operating as planned (Peterson, Homer, & Wonderlick, 1982).

Complete versus Incomplete Observation

We have already indicated that behavioral measurement should produce a record of the target behavior that is both complete and accurate. This ideal has implications for how much of the target behavior should be measured. The issue here is whether measurement will be designed to detect and record all instances of the behavior or to merely sample from all possible occurrences.

If observation is ongoing whenever target responses occur, it is possible to produce a complete record of the behavior. This is called **complete observation**. In this case, there are no concerns about sampling from among all possible target responses because all responses fitting the definition can be detected. When observation is scheduled in a way that may not detect all target responses, it is said to be **incomplete**. This involves designing observation periods so that they only sample from among all possible target responses.

> **Complete observation.** A schedule of observation that allows detection of all responses in the defined class.
>
> **Incomplete observation.** A schedule of observation that samples from the population of responses in the defined class.

Figure 6.1 diagrams the distinction between complete and incomplete observation. The event record labeled A represents a distribution of target responses during a period. Let us assume that this record represents all responses that occurred during a day. The line underneath this record (labeled B) represents an observation period. Because it covers the entire period during which responding occurred, it illustrates complete observation. The two lines

FIG. 6.1. Illustration of complete and incomplete observation.

on the bottom (labeled C) also represent observation periods. Because they fail to cover the entire period during which responses occurred, they illustrate incomplete observation.

Let us examine the effects of these two approaches on the resulting data. First consider the accuracy of the data they produce. Although complete observation is an ideal approach, it does not guarantee that the resulting data will be accurate. For example, even though all target responses can be detected it does not mean that they will be. Furthermore, responses that should not be recorded may be included. Incomplete observation provides no guarantees either. During observation periods, some target responses could be missed and responses could be recorded that should not be. In other words, regardless of whether an observation schedule is supposed to capture all target responses or merely sample them during limited periods of time, the data may be fully accurate or may involve some error.

Second, consider the matter of how well the data represent what they are supposed to represent. A schedule of observation that captures all responses in the target response class (putting aside the possibility of error) necessarily provides data that represent a complete picture of what is happening with that behavior. However, a schedule of incomplete observation raises the risk that the data may not fully represent what is going on with the target behavior. The seriousness of this risk depends on how the observation periods are scheduled, how long they are, and what the researcher or practitioner wants to learn.

For example, suppose that an investigator is measuring coffee drinking in individuals whose doctors have told them to cut back on their consumption of caffeine. If the researcher chooses to schedule observation sessions only in the morning between 7:00 and 10:00, the resulting (presumably accurate) data may not very well represent the participant's coffee-drinking practices. The data will almost certainly underestimate the total daily amount of coffee drinking by failing to measure the behavior during the rest of the day. They will also probably overestimate the amount of coffee drinking in the afternoon and evening, when most people drink less coffee.

In summary, although complete observation is clearly the ideal, incomplete observation is not necessarily a poor alternative. Both approaches can yield accurate measures of responding during observation periods, although there are no guarantees. In order for incomplete observation to yield data that represent responding during unsampled periods of time, however, it is important to arrange periods of observation that meet a study's needs for a meaningful picture of the amount and distribution of responding.

Continuous versus Discontinuous Observation

Let us now turn to the procedures operating during observation periods themselves, regardless of whether observation is scheduled to be complete or incomplete. When observation procedures are designed to detect every target response occurring during an observation period it is called **continuous observation**. Because complete observation involves detecting all target responses, whenever they occur, complete observation is necessarily continuous. However, observation can also be continuous during observation periods that only sample from the times during which responding can occur. For example, care-givers in a group home for individuals with mental retardation may be charged with observing certain social interactions with staff for a particular individual from the time she returns from a day program until dinner is ready. Although the behavior could occur at other times, observation can be continuous during the designated afternoon observation periods. As we have already seen, continuous observation has the potential to be accurate, although errors can always occur.

When observation procedures are not designed to detect all target responses during observation periods, it is called **discontinuous observation**. In other words, instead of detecting every target response when observation is in progress, discontinuous procedures only sample from among the responses that occur during an observation period. This means that some responses are likely to be missed.

Discontinuous observation procedures are often used in applied behavioral research and practice. They take many forms, but perhaps the most common is called **interval recording**. In a typical application, the observation period is divided into equal intervals, which might range from a few seconds to a number of minutes in length. In **partial interval recording**, the observer is charged with scoring each interval in which at least one response (or even part of a response) occurs. In **whole interval recording**, the observer scores the interval only if the target behavior occurs without ceasing throughout the whole interval. In either case, the total number of scored intervals is divided by the total number of intervals in the observation period, and the result is multiplied by 100 to yield a measure of the percentage of intervals that were scored.

Continuous observation. Observation procedures in which all target responses can be detected during observation periods.

Discontinuous observation. Observation procedures in which all target responses are not necessarily detected and recorded.

Interval recording. A discontinuous observation procedure in which observation periods are divided into equal intervals, which are scored according to some rule if the target behavior occurs.

Partial interval recording. A form of interval recording in which an interval is scored if at least one target response (or even part of a response) occurs during the interval.

Whole interval recording. A form of interval recording in which an interval is scored if the target behavior occurs without ceasing throughout the entire interval.

Although interval recording procedures are straightforward, they can result in potentially serious problems. First, discontinuous procedures produce data that cannot be clearly related to dimensional quantities such as count, duration, or frequency. In partial interval recording, for example, once the first response occurs in an interval, that interval is scored. This means that additional responses occurring in the same interval are ignored. Because the procedure does not measure the number of responses, the resulting "percent of scored intervals" data cannot be used as an estimate of count. Neither can you divide the number of scored intervals by session time and get a measure of frequency. Similarly, because the procedure does not measure response durations, "percent of scored intervals" data cannot be used as an estimate of duration. Whole interval recording requires scoring intervals only when the behavior occurs throughout the entire interval. Because intervals are not scored when the behavior occurs during an interval, but not throughout the entire interval, the same dimensional limitations apply.

A number of studies have investigated the seriousness of the discrepancy between the information provided by discontinuous observation procedures versus continuous observation of dimensional quantities such as count and duration (Gardenier, MacDonald, & Green, 2004; Green, McCoy, Burns, & Smith, 1982; Harrop & Daniels, 1986; Murphy & Goodall, 1980; Powell, Martindale, & Kulp, 1975; Powell, Martindale, Kulp, Martindale, & Bauman, 1977; Repp, Roberts, Slack, Repp, & Berkler, 1976). As might be expected, the studies generally show that partial interval recording data imply less responding (and whole interval recording data imply more responding) than continuous measurement of count or duration actually reveals. The size of this problem partly depends on the length of the intervals used: the longer the interval, the greater the discrepancy. The extent of this problem also depends on the distribution of responses during sessions.

A second problem is that the size of the intervals affects the percent of scored intervals data. Given a particular distribution of responding throughout a session, different size intervals will yield different values. Figure 6.2 illustrates this point by showing that, for a particular sample of responding, two different interval durations produce different pictures of responding. The event record labeled A shows that eight responses occurred during an 80-second period. The partial interval procedure labeled B, using 10-second intervals, resulted in five of the eight intervals (62.5%) being scored. Using 20-second intervals,

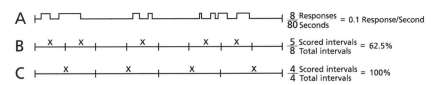

FIG. 6.2. Illustration of the effect of interval size on percent of scored interval calculations.

the same eight responses require that all four intervals be scored, resulting in a value of 100% of scored intervals.

These differences are especially problematic because they have nothing to do with the participant's behavior. This means that graphed data showing percent of scored interval data across a series of sessions for a participant would look different depending on the length of the intervals. Of course, without a continuous record, there would be no way to determine how the data would be affected by different intervals.

Another common version of discontinuous observation is called **momentary time sampling**. In this procedure, the observation period is also divided into equal intervals. However, the observer records the presence or absence of the target behavior at the moment that each interval ends. In other words, observation does not occur during intervals, only at the moment each interval ends. As with interval recording procedures, the data resulting from momentary time sampling are typically expressed in terms of percent of scored intervals. Momentary time sampling generally shares the same limitations as interval recording, although some studies have shown that momentary time sampling may yield less error than interval recording, particularly as interval length increases (Gardenier, MacDonald, & Green, 2004).

> **Momentary time sampling.** A discontinuous observation procedure in which observation periods are divided into equal intervals, but the observer only notes the momentary status of the target behavior at the end of each interval.

There are a variety of less formal ways by which observation can result in a discontinuous picture of responding. For example, conducting observation sessions by alternating periods of observing with periods of recording (during which observation does not occur) creates a discontinuous record. This is easy to see in a measurement procedure in which 10 seconds of observing is followed by 5 seconds devoted to recording, which means that observing is only occurring during two-thirds of each observation period. Another kind of observation procedure that results in a discontinuous record involves rotating brief periods of observation across different participants. For instance, observing each child in a classroom for 15 seconds before switching to the next child and then the next in rotation not only creates grouped data but involves a discontinuous picture of any one child's behavior during the session.

TACTICS OF OBSERVING AND RECORDING

Making Observations

Automatic. Any behavior involves movement, and all movement changes the environment in some way, even if only momentarily. These changes may be

---

BOX 6.2

What About Rating Scales?

You might be wondering why rating scales have not been discussed. It is because, as a way of measuring behavior, they represent a unique set of problems. In spite of serious shortcomings, rating scales have long been popular in the social sciences and come in many forms. When used to measure an individual's behavior, they generally require an observer to rate at least one, but usually many behaviors or behavioral categories. The procedure involves assigning each behavior or category a number on a scale. The scale's values typically range from 1 to 5 or 1 to 7. The extreme values, or even each value, may be loosely anchored or defined by a phrase. For example, an observer might rate the category of "acting out" as 2 on a scale of 1-5, in which 1 represents "all the time" and 5 represents "not at all."

Rating scales are most often used by asking the observer to make ratings based on their contact with a participant over a substantial period of time. For instance, although a rating scale might be completed at the end of a single observation session, it is common for a set of ratings to represent an entire day or even a week or more of the participant's behavior. Furthermore, although there is nothing about rating scales that prevents using precise definitions of specific behaviors, they typically incorporate relatively broad behavioral categories (e.g., misbehaving, sociability, autistic behavior, or staying on task) that include many different behaviors. When rating scales are designed for self-administration, the categories often refer to traits, feelings, and other mentalistic concepts. Individuals filling out rating scales do not usually receive training as observers.

Not surprisingly, this simplicity and convenience has a price, and the literature on rating scales has enumerated many problems (see Wittenborn, 1972). For example, agreement among different raters observing the same individual often suffers because of the looseness of the rating categories, the relatively long period that the ratings must cover, and the inherent subjectivity of the scale values. In spite of using behavioral references to anchor the numerical values, the task of assigning a number to represent the status of a loosely defined behavioral category over a period as long as a day or week simply ensures that observers will differ somewhat in their judgments. Although the researcher can work to reduce interobserver differences, there will still be no way to assess the accuracy of the data. This may not matter, however, because the vague nature of the data presents insurmountable interpretive problems anyway. In summary, although their convenience may be tempting, rating scales are an inferior approach to the challenges of behavioral measurement.

---

relatively permanent and obvious, as in the work products of an employee, or more transient and subtle, as in a child's play behavior during recess. With the target behavior clearly defined, however, it is sometimes feasible to measure the movements or their associated environmental changes automatically with the aid of equipment.

The first step is to identify those changes associated with the target behavior that invariably accompany responses. In the case of rumination of food in individuals with mental retardation, for example, key movements are associated with regurgitating food from the stomach into the mouth and reswallowing it. In this process, the Adam's apple unavoidably moves in a noticeable way. It is important to be sure that the movements or environmental changes are an invariant characteristic of responses, however. Although the behavior may often generate some reaction on the part of other individuals, for instance, such environmental changes are not usually consistent and should not serve as the basis for automatic measurement.

Once a list of accompanying features is available, the second step is to consider how one or more of them can be detected by some kind of device. Although laboratory researchers can turn to catalogs of equipment for measuring various behaviors under controlled conditions, automatic measurement under field conditions is not so convenient. On the other hand, there is an almost limitless array of devices available than can detect anything about behavior we might want to capture. Although some engineering may be required to create a suitable measurement tool, sometimes these devices are already available because they are used for other purposes. Sexual arousal in males, for example, can be measured by a penile strain gauge, which is used by physicians to assist in determining if reported problems of impotence have an organic basis (Barlow, Becker, Leitenberg, & Agras, 1970). Various features of the complex behavior of driving a vehicle can be measured by attaching a device to the car that records such things as speed, distance traveled, engine operation, and other response products (Schnelle, Kirchner, Casey, Uselton, & McNees, 1977).

Once a suitable device is identified, the third step is to establish procedures for making sure that it is working as intended. This process is called calibration and is covered in chapter 7. Calibration involves insuring that the equipment will accurately detect all target responses but no others. If its output is not within acceptable limits, the equipment must be adjusted until it performs to standards. Scientists routinely calibrate their equipment in this manner.

TABLE 6.2
Requirements for setting up automatic observation

- Identify changes invariably accompanying target responses
- Determine how changes can be detected by equipment
- Establish procedures to be sure that equipment is working as intended

---

One approach to automatic observation is widely used and merits special mention. Even when other devices are not a convenient option, it is often possible to make a video recording of a participant's behavior throughout observation periods. This creates a two-dimensional record of the target behavior, though mixed with other behaviors that are not of interest. This convenient approach to preserving a picture of responding means that human observers must later watch the videotape and detect and record target responses. In doing so, they have an important advantage over observers who must do the same job in real time. They can replay or manipulate the videotape as needed to be sure of their judgments. Of course, the disadvantage of this approach is that each observation period requires at least that much more time to "score" the videotape.

Human Observers. As we have already discussed, human observers are typically used to detect and record behavior under most field conditions. Although this approach is familiar to applied researchers and to practitioners, it is actually fairly complex and time-consuming.

The first step is determining the task requirements that observers will have to meet. That is, given the target behavior and the environmental circumstances in which it occurs, exactly what will observers be asked to do? Will participants be in one place or moving around? Will it be possible to see the target behavior whenever it might occur? Will participants be alone or interacting with other people? How many target behaviors will need to be observed simultaneously? What type of response class definition (functional or topographical) will be used? What dimensional quantities will be measured? What will observers have to do to record their observations?

The answers to these kinds of questions can result in a considerable list of performance requirements for observers. It is probably the case that the longer the list, the greater the risk that some aspects of observer performance might suffer. The second step, then, is to consider how the demands on observers can be minimized. It is often appropriate, for example, to provide equipment that will make recording easier. Using counting and timing devices can be less distracting than having to mark a recording form. Timers can provide interval signals to observers if needed. Hand-held computers can record button presses in real time, resulting in a record of when responses occurred or how long they lasted. Whatever the details, it is important to avoid burdening observers with more tasks than they can manage.

With a clear picture of what observers will be asked to do, the third step is selecting and recruiting the individuals who will serve in this role. Although observers will receive training to help them do their job, it can be important to select individuals who have a background that might give them advantages over others. For example, psychiatric nurses might be a better choice than undergraduate students if the task involves observing patients in a mental hospital. Similarly, engineering or science majors might have a greater respect for quantitative precision than fine arts majors. Assumptions about the influence of prior histories can be wrong, but it can still be useful to consider past experiences in selecting observers.

Whatever the background of the individuals selected to be observers, the fourth step is to design and implement a training program that will lead them to accurately detect and record target responses. More behaviorally, the objective of observer training is to bring their observing behavior under narrow control of the defined features of the target behavior. This objective

TABLE 6.3
Requirements for setting up human observation

- Determine task requirements that observers will have to meet
- Consider how observer demands can be minimized
- Select and recruit observers
- Design and implement observer training program
- Establish procedures for evaluating observer performance

will certainly involve detailed instructions, but it typically also requires modeling and repeated practice with feedback, often using video of typical participant behavior. Observer training usually involves a number of sessions, and there should be specific performance standards that must be met before trainees are qualified to serve.

Unfortunately, even though observers may meet training standards, their performance may wane once on the job. The fifth step therefore involves setting up procedures for evaluating their performance on an ongoing basis. (Chapter 7 will consider these procedures in detail.) There are many reasons why observer performance may vary over the course of a study, a phenomenon called **observer drift**. They may gradually change the criteria they use for detecting target responses, perhaps without even realizing it. The different phases of a study may have effects on how they follow response class definitions. Some conditions may change the behavior of participants in ways that make it more difficult to detect responses. Observer performance may also be affected by what is going on in the rest of their lives. For instance, on some days they may be tired, preoccupied, or not feeling well.

Depending on the nature of the study, researchers may choose to limit observer's access to information about the study as a way of minimizing the chance that it might influence their judgments. When this is done, observers are referred to as **blind**, although the procedure is not as cruel as it sounds. Blind observers are systematically prevented from having certain information about a study, such as why the study is being conducted, the nature of various experimental conditions or their rationale, any expectations the investigator may have about the effects of experimental conditions, or even the nature of the accumulating data. In most studies, especially practical interventions, observers can hardly help learning some things about the project from day to day, but this approach can help to minimize the risk that such information might systematically bias their performance.

> **Observer drift.** A change in the accuracy of an observer's performance, often gradual and for unknown reasons.
>
> **Blind.** A reference to being unaware of the goals of an experiment, the nature of experimental or control conditions, or the outcomes of each condition. May apply to the experimenter, observers, or participants. If both experimenter and participants are blind, it is called a *double-blind* experiment.

This approach may also be used with participants, and even experimenters as well, if knowing certain things about a research project might influence their behavior in undesirable ways. Studies in which neither experimenter nor participants know key features of experimental and control conditions are called *double-blind experiments*. This technique is commonly used in investigating the effects of drugs, for example. Neither physician nor patient would know whether the patient is receiving the experimental drug or the placebo.

Finally, as with any desirable behavior, it is important that the observer's compliance with procedures generates sufficient reinforcement to maintain their performance. Observers are sometimes paid, unless they are already employees and would therefore not receive extra pay for this duty. If paraprofessional employees in service delivery settings are simply expected to follow data collection protocols as part of their work, it is still important to make sure that their compliance leads to positive reinforcers, even if the reinforcers are only social in nature. Chapter 7 will show how formal evaluation of measurement procedures and data can provide opportunities to differentially reinforce the quality of each observer's performance. In the absence of such formal evidence, it is generally the case that reinforcers are contingent on following observer protocols, not on producing "good" data.

Participants as Observers. It might seem that the individuals who are the least appropriate candidates for serving as observers are participants themselves. After all, they are not exactly disinterested in what is going on, and their involvement may only insure that they are difficult to train, biased toward detecting either more or fewer responses than actually occurred, likely to be influenced by the data they are collecting, and sometimes not inclined to cooperate anyway. With these potential problems, why would anyone ever want to use participants as observers?

The answer is that participants have one notable advantage over other observers: they are always around. Using participants to observed and record their own behavior solves one of the most difficult challenges of using human observers—gaining access to the target behavior. Participants are always present when the behavior occurs.

In fact, participants do not present researchers or practitioners with problems that are any different than those faced with other observers. Both types of observers can have histories that may not encourage good observing, and their observations may be influenced by treatment conditions and the emerging data. As with other observers, participant-observers must be selected, trained, maintained, and evaluated with care, and their data must meet customary standards. However, when all this is done, those participants who qualify then have the important advantage over other observers in their unrestricted access to the behavior. In other words, if participants are treated the same way and held to the same criteria as other observers, they not only have no inherent disadvantages but they also have a big advantage.

BOX 6.3

The Problem of Measurement Reactivity

When a participant's behavior is in any way influenced by measurement pro-cedures, it is called **measurement reactivity**. If the procedures used to observe and record behavior are detectable by the participant, it is possible that the participant may behave differently than if he or she were not being observed.

Although we might assume that knowing that we are being observed would always have some impact on our behavior, investigators usually find under such circumstances either that there is no apparent effect or that any effect dissipates quickly. Nevertheless, the risk of measurement reactivity must always be con-sidered until it is clear that the problem does not exist.

It is sometimes easy to minimize reactivity, such as by how equipment or observers are used. For example, a video camera might be left in place all of the time, rather than just being set up just for observation sessions. Observers might be stationed unobtrusively rather than placed in an obvious location. If the risk of measurement reactivity seems especially great, it may be necessary to design observation procedures that are entirely invisible to participants.

Whatever preparations are taken to minimize measurement reactivity, there remains the question of whether they are successful. This can only be answered by devoting some experimental comparisons specifically to this issue. These manipulations would have to compare responding under routine observation procedures to responding under somewhat different (perhaps unobtrusive) observation procedures. Of course, it is not possible to compare responding in the presence versus the absence of measurement; without measurement, we would have no data at all.

Again, although measurement reactivity is certainly possible, it is usually a small and transient effect, if it occurs at all. At the least, because behavioral measurement continues throughout a study, any durable effects may at least be constant and may not complicate conclusions about the role of experimental conditions.

This advantage may sometimes be the only feasible way to collect needed data. If the target behavior can occur during all waking hours under varying environments, using others as observers will usually require restricting the times and situations under which observation will take place. These restric-tions can limit the representativeness of the data and the generality of the findings. Using participants as observers can avoid these constraints.

Scheduling Observation Periods

We have already considered the basic issues underlying decisions about how observation is scheduled. The ideal is that observation should be ongoing whenever target responses can occur. For behaviors that can occur only under limited conditions, such as in a classroom or during a training session, this is often an easy standard to meet. Some behaviors can occur during all waking hours in different settings, however, and it can be challenging to arrange for complete observation under these conditions. For example, self-injurious behavior in individuals with developmental disabilities is likely to be observed under varied conditions throughout the day.

If complete observation is not feasible, then observation periods must be scheduled that sample from the times and circumstances under which the behavior could occur. In making these decisions, the key questions are "How often should observation periods be scheduled?" and "How long should each observation period last?" The answers are straightforward: "As often as possible and as long as possible." In other words, the objective is to arrange observation periods that come as close as is reasonably possible to complete observation.

The reason for this approach is to minimize the risk that incomplete observational data do not adequately represent what was going on with the target behavior while it was not being observed. How important it is for the data from limited sessions to represent a complete picture of the target behavior depends on the nature of the question. In many practical circumstances, the data from limited daily sessions must reflect the occurrence of the behavior throughout the full day. It would be a problem, for example, if the data from limited observation periods showed that a problem behavior was decreasing to low levels as a result of an intervention but care-givers could clearly see that it was continuing to occur as much as ever during times of the day when data were not being collected.

On the other hand, in many research projects it is only necessary for the data to show how a target behavior is affected by experimental variables. For example, a study of variables influencing the effectiveness of reprimands only needed to show their effects on target behaviors during experimental sessions (Van Houten, Nau, MacKenzie-Keating, Sameoto, & Colavecchia, 1982). These results answered the research question about how these factors impacted the effectiveness of reprimands, and it was not necessary to show the effects on responding outside of sessions.

Finally, another consideration when deciding how often and how long observation should be scheduled concerns how often the target behavior occurs. Generally, the less often the behavior occurs, the more frequent or longer the observation periods should be in order to provide a good sample of responding. For example, if the behavior occurs only a few times each day, observation must be in place for much of the day in order to detect these few responses.

Conducting Observation Procedures

Continuous Observation Procedures. We have already pointed out that the ideal observation procedure involves observing throughout the entire session in a way that detects each response. This approach can yield accurate data because it is at least designed not to miss a single response. In order to implement this procedure, observers must be able to detect the occurrence of each target response, which means knowing when it is or is not occurring. If this is possible, it follows that it is also possible to determine when each response starts and stops. With these capabilities, observers can, in principle, measure count, duration, and interresponse time, as well as calculate frequency.

Continuous observation requires observers to attend to participants sufficiently closely to detect each target response. This can sometimes be challenging in service settings, where personnel typically have many duties that may distract them from observational responsibilities. For direct measurement, there is no way around this mandate, however. Discontinuous observation procedures do not provide a less demanding alternative. They tend to require the same level of attentiveness, especially if the intervals are brief, as they should be. Sound behavioral measurement simply takes some effort. Behavioral researchers and practitioners long ago learned that the benefits are always worth the cost.

Aside from this requirement, continuous observation is usually not difficult to implement, whether for research or practical purposes. However, when the target behavior can occur at high frequencies for brief periods, it may be necessary to adjust the response class definition to specify an episode of responding. Stereotypic behavior may be a good example of this problem. Stereotypy is generally defined as repetitive motor or vocal behavior that serves no obvious adaptive functions (Gardenier, MacDonald, & Green, 2004). Typical behaviors include body rocking, pacing, posturing, vocalizing, facial grimacing, manipulating objects, and repetitive movements and these are often observed in individuals diagnosed with autism spectrum disorders.

Self-stimulatory responding such as this often occurs frequently or for extended periods. These responses may be defined in such a way that individual responses can be differentiated. However, if the behavior occurs at high frequencies for periods of time, it may be more useful to define the behavior in terms of episodes. Depending on how often such episodes occur or how long they last, observers can be assigned to measure the number or the duration of episodes (or both). This is a good way to implement a continuous observation procedure when it might otherwise be difficult to detect individual responses.

Discontinuous Observation Procedures. We have already noted the inherent limitations of discontinuous observation procedures such as interval recording and momentary time sampling. Because they do not attempt to detect all responses that occur during observation periods, they yield data that do not reflect dimensional quantities and cannot be assessed by the accepted scientific standards of accuracy and reliability. Data described as percent of scored intervals are also affected by the interval duration used. Nevertheless, interval recording and momentary time sampling procedures are represented in the applied behavioral literature.

Some of the problems with interval recording and momentary time sampling can be minimized by selecting very short intervals. To make this point, consider that if intervals were only 3 seconds long, in most cases there would probably be fairly little discrepancy between scored interval data and count data. The rule, then, is to select an interval that is as brief as observers can handle. Even busy observers should be able to accommodate intervals less than 1 minute long, and 10-second intervals are not uncommon in applied research.

The differences between partial and whole interval recording alternatives do not really provide an opportunity to minimize their shared problems. The partial interval procedure ignores responses that occur during an interval that has already been scored, and the whole interval procedure ignores responses that do not last throughout the interval. The data generated by each procedure can be more or less misleading depending on the distribution of responses being measured, but there is no way to know in advance which alternative will be less problematic.

On the other hand, momentary time sampling does not share the bias associated with partial and whole interval recording. Momentary time sampling ignores responses in an even-handed way by scoring intervals based on whether the target behavior is occurring at the end of the interval. Studies have shown that momentary time sampling does not produce a systematically biased picture of actual responding, although it still shares the other limitations of discontinuous observations procedures (Gardenier, MacDonald, & Green, 2004). As with interval recording procedures, the key to minimizing these other limitations is in selecting very short intervals.

As with continuous observation procedures, interval recording and momentary time sampling procedures are straightforward to implement. Although the problems with discontinuous procedures can be minimized by selecting very brief intervals, such intervals require observers to stay on task without interruption or distraction. Of course, if observers are monitoring participant behavior continuously, continuous observation is an equally feasible and superior alternative.

Recording Observations

The effort put into defining and observing a behavior only counts when observations are recorded. It is at this point that facts become data. The goal of recording observations is to accurately preserve the observed facts regarding the target behavior.

When automatic observation is used, it is likely that the equipment that detects responses will also be used to make a record of those detections. An early example of this approach is a study by Barrett (1962) of extensive muscular tics in a 38-year-old man. His tics involved major contractions of his neck, shoulders, chest, and abdominal muscles, as well as eye blinking, opening of his mouth, and other facial movements. Barrett's way of measuring these diverse movements involved the patient sitting in a swivel-tilt armchair that had a large U-shaped magnet attached to the back of the chair top so that it could hang freely. An induction coil was nested in electrical tape between the poles of the magnet and was adjusted so that the patient's larger movements created a movement of the coil in the magnetic field. The resulting current operated a sensitive relay, which defined individual responses. The output from the relay also operated a cumulative recorder, which provided a continuous record of responding. Today's electronic technology would provide Barrett with much more sophisticated options, of course.

In field research and practice, human observers typically serve both observing and recording functions. When this is the case, the distinction between observing and recording can be especially important. Because the behavioral requirements of these tasks can sometimes be incompatible, there is a risk that the requirements of recording will interfere with the job of observing and result in inaccurate data. Of course, it is also possible for observational obligations to interfere with making an accurate record.

The challenge is to design observing and recording tasks so that their requirements are compatible. The most common problem is when the need to record responses requires an observer to break visual contact with the participant's behavior. Even a few seconds spent marking a recording form can cause the observer to miss responses in some situations. One solution is to use equipment that allows observers to record observations without looking away from the participant. As we have already mentioned, counters and timers are widely available, and hand-held computers programmed just for this type of application allow even more sophisticated recording options.

To recapitulate, recording is the terminal step in a complex sequence that begins with defining the response class of interest and selecting relevant dimensional quantities, proceeds through observing and recording, and culminates in a permanent record of the target behavior. All of these steps must contribute to creating a record that accurately preserves selected features of the participant's behavior because, after each observation session, that record is all that remains.

CHAPTER SUMMARY

1. The overarching goal of behavioral measurement is to produce data that will guide correct and meaningful interpretations by the researcher or practitioner. In order to accomplish this, our observations and recording of the target behavior(s) must be complete and accurate.

2. Scientists always prefer direct measurement over indirect measurement. Making assumptions about the indirect measure (e.g., survey data) and what they are intended to represent (i.e., specific behavior) is inherently incomplete and possibly misleading.

3. When deciding between automatic or human observation, we should decide which approach is most likely to provide us with accurate and

complete observations. Automatic observation may be most effective in detecting and recording target behaviors, but most machines are unresponsive to events that fall outside of their design parameters.

4. Although complete observation is an ideal approach, it does not guarantee that the resulting data will be accurate. Incomplete observation is not necessarily a poor alternative as long as the researcher is able to arrange periods of observation to yield data that provide a good description of what responding would look like during unsampled time periods.

5. The most common form of discontinuous observation is called interval recording. While easy to implement, interval recording procedures may result in several problems for the investigator. First, they do not record any data about a response's frequency, count, or duration. Second, dependent upon the type of interval recording method used, responding is often overestimated (partial interval) or underestimated (whole interval). Finally, changing the length of the interval affects the percent of scored interval data. This is especially problematic because it has nothing to do with the participant's behavior.

6. Momentary time sampling is another common version of discontinuous observation. Momentary time sampling generally shares the same limitations as interval recording, although some studies have shown it to be similar in accuracy to continuous recording.

7. In determining whether to observe and record behavior automatically, the first step is to identify those changes associated with the target behavior and determine how they could be detected with a particular device. Once a device is selected, the investigator must be sure that the machine is working properly and will accurately detect and record all of the target responses.

8. When human observers are to be used, the first step is to determine what exactly they will be required to do. Once these specific requirements have been determined, it is often beneficial to consider how the demands on the observer(s) can be minimized. The observers are then selected and trained on how to observe and record the target behavior in order to provide a complete and accurate account of the target responses. The investigator should also be sure to monitor their observers and evaluate their performance on an ongoing basis.

9. If complete observation is not feasible, observation periods must be arranged so that they come as close as is reasonably possible to complete observation. This approach will help to minimize the risk that incomplete observational data do not adequately represent what was occurring with the target behavior when it was not being observed.

10. Despite the inherent problems associated with discontinuous observation procedures, they continue to be used in the applied behavioral literature. Some of the problems associated with these procedures can be minimized by selecting very brief intervals. This still requires the observer to stay on task and monitor behavior continuously. Of course, if observers are

monitoring participant behavior continuously, then continuous observation would seem to be an equally feasible and superior alternative.

11. The goal of recording observations is to accurately preserve the observed facts regarding the target responses. One challenge that human observers face in applied settings is recording behavior while simultaneously observing the participant. One solution to this problem is using equipment that allows the observer to record observations without looking away from the participant (e.g., counters, timers).

TEXT STUDY GUIDE

1. Explain how behavioral measurement is a filtering process.
2. What is the goal of behavioral measurement?
3. Explain the difference between direct and indirect measurement.
4. Why is direct measurement preferred over indirect measurement?
5. What advantage does automatic observation have over human observation?
6. How can human observation supplement automatic observation?
7. What is the difference between complete and incomplete observation?
8. Compare complete and incomplete observation with regard to the accuracy of data.
9. What issue does incomplete observation raise?
10. Explain the difference between continuous and discontinuous observation.
11. What is the primary weakness of discontinuous observation?
12. Explain partial and whole interval recording procedures.
13. Describe how partial interval recording misrepresents actual responding.
14. Describe how whole interval recording misrepresents actual responding.
15. Explain how interval size affects percent of scored interval data.
16. What is the consequence of the fact that percent of scored intervals is a dimensionless quantity?
17. Explain the momentary time sampling procedure.
18. List the steps involved in designing an automatic observation procedure.
19. List the steps involved in designing a human observation procedure.
20. What is observer drift?
21. What are blind observers? When would you use this procedure?
22. Explain how participants can be considered as suitable observers for their own behavior.
23. What are the key questions, and their answers, associated with incomplete observation?

24. What is the impact of response frequency on how observation periods are scheduled?
25. What observation capability is minimally necessary to implement continuous observation procedures?
26. Under what circumstances might it be useful to define the target behavior in terms of episodes?
27. What is the best way to minimize the disadvantages of discontinuous observation procedures such as interval recording and momentary time sampling?
28. What is the goal of recording observations?
29. Why is it useful to distinguish between observing and recording?

BOX STUDY GUIDE

1. Describe the use of rating scales in behavioral measurement.
2. What are the major problems with rating scales?
3. What is measurement reactivity?

SUGGESTED READINGS

Barrett, B. H. (1962). Reduction in rate of multiple tics by free operant conditioning methods. *Journal of Nervous and Mental Disease, 135*, 187–195.
Gardenier, N. C., MacDonald, R., & Green, G. (2004). Comparison of direct observational methods for measuring stereotypic behavior in children with autism spectrum disorders. *Research in Developmental Disabilities, 25*, 99–118.

DISCUSSION TOPICS

1. Select a target behavior occurring in some situation and discuss how direct versus indirect measurement might be used.
2. Select some examples of target behaviors and discuss how automatic measurement procedures might be developed.
3. Select some "real world" examples of specific behaviors and discuss how the frequency and duration of incomplete observation sessions should be scheduled.

EXERCISE

1. Select a student who will be asked to engage in the behavior of finger snapping during a 5-minute period. Select another student to serve as

observer who will record the exact time of each response. After these data are available, divide the 5-minute session into intervals. In one case, use 10-second intervals. In a second case, use 30-second intervals. In a third case, use 1-minute intervals. Then score each set of intervals based on the continuous record of responding using the partial interval rule, and calculate the percent of scored intervals. Discuss the results in terms of the issues raised in the chapter.

Assessing Measurement

Although this may seem a paradox, all exact science is dominated by the idea of approximation.

—Bertrand Russell

139

STRATEGIC ISSUES

Estimation

The goal of scientific measurement is to arrive at the best possible estimate of the true value of some event that has occurred. The product of measurement is considered only to be an estimate of what really happened because researchers find it useful to admit the possibility that data include some error. Based on their experience, researchers generally acknowledge that it is not uncommon for there to be discrepancies between what actually happened and their measurements of it. Fortunately, these differences are often so small that they do not prevent investigators from drawing accurate conclusions.

One of the advantages of conceding that data are only estimates of the facts is that it encourages researchers to try to obtain the best estimates possible. (Chapter 6 considered some of the ways of avoiding measurement error.) This approach helps minimize the risk of basing conclusions on data that are tainted with substantial error. The possibility of error also confronts researchers with the obligation of determining the extent to which error is present in the data, in spite of their best efforts. This chapter focuses on ways of evaluating data and, by extension, the measurement procedures that produced them.

Observed versus True Values

Let us begin by making a distinction between observed values and true values. **Observed values** are simply the values that result from observation. They are usually in the form of numbers representing some amount of a dimensional quantity (e.g., 2.6 minutes of duration or 0.75 cycles per minute of frequency). It is observed values that will, if they pass muster, serve as the data from the study that will be examined by the researcher, practitioner, and others.

True values are also obtained through observation; after all, there is no other way to find out what happened. However, in order to say that observations result in true values, the investigator must take special precautions to insure that possible sources of error have been avoided or minimized in some way. The special steps that might be taken depend on the nature of the target behavior and how it is being observed. At the very least, the procedures that are used to obtain true values must be somewhat different from those used to obtain the observed values being evaluated.

> **Observed values.** Values resulting from observation and recording procedures used to collect the data for a study.
>
> **True values.** Values resulting from special observation and recording procedures that are somewhat different from those used to collect the data being evaluated and that involve special efforts to minimize error.

For example, researchers studying the performance of employees cleaning items in a salvage business set up procedures by which the employees would measure their own work behavior throughout the day. In an effort to evaluate these data, the researchers set up special procedures to obtain true values. Members of the research team periodically took boxes of clean items leaving the work area and compared the employees' counts with their own counts. The availability of the cleaned items as permanent products of the target behavior gave the researchers the luxury of making this special count using counting procedures that minimized error and counting the contents of each box being sampled multiple times (Stoerzinger, Johnston, Pisor, & Monroe, 1978).

Of course, just because special efforts are made to avoid or remove possible sources of error in obtaining true values does not guarantee that such data are error free. In fact, there is no way to be sure that any set of data are fully accurate. Someone can always argue that the true values being used to assess observed values might themselves contain some error. This is why scientists are always looking for more accurate measurement procedures.

Accuracy

Accuracy is the term used to describe the extent to which observed values approximate what actually happened. There are two requirements for evaluating the accuracy of a set of observations. First, the data must represent real (physical) events. This means that the data must not be the only evidence that what is supposedly being measured actually exists. Second, it must be possible to measure these events directly. Behavior certainly meets these requirements, so assessing the accuracy of behavioral measurement is feasible in principle. In contrast, although we speak of intelligence as if it is a physical phenomenon, the only evidence of its existence is in the measures of behavior generated by intelligence tests. It cannot be measured directly, which requires basing inferences about the amount of "intelligence" present on this indirect evidence. Therefore, neither of these two requirements can be met in the case of intelligence.

> **Accuracy.** The extent to which observed values approximate to the events that actually occurred.

Reliability

If data are found to be less than fully accurate, the next question concerns the nature of the error. Is the error consistent in some way (as in when a scale is always high by 3 kilograms), or does the size of the error or its direction vary unpredictably? When we are talking about the nature of the error, we are

BOX 7.1

Reliability in the Social Sciences

The conception of reliability offered here is consistent with well-established usage in the natural sciences. However, certain applications in the social sciences have led to an alternate perspective. These applications typically involve some kind of psychometric test or instrument administered by researchers or clinicians as a way of making statements about general features of behavior or about mental qualities.

This approach to measurement is quite different from direct measurement of a specific target behavior, and different procedures have been developed for assessing what is described as the reliability of such tests. For example, the *split-half method* involves dividing the items on the test into two halves, such as odd versus even numbered items, and using the correlation between the two versions as an estimate of the whole test's reliability. Another method is said to estimate *test–retest reliability* because it uses correlations between scores from two administrations of the same test.

It should be clear that these procedures represent a fundamentally different conception of reliability from that used in the natural sciences. They do not involve assessing the relationship between directly observed measures and the events they actually represent.

BOX 7.2

The Relationship Between Accuracy and Reliability

It can be easy to get confused about accuracy and reliability. If a set of observations are determined to be completely accurate, they are also completely reliable. In fact, if the data are fully accurate, there is no reason to even raise the issue of reliability. After all, reliability is only an issue if there is some error. Only then can we ask whether the error is small or large, high or low, or consistent or variable.

Let us assume that the data are not completely accurate, however, and we are assessing the reliability (consistency) of the error. If our evaluation shows that the observed values are very reliable (e.g., always low by the same amount), we might describe the data as very reliable. As we can see from the example, this does not mean that the data are also accurate. Accuracy and reliability are very different aspects of the relationship between what was measured and what really happened. If data are reliable, it says nothing at all about their accuracy. The error might be very consistent but quite large, for example.

talking about reliability. **Reliability** refers to the consistency of the relationship between observed values and the events that actually occurred. A measurement procedure or device is said to be reliable if it yields the same result every time it is used to measure the same events. For example, measurement would be considered highly reliable if a scale always gave measures of the weight of a particular object that were low by 3 kilograms. On the other hand, we might consider measures at least somewhat unreliable if an observer viewing a video-tape of a participant's behavior during a session reported values that vary considerably from one viewing of the tape to another.

> **Reliability.** The stability of the relationship between observed values and the events that actually occurred.

Validity

When it is not clear that the data represent what they are supposed to represent, the issue of **validity** arises. This is typically a problem when indirect measurement is used. Recall the example in chapter 6 about evaluating

---

BOX 7.3

Validity in the Social Sciences

Questions about the validity of data are unusual in behavioral research because investigators are usually able to find a way of directly measuring the behavior of interest. However, much research in the social sciences involves indirect measurement. This means that the behavior actually measured (e.g., completing a questionnaire) is only used to make inferences about other behaviors or even mental qualities.

Assessing the validity of an indirect measurement procedure is therefore a common challenge in social science fields such as psychology, and a number of techniques have been developed. For instance, *criterion validity* refers to comparing the procedure under examination to an existing instrument that is already accepted as an adequate indicator of the characteristics of interest. The validity of an aptitude test might be evaluated by seeing how well it predicts performance as defined by some objective measure. (This is also called *predictive validity*.) The weakness of this approach lies in how the validity of the criterion was established. It may simply be that it is popular or has been around for some time.

Another approach concerns *content validity*. Here, the validity of a measurement procedure is assessed by inspecting its content, rather than by using an empirical method. The usefulness of this technique clearly depends on who is doing the assessment. *Construct validity* raises the question of how well the test measures the underlying construct it is intended to measure. This approach is also quite subjective because it involves the hypothetical nature of the underlying construct. After all, it is what the measurement procedure is supposed to illuminate.

> **Validity.** The extent to which observed values represent the events they are supposed to represent and that will be the focus of interpretation.

employee performance under an old versus a new lighting system in which employees completed a questionnaire about how their work was affected by the change. The validity of the questionnaire data would raise the issue of validity because it would not be clear whether they constituted a proper measure of work performance.

In this example, it would at least be possible to address this issue by collecting direct measures of work performance and comparing them to the questionnaire data. In many cases, this kind of option is not available. There is often no evidence that the focus of the indirect measures actually exists independently of the measurement operation. Measures of hypothetical psychological qualities resulting from various psychometric tests, inventories, and rating scales leave researchers and clinicians unable to assess whether such data are valid measures of these qualities because there is no way to measure such qualities directly.

Believability

Accuracy, reliability, and validity all involve some assessment of the relationship between observations and the actual events they are intended to represent. Sometimes the outcome of this assessment is not satisfactory. For instance, the accuracy of the data may prove to be less than desirable, reliability may be poor, or the evidence for validity may be weak. Worse still, it may not be feasible to even assess these relationships. Such circumstances constitute a real problem for the investigator and others who might be interested in a study. They cannot be sure that the data properly represent what actually happened. This means that conclusions based on these data could be misleading.

This situation does not necessarily mean that the data are worthless, but it does mean that their worth cannot be clearly established. (In mature sciences, this would usually preclude a study from being published.) This leaves the investigator in the unfavorable position of trying to enhance the **believability** of the data. Unlike accuracy, reliability, and validity, believability does not refer to the relationship between the data and the events they are supposed to represent. The term indicates that this approach focuses on convincing others to believe that the data are "good enough" for interpretation, even though there is no direct evidence that would clearly support such a belief.

> **Believability.** The extent to which the investigator can, in the absence of direct evidence, convince others to believe that the data are good enough for interpretation. Does not involve direct evidence about the relationship between data and the events they are intended to represent.

TACTICAL OPTIONS

Assessing Validity

It is most often the case in both behavioral research and practice that the target behavior can be directly measured. When this is done, the data are valid by definition because they represent exactly what investigators or clinicians will be drawing conclusions about. When indirect measurement procedures are used, however, they raise the question of whether the data are valid reflections of the real focus of interest. It is important to find an acceptable answer to this question. If there is no evidence that indirect measures of behavior are valid, it forces those using the data to make an uninformed assumption one way or the other.

The ideal approach to assessing the validity of indirect measures involves finding a way to collect evidence about the correspondence between the indirect measures and what they are intended to represent. For example, it can be difficult to directly measure the exercise behavior of individuals whose medical conditions require that they exercise regularly. This might lead a researcher or practitioner to ask participants to complete a weekly questionnaire as a way of measuring certain features of their exercise behavior. It remains possible to measure exercising directly, however, even though that option may present some challenges for routine use. Direct measures might be obtained from family members or health club computers, for instance, that could be compared to the questionnaire data.

Even if direct measurement of the behavior of actual interest is not feasible, it may be possible to collect data that would at least bear on the question of the validity of the indirect measures. In the case of exercising, for example, if an individual is reporting certain exercise routines on a questionnaire, it might be reasonable to expect that there would be some correspondence between questionnaire data and certain measures of physical functioning that could be directly obtained.

There are, then, two approaches to assessing the validity of indirectly measured data. One option is to arrange for direct measurement of the target behavior on a periodic basis. This will usually require special arrangements— after all, if it were easy to measure the behavior directly there would be no reason to resort to indirect measurement. However, it will often be sufficient to show close correspondence between indirect and direct measures for only a sample of all of the sessions. A second option provides more ambiguous evidence but can be convincing. This involves collecting corroborative data that, although not direct measures of the behavior, are at least consistent with the assumption that the indirect measures are valid.

TABLE 7.1
Procedures for assessing validity

- Arrange for direct measures of target behavior on a periodic basis
- Collect corroborative evidence consistent with assumption of validity

Assessing Accuracy and Reliability

Sequence of Assessment Efforts. The overriding interest in assessing experimental or clinical data lies in establishing their accuracy. If the data can be shown to be completely accurate, there are no further questions about their suitability for research or practical purposes. If the evidence shows that the data are less than fully accurate, it raises the question of what kind of error is acceptable. This issue is discussed in a later section.

When the degree of error is within acceptable limits, interest turns to the stability of the error. That is, is the error relatively consistent from measurement to measurement, as when a bathroom scale is always high by 2 kilograms? Or, is the error unstable, varying substantially from occasion to occasion? This concern is about the reliability of the data. When the data involve some degree of inaccuracy, the researcher must determine the characteristics of the error, including how large the errors are and how consistent they are. These characteristics must then be evaluated in terms of the needs of the study and the literature.

For example, if the data are only somewhat inaccurate but fairly reliable, they might be usable. If the data are unacceptably inaccurate but highly reliable, it may be possible to correct the data by adding or subtracting the consistent error. (A better approach would be to fix the problem that is producing inaccurate data.) If the data are both moderately inaccurate and unreliable, they may not be usable. There is no clear standard in judging the balance between accuracy and reliability, however. In addition to the considerations discussed in an upcoming section, decisions partly depend on the practices of other investigators in the same research area.

Procedures for Assessing Accuracy. The procedure for assessing accuracy is straightforward: Observed values are evaluated by comparing them to true values. In practice, this involves first determining a procedure for obtaining true values. There is no single way to obtain true values. There are only the requirements that: (a) the procedure must be different from that used to collect the data that are being evaluated; and (b) the procedure must incorporate extraordinary steps that avoid or remove possible sources of error. For example, a practitioner interested in measuring the compliance of arthritis patients with physician recommendations for walking exercise may use pedometers to measure the distance walked each day. Aside from the problem of whether the patients wear their pedometers as instructed, the accuracy of the instruments themselves can be measured by comparing their output on a course with a known distance (e.g., a football field) or with measures obtained by another device for measuring distance, such as a distance-measuring wheel.

When the data come from human observers rather than equipment, a common approach to evaluating accuracy involves making a videotape of the participant's behavior. The images can then be played back as many times as necessary to allow a different observer to obtain what can then be called true values. Still another procedure is possible when a target behavior observed in real time also results in response products that can later be measured in some manner. For example, this might be the case if a client's job performance in a supported employment setting resulted in completed tasks that could be measured after observation sessions were completed.

In assessing accuracy, comparisons between true and observed values can involve individual responses or summaries of responding. For instance, measures of individual responses during an observation period are often summarized into a session total. If these totals are used in comparing observed and true values, conclusions about accuracy can be made only about session totals. This limitation results from the possibility that even though observed and true value session totals may agree it does not mean that each represents measures of the same responses. In order to state that accuracy was obtained at the level of individual responses, it is necessary to show agreement between both types of observations for each response.

Actual calculation of accuracy involves comparing the obtained measures with measures of the true values. Suppose, for example, we want to determine the accuracy of observer measures of the latency of responses in a discrete-trial training procedure being employed with autistic children. To make this assessment, we might supplement observer data by making a video recording of one or more training sessions. We would arrange for careful scoring of the videotape by a different and highly trained observer, who can study the videotape as needed to minimize the risk of error. We would then compare these true values with those obtained by the regular observer working in real time. One way to make this comparison is to calculate a correlation coefficient between these two data sets, and this would serve as an index of accuracy.

Procedures for Assessing Reliability. There are two ways to assess reliability. One way to do this is as a byproduct of assessing accuracy. That is, when comparing observed and true values, it is easy to also track the nature of any error. If the consistency of the error is relatively high, for instance, the data might be described as acceptably reliable. Of course, this would have nothing to do with whether the data were acceptably accurate (see Box 7.2). This way of calculating the reliability of observations involves the same methods described above for assessing accuracy.

A second way of assessing the reliability of observed values does not require true values. In this approach, the behavior of interest must be preserved in some way, such as in a videotape format. With this advantage, the observer can

TABLE 7.2
Procedures for assessing accuracy and reliability

- Accuracy: Obtain true values and compare with observed values
- Reliability: (1) Obtain true values and compare with observed values
                      (2) Present observer with same sample multiple times

---

be presented with the videotape two or more times so that the consistency of observational judgments can be evaluated. In other words, it is not necessary to have independently measured the target behavior in the videotape. The fact that this sample of the participant's behavior is unchanging from one viewing to another is sufficient to determine whether an observer's judgments are reliable.

Calibration. When accuracy and reliability are found to be unacceptable, the investigator has two choices. The project can be abandoned, or the problems with measurement procedures can be identified and fixed. This latter approach is called calibration. **Calibration** involves evaluating the data from a measurement procedure and using the findings to adjust the procedure so that its output meets desired standards. Scientists and engineers is all fields of endeavor whose work depends on sound measurement routinely calibrate measurement systems.

> **Calibration.** Evaluating the accuracy and reliability of data produced by a measurement procedure and, if necessary, using these findings to improve the procedure so that it meets desired standards.

Enhancing Believability

Interobserver Agreement. In applied behavioral research and practice, the most common approach to evaluating measurement procedures and data does not involve assessing either accuracy or reliability. Instead, it is typical to arrange for simultaneous but independent observation by two or more observers for at least some sessions. This procedure allows researchers or practitioners to calculate the degree of agreement between observers. The outcome of this procedure is called **interobserver agreement**.

> **Interobserver agreement.** A procedure for enhancing the believability of data that involves comparing simultaneous but independent observations from two or more observers. Provides no information about accuracy or reliability.

It is important to be clear that interobserver agreement provides no information about either accuracy or reliability. As we have seen, assessing accuracy unavoidably requires access to true values so that they can be compared with observed values. Reliability is usually evaluated in the same manner (although it can also be determined by repeated observation of the same sample of behavior). A second observer used in the same way as the primary observer cannot be assumed to create true values just because they are being used to evaluate the primary observer's performance. When two (or more) observers are used, there is presumably no information regarding the accuracy of either. After all, if one observer was known by some assessment procedure to be accurate, there would be no reason to use a second observer.

The fact that two observers reported the same measure of the target behavior for a session says nothing about the accuracy or reliability of either. Perfect agreement between observers watching the same participant during a session may be a comforting fact, but it only allows the conclusion that their total observations agreed. As usually practiced, it does not even mean that the two observers detected the same responses. Each observer may have failed to detect, or erroneously detected, different responses, while still arriving at the same total measures.

In other words, just because two observers obtain the same total measure of responding does not provide any guarantee that either report reflects exactly what happened with the target behavior. Such information merely encourages the investigator and others to accept the data as believable or "good enough." This assessment might seem reasonable based on our shared experiences in everyday life. After all, independently verified reports often are true, or at least they may appear to be. There is nothing about independent agreement per se that assures this result, however.

In spite of these limitations, interobserver agreement procedures are widely used in behavioral research and practice. The following steps are based on a simple observational situation requiring only a single observer. First, the individuals who will serve as the primary and secondary observers must be selected and trained. The sole distinction between them is that the primary observer's data will serve as the project's results, and the secondary observer's data will be used only for comparison. Although it might be tempting to suppose that the "best" trainee should be selected as the primary observer, the secondary observer must be no less skilled. When comparisons in their data do not agree, it will not be known which is correct, or if either of them are.

Second, each must also not be able to tell when the other is detecting and recording a response. That is, their judgments must be independent of each other. If either can tell when the other is recording a response, it could influence their judgment. What further complicates this requirement is that, during sessions when both are scheduled to observe, each must be positioned so that neither is at a disadvantage in viewing the participant's target behavior. This can be difficult to arrange in some field settings.

Third, the two sets of observations must be compared in some manner.

TABLE 7.3
Procedures for determining interobserver agreement

- Select and train primary and secondary observers
- Set up independent observation procedure
- Select agreement formula and calculate agreement

There are a number of ways of doing this, depending on what aspect of the target behavior is being observed and recorded. We will describe four procedures for calculating agreement.

First, the **total agreement** procedure is typically used when observers are recording dimensional quantities such as count, duration, or latency. When the number of responses is being recorded, the investigator sums the total count for each of the two observers, divides the smaller total by the larger total, and multiplies the result by 100 to arrive at the percent agreement. The formula for this calculation is:

$$\text{Smaller total} \div \text{Larger total} \times 100 = \% \text{ Agreement}$$

This formula can also be used to calculate interobserver agreement for duration or latency data. For example, if the total duration of responding recorded by the primary observer during a session was 180 seconds and the total duration recorded by the secondary observer was 200 seconds, there would be 90 percent agreement (180 seconds divided by 200 seconds multiplied by 100).

A second procedure is a more demanding variation of the total agreement procedure and is called **exact agreement** (Repp, Deitz, Boles, Deitz, and Repp, 1976). With this approach, the observation period is divided into equal intervals but observers record the actual number of responses in each interval, rather than scoring the interval by partial or whole interval rules. Only intervals in which the two observers agreed on the exact count are considered agreements. When these intervals are very short, for instance a few seconds, this procedure may come close to insuring that the observers are recording the same responses. In order to obtain the percent agreement, the total agreements are divided by the total number of intervals (total agreements plus total disagreements) and the result is multiplied by 100. The formula for this calculation is:

$$\text{Total agreements} \div \text{Total number of intervals} \times 100 = \% \text{ Agreement}$$

Total agreement. A procedure for calculating interobserver agreement typically used with dimensional quantities such as count, duration, and latency that involves summing the total count for each of two observers, dividing the smaller total by the larger total, and multiplying the result by 100 to arrive at the percent agreement.

Exact agreement. A procedure for calculating interobserver agreement that involves dividing the observation period into intervals in which two observers record the actual number of responses. In order to obtain percent agreement, only intervals in which the two observers agreed on the exact count are considered agreements.

A third procedure is called **interval agreement** and is used when the two observers are using interval recording or time sampling procedures. Each interval scored by both observers is counted as an agreement. Each interval that is scored by neither observer is also called an agreement. Intervals scored by only one observer are counted as disagreements. In order to obtain the percent agreement, the total agreements are divided by the total number of intervals (total agreements plus total disagreements) and the result is multiplied by 100. The formula for this calculation is the same as for exact agreement:

Total agreements ÷ Total number of intervals × 100 = % Agreement

This calculation is widely used, but there is an important limitation of this procedure. If the participant's responding occurs very frequently or very infrequently, the number of agreements could be misleading. For instance, suppose that responses occurred in only five out of 180 intervals. Even if the two observers disagreed on the five intervals when responses occurred, they would probably agree on most of the many unscored intervals when the behavior did not occur. As a result, the percent agreement would be very high, which would improperly imply that they usually agreed on scored intervals (Bijou, Peterson, Harris, Allen, & Johnston, 1969).

The solution to this problem is to use a fourth procedure called **occurrence/nonoccurrence agreement**. This is a more conservative approach because it involves calculating and reporting agreement separately for both occurrences (scored intervals) and nonoccurrences (unscored intervals). This prevents percent agreement from being inflated by especially frequent or infrequent responding (Bijou, Peterson, Harris, Allen, & Johnston, 1969; Hawkins & Dotson, 1975). This means that agreements are counted when the two observers score an interval or when both fail to score an interval. Disagreements occur when one scores an interval and the other does not.

> **Interval agreement.** A procedure for calculating interobserver agreement when interval recording or time sampling is used. Each interval scored by two observers is counted as an agreement, and each interval that is scored by neither observer is also called an agreement. Intervals for which only one observer scored the behavior are counted as disagreements.
>
> **Occurrence/nonoccurrence agreement.** A conservative approach to calculating interobserver agreement when interval recording or time sampling is used that involves calculating and reporting agreement separately for both occurrences (scored intervals) and nonoccurrences (unscored intervals).

The formula for calculating occurrence and nonoccurrence percent agreement is the same as for interval agreement, except that occurrence agreements and nonoccurrence agreements are calculated separately. In other words, to calculate occurrence agreement the number of intervals for which the two

TABLE 7.4

Formulas for calculating interobserver agreement

Procedure	Formula
• Total agreement	Smaller total ÷ Larger total × 100
• Exact agreement	Total agreements ÷ Total number of intervals × 100
• Interval agreement	Total agreements ÷ Total number of intervals × 100
• Occurrence/nonoccurrence agreement	Total agreements ÷ Total number of intervals × 100

observers agreed that the behavior occurred are divided by the number of occurrence agreements plus the number of intervals when only one observer scored. To calculate nonoccurrence agreement, the number of intervals for which the two observers agreed that the behavior did not occur are divided by the number of nonoccurrence agreements plus the number of intervals that only one observer scored.

Other Corroborative Evidence. Obtaining evidence that two observers more or less agreed in their reports of what they independently observed is not the only way to augment the believability of the data. Any evidence that might persuade others that the data are good enough to warrant interpretation may be used. For example, a project to measure study behavior in college students involved the development of a form that students were asked to complete each time they studied, which naturally involved a wide range of circumstances (Johnston, O'Neill, Walters, & Rasheed, 1975). Because it was not feasible to assess the accuracy or reliability of their self-reports, it was necessary to gather evidence that their data were at least believable.

Here are some examples of evidence that was useful. First, if the form was soliciting valid and meaningful reports of study behavior, certain types of errors should have been found only rarely. For example, they should have reported "reading" material prior to reporting "rereading" for the same assignment. Second, given the type of testing used in their course, students should not have reported certain types of study behavior. For example, if a course did not have formal lectures and tests covered only text material, transcribing and rereading lectures should have been rarely reported. Third, courses being used in these studies required students to test repeatedly until they met mastery criteria. If the amount of study was generally related to test performance, this relationship should have been evident in the correspondence between study data and test performance across successive attempts. Finally, one of the variables investigated in the course was the amount of material assigned and tested from one unit to another. This should have corresponded to predictable variations in the amount of time spent reading the material (e.g., more material should have resulted in more reported reading time). In all of these instances, the data suggested that students were filling out the study reporting form correctly and providing meaningful reports of their study efforts (O'Neill, Walters, Rasheed, & Johnston, 1975; Walters, O'Neill, Rasheed, & Johnston, 1975).

Procedural Issues

Implementing Assessment Procedures. Regardless of whether data assessment focuses on accuracy, reliability, or believability, there are a number of procedural details that must be decided. One concerns *when assessment efforts should be made.* As a general rule, it is important to start evaluating data as soon as a project begins. If problems are discovered they can be fixed right away, which will minimize the amount of data that might have to be discarded if serious problems are discovered. Furthermore, because problems with measurement procedures can occur at any point, assessment efforts should continue throughout all phases of the study.

Although assessment efforts should be ongoing, investigators still need to decide *how frequently data should be evaluated.* If observation sessions occur every weekday, for example, should assessment efforts be scheduled multiple times each week, only once per week, or even less often? There is no simple rule to guide this decision. Although some authors suggest that about one-third of all sessions is appropriate (Bailey & Burch, 2002; Kennedy, 2005), this standard is arbitrary. The decision partly depends on the complexity of the measurement procedures. If measurement involves observing only a single behavior that is clearly defined and easily detected, the data may not need to be assessed very often. On the other hand, if observers must detect multiple behaviors in multiple participants in a complex setting, it may be wise to evaluate the data fairly often. More frequent assessment may also be necessary when observers must also record the status of treatment conditions or behavior of individuals other than participants who are involved in key ways. The frequency with which data assessment is conducted also depends on what these evaluations reveal. That is, the better the assessment outcomes, the less often such assessments may need to be made. On the other hand, if assessment data show certain kinds of problems, it is best to be cautious and conduct assessment frequently.

Another factor to consider when scheduling data assessments concerns *sampling different circumstances throughout a study.* There are many factors in a study that might affect how well measurement procedures work and the quality of the resulting data. In scheduling assessment activities, it is important to make sure that data are evaluated under all of the different circumstances represented in a study. For example, different experimental or treatment phases usually affect participant behavior but can also affect measurement operations. The nature of certain conditions can make observation more difficult or even affect how observers make judgments. Data assessment should therefore be conducted under each phase of a study. The identity of observers can also change during a study, so it is important to make sure that the performance of each observer is evaluated.

Standards for Assessment Results: Origins. The reason for assessing the quality of the data in a study is to allow an informed decision about whether they properly represent what they are supposed to and are therefore acceptable for interpretation. Researchers and practitioners are interested in taking whatever actions are necessary as the study is being conducted to insure that the accumulating data meet accepted standards. Once a study is completed, others will make their own decisions about the quality of the data.

The standards for the quality of experimental or clinical data vary somewhat from one scientific discipline to another. The nature of the phenomena being investigated, how well it is understood, the measurement technology available, and the data quality typically achieved by investigators all contribute to informal standards within a particular literature.

Sometimes standards for assessing data can depend on certain strengths and weaknesses in a study's methods. For example, consider two studies that used partial interval recording procedures. Assume that interobserver agreement findings were weak in both cases but that one study used 2-minute intervals and the other used 15-second intervals. Would the disadvantage of weak assessment data be overcome by the advantage of the shorter interval? Consider a second example. Would weak accuracy data be more acceptable if the observation procedure involved continuous observation than if it used momentary time sampling? The answers should depend on the details in each case, but it is sometimes reasonable to balance the strengths and weaknesses of the particular measurement procedures used. This is a risky practice, however. When measurement procedures or assessment outcomes are seriously flawed, no compromises are appropriate.

Standards may even depend on the uses to which a study's conclusions may be put. This is also a risky consideration because the truth of a study's conclusions does not depend on how they will be used. Nevertheless, when setting a standard for the credibility of data, it may be reasonable to consider the uses to which the findings will be put. For example, when the findings of a project might lead to a badly needed but expensive intervention program for an at-risk population, it is certainly important that the quality of the data fully justifies the study's conclusions.

Standards for Assessment Results: Interpretation. Even though there may be no general standard for accuracy, reliability, or approach to believability such as interobserver agreement, it is important to understand what any particular standard might mean. For instance, it is not uncommon for applied behavioral research published in respectable, peer-reviewed journals to report interobserver agreement values as low as 80% (Bailey & Burch, 2002; Cooper, Heron, & Heward, 1987; Kennedy, 2005). Does this mean that if a researcher obtains about 80% agreement from data assessment procedures that it is therefore appropriate to continue the study and confidently draw conclusions when it is completed?

One way to think through what a standard such as 80% means is to figure out the impact that this outcome could have on how the data are interpreted. This is fairly straightforward in the case of accuracy and reliability. If we know that the data are 80% accurate, we know not only the exact amount of the error but its direction. That is, because true values were available to assess observed

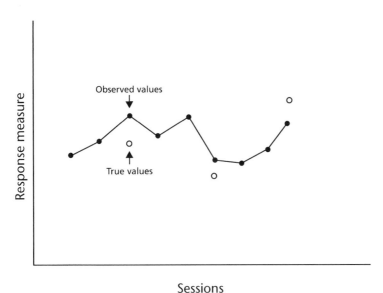

FIG. 7.1. Graphical display of primary data and associated true values.

values (the only way to assess accuracy), we know which data points are incorrect and by how much. In fact, if we have this information for each observation we could simply correct the errors, just as if you know your bathroom scales are high by 2 pounds you can subtract this amount from its reading. Even if we have accuracy data for only some of the values, we could plot both the observed and true values on a graph. This would not only show the extent of the error but also how it is distributed (its reliability), and allow us to evaluate how it might influence our interpretation of the observed data (see Figure 7.1).

If the data assessment procedure were based on interobserver agreement, the meaning of 80% would be more complicated and uncertain. Let us take the relatively simple case in which two observers independently count responses using continuous observation. Here, 80% agreement simply means that one observer's total count for a session was 20% higher or lower than the total obtained by the other. Although the investigator would know which observer had the high and low value, there would be no evidence about whether either count was accurate. In fact, unless the procedure determined point-by-point correspondence, it would not be known if 80% agreement even represented agreement on specific responses.

All we would know is that two observers watching the same participant came up with total response counts that disagreed by 20%. Let us extend this example by assuming that interobserver agreement was determined for one out of every five sessions across baseline and treatment phases and that the two observers averaged 80% agreement across all such comparisons. Because interobserver comparisons are not available for four out of five sessions, we might assume that the same level of agreement holds for these unchecked sessions.

One way of looking at a graph of these data is to consider what they might look like if each data point from the primary observer was displaced by 20% in either direction. This is a good test because we have no information about the accuracy of either observer's data. (The secondary observer's data could be just as "good" as the primary observer's data.) Figure 7.2 shows hypothetical data illustrating this kind of comparison. The data from the primary observer are surrounded by data sets that are 20% higher and lower. This view helps to show what 80% agreement (or 20% disagreement) could mean.

An even more conservative interpretation would be to assume that the 20% disagreements were not random but represented systematic bias in a way that could change how we might interpret the study's outcome. In this worst-case scenario, this would mean assuming that the study's results could be represented by the upper data set in the baseline phase and by the lower data set in the treatment phase. This assumption minimizes the differences in responding between the two conditions and brings into question whether the changes in responding are sufficient to conclude that the treatment condition had an important effect on responding.

Finally, if the interobserver data being considered were based on interval recording procedures, their interpretation would require a slightly different procedure. When two observers are simply counting a participant's responses, 80% agreement means that one count was 20% higher or lower than the other. However, when two observers are scoring intervals according to either partial or whole interval rules, 80% agreement means that they disagreed on whether the behavior occurred at all on 20% of the intervals. We cannot know how

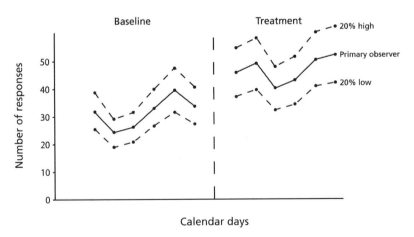

FIG. 7.2. Graphical display of primary observer data and data sets representing 20% disagreement in both directions.

much disagreement 20% might represent in terms of a dimensional quantity such as count, duration, or latency.

Standards for Assessment Results: Failing to Meet Standards. What if the assessment process shows that the data fall short of the field's standards? The researcher sees the data as they accumulate day by day and can respond to such situations by fixing problems with measurement procedures and improving the data. Sometimes the corrective actions will involve only minor improvements, such as giving observers refresher training. However, it may be that more significant improvements in measurement procedures are necessary. Such changes might include revising definitions of the target behavior or modifying measurement procedures in some way. If data collected following such changes cannot be interpreted in the same way as those collected under the original measurement procedures, it is likely that the old data must be discarded. This is why it is important to identify and resolve problems with the quality of the data as soon as possible. The sooner any problems are discovered, the fewer observations may have to be thrown out. (Chapter 13 will consider the issue of discarding data in more detail.)

If accuracy or interobserver agreement data are available weekly, for example, an unacceptable assessment made on Friday casts doubt on all of the data collected since the last assessment. This means that an entire week's data might have to be discarded. However, this is certainly less painful than it would be if data assessments were made only once in each phase. Then it might be necessary to throw out the entire phase, fix the measurement problems, and run that phase again.

Readers of a published study can only passively evaluate the researcher's choices and the assessment evidence. When a reader is interested in a study's findings but has concerns about a study's measurement procedures or the quality of the data, this can be a frustrating limitation. The journal's editor and the peers who reviewed the paper are supposed to represent the field's standards in reaching a decision about whether to publish the paper. In mature sciences, the peer review system generally works well and only methodologically sound research is published. Social and behavioral science fields are still struggling with methodological issues, however. Most research projects can find a journal outlet, even when they have significant measurement or design problems. Although readers can correspond with investigators and ask questions about any features of a study, this is uncommon. More often, readers simply make their own judgments about the quality of the data and whether conclusions seem justified.

Reporting Assessment Results. The fact that an investigator continues a project to its conclusion presumably means that he or she is satisfied with the quality of the data generated by measurement procedures. In disseminating the results of the study, whether at a conference or by submitting a report to a professional journal, the task is to report evidence about the quality of the data in such a way that others can make their own evaluations. There is no standard way of reporting data assessment findings, and practices vary from one field to another. How such evidence is reported most often depends on the measurement procedures themselves and the nature of the assessment outcomes.

At the very least, the methods section of a study must describe the details of data assessment procedures. When true values are used to assess accuracy and reliability, the investigator should describe how these special observations were made. When interobserver agreement procedures are used, it is important to describe how both primary and secondary observers were trained and deployed. When assessment procedures are not conducted for each observation period but on some intermittent schedule, their frequency and distribution must be described. It can be especially important to be clear about how an assessment was distributed across different conditions, observers, or other important features of a study. It is also important to clarify the formula used for calculating assessment results.

All of this information is usually described in the text of a report. Sometimes the results of assessment procedures may be summarized in a brief statement as well. For example, if the accuracy and reliability of data were regularly assessed and consistently found to be very good, it might be sufficient to describe the assessment procedures and a simple summary of their results. When assessment outcomes are less than ideal, it is usually important to report separate assessment data in more detail, including data for each phase of a study or even for different observers.

When reporting complex assessment information, it is sometimes easiest for readers to understand if it is described in a table or graph instead of in text. Tabular presentations are typically straightforward row and column layouts of assessment results for each condition response class, setting, or other important feature of the project (see Table 7.5). Graphical descriptions of assessment outcomes might add assessment data to graphs showing the study's primary data, as in Figure 7.1.

In sum, one of the key features of scientific method is a relentless focus on measuring events of interest with great care. It is not enough to be careful, however. Researchers must demonstrate that their efforts have paid off with data that meet at least the minimum standards of the field. For each discipline, these standards ultimately come from the reactions of reviewers and readers of published reports as they decide whether reported data are worthy of interpretation.

TABLE 7.5
Example of tabular presentation of interobserver assessment results

	Control condition 1	Intervention condition 1	Control condition 2	Intervention condition 2
Initiating social interactions	83%	85%	92%	80%
Complying with requests	89%	93%	86%	94%
Classroom	87%	92%	85%	95%
Playground	79%	77%	85%	81%

CHAPTER SUMMARY

1. The goal of scientific measurement is to arrive at the best possible estimate of the true value of some event that has occurred. By acknowledging that data are often only estimates of the facts, this may encourage researchers to try to obtain the best possible estimates and minimize measurement errors.

2. Observed values are those values that are recorded from simple observation. True values are obtained by the investigator by taking special precautions to minimize or avoid error.

3. In order to evaluate the accuracy of a data set, the data must represent a specific behavior, and this behavior must be able to be measured directly. If the data are not accurate, we must consider the nature of the error that is contributing to the inaccuracy. Reliability examines this issue by looking at the consistency of the relationship between observed values and the events that actually occurred. A measurement procedure is reliable if it yields the same result every time it is used to measure the same responses.

4. Validity addresses whether the data represent what they are actually supposed to represent. Validity is usually of concern when indirect assessment is used, because there is often no evidence that the focus of the indirect measures actually exists independently of the measurement operation.

5. The ideal approach to assessing the validity of indirect measures involves finding a way to collect evidence about the relationship between the indirect measures (e.g., survey, questionnaire) and what they are intended to represent (physical behavior).

6. In order to assess the accuracy of a data set, the observed values are compared to true values. True values must be collected using a procedure that is different than what was used to collect the observed values, and the procedure must incorporate very specific steps to avoid or remove any possible source of error (e.g., video recordings).

7. The reliability of a measurement procedure may be assessed in conjunction with measuring accuracy. When comparing observed and true values, the researcher can examine the nature of any error. If the pattern of the errors is consistent, the data may still be described as reliable.

8. If accuracy and reliability are both unacceptable, researchers will often evaluate the data and use their findings to adjust the procedure until the output meets their standards. This process is known as calibration.

9. Applied researchers will often evaluate their measurement procedures by occasionally using two independent observers. In an interobserver agreement procedure, the independent observers record their observations and then compare them to see if they agreed on the occurrences and nonoccurrences of the target behavior. This procedure does not provide information about accuracy or reliability; it only informs the investigator whether both observers obtained the same total measure of responding.

10. Dependent upon what dimension of behavior the researcher is recording, there are several ways of calculating interobserver agreement. The most conservative of these approaches is a procedure called occurrence/nonoccurrence agreement. This procedure requires the observers to calculate their scores separately for both occurrences (scored intervals) and nonoccurrences (unscored intervals). This prevents the percent agreement from becoming inflated by behaviors that are especially frequent or infrequent.

11. The assessment of data should begin immediately and continue throughout all phases of the study. This will allow the researcher to identify any problems with the procedure and minimize the amount of data that must be discarded.

12. The reason for assessing the quality of the data is to allow the investigator to make an informed decision about whether the data are valid and acceptable for interpretation.

13. Most disciplines have certain general standards that their data must meet in order to make interpretations. If the data do not meet these standards, the researcher must alter the measurement procedures in an attempt to improve the study and the data collected.

14. When an investigator is satisfied with the quality of the data generated by the measurement procedures, the results may be disseminated. There is no standard way of reporting data assessment findings, but at the very least the researcher must be sure to fully and accurately describe the data assessment procedures.

TEXT STUDY GUIDE

1. Why is the concept of estimation a useful way to approach behavioral measurement?

2. What is the distinction between observed and true values? Given that true values must be created through some form of observation, why might they be considered "true" values?

3. What is the difference between accuracy and reliability? How are they often confused?

4. What is validity, and why is it not usually a concern in behavioral research and practice?

5. How is believability fundamentally different from accuracy, reliability, and validity?

6. Validity is an issue when indirect measurement procedures are used. What must you collect evidence about in order to validate indirect measures? What can you do when such evidence is not available?

7. What are two approaches to assessing the validity of indirectly measured data?

8. With directly measured data, what should be the sequence of assessment questions?

9. What are the two requirements for obtaining true values?

10. If observed and true values agree at the level of session totals, what can you say—and what can you not say—about accuracy?

11. What are two basic ways of assessing the reliability of data?

12. Explain the concept of calibration with regard to behavioral measurement.

13. What is the basic procedure for obtaining interobserver agreement?

14. What does interobserver agreement not tell you?

15. What is the formula for calculating total interobserver agreement?

16. What is the rationale and formula for calculating exact interobserver agreement?

17. What is the formula for calculating interval interobserver agreement?

18. What is the rationale and formula for calculating occurrence/non-occurrence interobserver agreement?

19. When should data assessment activities begin?

20. What factors influence the decision about how frequently to assess data?

21. How should you decide when to schedule data assessment throughout a study?

BOX STUDY GUIDE

1. How is reliability interpreted in psychometric assessment?

2. Distinguish between split-half and test–retest reliability.

3. Complete the following sentence using the terms "accurate" and "reliable." If data are _____, they must be _____. Why is the converse not true?

4. Distinguish between criterion, content, and construct validity in psychometric measurement.

SUGGESTED READINGS

Hawkins, R. P., & Dotson, V. A. (1975). Reliability scores that delude: An Alice In Wonderland trip through the misleading characteristics of interobserver agreement scores in interval recording. In E. Ramp & G. Semb (Eds.), *Behavior analysis: Areas of research and application* (pp. 359–376). Englewood Cliffs, NJ: Prentice-Hall.

Repp, A. C., Deitz, D. E. D., Boles, S. M., Deitz, S. M., & Repp, C. F. (1976). Differences among common methods for calculating interobserver agreement. *Journal of Applied Behavior Analysis, 9*, 109–113.

DISCUSSION TOPICS

1. Discuss ways of obtaining true values in field research.
2. Discuss the limitations of interobserver agreement.
3. Select a published study and discuss the options for assessing measurement procedures and data.
4. Using Figures 7.1 and 7.2, discuss the implications of 80% as a standard for accuracy and for interobserver agreement.

EXERCISES

1. Provide observed and true value data sets and calculate the accuracy and reliability.
2. Provide interobserver data sets and calculate the different types of interobserver agreement.

PART THREE

DESIGN

Behavioral Variability

I can, if the worst come to the worst, still realize that the Good Lord may have created a world in which there are no natural laws. In short, a chaos. But that there should be statistical laws with definite

solutions, i.e., laws that compel the Good Lord to throw the dice in
each individual case, I find highly disagreeable.

—A. Einstein

STRATEGIC ISSUES

A Definition of Behavioral Variability

It is often the case that objects or events that may seem to be the same are not
actually identical. Scientists have learned that if we measure carefully enough,
differences can almost always be found. It seems especially easy to agree with
this assumption when behavior is the subject matter. Even when we study very
simple behaviors such as a pigeon pecking a key under restricted laboratory
conditions, responses that at first seem very stereotyped can be shown to be
different from one another (Schwartz & Gamzu, 1977).

It is the differences among individual members of a response class that are
at the root of what we refer to as **behavioral variability**. If a researcher is
measuring self-injurious behavior by an autistic child, for example, each
response will be a bit different from the next in topography, duration, interresponse time, force, velocity, or other features. From session to session, these
differences will add up to variation in whatever dimensional quantity the
researcher is measuring. In fact, it is uncommon for measures of responding to
be the same from one session to another. Each data point is usually different
from the next.

> **Behavioral variability.** Variations in features of responding
> within a single response class, as well as variations in summary
> measures of that class.

Levels of Behavioral Variability

Although variability in a behavior always comes down to differences among
individual responses, there are many ways of looking for and describing it.
Behavioral researchers look at variability in their data much as other
researchers use a microscope. By switching lenses, different degrees of magnification become available. This means that viewers can make choices about
what the level of "magnification" (summarization) might be revealing in each
case.

There are at least three levels of summarization in which researchers and
practitioners are often interested. The greatest detail can be found by looking
at the distribution of individual responses over time during an observation
period. There are a number of ways of doing this. One way is to locate each
response in time by identifying each response with an upward step of a pen,

leaving a cumulative trace on a roll of paper (see chapter 12). B. F. Skinner developed a device called a cumulative recorder just for this purpose, and laboratory investigators routinely examined behavioral data in this format for many years (Skinner, 1956). Panel A in Figure 8.1 shows an example of a cumulative record. These data show key-pressing responses of a nonverbal individual diagnosed as profoundly mentally retarded working under a fixed-interval 40-second schedule contingency. The graph shows that responding was characteristically infrequent immediately following reinforcement (indicated by the downward slashes) but increased considerably toward the end of the intervals.

Panel B of Figure 8.1 illustrates a noncumulative display of responding. This graph shows continuous variation in penile erection responding (Henson & Rubin, 1971). The participant was watching an erotic film during both phases. He was instructed not to inhibit responding during the first phase, but to inhibit responding during the second phase.

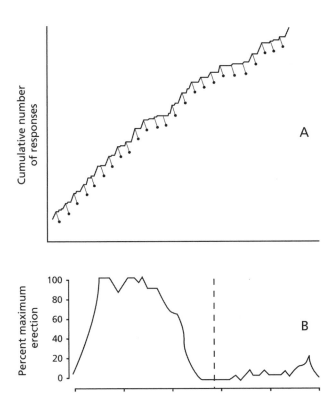

FIG. 8.1. Examples of data displays showing the distribution of individual responses during observation periods. Panel B is adapted from Henson, D. E., & Rubin, H. B. (1971). Voluntary control of eroticism. *Journal of Applied Behavior Analysis, 4*, 37–44, p. 42. Copyright 1971 by the Society for the Experimental Analysis of Behavior, Inc. Used by permission.

Another level of summarization results from combining response measures during each session into a single value. Variability at this level is evident in the differences among these session summary values. Although this approach prevents seeing variability among individual responses, it has the advantage of revealing variability that might be difficult to detect by looking only at individual responses.

Investigators typically find this view of variability very informative. It does not allow them to see what is going on during each session, but this perspective helps to highlight changes in behavior from one session to another under the same phase. Because conditions during a phase are usually intended to be relatively consistent from session to session, changing patterns of responding can be especially meaningful. For instance, they might suggest that extraneous influences are operating. This view also aids comparisons of responding under two or more different conditions. Chapter 9 will show that this picture of variability is especially important in helping to make decisions about when to terminate one phase and initiate the next phase.

Figure 8.2 shows two examples of this level of summarization as a way of looking at behavioral variability. Panel A shows the percent of correct trained letter strokes across sessions under baseline and feedback conditions in a project focusing on training cursive handwriting (Trap, Milner-Davis, Joseph, & Cooper, 1978). Panel B shows the performance of a nonvocal adult diagnosed as profoundly mentally retarded participating in a project on training in basic communication skills (Reid & Hurlbut, 1977). The graph shows the number of correct pointing responses under baseline conditions and following training sessions. Both graphs make it easy to see changes in responding within each phase and from one phase to the next.

A third view of variability involves summarizing measures of responding across individual sessions. The resulting values represent measures of responding for a number of sessions, such as all of the sessions under a particular condition. This view prevents seeing changes in responding from one session to another but helps to highlight differences between conditions. A researcher may want to compare responding under a pair of control and experimental phases, for example, or between the same treatment phase implemented at two different points in time.

The panels in Figure 8.3 show examples of this view of variability. Panel A shows the average number of cigarettes smoked per day for 14 participants. Their self-reported data have further been averaged across days for each of four conditions (Glenn & Dallery, 2007). This bar graph or histogram also shows data points representing the means for individual participants for each phase.

Panel B shows data from a project evaluating the use of computer-based instruction for teaching young children prereading skills (Connell & Witt, 2004). The graph summarizes performance over multiple sessions for a series of tasks under various conditions (before training, after training Task 1, and so forth). This view makes it easy to compare each participant's performance across the important features of the study.

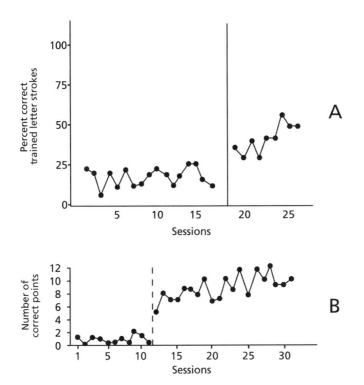

FIG. 8.2. Examples of data displays showing responding in the form of session summary values within and across conditions. Panel A is adapted from Trap, J. J., Milner-Davis, P., Joseph, S., & Cooper, J. O. (1978). The effects of feedback and consequences on transitional cursive letter formation. *Journal of Applied Behavior Analysis, 11*, 381–393, p. 389. Copyright 1978 by the Society for the Experimental Analysis of Behavior, Inc. Used by permission. Panel B is adapted from Reid, D. H., & Hurlbut, B. (1977). Teaching nonvocal communication skills to multihandicapped retarded adults. *Journal of Applied Behavior Analysis, 10*, 593–613, p. 597. Copyright 1977 by the Society for the Experimental Analysis of Behavior, Inc. Used by permission.

The degree of summarization represented in the graphs in Figure 8.3 is substantial, so there is a risk that interesting features of responding are being missed. Behavioral researchers tend to use this view of variability to summarize their data only after they have examined less summarized versions of the same data.

TABLE 8.1
Levels of summarizing variability

- Displaying the distribution of individual responses over time
- Displaying summaries of response measures for each observation period
- Displaying summaries of response measures across multiple observation periods

---

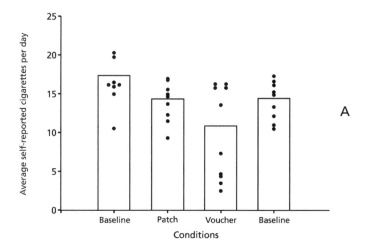

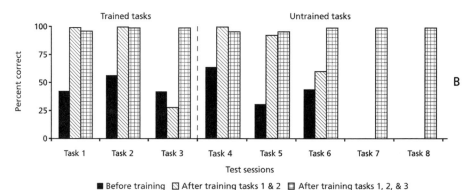

FIG. 8.3.   Examples of data displays showing responding summarized across conditions or phases. Panel A is adapted from Glenn, I. M., & Dallery, J. (2007). Effects of internet-based voucher reinforcement and a transdermal nicotine patch on cigarette smoking. *Journal of Applied Behavior Analysis, 40,* 1–13, p. 8. Copyright 2007 by the Society for the Experimental Analysis of Behavior, Inc. Used by permission. Panel B is adapted from Connell, J. E., & Witt, J. C. (2004). Applications of computer-based instruction: Using specialized software to aid letter-name and letter-sound recognition. *Journal of Applied Behavior Analysis, 37,* 67–71, p. 70. Copyright 2004 by the Society for the Experimental Analysis of Behavior, Inc. Used by permission.

The Nature of Behavioral Variability

Variability as Intrinsic.   Having defined behavioral variability and discussed different ways of looking at it, we can turn to considering where variability comes from. In general, there are two conflicting perspectives about the nature of behavioral variability. The traditional assumption is that variability in behavior is **intrinsic**. This point of view says that behavioral variability is in one way or another inherent in the nature of humans and other animals. This

> **Intrinsic variability.** The assumption that variability in behavior is in one way or another inherent or built into the nature of organisms. See *Extrinsic variability*.

implies that the origins of variability are somehow simply part of what it means to be a human being, for example. If variability is inherent, it also implies that the causes for behavior are built into our nature and therefore cannot be influenced by environmental factors.

Although most people acknowledge that behavior is at least partly influenced by experiences, it is also common to hear someone say that people may do things for no reason, that they can make free choices, or that some aspects of behavior are beyond scientific explanation. Such comments all suggest an underlying assumption that variability in behavior is intrinsic. In fact, most philosophical, religious, and cultural explanations of behavior rest on an implicit assumption of intrinsic variability. It is easy to see why this perspective is so comfortable. Variation in human behavior from occasion to occasion in daily life may be obvious, but its causes are often subtle and difficult to identify. Without an understanding what influences are actually at work, it is convenient to invent causes such as the mind ("I just made up my mind to quit smoking") or to assume that behavior has no causes ("I am free to choose any item on the menu").

Variability as Extrinsic. The contrasting position taken by behavioral researchers is that the variability we observe in behavior is **extrinsic**. To say that behavioral variability is extrinsic means that it is describable, explainable, and predictable with reference to other natural phenomena. Scientists long ago learned that an organism's behavior is the result of its biology and its environmental experiences. This position therefore holds that the variations we see in a particular behavior from moment to moment or day to day are the result of biological and environmental influences. Contrary to the intrinsic assumption, variation in responding is not assumed to be the result of a fundamental quality of variability that is supposedly an inherent property of all organisms.

> **Extrinsic variability.** The assumption that variability in behavior is describable, explainable, and predictable in terms of variation in other phenomena, whether biological or environmental. See *Intrinsic variability*.

Of course, in practice we often have to admit that we do not know why a particular behavior occurs, especially at a specific moment. The extrinsic perspective at least allows us to optimistically argue that its causes are within the realm of science and can, in principle, be found. This means that we can continue to improve our understanding about the causes of behavior and our ability to resolve behavioral challenges in daily life.

Practical Outcomes. It is important to remember that the intrinsic and extrinsic positions about the nature of behavioral variability are only assumptions. We cannot decide between these two points of view by proving that one is correct and the other is wrong. As Sidman (1960) observed, the methods of science lend themselves not to proving that something is untrue, but to demonstrating the plausibility of the alternative. Proving the extrinsic argument, for example, would require finding causes for every instance of behavior in order to show that such causes exist. This would not only be impossible, but an unwise use of scientific resources.

From a practical perspective, it may be sufficient to consider the consequences of taking the intrinsic versus the extrinsic view. For instance, if the operating assumption is that variability is intrinsic, it might encourage researchers, as well as practitioners, to view variability in their data as an unavoidable aspect of behavior. This position might in turn lead to accepting excessive variability in behavioral data, rather than taking steps to establish improved control over extraneous influences.

In contrast, the extrinsic assumption tends to encourage researchers to design experiments that minimize the contribution of these extraneous factors so that the impact of treatment conditions can be more clearly identified. As we have already seen, the choices involved in designing measurement procedures provide many opportunities for minimizing extraneous influences. Later chapters will show many more such opportunities associated with creating experimental comparisons and analyzing data.

Functions of Behavioral Variability

In the most general sense, variability is the subject matter of all sciences. It is the task of behavioral scientists to describe variability in behavior through measurement procedures and to discover why behavior changes as conditions change. Such discoveries are the foundation of basic and applied research literature. Practitioners may even arrange brief experimental manipulations in order to understand the variables maintaining a target behavior so that they can develop more informed treatment procedures (Handley, Iwata, & McCord, 2003; Lalli, Browder, Mace, & Brown, 1993).

There are three general functions served by behavioral variability. First, variation in responding motivates and guides a researcher's curiosities. The focus of experimental questions about a particular kind of variability tends to direct such curiosities. One study might ask why different individuals respond differently to the same set of conditions. For example, why might some children have no difficulty in learning to read using a particular teaching procedure but others fail to progress? The objective might be to develop procedures for reducing that variability so that the procedure will be effective

BOX 8.1

Free Will versus Determinism

The argument about whether variability in behavior is intrinsic or extrinsic is just another way of talking about free will versus determinism. As human culture and language evolved, people tended to invent explanations for the events in their daily lives for which they had not yet discovered explanations. Of course, these invented explanations were usually false. Scientific discoveries of the last century or two have greatly reduced the popularity of invented causes for most physical phenomena. (We no longer believe that life generates spontaneously or that the Earth is flat.) It has been more difficult to overcome the endless assumptions about the nature of human nature.

One of the most persistent convictions people often share is that each person is free to make decisions and take actions that are not influenced by outside events. In other words, many assume that human behavior is often free, in the sense that it is not caused by any specific factors. It is easy to appreciate why this seems so obvious. Most people do not understand the real causes of human behavior, which are complex and sometimes poorly understood by even scientists. As a result, we are usually unaware of the factors that actually influence our actions. Our language encourages us to assign causation to "ourselves" rather than to influences in the physical world. So, we say that we did something because "we wanted to" or that we "changed our mind."

In his book, *Beyond Freedom and Dignity* (1971), B. F. Skinner tried to show that such assumptions about human nature are actually quite troublesome. They get in the way of understanding how our behavior is affected by our experiences. In turn, this limits our ability to grow personally or to learn to be more successful in our daily lives. In fact, if it were really true that some aspects of human nature were without natural causes, it would be very discouraging. Assuming that certain aspects of behavior are "free" means they are without causes, which is the same thing as saying they are random or capricious. If this were so, it would be pointless for scientists to study behavior because it would be impossible to find consistent relationships between behavior and environmental variables.

It should not be surprising, therefore, to learn that when scientists go to work every morning, they assume that the events they are studying are not free but are determined by other events. This simply means that they assume that all events have causes, even though they do not know what all of the causes are in each case.

with more children. Another study might investigate what it would take to induce changes in behavior. For instance, what kinds of compounds in explosives are detector dogs alerting to? If we can learn about these compounds, handlers can train dogs to be more effective in responding to explosive materials. Still another experiment might focus on ways of increasing variability. For example, what procedures can be effective in training people to perform in ways that might be called creative?

Second, variability in behavior guides decision-making as a study proceeds. Both researchers and practitioners make many decisions guided by the patterns of responding they observe during the course of a project. Modifying measurement procedures, adjusting intervention conditions, identifying and controlling extraneous variables, beginning and ending phases, and selecting data analysis techniques all involve choices that depend on how responding varies across time and conditions. The influence of these factors is what we described in chapter 1 as bringing the researcher's behavior under control of the subject matter.

For example, as we saw in the discussion of defining target behaviors (chapter 4) when a definition of the response class is first used for data collection, the initial data may suggest the need for some adjustments. If the data are highly variable, it could be the result of problems with the definition. The definition might be too broad, encompassing two or more behaviors that have different sources of influence. This might result in variability from session to session as one behavior or the other increases or decreases. The definition might also present problems for observers, who might therefore make their own judgments about what responses should be included. The variability that results from these problems is an indication that the definition may need to be modified.

Third, variability in responding provides the foundation for how we interpret experiments. Here, graphical displays of variations in responding within each phase, as well as changes in responding from one condition to another, are especially important. They prompt researchers to draw certain conclusions about the role of treatment variables, as well as the influence of extraneous factors that might complicate the picture.

For instance, let us suppose that after exposure to a baseline condition responding decreased when an intervention started but then gradually increased to baseline levels as the intervention phase continued. This change in responding during the intervention phase, when the intervention procedures were presumably the same from day to day, might suggest that it would not be appropriate to conclude that the intervention produced only a decrease in responding from baseline. It would also be important to note the gradual recovery of responding to baseline levels, suggesting that the effects of the intervention were not very durable. The remaining chapters in the book describe ways of using variability to draw conclusions that reflect what really happened in the study.

TABLE 8.2
Functions of behavioral variability

- Motivates and guides researcher curiosities
- Guides decision-making as a study proceeds
- Provides the foundation for interpreting experiments

Managing Variability

Variability due to Independent Variables. Researchers pursue these three ways of using behavioral variability with a two-part approach: (a) producing variability in responding by manipulating independent (treatment) variables, whose influence is in question; and (b) reducing variability in responding by identifying and controlling extraneous factors. The first part of this approach is the primary focus of experimentation—to see if a certain condition will affect behavior and, if so, what kind of effects it will have. A particular treatment or experimental condition is selected because it seems likely that it will produce a change in responding. Researchers hope that this change, which represents a particular form of variability of the target behavior, will help to answer the experimental question.

In applied research, for example, questions often concern the impact of a procedure on a behavior having some practical importance. The researcher is interested in seeing if the stable responding achieved under control or baseline conditions will change in particular ways when the treatment condition is present. If so, these changes in responding may allow conclusions about the practical effects of the intervention. The more substantial and distinctive the intervention's impact on responding compared to baseline performance, the more confident the researcher and others might be about the role of the treatment condition. Researchers generally try to maximize the impact of the treatment variable on the target behavior serving as the dependent variable.

This is a good occasion to more fully define what we mean by an independent variable condition (also called a treatment or experimental condition). In some studies a single, narrowly defined change in the environment may serve as the independent variable. This might be the case in a laboratory project, for instance, that varied the dosage of a drug or parameter of a reinforcement schedule. However, in most studies, the independent variable is a coordinated set of environmental changes. This is typical in much applied research. When an intervention involves even a relatively simple procedure such as differential reinforcement, for example, what is introduced (and later withdrawn) is actually an array of factors, including a particular reinforcer in a particular amount, a certain reinforcement contingency, a schedule of reinforcer delivery, and an extinction contingency, among other variables. We will see later that clearly defining each independent variable condition is especially important in deciding what might have caused any changes in the dependent variable.

Variability due to Extraneous Variables. The second part of this approach—reducing behavioral variability by controlling extraneous factors—is necessary in order to be sure that the treatment condition is the only factor responsible for observed changes in responding. It might be that other factors unrelated to the researcher's interests also contributed to observed changes in responding, perhaps even substantially. If an experimental condition is introduced but is also accompanied by changes in other variables, it will not be clear what actually caused any changes in responding.

As an example of this risk, suppose that a researcher is interested in learning about the effects of a new, behaviorally active drug on the aggressive behavior of dually diagnosed clients (individuals diagnosed as both mentally retarded and mentally ill). First, a baseline condition might be introduced so that the researcher can examine the pattern of responding characteristic of this control condition. Next, the researcher would introduce the experimental condition— a particular dosage of the new drug—so as to watch for any changes in responding. Suppose, however, that at about the same time as the drug phase of the study started the participants were relocated to a new residential facility. This change might by itself be expected to produce changes in their behavior, possibly including their aggressive behavior. Because the initiation of the drug regimen and the facility relocation occurred together, it would not be clear which factor contributed to any observed changes in the target behavior.

There are two ways of managing the contribution of extraneous variables. One involves *holding the extraneous factors constant* across all phases of a study. If this is feasible, it will mean that their effects will still be present but will at least be the same across control and experimental phases. In the above example, the researcher would make sure that the living arrangements of the participants would not change during the study. Although what is happening every day on the residential unit might well influence the behavior of participants, those influences would be more or less the same throughout all phases of the study. They would therefore be unlikely to be responsible for changes in behavior observed only when the drug condition was present.

This tactic of holding extraneous variables constant may not help if the effects of extraneous factors are so powerful that they obscure the effects of the treatment variables. If it turns out that staff members are unwittingly reinforcing aggressive behavior in the residence, for instance, such behavior may remain quite frequent, making it more difficult to see any decrease that might otherwise result from the new drug.

Another way to manage extraneous variables is to *completely eliminate the problematic factors* from the situation so that they cannot have any influence. For example, consider the challenge for a researcher interested in studying how social factors influence alcohol consumption. Even though it might be preferable to measure drinking patterns under everyday conditions, there are so many factors in daily life that can affect drinking besides social variables (such as money and opportunity) that it would be difficult to get a clear picture of the effects of social variables by themselves. The solution might be to conduct studies in a residential treatment setting, where these other factors can be largely, if not entirely, eliminated.

These two tactics—holding extraneous variables constant or eliminating them—can be implemented to varying degrees. At a minimum, the investigator can either control or eliminate sources of extraneous variation one by one until the desired degree of control over responding is achieved. This approach may be time-consuming, but it has the advantage of managing only those extraneous factors that are significant, and ignoring more trivial variables. This option may therefore be more economical in terms of the researcher's time and effort.

At the other extreme, the investigator can attempt to control or eliminate all possible sources of extraneous variability from the outset, regardless of their potential impact. Although this approach can be quite effective, it can be challenging to accomplish and there is a price. The more that experimental circumstances differ from the situation of ultimate interest, the more difficult it is to know whether the same results would be obtained under those more realistic situations. This is a particularly important question for applied research. The reason for an applied research project is usually to find results that will hold up under particular real-world situations. For example, if a research project is investigating procedures for training care-givers, it is important that practitioners who apply its findings get the same results. If the research was conducted under highly artificial circumstances, the results might depend on these circumstances and not be obtained under everyday conditions.

Although dealing with extraneous factors might seem a distraction from the investigator's primary interest, it is not unusual for this effort to require more attention than arranging the experimental conditions themselves. Scientists have learned, however, that reducing the effects of unwanted factors is worth the time and trouble in order to increase the chances that their conclusions about the effects of treatment conditions will be true and can be depended upon by others.

SOURCES OF BEHAVIORAL VARIABILITY

Organism

One might get the impression that an organism's environmental experiences have a greater influence on its behavior than does its biology. It might seem this way because we can often get at environmental variables more easily than biological factors. Although environmental factors are undeniably potent, it would be a mistake to fail to acknowledge the pervasive influence of an organism's biology.

We often think of an organism's genetic endowment and physiological functioning in terms of the limits they place on behavior. What we can sense about the world we live in and how we can react to everyday events is indeed limited by our physical features and capabilities. No matter how fast we might flap our arms, we cannot fly, and although we have good eyesight compared to many species, we still cannot see in the dark as well as a cat.

In contrast, many features of our biology provide not so much limits as a powerful array of ongoing influences. Some are relatively stable, such as the physiological processes that maintain various life functions. For instance, the behavior of breathing is controlled by the body's need to maintain homeostatic oxygen levels in the blood, and the behavior of eating is partly controlled by the need to balance energy consumption and expenditure.

A different set of organismic variables are developmental in nature and thus change over time. Some changes in behavior are the result of genetically mediated physiological changes that influence the way the body ages. For example, changes in infant brains in the early months of life have subtle but significant effects on behavior. Puberty is later defined by hormonal changes that have broad and noticeable effects on behavior. As we grow into old age, cellular changes in the body contribute to changes in behavior in obvious (posture and gait) and more subtle (memory) ways.

Sometimes categorizing influences on behavior as environmental or biological seems arbitrary. There are many environmental events that lead to changes in biology, which in turn lead to behavioral changes. For example, drugs and other environmental chemicals (e.g., toxic substances) can contribute to behavioral variability by how they affect the organism's physiology. Even food can be thought about in this way. Geophysical variables affect behavior in ways we are still learning about. Jet lag, which results from abruptly modifying sleep cycles by rapidly moving around the Earth across time zones, is a good example of this kind of phenomenon. Physical injuries and some diseases might also be thought of as the result of environmental influences on the organism's biology that often have behavioral effects.

Finally, although we think about an organism's history as largely the result of environmental factors, these influences are actually mediated by the organism's biology. For example, we often speak as if the environment is changed by conditioning processes ("the neutral stimulus has now become a conditioned reinforcer"), but it is the organism that has changed at a biological level in ways we do not yet fully understand.

Each experimental participant brings a unique history with them, of course, and it can be a potent source of behavioral variability. Sometimes these pre-experimental historical influences are more powerful than experimental variables. Because the effects of pre-experimental history are often unrelated to research interests, selecting participants whose behavioral characteristics suit the needs of each study is a key feature of research methods.

For example, it is well-established that human participants with well-developed verbal repertoires are likely to talk to themselves during experimental sessions about what is going on (Catania, Shimoff, & Mathews, 1989). Studies have shown that this kind of talk can have a substantial influence on how they react to experimental procedures. Participants who do not have this repertoire (including babies, individuals with profound mental retardation, as well as nonhuman species) often respond differently than participants who can talk to themselves when exposed to similar procedures (Lowe, 1979).

BOX 8.2

What is Inside the Organism?

Our language makes it easy to talk about what seems to be going on inside the organism. As we learn to talk in childhood, we learn to explain behavior by reference to memory, intelligence, abilities, ego, mind, compassion, wants, impulses, images, information, attitudes, inhibitions, virtues, habits, intentions, beliefs, knowledge, and so forth. Instead of replacing colloquial language in its scientific pursuits, however, psychology has tended to incorporate and elaborate such terms, as well as add many of its own contributions.

As nouns, these words almost seem to refer to things, even if no one has actually seen them. Our language needs agents for verbs that express action, and these kinds of terms are often given the function of causing behavioral actions. So we say that "He does well in school because he is smart," "She has a big ego, so she is always talking about herself," or "If you think about what you were doing, it will help to jog your memory."

Of course, all that anyone can actually find inside the organism is the physical equipment of its biological functioning. This does not mean, however, that all inner "causes" of behavior that such words seem to refer to have nothing to do with behavior. To propose that the qualities that such words suggest do not exist in some sense might be as naïve as arguing that they refer to real, physical events.

Instead, the critical issue is what is *really* there and how we should talk about it. When scientists are not completely sure about the physical status of some supposed phenomenon, they pay special respect to the notion of parsimony (see Box 2.6). The scientific attitude of parsimony means that we should be careful to try to explain aspects of the behavior of human and nonhuman animals in terms of principles or laws that are already well-established scientifically before turning to less understood or more troublesome causes. Inventing a nonphysical or mental universe of causes for behavior certainly leads to endless problematic explanations.

Being careful about how we talk about the causes of behavior is also critical to avoiding scientific dead ends. Although it might seem harmless to say that expectations influence behavior, for example, if it encourages some researchers to spend the field's resources trying to study expectations then considerable harm has been done. Refining our professional language to avoid this kind of trap is difficult, but it can be done. It involves making sure that we only assign causal roles to phenomena that we are reasonably certain physically exist, although it is more complicated than this. For an introduction to how to talk about behavior in a scientifically cautious manner, you should read B. F. Skinners' books, *Science and Human Behavior* (1953), or *About Behaviorism* (1974). He spent much of his career trying to improve our scientific vocabulary about human affairs.

Experimental Setting

In any investigation, the behavior of interest occurs in a setting composed of many potential sources of variability. One or more of these variables will be considered independent variables because they are the primary focus of experimental attention. The remainder are considered extraneous variables, signifying that they are not the researcher's primary interest.

Let us consider the kinds of extraneous variables that might be present. First, some extraneous factors may have nothing to do with the experimental setting itself, such as when a participant gets sick or is under stress for reasons unrelated to the study. Second, some extraneous variables are part of the general physical space in which a study is conducted. The lighting or ventilation in a room or noises coming from outside the room are typical examples. Third, still other extraneous influences are in some way associated with the general experimental procedures in which the independent variable is embedded. These might include the nature of the task, instructions from the experimenter, or the kind of reinforcers used. Fourth, sometimes extraneous factors can be associated with the treatment condition itself, even though they are not formally defined as part of it. For instance, in a study examining a particular teaching technique, the social interactions between a teacher and students might not be considered part of the procedure being evaluated even though they are intermingled with the teaching procedures.

Although investigators carefully distinguish between independent and extraneous variables, all environmental variables have the potential to affect behavior. It is tempting, however, to ignore extraneous factors or at least suppose they will have little or no effect on the target behavior. Unfortunately, once extraneous influences have occurred, their effects cannot be disentangled from the impact of the independent variable by argument or speculation. In other words, the best time to address the role of extraneous factors is when the study is being planned.

Measurement

Defining Response Classes. Sometimes variability in the data can be traced to how the target behavior is defined. Definitions may unintentionally

TABLE 8.3
Types of extraneous variables

Category	Example
• Unrelated to the experiment	Sickness, stress
• Part of the general experimental space	Lighting or ventilation
• Associated with general procedures	Task features, instructions
• Associated with the independent variable condition but not part of it	Social interactions tied to nonsocial independent variable

include responses that belong to different classes. (Chapter 4 discussed this possibility in some detail in considering functional versus topographical response classes.) When this is the case, the resulting data may show more variability than would be found if the target behavior were more carefully defined.

To understand one way in which this possibility might come about, consider a project focusing on the tantrum behavior of an individual diagnosed with severe mental retardation. Suppose the definition includes hitting, kicking, throwing (objects), and cursing responses, all of which tend to occur together during tantrum episodes. The fact that some responses (hitting, kicking, and throwing objects) involve safety risks may mean that they pretty consistently result in intervention by care-givers. However, cursing may not by itself typically generate staff intervention and may also occur when other tantrum responses are not occurring.

The possibility that cursing often results in different consequences than the other tantrum behaviors suggests that it might be a separate functional response class. If we assume this to be the case for this illustration, the inclusion of cursing in the definition of tantrum behavior may result in greater variability than we might see if we only measured hitting, kicking, and throwing responses. The variables in the everyday environment, as well as a treatment procedure, may influence these two functional response classes somewhat differently. This means that the day-to-day frequency of cursing versus hitting/kicking/throwing responses would ebb and flow as functionally related parts of the environment changed. This would show up as variability in the data from day to day. This problem could even mask the effect of a treatment procedure. For example, an intervention might reduce hitting/kicking/throwing but increase cursing. As a result, the data could imply that there was not much change in the defined target behavior.

Selecting Dimensional Quantities. Chapter 5 explained that any behavior can be described in terms of different dimensional quantities. Both researchers and practitioners are naturally interested in selecting those quantities that will reveal changes in responding generated by experimental or treatment conditions. If a quantity is chosen for measurement that does not reveal meaningful changes in responding, the data may prompt misleading conclusions about the effects of treatment conditions.

For example, if a therapist uses a discrete-trial training procedure to teach a skill, measuring progress in terms of frequency of responding is likely to be misleading. This type of procedure involves conducting repeated trials, each of which is initiated by the trainer. Therefore, the pace (frequency) of responding is at least partly determined by the trainer. (The learner cannot respond until the trainer starts a new trial.) Measures of the learner's performance in terms of response frequency would therefore be misleading because this dimensional quantity would partly reflect the behavior of the trainer, not the learner.

Observing and Recording. As chapter 6 indicates, decisions about observing and recording procedures can have a major impact on variability in the data. For instance, decisions about when observation takes place and how long sessions last will influence the picture of variability in the same way that a documentary film-maker making a movie about a foreign country determines viewers' impressions by how scenes are selected. Researchers and practitioners can easily see the impact of their choices on the data by trying out alternative observation plans. Moving observation sessions to a different time of day or setting or increasing the length of observation periods is a good way to test whether different sampling procedures might show different patterns of responding.

Of course, the choice of continuous versus discontinuous observing procedures is likely to have a substantial impact on the nature of the data collected. One limitation of discontinuous procedures such as interval recording is that they fail to provide a picture of what is happening with dimensional quantities because the data reflect only the number or percent of scored intervals. Another problem is that the number of intervals scored unavoidably depends on the length of the interval chosen.

These issues make it difficult to compare the picture of responding obtained by discontinuous observation procedures with data resulting from continuous observation procedures, such as counting the number of responses during an observation period. As chapter 6 noted, studies have shown that interval recording procedures often show the same general increases or decreases from one condition to another as continuous observation data collected during the same sessions. However, more specific aspects of variability inevitably differ in such comparisons, and the data points in the two kinds of samples represent fundamentally different information.

Experimental Design

Alternative Approaches. The phrase **experimental design** refers to how researchers arrange comparisons between control and experimental conditions so as to permit inferences about any effects independent variables may have on responding. Decisions about how these comparisons will be made can have a profound impact on the variability the data reveal. Perhaps the most fundamental decision concerns how comparisons will be made. There are two distinct alternatives. One approach is to compare each participant's behavior as he or she is exposed to control and experimental conditions in sequence. That is, the researcher looks at the data from each participant separately and compares responding under a control condition with responding under an intervention condition for each individual. This approach is called **within-subject design**. A different approach typically involves dividing the participants into two groups, one of which will be exposed to a control condition and the other to an experimental condition. The data from each set of participants is grouped into a collective outcome, and these outcomes are then compared. This approach is called **between-group design**.

Experimental design. Arrangement of control and treatment conditions that permit comparisons that help to identify the effects of the independent variable on the dependent variable.

Within-subject design. A method of arranging comparisons between control and experimental conditions in which each subject is exposed to both control and experimental conditions in sequence so that the data represent the performance of individual participants.

Between-group design. A method of arranging comparisons between control and experimental conditions in which different groups of subjects are exposed to control and experimental conditions so that the data represent the combined performance of individual participants who have experienced only one of the conditions.

Behavioral Requirements for Experimental Design. These two approaches to experimental design result in very different pictures of participant behavior. To understand these differences, consider the following points. First, recall that behavior is a biological phenomenon and is therefore a characteristic of individual organisms. It is a result of interactions between individuals and their environments, and it is only by understanding this relationship that we can understand how behavior is influenced by particular environmental factors.

Second, it follows that no two individuals behave exactly alike. Even identical twins raised in the same family do not share exactly the same histories. If they did, the twins would behave identically from moment to moment, just as a shadow follows its owner. Each person has a unique history and is likely to respond to similar events at least a little bit differently—and perhaps very differently.

Third, a description of a single individual's behavior under some condition represents something very different than a description of the combined behavior of two or more individuals under the same condition. Let us suppose, for example, that we have measured the performances of two participants (Harry and Sally) on a problem-solving task. If we look at their data separately for a single session, we will know exactly how each performed. However, if we combine their individual performances in some way (e.g., by averaging their responses), we will not know the performance of either Harry or Sally. Furthermore, they may well have performed differently, which means that the average will not correctly represent the performance of either person.

Let us add some detail to this example by stipulating that Harry solved 10 problems correctly and Sally solved 16 correctly. These are measures of each one's behavior. It is clear that the average (13 correct responses) is not an accurate measure of either individual's behavior. Hidden in this average is the difference (six) between the two individual's performances. This difference is not a measure of either individual's behavior, which is why it is misleading to describe the difference between the performances as "six correct responses." If six correct responses was a measure of behavior, whose behavior would it represent? Neither Harry's nor Sally's, because we know they got 10 and 16 problems correct, respectively. Instead, this difference is an artifact of combining data in this way. This artifact is called **intersubject variability**, which here refers to the differences between the behavior of two or more participants.

> **Intersubject variability.** Differences in responding between participants.

Fourth, because intersubject variability has nothing to do with the description of behavior (an intraorganism phenomenon), it is not helpful in explaining the behavior of a single organism. Knowing the difference between Harry's and Sally's performances says nothing about why either behaved as he or she did. On the other hand, an adequate account of why each behaved as he or she did will be sufficient to explain any differences between their performances. This point certainly does not mean that the differences among individuals are unimportant. However, if researchers want to explain those differences, their data must reflect pure measures of behavior, undiluted by intersubject variability.

Fifth, one of the reasons for this guideline is that the differences in each participant's reaction to a condition are the actual effects of the condition. Combining Harry's and Sally's data will only hide the true effects of the condition, which will partly depend on certain factors unique to each individual. Any environmental condition produces individual effects, not average effects. The usefulness of studies reporting average effects will therefore often be limited because those outcomes do not necessarily reflect the actual effects on participants' behavior resulting from the experimental conditions.

Sequence Effects. Another way to consider the differences in these two approaches to experimental designs is to examine the experiences of participants. Individuals in a typical between-group design are often assigned to either a control or an experimental condition and therefore do not have contact with both conditions. In contrast, each participant in a "within-subject"

TABLE 8.4
Arguments for analyzing individual data

- Behavior is a characteristic of individual organisms
- No two individuals behave exactly alike
- A description of one individual's behavior is fundamentally different from a measure of the behavior of multiple individuals, which creates intersubject variability
- Intersubject variability has nothing to do with the description of behavior
- The effects of a variable are on the behavior of individuals, not on aggregate measures across individuals

design experiences both types of conditions. In fact, they may respond under a sequence of conditions throughout a study, such as an initial control condition (baseline), a subsequent treatment condition, a return to the control condition, and a return to the treatment condition. Many different sequences of this sort are common.

As we will learn in upcoming chapters, there are important advantages of measuring the behavior of each participant under different conditions. For now, it is sufficient to understand that moving from one set of environmental conditions to another creates the possibility that the experience of one condition may influence a participant's reaction to a subsequent condition. This kind of variability is called a **sequence effect**, and the possibility of such effects is inherent in within-subject designs. In fact, it is unavoidable that responding can be influenced by an individual's prior experiences under similar conditions. This is simply how conditioning processes work, and it helps our behavior adapt to different circumstances as we go about our daily lives.

> **Sequence effect.** An effect of a participant's behavior resulting from exposure to a prior condition.

Sequence effects may be useful or problematic. For example, an investigator may be interested in studying how prior contact with one condition (a training regimen) will affect performance under a subsequent condition (under which the trained performance must be exhibited). In this case, the sequence effect is experimentally useful. On the other hand, it is often desirable that performance under a treatment condition reflects only the effects of that condition, uncontaminated by the participant's experience under a prior condition. In this situation, the investigator must find ways to minimize sequence effects and to evaluate the extent of their impact on responding.

Fortunately, the likelihood of obtaining sequence effects can be either enhanced or minimized, depending on the researcher's interests. For instance, giving participants a long history with one condition and then switching to a different condition augments the chances that experience with the first condition will affect responding in the second condition. However, the influence of the first condition will usually weaken as a participant gains exposure to the second condition.

One way to separate sequence effects from treatment effects is to use the fact that behavior gradually adapts to new circumstances. Making sure that participants are exposed to the second condition long enough for any impact of the first condition to wear off can leave a clear picture of the effects of the second condition alone. This common tactic will be discussed in detail in the next chapter. Later chapters will also discuss ways of assessing the extent of possible sequence effects.

Data Analysis

As the raw data in a study accumulate, researchers must choose how to display and analyze them so that the data can aid in evaluating the progress of the project and its outcomes. Chapter 12 considers this topic in detail, but for now it is important to recognize that different pictures of variability can result from different analytical techniques. Some views of variability can be valuable in helping the investigator to recognize what the data reveal, but other views of variability can obscure important information or even be misleading.

For example, Figure 8.4 shows hypothetical data from control and experimental conditions displayed in terms of individual sessions (Panel A) and as averages summarizing all sessions within each condition (Panel B). Both displays show correct and potentially useful information, depending on what the researcher or others need to know. However, it is clear that the two pictures of variability in the data differ markedly. The level of summarization in Panel B

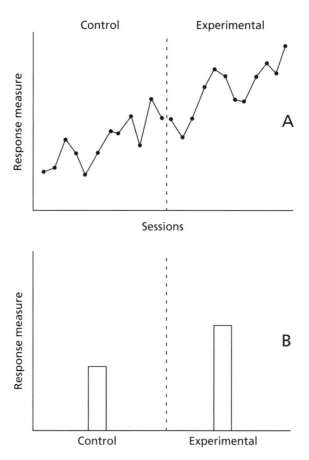

FIG. 8.4. An example of data from control and experimental conditions displayed by sessions (Panel A) and by conditions (Panel B).

hides the fact that responding gradually increased throughout the control condition and continued increasing throughout the experimental condition. As the next chapter will show, being aware of the pattern of variability shown in Panel A is important in evaluating the role of extraneous factors, which could be confused with the contribution of the experimental condition.

Independent Variable

Finally, the independent variable is an obvious source of behavioral variability. In fact, it is the only source of variability whose impact is intentional and the primary focus of interpretation. All other features of the experiment are designed to clarify the effects of the independent variable on the target behavior. Upcoming chapters will consider how to arrange experimental comparisons so that the role of the independent variable is clearly revealed.

Unfortunately, researchers cannot assume that an independent variable condition will be exactly the same from day to day throughout an entire phase, which may last for some time. Any of its features may vary in unplanned ways over time, which might result in variability in the data. This means that researchers must take steps to insure that the independent variable and the circumstances in which it is embedded operate exactly as planned.

This can be a considerable challenge, especially in applied research. As we have already pointed out, in applied settings the treatment conditions are often complex arrangements involving the behavior of others such as parents, teachers, or other personnel. For example, an experimental condition may require a teacher not only to respond in a specific way each time a child emits the target behavior but to behave in a different way the rest of the time. Merely training the teacher how to respond may not be sufficient to insure consistent reactions over a period of weeks. This is why it is often necessary to collect and report evidence that experimental and control conditions actually operated as designed (Peterson, Homer, & Wonderlick, 1982).

CHAPTER SUMMARY

1. There are many ways of looking for and describing behavioral variability. There are at least three levels of summarization in which researchers and practitioners are often interested. The greatest detail can be found by examining individual responses over time.

2. Another level of summarization requires the investigator to combine response measures during each session into a single value. While this approach prevents seeing variability among individual responses, it can reveal variability that might have been difficult to see by only looking at single responses. This approach is informative because it highlights changes in behavior from one session to another session in the same phase.

3. A third view of variability requires the researcher to summarize measures of responding across individual sessions. This view prevents seeing changes in responding from one session to another, but it helps to highlight differences between conditions.

4. The traditional assumption is that variability is intrinsic or inherent in the nature of organisms. If this logic is used, it also implies that the causes of behavior are built into our nature and cannot be influenced by the environment.

5. The contrasting position is that variability is extrinsic and may be described and explained with reference to environmental and biological events. This approach encourages researchers to minimize the contribution of extraneous factors to reduce variability, rather than just accept variability as an unavoidable aspect of behavior.

6. There are three general functions served by behavioral variability. The first is that variation in behavior may guide and motivate a researcher's curiosities. Second, variability in behavior guides the researcher's decision-making throughout the study. Finally, variability provides a foundation for how we interpret experiments.

7. Researchers pursue these three ways of using behavioral variability by producing variability in responding by manipulating independent variables and by reducing variability in responding by identifying and controlling extraneous factors. The first part of this approach is the primary focus of experimentation—to see if a specific variable will affect behavior and, if so, what kind of effects it will produce.

8. Controlling extraneous factors to reduce behavioral variability is necessary in order to be sure that the change in responding during a particular phase is due only to the independent variable.

9. Extraneous factors may be managed by either holding extraneous variables constant across all phases of the study or by completely eliminating the problematic variables. At a minimum, the investigator should control or eliminate sources of extraneous influence individually until the desired degree of control over responding is achieved. The other possibility is attempting to eliminate or control all of the extraneous variables from the outset, regardless of their potential impact.

10. Behavioral variability may occur for a number of reasons, including the genetically mediated physiological changes. Variability may also occur due to the experimental setting. Extraneous variables may be embedded within the general experimental procedure, be a part of the general physical space, or even be associated with the treatment condition.

11. Variability in the data can also be traced to how the target behavior is defined. Definitions may unintentionally include responses that belong to different classes.

12. The experimental design may also influence how the researcher views variability. The use of a within-subject design or a between-subject design will present a very different representation of participant's behavior.

13. Moving from one set of conditions to another creates the possibility that the experience of one condition may influence a participant's reaction to a subsequent condition. This kind of variability is called a sequence effect. Sequence effects are inherent in within-subject designs and may be useful or problematic. Depending on the researcher's interests, sequence effects may be enhanced or minimized.

14. The most obvious source of behavioral variability is the independent variable. This is the only variable whose impact is intentional and the primary focus of interpretation.

TEXT STUDY GUIDE

1. What is behavioral variability?
2. Distinguish among three levels of behavioral variability.
3. What does it mean to propose that variability in behavior is intrinsic?
4. Describe the position that variability in behavior is extrinsic in nature.
5. What are the practical outcomes of assuming that behavioral variability is intrinsic?
6. What are the practical outcomes of assuming that behavioral variability is extrinsic?
7. Describe the three functions of variability for researchers.
8. What are the two tactics that are together used to deal with variability?
9. Explain how it can be experimentally useful to increase variability.
10. What are synonyms for the independent variable condition?
11. Describe two ways of managing extraneous sources of variability and the limitations of each.
12. Describe three types of biological influences on behavioral variability.
13. Why is it appropriate to view an organism's environmental history as a biological influence?
14. What are some of the types of extraneous variables that researchers might encounter?
15. How can behavioral variability be influenced by the response class definition?
16. How can behavioral variability be influenced by the selection of dimensional quantities?
17. How can behavioral variability be influenced by observing and recording procedures?
18. What is experimental design?
19. Describe the argument that the study of behavior must be based on comparisons of the behavior of individual participants under control and experimental conditions.

20. What is intersubject variability?

21. What is a sequence effect?

BOX STUDY GUIDE

1. What are the implications for a science of behavior of saying that people are "free" in the sense that their behavior does not have causes?

2. Why do we tend to explain behavior by referring to causes inside the organism?

SUGGESTED READINGS

Sidman, M. (1960). *Tactics of scientific research*. New York: Basic Books. [Chapter 5: Intrinsic vs. imposed variability]

Skinner, B. F. (1971). *Beyond freedom and dignity*. New York: Alfred A. Knopf.

DISCUSSION TOPICS

1. Discuss ways in which colloquial language suggests that variability is intrinsic to human behavior.

2. Discuss everyday observations about behavioral variability that might suggest experimental studies.

EXERCISES

1. Find or create a data set with values in at least two phases. Analyze the data graphically at each of the three levels of summarization.

2. Select three published studies and, for each, decide exactly what the experimenter designated as the independent variable. For each, identify those factors in the independent variable condition that are not part of the independent variable itself.

3. For each of these three studies, identify possible extraneous variables. Did the investigator attempt to manage these extraneous factors? If so, how?

4. Let three people independently create a data set with 12 values in each of two phases and graph each data set. Do not let others see these graphs. Calculate a mean for each of the 24 sets of "observations" and graph the mean data. Discuss what the mean data set shows across the two phases. Then compare the mean graph to the individual graphs.

Steady States and Transitions

Manipulation of new variables will often produce changes, but in order to describe the changes, we must be able to specify the baseline from which they occurred.

—Murray Sidman

THE STEADY-STATE STRATEGY

Collecting Repeated Measures

Let us suppose that we have defined a response class, selected a dimensional quantity, set up observation procedures, and are ready to start collecting data under a baseline (control) condition. The first graphed data point summarizing responding during a session will tell us something we never knew before, but it will only make it obvious that one data point does not tell us very much about what responding looks like under this condition. In particular, we would not know whether this value is typical of what we should expect under this baseline condition.

The only way to answer this question is to observe for another session. What we are likely to find is that our second data point is not the same as the first. Our question then becomes: "Which of these two values is more representative of the impact of this phase?" Again, there is no way to settle this issue except to observe for another session.

We should not be surprised if the third value is at least somewhat different from the other two. However, if the three values are not wildly different, they may begin to tell us something about responding in this phase. Still, it would be easy to admit that we do not yet have a very complete picture of what responding is like in this phase. After all, our participant has had only limited exposure to this condition, and we know it can take a bit of time for responding to adapt to a new set of influences. In other words, there is good reason to anticipate that the initial impact of our baseline condition may not be a very good prediction of how responding might change with increasing experience.

As we keep collecting data from one session to the next, our graph will gradually draw an increasingly comprehensive picture of responding. With some luck, we may find that responding under this initial condition is relatively stable. This means that responding is neither generally increasing nor decreasing and that the variability from one value to another is not excessive and is fairly consistent. We may even begin to feel some confidence in answering the original question: What kind of responding represents the typical impact of this condition?

BOX 9.1

**Measuring One Participant Many Times versus
Many Participants Once**

There are two different approaches to obtaining a picture of the effects of
experimental conditions on responding. Under both control and treatment conditions, the researcher can measure the behavior of one participant many times
or many participants once. Although you can wind up with lots of data either way,
there is a big difference between these alternatives for our ability to discover
things about behavior.

To understand this argument, remember the discussion in chapter 2 about the
fact that behavior is a biological phenomenon. This means that behavior can be
clearly observed only at the level of the individual organism. In other words, the
influence of any variables on behavior can be clearly seen only as they impact
the behavior of each participant. Although we might wish that treatment
variables would affect different participants in exactly the same way, we cannot
assume that this will be the case. In fact, this is part of what we are trying to learn,
and using grouped data from many different individuals makes it difficult to
answer this question.

As this chapter shows, observing the behavior of a single participant repeatedly under a condition gives the researcher the opportunity to obtain a complete
and clear picture of the effects of that condition on responding. It should be easy
to see that observing the behavior of a participant only once cannot provide the
same information. It may not be so obvious that measuring the behavior of a large
number of individuals once for each does not improve the completeness or
clarity of the picture of the effects of the condition on behavior. Although this
tactic would provide many observations, each would show only the smallest
sample of how different participants, each with his or her unique characteristics
and histories, might react to the condition. We would know no more about the
effects of the condition on the behavior of each participant than we would if we
measured a single individual once. In other words, the point is not merely to get a
lot of data but to get enough of the right kind of data. What we need are data that
reveal exactly how each participant's behavior is influenced by a condition.

Comparing States of Responding

With this answer, we may decide that we are ready to see how responding
changes when our participant encounters an intervention condition. In order
to make this comparison, we must first determine what kind of responding
is typical of the effects of this new condition. As we accumulate data points
across repeated sessions, the graph will gradually reveal a new picture of
responding. We might find that responding is initially like that observed in
the first phase but gradually transitions to a different level. On the other hand,
it might be that responding immediately changes in some way. Whatever the

initial changes, we would probably find that the more sessions we observe, the better we understand the effects of the intervention condition.

By giving our participant repeated exposure first to the baseline condition and then to the intervention condition, we are trying to get a graphical picture of responding under each condition that is *complete* and *representative*. That is, we want to make sure we obtain enough data to be confident that we have learned what responding looks like under each condition after its effects on the target behavior are fully developed. This will allow us to compare responding under the two conditions and be sure we are comparing data that fully represent the impact of each condition. This is important because we want to be able to conclude that any differences in responding we see are due to the differences between the two conditions themselves.

The Risk of Extraneous Variables

What complicates this conclusion is the risk that responding under either condition might be influenced not just by the condition itself, but by extraneous factors. Making repeated observations of a participant's responding under each condition provides one way of assessing this risk. This approach depends on trying to make sure there is relatively little variation from session to session in the key features that define each condition. This certainly does not mean that a participant's experiences are identical across sessions within each of these two phases. However, it does mean that the key factors that make up each condition are relatively consistent from session to session.

Given this consistency, if the data show that responding is unstable under either condition, we should assume that there are factors responsible for these variations in responding. We might reason that if these variations are not due to changes in the condition, which is being held constant, they must be due to extraneous factors. More optimistically, if the data are relatively stable during a condition we might assume that either extraneous factors are not having noticeable effects or that any extraneous effects are at least consistent.

In other words, when the data within a phase are relatively stable it provides limited assurance that extraneous influences are relatively minor. As we shall see, this conclusion is not necessarily true. However, it is at least reassuring that the data are not noticeably or systematically variable. This would leave us no choice but to worry that extraneous factors may be causing this variability. Unstable patterns of responding from session to session in a phase would require us to admit that the data may represent not just the effects of the condition, but the effects of the extraneous factors as well. If this were the case, we would therefore not be in a good position to compare responding under that condition with responding under another condition. Such a comparison would not allow us to conclude that differences in responding were due only to differences in the conditions.

In other words, a graphical picture of stable responding across sessions under a condition provides some encouragement that the data represent the effects of that condition and that the contribution of extraneous factors is minimal or at least constant. Stable responding—a steady state—is therefore a kind of marker for two important characteristics of the data. First, as just discussed, stable responding suggests that extraneous influences are minimal, unless they are consistent throughout the condition. Second, stable responding suggests that any transition from the initial effects of the condition to its more enduring effects is complete.

Summary

The **steady-state strategy** is an approach to making experimental comparisons that involves measuring responding for each participant repeatedly under both control and experimental conditions in succession. The objective is to assess and manage extraneous influences and thereby obtain a stable pattern of responding that represents the full effects of each condition. This strategy evolved in the work of B. F. Skinner and his students (Skinner, 1956), and was first described in detail by Sidman (1960). It has been a powerful and effective way of managing extraneous influences and obtaining a clear picture of the effects of each condition. This outcome allows comparisons of responding under control and intervention conditions that focus on actual differences resulting from treatment variables. This focus in turn facilitates conclusions that are likely to hold up when tested by other researchers or used by practitioners.

> **Steady-state strategy.** An approach to making experimental comparisons that involves measuring responding for each participant repeatedly under each condition in an effort to assess and manage extraneous influences and thereby obtain a stable pattern of responding that represents the full effects of each condition.

The steady-state strategy is equally useful in basic and applied research projects. Although it can be more challenging to obtain stable responding in nonlaboratory settings, the costs of failing to do so are unavoidable. If researchers collect only a few observations under a condition, the data cannot help to identify extraneous influences and will not provide a full picture of the effects of that condition. This limitation increases the risk that comparisons of responding under control and treatment conditions will be misleading. As a result, when others use this information, there is a greater chance they will not get the same results.

Practitioners often have the opportunity to measure a client's behavior repeatedly over a number of days or even weeks. A baseline or pretreatment phase is typically followed by an initial intervention designed to change responding in some practical way. The initial treatment procedure is often followed by adjustments required to make the procedure more effective.

Adjustments may also be needed to accommodate changes in the behavior or surrounding circumstances as the intervention proceeds. Repeated measurements throughout each phase allow practitioners to monitor changes in the target behavior as the project continues.

Of course, the primary interest of practitioners is delivering effective services, not arranging experimental comparisons for the purpose of publishing research findings. This obligation usually discourages efforts to distinguish between the effects of treatment procedures and the many other events going on in applied settings. Decisions about when to make changes in conditions are often driven more by clinical considerations than by steady-state criteria. As a result of these service delivery priorities, practitioners are not usually in a strong position to be confident about exactly why their client's behavior changes. This is simply one of the distinctions between research and practice.

STEADY STATES

Definition

A **steady** (stable) **state** of responding may be defined as a pattern of responding that shows relatively little variation in its measured dimensional quantities over some period of time. Let us examine some implications of this definition.

> **Steady state.** A pattern of responding that shows relatively little variation in its measured dimensional quantities over some period of time.

First, it is important to understand that the meaning of the term *steady* is relative. Exactly how much variability or what patterns of variability are required to describe responding as stable or unstable will vary from one research project to another. Such factors as the characteristics of the response class, the features of the general environment, the details of experimental procedures, and the focus of the experimental question may influence the researcher's judgment. For example, an investigator conducting a laboratory study of the effects of toxic chemicals on the behavior of rats may expect a very low level of variability, given similar studies already published. On the other hand, a researcher conducting a project in a group home for individuals with mental retardation may need to accommodate the effects of day-to-day variations in extraneous factors that cannot be easily managed. Such differences from one study to another mean that it is usually not feasible to define steady-state responding with a rigid formula.

Second, although the dimensional quantity being measured might be stable, this does not mean that other quantities not being measured are also stable. For example, although the number of responses from session to session might show good stability, their duration could be systematically changing in some way. In fact, when two or more quantities are being measured, it is not uncommon for them to vary in different ways. Of course, there is no way to know about the stability of quantities that are not being measured. This is why evidence of stability in a dimensional quantity should not prompt the researcher to make the general statement that responding is stable. Instead, it is more appropriate to say that a particular feature of responding is stable.

Third, just because some aspect of responding is stable, it may not be correct to conclude that the environment is also stable. A relatively consistent pattern of responding can result from a mix of changing variables whose net effect is stable responding. Some environmental factors may even change in obvious ways but not influence the target behavior. For example, a substitute teacher would seem to be an important change in a classroom environment. However, this change may not be evident in the data. All we can say about the experimental environment from observing stable responding is that any extraneous environmental changes affecting responding are either weak or have effects that are balanced by other environmental factors.

Uses

Evaluates Measurement Decisions.   The steady-state strategy is valuable because it guides the researcher's decisions as the study progresses. This benefit begins by helping the researcher to evaluate prior decisions about how the target behavior is defined and measured. Collecting data under such rules for a number of sessions provides a picture of responding that may prompt second guesses about how the response class is defined, which dimensional quantities are measured, and how and when observation is conducted.

For example, the pattern of variability across sessions might suggest reconsidering the response class definition. If the data tend to fall into distinct patterns from one session to another (such as higher versus lower values), it could mean that the definition has combined different functional classes. For instance, a definition of "aggressive" behavior may include both hitting and cursing. In some sessions, the target responses may be largely in the form of hitting, and on other days measured responses may be mostly cursing. If cursing generally tends to occur at higher frequencies than hitting, the data could show some sessions with higher values than others. That is, sessions in which responding was mainly in the form of cursing would have higher values than sessions in which responding was mostly hitting. This pattern of variability might prompt the researcher to wonder if the data are suggesting a problem with how the target behavior is defined. Perhaps it would be more useful to define and measure hitting and cursing separately.

Collecting repeated measures under each condition can also encourage curiosity about other measurement decisions. For example, if the data showed very little change from one session to another, it might be tempting to conclude that responding was stable. We have already pointed out, however, that stable data only provide assurance that the dimension quantity being measured is stable. Such data may not reveal the reason for this stability. Informal observation of what is happening during sessions might show that the target behavior varies a good bit from session to session in other ways. Together with the overly stable data, these observations could suggest that the measurement procedure is insensitive to changes in the target behavior for some reason. One solution is to address the reasons for this insensitivity. If the problem was that observation periods were too brief or not scheduled appropriately, they could be adjusted. Another solution is to measure other dimension quantities, which might provide a more informative picture of what is happening with the behavior.

As an example of these situations, consider data from partial interval recording using 5-minute intervals that showed consistently high percentages of scored intervals. It could be that the relatively long intervals result in most being scored as containing at least some of the target behavior. Interval recording procedures do not measure dimensional quantities, however, so the researcher might worry that there is interesting variation being missed in quantities such as count, duration, or frequency. Again, steady-state data might not always mean that all aspects of responding are stable. Such data must be examined in light of what is being measured and how it is being observed.

Reveals the Influence of Conditions. The steady-state strategy is especially valuable in revealing what is going on with the target behavior as it accumulates contact with a condition. It is typical that when a behavior is exposed to a new condition the behavior changes in some way. Although the new condition may have some immediate impact, the still recent experience with the previous condition may still be having some effect. In other words, the data often show a mixture of influences at the beginning of a new phase that reflects a transition in control from the previous condition to the new condition. Although this transition is sometimes a particular focus in some research projects, more often it is merely a nuisance because it complicates seeing a clear picture of the effects of the new condition alone.

As the data show an end to the transition in responding that started when conditions changed, it is tempting to assume that the full effects of the new condition are finally evident. The data may now represent a level of responding that is notably higher or lower than in the previous condition. Although this change in the level of responding may show the impact of the current condition, the steady-state strategy asks for evidence that the new level of responding is durable. That is, the researcher needs to be sure that the apparently stable responding will continue as long as the condition is in effect. If responding were to eventually change in some way, it would be important to include this change as part of the effects of the condition. For instance, responding might gradually decrease when an intervention is started. However, with continued exposure, this low level of responding might gradually climb back to the higher level that existed in the previous condition. The steady-state strategy helps to capture all of these changes that might be characteristic of the condition.

Evaluates Experimental Control. Measuring a behavior repeatedly under the same condition can also alert the investigator to the role of extraneous variables. Remember that any factors that are not explicitly part of the independent variable are extraneous to experimental interests. As chapter 8 described, such extraneous factors may be unrelated to the experimental preparation and may occur unsystematically (a fire drill in a preschool). However, they may also be attached to the general circumstances of a study and may therefore have continuing or systematic effects (influence from coworkers for a study conducted in the workplace). They can even be attached to the independent variable itself and therefore come and go as it is presented and withdrawn. (Instructions associated with treatment procedures are a good example of this last category.)

The steady-state strategy creates a good opportunity to detect the influence of unsystematic extraneous factors that might occur at some point in a phase. As we will see, instability in the data can be relatively easy to identify, although its sources must usually be guessed from observing what is going on during sessions. It is usually more challenging to identify the influence of extraneous factors that are consistent throughout a condition. If their impact is stable as well, their contribution may be missed. If their impact ebbs and flows from session to session, however, changes in responding may hint at their presence under an otherwise stable set of conditions.

The steady-state strategy can help to identify unstable responding, but the real question is what the researcher is able to do about excessive variability once it is evident. Studies differ from one another in how carefully extraneous influences must be managed. Some experimental questions and procedures require a high level of control, perhaps even a laboratory setting. However, even studies conducted in messy, real-world settings often require some management of extraneous influences. Whatever the requirements of an individual study, the level of stability in responding reflected in the data is a measure of the level of experimental control that the investigator has achieved.

Facilitates Experimental Comparisons. As we will see in more detail in the upcoming chapters on experimental design, the steady-state strategy provides the foundation for making comparisons between the effects of control and intervention conditions. Drawing conclusions about the effects of an intervention condition that have a good chance of being true, and therefore dependable, depends on how well the effects of both control and intervention conditions can be described and understood.

Efforts to establish stable responding under each condition help the investigator to do this in two key ways. First, repeatedly measuring responding under each condition helps to identify both the initial and final patterns of responding in each phase. Second, these data also encourage efforts to manage extraneous variables, which helps to minimize their influence and thereby clarifies the effects of each condition. These two outcomes of the steady-state strategy help the investigator to distinguish between effects of the conditions and the effects of other factors. The resulting comparison is therefore more likely to be an accurate description of the effects of the intervention. This also means that the findings have a good chance of holding up when others use them in some way.

As an example, let us suppose that a researcher is conducting a study in a developmental center looking at the possibility that a certain psychotropic drug may make it more difficult for individuals with mental retardation to learn new skills. Each individual's performance, measured repeatedly under control and drug conditions, will be partly a function of the basic testing procedures used throughout both conditions. In addition, performance under the experimental condition should reflect any influence of the drug. However, what if there are events going on in the participant's daily living conditions that vary from one day to another and that might affect their performance in daily testing sessions? One individual may be moved from one living unit to another, a kind of disruption that often has broad effects on behavior. Another may go home on some weekends and behave differently on Mondays as a result. Still another may have health problems and may not be feeling well on some days.

Any effects of these extraneous factors may show up as variations in acquisition performance from one session to another. If the researcher ignores these variations and concludes that the difference in learning performance between the two conditions is due solely to the drug, this finding may not hold up very well for other researchers or practitioners. On the other hand, if the variations in responding within each condition are used to identify the contribution of the extraneous factors so that they can be better managed, it will be easier to identify the influence of the drug.

Identification

Trends. One of the challenges of the steady-state strategy is recognizing when the data show stable responding and when they do not. There are particular features of variability in a series of data points that often bear on this decision. One pattern of variability is called a trend. A **trend** may be defined as a relatively consistent change in a single direction. Although there are some exceptions, steady-state data do not show strong or consistent trends in either a decreasing or an increasing direction.

> **Trend.** A relatively consistent change in the data in a single direction.

It is not necessarily easy to tell if the data in a phase are generally trending upward or downward. There are endless ways in which a sequence of data points can show trends. The graphed data sets in Figure 9.1 shows some possibilities. The data in both Panels A and B show a slightly increasing but consistent trend. However, the greater range of the values in Panel B might mask the fact that the slope of the trend in these two data sets is the same as in Panel A.

BOX 9.2

One Data Point at a Time

A trick that can help you appreciate the importance of measuring responding repeatedly under each condition is to look at the data in the same way the investigator sees them—one value at a time. Place a piece of paper over all but the first few data points on a graph. Then slowly slide the paper to the right, uncovering successive values one at a time.

If you do this for the graphs in Fig. 9.1, you will see how difficult it can be to decide when the data show a trend. In Fig. 9.2, you will see that it is challenging to determine when the data are stable. In most cases, this exercise shows how valuable it is to see additional data points.

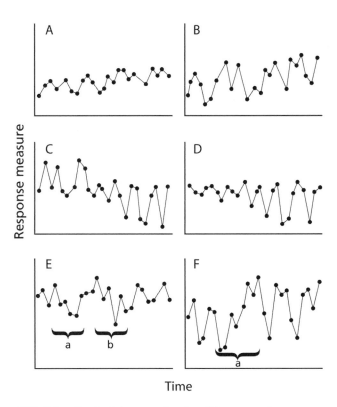

FIG. 9.1.   Graphed data sets showing different trend patterns.

In Panel C, most of the data points fall in the middle range of the vertical axis. The existence of a downward trend results from the fact that there are four high values in the first half of the data set and four low values in the second half. This type of trend is also shown in Panel D. Here, although most points fall in the middle of the vertical axis, a number of lower values begin appearing in the latter half of the data set. In both of these graphs, the trends result from the pattern of only a few of the data points in the set.

Panels E and F show what are called "local" trends because they are embedded in otherwise relatively stable patterns of responding. In Panel E, the values marked *a* and *b* reveal brief decreasing trends, just as the values marked *a* in Panel F show a sharp increasing trend. It is tempting to ignore such local trends because they are temporary and are surrounded by more stable data. This might not be a problem, but if such changes happened to occur at the beginning of a new condition it would be easy to mistake them for the effects of the new condition.

Trends that appear under a constant set of conditions suggest that there may be extraneous factors at work. As we have already pointed out, if the researcher is successfully managing the conditions defining a control or intervention phase, the participant's experiences should be very similar from session to session. Under such conditions, it is reasonable to assume that responding would be relatively stable. If a consistent increase or decrease in responding occurs, there must be something producing this change. If the trend appears at the beginning of a condition, it may be that it represents the initial effects of the condition. However, if it occurs after the phase is well underway, it may mean that extraneous factors are at work.

In sum, there are at least three reasons for worrying about trends that have no obvious explanation. First, a trend means that some variables are influencing behavior in significant ways, which might interfere with seeing the impact of either the control condition or the intervention condition. Second, when the researcher is unaware of what is causing a trend, it is not clear how to more effectively control the environment to reduce the impact of these factors. Third, trends make it more difficult to determine the effects of an intervention. If the effects of either of the two conditions being compared are unclear, this distorts their comparison. The result can be that the effect of the intervention condition is seen as greater or smaller than it really is.

Finally, there are circumstances in which trends may be considered stable patterns of responding. This would be the case when procedures produce a repeating pattern of brief trends throughout both control and intervention conditions. The data in Figure 9.2 showing measures of a student's correct digits on multiplication problems illustrate this kind of pattern (Johnson & Layng, 1992). The data show increasing trends within each type of problem assigned in each of the four conditions. When each type of problem was assigned, performance improved somewhat over successive measures. Because this same local trend pattern is clear in each phase, the repeated trends do not interfere with making sound comparisons between the multiplication fact phases and the alternating phases assigning double digit multiplication computations. In this case, the data show an initial multiplication fact performance of about 70 digits per minute. When the teacher attempted to build the student's fluency in complex multiplication computations, performance was poor (about 15 digits per minute). A successful effort to build multiplication

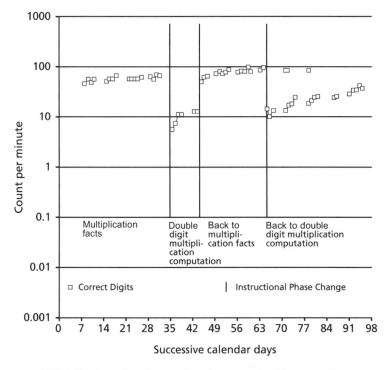

FIG. 9.2. Data showing trends as a pattern of stable responding.

fact skills in the third phase then led to improving performance on the more difficult problems in the final phase.

Range. Another feature of variability that is important in identifying steady states is range. **Range** is defined by the highest and lowest values in a data set. It is particularly easy to determine the range of a set of values when data are plotted on a graph. Figure 9.3 shows some different patterns of variation in range that can influence decisions about steady states.

> **Range.** A measure of variability defined by the highest and lowest values in a data set.

The data sets in Panels A and B each show a fairly consistent range from beginning to end. Whether the range of either data set would be acceptable for an investigator would depend on the actual values that these data points represent, as well as various features of the study. For example, the nature of the experimental question, the relevant literature, the response class being measured, the general preparation under which responding occurs, and the independent variable all contribute to a standard of acceptable variability. For these reasons, a laboratory study of the effects of a drug on the performance of

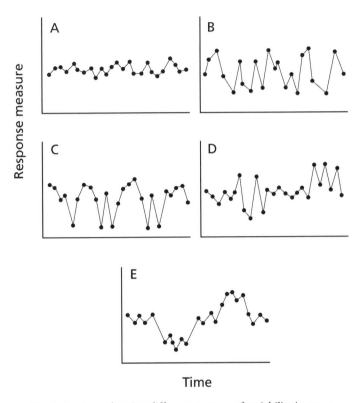

FIG. 9.3.   Data showing different patterns of variability in range.

rats under particular schedules of reinforcement might require less variable data than a field study of the effects of an intervention on the behavior of individuals living in a developmental center.

Although most of the data points in Panel C fall in the same range, five values are markedly lower. These lower values seem consistent and are not apparently occurring more often. Nevertheless, they suggest that some influence is at work for some sessions that is different from what is going on in most other sessions. If the researcher is aware of why responding is lower on some days, it might be acceptable to ignore these values. However, if they have no obvious explanation, it should be worrisome that they might become more frequent, possibly making it more difficult to see the effects of an intervention condition.

Panel D presents a similar problem. In this case, however, there are more than a few data points that exceed the range otherwise defined by the majority of the values. This kind of variation in range from one local group of values to the next does not seem like a very good basis for predicting the outcome of future measurements. Again, there are two problems: (a) we should wonder what extraneous factors are producing these changes in local range; and (b) it would not be clear what level of responding would be used to represent the effects of this phase. If the next phase was started at this point, the net effect of these problems is that conclusions about the effect of an intervention would be uncertain and might not hold up for others.

The data points in Panel E represent a particularly troubling situation. Although we could determine the range of the entire data set, it would be more meaningful to focus on what is happening with the local range. It is generally fairly small, but it keeps moving around. This pattern of local range values provides a poor basis for describing the effects of the present condition. In turn, this would make it difficult to determine by comparison the effects of a subsequent condition.

Cycles. A cycle is a locally complex pattern of variability that, like trends, can sometimes be considered a stable pattern of responding. A **cycle** is a repeating pattern of local variability that often involves sequences of increasing and decreasing trends (in either order). The highest and lowest values in each cycle define its range, and the time taken from beginning to end is called its period. The periodicity of the cycles may be either regular or unpredictable. Furthermore, the cycles may appear consistently or on an irregular basis. Cycles may be considered stable or unstable in their different features, including their form, the level of responding involved, and their frequency of occurrence.

> **Cycle.** A repeating pattern of local variability, often involving sequences of increasing and decreasing trends (in either order).

Cyclic patterns of variation in behavior are not uncommon. However, identifying them requires good environmental control, not to mention careful measurement. They are therefore more likely to be clearly detected under laboratory than field conditions. However, a weekly pattern of cyclic responding is sometimes found in applied research and practice. Regularities in environments and activities from one week to another may show up in fairly consistent changes in responding throughout each week. A consumer living in a group home who goes home to visit her family each weekend may typically behave differently on Mondays or Fridays, for example.

Figure 9.4 shows three examples of cyclic patterns of variability. In Panel A, the cycles are regular in their form and frequency of occurrence within each phase. The fact that a number of cycles occur under each condition helps to provide a good basis for comparing differences in responding under the two conditions. Panel B shows cyclic variations that are less regular. They vary in their form and frequency of occurrence. Nevertheless, the cyclic patterns show one general level of responding throughout the first phase and a different but consistent level of responding in the second phase. For this reason, the investigator is in a good position to compare responding under the two conditions.

The data in Panel C show the greatest risk associated with cyclic data. In this case, the cyclic character of the data is not recognized, and the phase changes

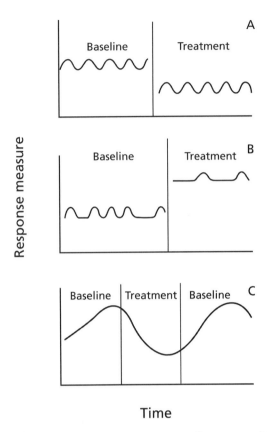

FIG. 9.4. Stylized data showing various cyclic patterns of data.

happen to correspond to the local trends defining the cycle. With the advantage of hindsight, it is easy to see that the decrease in responding under the treatment condition might be at least partly due to the factors causing the cycle, rather than the treatment condition alone. This risk is another reason to avoid changing conditions when the data show a clear trend, especially when the expected change in responding is in the opposite direction.

Criteria

Uses. Deciding when steady-state responding has been attained is such a frequent challenge that some informal criteria or rules have evolved to help researchers. There is certainly no denying the importance of the decision. It is not just about whether responding is stable. It is about whether to continue the present condition unchanged, modify the environment by managing more variables to improve stability, or end the condition and begin the next phase. It is also an assessment about whether the effects of the present condition have been fully determined and represent its typical influence on responding. It is therefore a decision about whether there is a sound basis for comparing one condition with another condition. Of course, this judgment is the same for both control (baseline) and independent variable (treatment) conditions.

The function of a decision rule is not necessarily to force identification of a steady state as much as it is to help the researcher to focus on some important considerations. Remember that the decision about when stable responding has been achieved should be partly guided by the nature of the question, the procedures used in the study, and the standards evident in the literature. Sidman (1960) summarized the task nicely:

> The utility of data will depend not on whether ultimate stability has been achieved, but rather on the reliability and validity of the criterion. That is to say, does the criterion select a reproducible and generalizable state of behavior? If it does, experimental manipulation of steady states, as defined by the criterion, will yield data that are orderly and generalizable to other situations. If the steady-state criterion is inadequate, failures to reproduce and to replicate systematically the experimental findings will reveal this fact. (pp. 257–258)

Statistical. One kind of criterion involves a statistical description of variability. This approach usually specifies a limited amount of variability that will be permitted over a certain number of data points. For example, such rules might describe the maximum range for a number of sessions: "No data point may deviate by more than 5% from the median of the last five sessions." They might instead impose a limit on the difference between the means or ranges of two successive series of sessions: "The means of two consecutive sets of 10 data points may differ by less than 10% of the total range." The possible specifications of this type of rule are nearly endless.

Although the mathematical precision of this type of criterion might seem reassuring, it has some risks. Consider that the degree of variability in the data may well change from one condition to the next. It is not uncommon, for instance, for an intervention condition to produce less variability than a control condition. In this situation, it is possible that a fixed criterion would select good stability in one phase but would be immediately met in another phase. This might not provide sufficient exposure to the second set of conditions.

In other words, suppose that a baseline condition with fairly variable data was followed by a treatment condition that generated much less variable responding. A statistical decision rule might lead to a decision to terminate the treatment condition before its effects on responding were fully developed. This possibility means that researchers who decide to use a statistical criterion of stability should not do so blindly. They need to remain alert to the need to adjust the criterion if the data warrant.

Graphical. The most popular approach to stability criteria is based on ongoing visual inspection of graphically displayed data. This preference avoids the risky commitments of statistical rules in favor of thoughtful judgments. These intentionally subjective judgments involve carefully studying the evolving graphical picture of variability in a phase as each new data point is added. Researchers look at the characteristics of variability in their data and wait until their professional history tells them when stability has been attained. We might call this type of criterion the Supreme Court standard: "I can't tell you in advance what it is, but I'll know it when I see it."[1]

It would be a mistake to view this kind of criterion as less demanding than the statistical approach just because it does not involve an a priori mathematical statement. For well-trained researchers, this graphical approach is more sophisticated than a quantitative rule, and it may yield a more meaningful picture of stable responding. Investigators using a graphical standard should be able to specify each aspect of the data they are considering and why those features might be important.

Figure 9.5 shows data in baseline and intervention phases that illustrate this approach to steady-state criteria. (We again suggest putting a piece of paper over the graph and uncovering the data points in chronological sequence one at a time.) The early data points in the baseline phase labeled *a* show a sharp decreasing trend, and there should be no temptation to describe them as stable. As the data labeled *b* are fully revealed, we see that this was a wise decision because an increasing trend becomes unmistakable. Additional data points (labeled *c*) tend to mostly fall in the upper end of the overall range. However, we keep finding an occasional low value, which should make us a bit concerned about the influence of extraneous factors. This might even prompt an effort to identify and control the suspected factors. Finally, we see more data points (labeled *d*) in the upper part of the range, though with no lower values intruding. Perhaps, most importantly, these values show no further evidence of the trend. We might find the data labeled *d* an adequate steady state of responding.

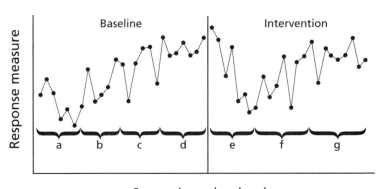

FIG. 9.5.   Data illustrating the complexity of decisions required by graphical steady-state criteria.

---

[1] Based on the well-known statement of Justice Potter Stewart in his concurring opinion in the Supreme Court's pornography decision in Jacobellis v. Ohio, 1964.

The intervention phase begins with a relatively rapid decreasing trend (labeled *e*), which "bottoms out" at a lower level than was seen under the stable portion of the baseline phase *(d)*. In contrast, the accumulating data labeled *f* show an increasing trend. However, as we see the data points labeled *g*, it becomes clear that the trend has "topped out" and responding has become relatively stable. In sum, the successive values in each phase show some local trends that eventually end in a series of relatively stable values. In hindsight, it is easy to see that neither phase showed stable responding until the last ten or so values were obtained. Even without the benefit of hindsight, the data in each phase show enough evidence of a trend or outlying values to encourage the investigator to continue the phase a bit longer and look for a clearer picture of stability.

Nondata. Investigators often face limits on the amount of time available to complete a project. The limiting factors might be participants who will only be available for a certain time, restrictions on access to a research setting, pressure to move quickly to a treatment condition that will resolve clinical problems, or financial constraints. In such situations, it may be necessary to set advance restrictions on the number of sessions for each of the planned phases of the experiment. For instance, this might mean allotting 10 days for a control or baseline phase, 3 weeks for an intervention phase, and so on.

In this approach to steady-state criteria, each phase therefore lasts for a predetermined number of sessions. We may call this a nondata criterion because it is based on considerations that have little to do with the nature of the data obtained under each condition. This means that each phase would be terminated without regard for what the data reveal about responding. Even though responding might be unstable throughout a phase, the next condition would be implemented at a certain point because the study's schedule requires it. This kind of decision-making might result in a weak basis for comparing the effects of control and intervention conditions.

Although nondata criteria for deciding when to change phases are risky, there is no denying that researchers might sometimes feel it necessary to limit the length of phases. The ideal solution to this situation is to try to confront the factors that are pressuring the investigator to compromise sound method-ological standards. If it is not feasible to resolve these pressures, the investigator may need to consider whether the planned study can be successfully con-ducted under the presenting circumstances.

Establishing Stable Responding

It is easy for discussions of the steady-state strategy to create the impression that obtaining stable responding is largely a matter of being patient. It might seem that all an experimenter has to do is continue a phase for long enough so that, eventually, acceptably stable data will accumulate. Sometimes this passive approach does indeed work. For example, unwanted variability may be due to the effects of the previous condition "wearing off" or the effects of the present condition becoming fully established. In this situation, simply continuing a phase until these transitions are complete may yield satisfactory stability.

On the other hand, the excessive variability may result from poor control over the procedures in a phase or from uncontrolled extraneous variables. Merely continuing the phase will not often resolve such problems. They will probably require specific efforts to improve experimental control. Continuing data collection will then assess whether these efforts were successful in drawing a clearer picture of responding.

Establishing stable responding can sometimes be challenging and time-consuming. When this is the case, it is important to avoid the temptation to manipulate data in ways that imply a level of stability that has not actually been achieved. The three panels in Figure 9.6 show how combining data over

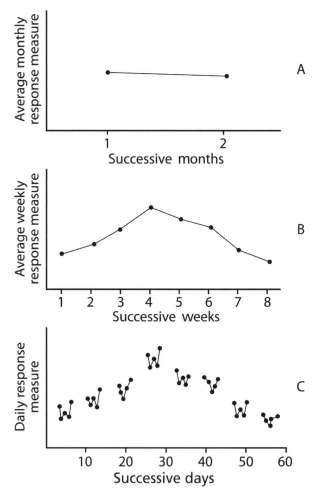

FIG. 9.6.   Graphs showing the effects of combining data over different units of time on displayed variability.

different units of time affects the resulting picture of variability. All three graphs are based on the same hypothetical values collected over a 2-month period. When these values are combined into monthly averages (Panel A) the two data points are similar, suggesting good stability. When the data are averaged on a weekly basis (Panel B) we can see that they form an upward trend followed by a downward trend. When the data are displayed on a daily scale (Panel C) the weekly trends are again evident. However, the daily time unit also reveals a weekly cycle in which Monday and Friday values tend to be higher than the other days of the week. Seeing the data in Panels B or C, we can appreciate that the display in Panel A would be a misleading description of stability.

TRANSITIONS

Transition States

When responding is unstable, we describe it as being in transition. Of course, being able to identify changes in responding requires distinguishing these changes from periods of stable responding going on before and after the transition. One kind of transition is called a **transition state**. In transition states, responding is changing from one steady state to a different steady state.

> **Transition state.** A pattern of responding involving change from one steady state to a different steady state.

Given the emphasis on steady states, it might seem that researchers might not be especially interested in transition states. After all, they often result from switching from one condition to the next. When this is the case, they reflect an expected, though usually temporary, mixture of influences from the old and new conditions. Because the researcher is typically interested in identifying the effects of each condition alone, this transitional interlude would seem to be a distraction.

In fact, understanding what makes behavior change and what these changes look like is the central focus of behavioral research. It is useful to obtain stable responding because it tells us that a transition is completed. When responding stabilizes following a switch from one condition to another, for instance, it means that we may now have a picture of the behavioral changes associated with that switch. What we are really interested in, however, is what kind of changes in responding were produced by initiating a new condition. The steady state is an endpoint for those changes in responding, but it is not the only effect of switching conditions. The effects of the new condition include the nature of the transition just as much as the steady state that eventually emerges.

Figure 9.7 shows a schematic representation of different kinds of transitions

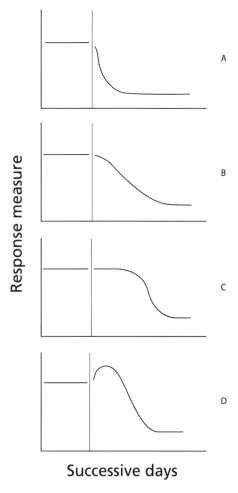

FIG. 9.7. Schematic representation showing different types of transitions resulting from introducing a new condition.

that might result from changing from one condition to another. In each example, steady-state responding in the first and second conditions is the same, thereby highlighting differences in transitional responding at the beginning of the second phase. In Panel A, the transition between the two steady states begins as soon as the second condition starts and quickly terminates in the new steady state. In contrast, Panel B shows a transitional pattern between the two steady states that is relatively gradual. Panel C shows a transition that does not start for some time after the second condition begins. The transition in Panel D is unlike the others in that a temporary increase in responding occurs before the decrease that then leads to the lower steady state. Depending on the features of the study, these differences in transitional responding may be no less important than the fact that changing from the first to the second condition eventually resulted in a decrease in responding.

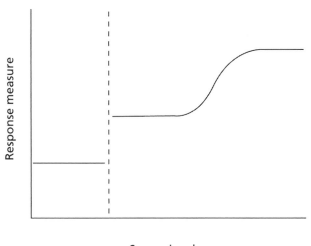

FIG. 9.8. Data showing a transition state occurring well after the implementation of a new condition.

Transition states do not only follow changes in the environment initiated by the experimenter, of course. Extraneous variables can just as easily lead to behavioral changes at any time during a phase that terminate in a different level of responding. Such transitions can be mistaken for the effects of treatment conditions, so it is important to describe them fully. If an unanticipated transition state appears well after the condition has begun, for example, it may be wise to suspect an extraneous influence.

Figure 9.8 shows an example of this situation. Responding increases immediately following the start of the second phase, suggesting that in this case there may not be a gradual transition initiated by switching conditions. However, well after the new phase is underway, responding abruptly increases further and eventually levels off. This transition state is a problem because it is now unclear whether it is a delayed effect of exposure to the new condition or the result of some extraneous factor. Because we cannot answer this question, we also do not know whether the real effect of the condition is reflected by the level of responding at the beginning or at the end of the second phase. One way to resolve this dilemma is to identify and hold constant or eliminate the suspected extraneous factor and see how responding changes.

Transitory States

We have so far considered transitions from one steady state of responding that eventually result in a different steady state. Transitional patterns may instead end in a return to the original level or pattern of responding, however. These are called **transitory states**.

Transitory state. A pattern of responding involving a deviation
from a steady state that ends in a return to the same steady state.

Distinguishing between transition states and transitory states is very important. In one case (transition states), changes in responding lead to a different
level of responding than before. In the other case (transitory states), changes in
responding return to the original level of responding. If one was mistaken for
the other, it might result in misunderstanding the effects of an intervention.

Here is one way this can happen. Although transitory states often result from
extraneous factors that occur during a phase, they can also be the outcome of
treatment conditions. In other words, the investigator may expect an intervention not only to change the participant's behavior but to maintain that
new level of responding as long as the condition is present. However, it may
be that the impact of the intervention is only temporary. An initial change in
responding may dissipate, eventually leaving responding at the level that
existed before the condition was introduced. This kind of change in responding would be a transitory state.

In this situation, it would be critical to determine whether the initial change
in responding was going to lead to a new steady state or back to the original
one. If an intervention phase only lasted long enough to capture the initial
change, we would not know whether the effect of the intervention was
durable or temporary—a very important distinction. Figure 9.9 shows a
schematic representation of this situation, as well as what can be done to avoid
this confusion. The initial steady states (from point *a* to point *b*) and transitions
(from point *b* to point *c*) are the same for both functions. At point *c*, the
experimenter cannot tell which type of transition is happening. In order to find
out, the phase must be continued until at least point *d*, at which time we can
see that stable responding has developed in both cases, though at different
levels. If the condition was terminated at point *c*, we would not know whether

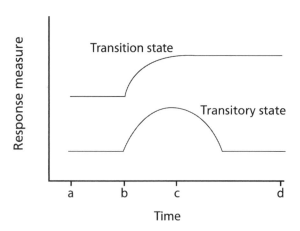

FIG. 9.9. Schematic representation of transition and transitory states.

the transition resulted in a durable or only a temporary change in behavior. In other words, any conclusion about the effect of this condition might be wrong and the experimenter would not know it. This is why it is so important to obtain a period of stable responding under each condition.

Identification

Identifying transition and transitory states is a matter of identifying the steady states preceding and following the transition. The frequency with which measurement occurs can affect how well an investigator can describe the transition and distinguish it from the surrounding steady states. The more often responding is measured during a transition, the more precisely the transition's boundaries can be described.

Figure 9.10 illustrates this point. The three panels show the same transition, but the features of the transition depend on how often measurements were made. The infrequent measures shown in Panel A give a false impression that responding simply jumped to the new steady state by the second data point in the new condition. The increased frequency of measurement in Panel B begins

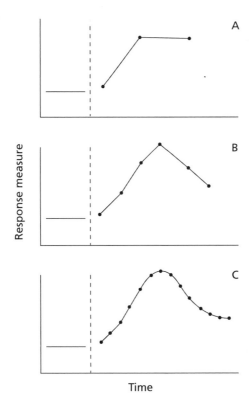

FIG. 9.10. Data showing the results of different frequencies of measurement during a transition state.

to capture the true form of the transition. However, this picture fails to locate the point at which stable responding begins to reappear. The data in Panel C remedy this shortcoming because the frequency of measurement is sufficient to provide a full picture of the transition and to identify its endpoints.

Making Phase Change Decisions

We have already emphasized the general risks associated with making a decision to change from one condition to another when responding is unstable. There are some special cases of this scenario that warrant discussion. The graphs in Figure 9.11 represent situations in which there may be some temptation to change phases even though stable responding has not been obtained. It may again be useful to look at these graphs one data point at a time by sliding a piece of paper from left to right.

Panel A shows an increasing trend in the first phase followed by a continuation of this trend in the second phase. If the researcher anticipated that the second condition would lead to an increase in responding, it might be tempting to conclude that the variables defining this condition were responsible for the increasing trend. Although a new condition might initially produce a transition like this, we should be concerned that this trend started under the first condition. Because the researcher is trying to hold the features of each condition constant throughout each phase, we should assume that this initial trend may reflect uncontrolled extraneous factors. These extraneous factors are likely to be unknown, otherwise the researcher would presumably

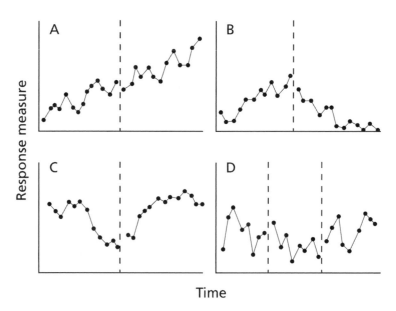

FIG. 9.11.   Data from control and intervention phases involving different types of instability.

BOX 9.3

How Long Should Each Phase Last?

By now, you should realize that this is not the right question. You should also know that there is no general answer in terms of a certain number of sessions that can be correct. If there is any rule, it is only that phases should last until satisfactory stability has been obtained. The level of stability that is necessary depends on the unique features of each research project. For each study, the standards in the existing literature, the nature of the experimental question, the features of the response class, the details of measurement procedures selected, and the characteristics of control and intervention conditions are all factors that should be considered.

Notice that this list does not include the difficulty of obtaining stable responding. It is certainly true that some projects provide insurmountable limitations on the researcher's ability to engineer stable responding. However, these challenges do not lessen the value of the steady-state strategy. Neither do they reduce the risks of proceeding without them.

Finally, it is important to understand that obtaining stable responding is not merely a "ticket" to the next phase, like touching each of the bases on your way to the home plate in order to get a home run. Getting stable responding is part of the larger strategy of obtaining a sample of responding that fully represents the effects of each condition. This information then allows comparisons between conditions that have a good chance of being both reliable and general.

---

have tried to minimize their influence. If they are unknown, there would be no basis for assuming that these influences stopped when the second phase was started. This means that they could be responsible for the continuing trend in the second phase, which raises doubts about the contribution of the condition itself. In sum, the data in Panel A cannot support a conclusion that the increased responding in the second phase is due to the variables defining this condition.

Panel B shows a similar increasing trend in the first phase but a contrasting downward trend in the second phase. This change in responding associated with the second condition might seem to allow a clear basis for attributing the change to the new condition. Although it might be reasonable to assume that the contrasting pattern of responding is related to implementing the new condition, this is not exactly what the researcher should be trying to learn. The real question is not whether an intervention can change behavior but what kind of effects the condition produces by itself (in the absence of extraneous factors). The problem here is actually the same as in the case of Panel A. Because the researcher does not know what extraneous factors are operating in the first condition that are producing the increase in responding, there is no reason to assume that they disappeared in the second condition. The proper interpretation of the second-phase data is that they may represent the effects of the condition itself plus the extraneous variables producing the trend in the first phase. The researcher does not know what responding in the second phase would have looked like without the contribution of these extraneous factors.

In the first phase of Panel C, an initial period of relatively stable responding is followed by a clear downward trend. Responding then increases under the second phase, terminating at about the same level as observed early in the first phase. As in the case of Panels A and B, this increase could reflect the influence of the unknown variables producing the variable data in the first phase, the impact of the new condition by itself, or an interaction of these two factors. The data provide no basis for concluding that one alternative is more likely than another.

Finally, Panel D shows three phases containing relatively variable data that overlap considerably across conditions. Although the values in the second phase are collectively lower than in the other two conditions, the decrease is modest. This level of variability begs for not only a greater number of observations under each condition but efforts to either reduce variability or at least strengthen the effects of the intervention. Reducing variability need not focus only on controlling extraneous factors. Sometimes the best solution is to reconsider the general conditions running throughout control and experimental phases, not to mention the features of the intervention condition itself. The full array of measurement decisions can also be reviewed.

Of course, all four examples suffer from the fact that stable responding was not obtained under most conditions. Obtaining the needed steady states might well have resolved the problem presented by each case. Having a clear picture of stable responding under each condition will not decide all interpretive issues, but it is at least a necessary component of any solution.

CHAPTER SUMMARY

1. The steady-state strategy involves measuring responding for each participant repeatedly under both control and experimental conditions, with the objective of obtaining a stable pattern of responding that represents the full effects of each condition.

2. By providing repeated exposure to the baseline and then treatment condition, we are attempting to receive a graphical representation under each condition that is complete, accurate, and representative. The researcher must be sure that the data being compared fully represent the impact of each condition, so that any differences in responding that are seen may be attributed to the independent variable.

3. Stable responding across sessions is a strong indication that the data fully represent the effects of that condition and that the contribution of extraneous factors is minimal or at least constant.

4. The failure to achieve stable responding under a condition in applied settings does not allow the practitioner to see the full effects of that

condition and increases the risk that comparisons between control and treatment conditions will be misleading.

5. It is important to remember that just because the dimensional quantity being measured may be stable, this does not mean that other quantities that are not being measured are also stable. Likewise, just because some aspect of responding is stable, one should not conclude that the environment is also stable. A relatively consistent pattern of responding can result from a mix of changing variables whose net effect is stable responding.

6. The steady-state strategy is valuable because it guides the researcher's decisions as the study progresses. It can help the investigator to evaluate how the target behavior is defined and measured, as well as help to capture all of the possible changes that might be characteristic of a specific condition.

7. Drawing accurate conclusions about the effects of an intervention condition depends on how well the effects of both control and intervention conditions can be described and understood. By repeatedly measuring responding under each condition, this helps the researcher to identify both the initial and final patterns of responding under each phase. These data also aid the researcher in being able to manage extraneous variables, which helps to minimize their influence and thereby clarifies the effects of each condition.

8. There are several reasons why trends that do not have an obvious explanation are of concern. First, a trend means that some variables are influencing behavior in significant ways, which might interfere with seeing the impact of either the control condition or the intervention condition. Second, if a researcher is unaware of what is causing a trend, it is not clear how to effectively control the environment and reduce the impact of possible extraneous factors. Finally, trends make it more difficult to determine the effects of an intervention.

9. Deciding when steady-state responding has been attained is not just about whether responding is stable. It is about whether to continue the present condition unchanged, modify the environment to improve stability, or end the condition and begin the next phase. Ultimately, it is a decision about whether there is a sound basis for comparing one condition to another condition.

10. There are several ways to aid in determining if stability has been met. Statistical criteria usually specify a limited amount of variability that will be permitted over a certain number of data points. While this approach may prove useful, it is possible that a fixed criterion would select good stability in one phase and not in another. This might not provide sufficient exposure to the second set of conditions.

11. The most popular approach to stability criteria is based on ongoing visual inspection of graphically displayed data. This approach requires the researcher to be able to specify each aspect of the data they are considering and why those features might be important.

12. It might seem that all an experimenter has to do is continue a phase long enough so that eventually stable responding will occur. This approach may in fact be sufficient; however, excessive variability may result from poor control over the procedures in a phase or extraneous variables. Simply continuing the phase will often not resolve this form of variability.

13. Identifying transition and transitory states is a matter of identifying the steady states preceding and following the transition. The frequency with which measurement occurs can affect how well an investigator can describe the transition and distinguish it from the surrounding steady states. The more often responding is measured during a transition, the more precisely the transition's boundaries can be described.

TEXT STUDY GUIDE

1. Why should a researcher collect repeated measures of responding under a condition?

2. What do you need to know about responding under each of two conditions in order to compare their effects?

3. What does having unstable data infer about the role of extraneous variables?

4. What does having stable data generally say about the role of extraneous variables?

5. What are two particular conclusions that stable responding allows?

6. Explain the steady-state strategy.

7. How is the circumstance of researchers and practitioners different with regard to the steady-state strategy?

8. What is a steady state?

9. What does it mean to say that the meaning of the term "steady" in the phrase steady state is relative?

10. What can you not say about responding when the data show a steady state?

11. What does stable responding say about the environmental conditions under which it occurred?

12. Explain how stable data allow the investigator to evaluate measurement decisions.

13. How does the steady-state strategy reveal the influence of a condition?

14. How does the effort to obtain stable responding under each phase help the researcher to evaluate experimental control?

15. Explain how the steady-state strategy facilitates experimental comparisons.

16. What is a trend?

17. What are three reasons why an investigator should be concerned about trends in the data that have no obvious explanation?

18. Under what conditions can trends be considered stable responding?

19. Define range. How is it relevant to steady-state decisions?

20. What is a cycle? Under what conditions might cycles be considered steady states?

21. Explain the following statement: The usefulness of a data set depends on the reliability and validity of the criteria that define their stability.

22. What are the pros and cons of statistical steady-state criteria?

23. Why can it be said that graphic steady-state criteria are more complex and potentially useful than statistical criteria?

24. What are the risks of nondata steady-state criteria?

25. What does it mean to say that obtaining stable responding is an active rather than a passive process?

26. Distinguish between transition and transitory states.

27. How do you identify transition states?

28. How is frequency of measurement important in describing transitional responding?

29. Why is it important to distinguish between transition and transitory states?

30. What are the consequences of introducing a new condition when responding is unstable?

BOX STUDY GUIDE

1. What are the differences in the resulting data of measuring one participant many times versus many participants once?

2. How does the choice between measuring one participant many times versus many participants once relate to the fundamental nature of behavior?

3. Why can it help to look at a series of data points one at a time in sequence?

4. How long should each phase of an experiment last?

SUGGESTED READINGS

Sidman, M. (1960). *Tactics of scientific research*. New York: Basic Books. [Chapter 8: Steady states]

Sidman, M. (1960). *Tactics of scientific research*. New York: Basic Books. [Chapter 9: Steady states (continued)]

Sidman, M. (1960). *Tactics of scientific research*. New York: Basic Books. [Chapter 10: Transition states]

DISCUSSION TOPICS

1. Discuss why practitioners should be cautious about drawing conclusions about why their treatment procedures were effective in changing consumer behavior.

2. Using articles published in behavioral journals, select a graphed data set representing a single phase that contains at least 20 values. Present the data to students one value at a time, asking them to independently decide exactly when they believe stable responding has been shown. Discuss the factors they considered in reaching their decisions.

EXERCISES

1. Using articles published in behavioral journals, such as the *Journal of Applied Behavior Analysis*, find examples of graphed data sets for individual phases in which the data suggest the presence of uncontrolled extraneous influences.

2. Using articles published in behavioral journals, find graphed data sets from individual phases that exemplify different patterns of values across sessions that reveal trends.

3. Using articles published in behavioral journals, find graphed data sets from individual phases that exemplify different patterns of variability in range.

4. Using articles published in behavioral journals, find graphed data sets from individual phases that exemplify cyclic variability.

5. Using articles published in behavioral journals focusing on basic research, such as the *Journal of the Experimental Analysis of Behavior*, find examples of statistical rules used to define stable responding.

Strategic Issues in Experimental Design

So far as I can see, I simply began looking for lawful processes in the behavior of the intact organism.

—B. F. Skinner

EXPERIMENTAL DESIGN AND REASONING

Experimental and Control Conditions

The steady-state strategy can provide a clear and complete picture of each participant's behavior under each phase or set of conditions in an experiment. This ongoing measurement can be made into an experiment by arranging two different types of phases so that their effects on responding can be compared. When the factors that make up a phase are not the specific focus of the researcher's interest, it is called a **control** (or baseline) **condition**. In other words, in this type of condition the independent variable is not present.

Baseline or control conditions serve as a background or context for looking at the effects of another type of condition or phase called an **experimental, treatment, intervention**, or **independent variable condition**. In this type of condition, the independent variable is present. The **independent variable** is made up of environmental events that the researcher has arranged in order to see how they might affect the participant's behavior. The particular behavior or response class being measured serves as the **dependent variable**. It is called the dependent variable because what happens with it depends on the independent variable controlled by the researcher.

> **Control** or **baseline condition.** A condition or phase of an experiment in which the independent variable is not present.
>
> **Experimental, treatment, intervention**, or **independent variable condition.** A condition or phase in which the independent variable is present.
>
> **Independent variable.** Those environmental events that the investigator manipulates in order to determine their effects on the dependent variable.
>
> **Dependent variable.** In behavioral research, usually a response class, at least one dimensional quantity of which is measured throughout all phases of a study.

In other words, the objective in an experiment is to determine the effects on responding of an experimental condition containing the independent variable compared with the effects of its control condition, which does not include the independent variable. The reason for making this comparison is to be sure that the changes in responding observed when the experimental condition is present, compared to when it is absent, are solely the result of the variables of interest in the treatment phase. Experimental designs are ways of arranging control and experimental conditions that permit comparisons to help isolate the effects of the independent variable on the dependent variable. Because the experimental question typically asks about the effects of the independent variable, this information should help to answer the question.

Experimental Reasoning

The key to identifying the effects of the independent variable in a study is making sure that the only thing that differs between an experimental condition and its matching control condition is the presence of the independent variable. In other words, the experimental and control conditions should be exactly the same, except that the independent variable is present only during the experimental condition. If this is the case, the only way to explain differences in responding under the two conditions is in terms of the presence or absence of the independent variable.

As an example, consider a simple study focusing on the impact of a procedure intended to decrease the occurrence of a problem behavior of an autistic child in a preschool setting. The preparation involves measuring the occurrence of a target behavior during group free-play sessions, which are scheduled two or three times each day. The free-play sessions are essentially the same in their basic features from one day to another. After measuring the occurrence of the target behavior during a number of these free-play sessions, the researcher should have a good picture of how often the behavior occurs under these circumstances. This is the control or baseline condition, which shows what the target behavior is typically like in these situations. When the intervention phase is then implemented for a number of sessions, measurement will provide another picture of this behavior. In order to see if any observed changes in the target behavior are reliable, let us assume that after implementing the intervention condition for a number of successive sessions the researcher goes back and repeats the initial control condition and then repeats the intervention condition.

Figure 10.1 shows measures of the target behavior across these four phases. We can see that the behavior consistently occurred less often when the treatment condition was in effect. The figure also describes the conditions present

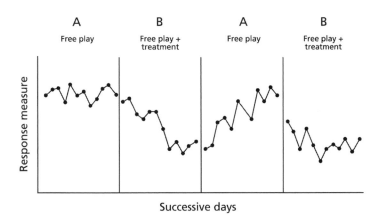

FIG. 10.1. Data showing responding under successive control and experimental conditions.

in each phase. Because the group free-play circumstances were the same across all four phases, the only apparent explanation for this difference in responding is the treatment procedure implemented during each session throughout the intervention phases. This is a defensible interpretation only if the free-play sessions are essentially the same under both control and intervention phases. In other words, the treatment procedure must be the only change in the environment that could explain changes in the target behavior.

If free-play sessions had systematically changed in some other way during the intervention phases (such as more teaching personnel being present in order to implement the procedure), it would be possible that this extraneous factor could have contributed to changes in responding. The problem is that we would not know if the decreases in responding were due to the treatment procedure, the fact that more staff were present, or both. If we concluded that the changes were the result of the treatment procedure, we might be right, but we also might be partly or even entirely wrong. This risk is why it is important that control and experimental conditions differ only in the absence or presence of the independent variable. This kind of reasoning underlies all experimentation in science.

STRATEGIC ISSUES

Making Experimental Comparisons

Independent Variable Condition. We often discuss the independent variable as if it is a single, narrow feature of the environment. In some laboratory experiments, this may be the case. For instance, an investigator may be interested in the effects of changing the dosage of a drug. Under the control condition, an animal might be receiving the drug at one dosage, and implementing the experimental condition might then involve nothing more than changing that dosage. The independent variable is simply the new dosage.

In most behavioral studies, however, the independent variable is a complex mix of multiple variables, and this is especially true in applied research. For example, in a study on staff training methods, the independent variable presented in the experimental phase may incorporate instruction in the specific skills to be learned, modeling of those skills, role-playing, and video feedback—all delivered as a coordinated intervention package. When experimental interest lies in the collective effects of multiple variables, it is still appropriate to refer to them collectively as *the* independent variable.

It is also important to distinguish the independent variable from the experimental condition itself. As Figure 10.1 suggests, it may help to think of the experimental condition as consisting of two parts. One part is the independent variable. The other part includes all of the factors that were also present in the control condition. Recall that everything going on in the control condition must also be going on in the experimental condition to be sure that any changes in behavior are due to the independent variable alone. The factors making up the control condition are often described as the general preparation of the experiment or its baseline procedures.

In the study on staff training, these baseline procedures might include the particular personnel who are participating, the training procedures they use in working with consumers, the consumer target behavior being trained, the consumers themselves, the setting in which training takes place, and the procedures used to measure staff and consumer behavior. All of these variables operate throughout both control and experimental phases and provide the context for evaluating the independent variable.

Finally, it may seem that the independent variable is usually something that is added to the baseline preparation from the control condition. However, the independent variable may also involve removing or merely modifying some factor in the baseline procedures. In our earlier example of a laboratory study of the effects of different dosages of a drug, the new dosage used in the experimental condition is not so much a matter of adding something to the baseline procedures as changing one of the baseline variables. Sometimes the independent variable involves removing a variable in the baseline preparation. This might be the case when a researcher is interested in evaluating the effects of terminating a particular feature of a procedure and seeing what effects the remaining components have.

For example, consider that a study is examining various features of a group contingency designed to minimize the disruptive behavior of students in an elementary classroom setting. The procedure may involve a number of elements, including announcement of the contingencies, dividing the class into teams, a point system with certain values, and the consequences associated with earning points. The study may begin with the group contingency procedure in place, and experimental phases may systematically manipulate some of these components. Working with the teacher, the researcher may revise the point system, drop the team component, or change the consequences. Any such changes constitute an independent variable.

Control Condition. There are two jobs that the control condition must do. First, it must establish the general conditions under which participants will behave. The control condition defines the basic preparation for at least part of an experiment. In the earlier example concerning staff training, we pointed out that the preparation included the staff, the training procedures, the target behavior being trained, the consumers, the training setting, and the measurement procedures. The researcher's interest in designing a control condition is selecting features that will help to highlight the effects of the independent variable. The resulting preparation must generate responding by participants that will be sensitive to any effects of the independent variable.

The risk is that some decisions might actually make it difficult to detect the effects of the independent variable. For example, choosing to target out-of-seat behavior exhibited by a hyperactive child in a classroom might be problematic because it is too much under the control of biological influences. This might mean that it will not be sensitive to the classroom contingencies serving as the independent variable. As a different example, a classroom setting might involve such powerful control by peers over disruptive behavior that it would be difficult for target academic behaviors to reflect any effects of an instructional procedure. As still another example, a decision to measure behavior at a particular time of day might lead to data that do not represent intervention effects at other times. These examples suggest that the control condition, which serves as the context for studying the influence of the independent variable, should be constructed with great care.

As we have indicated, the control condition runs throughout its matching experimental condition. It is the foundation for seeing any changes that might be generated by the independent variable. For this reason, the researcher should design the control condition and its associated experimental condition as a pair or unit. This leads to the second task that control conditions must accomplish. As a control condition, it must control for something, but what does it control for? The control condition controls for all of those factors in the experimental condition that are *not* the independent variable. In other words, in evaluating the effects of the independent variable itself, all of the other variables making up the experimental condition should be eliminated from consideration. Because the factors making up the experimental condition are also present throughout the control condition, they cannot explain any changes in responding that occur during the experimental condition. That is, they are controlled for.

This is why each different experimental condition must be matched to its own control condition. This means that a study that includes two different independent variable conditions must match each to its own control condition that serves this necessary control function. For example, consider a study examining the effects of different reinforcement contingencies on the behavior of patients with arthritis who are supposed to comply with exercise routines as part of a health club program. Aside from other general factors, an initial baseline condition may involve no explicit reinforcement contingencies. This condition might provide a good basis for comparing exercise compliance without reinforcement (the control condition) to compliance under an experimental condition in which participants earn praise when their performance meets certain standards. This pair of conditions will allow conclusions about the effects of a praise reinforcement contingency compared to a no-reinforcement condition.

Following the praise reinforcement phase, the investigator might then wish to see what effects would result from adding a points contingency to the praise contingency (points earned would be exchanged for backup reinforcers). Answering this second question about the effects of praise plus points compared to praise alone will require a different control condition than used in the first comparison. Now the praise contingency that served as the experimental condition in the first comparison will serve as a control condition for comparison to a praise plus points condition. Table 10.1 summarizes these two pairs of control and experimental phases.

TABLE 10.1
Control and experimental comparisons

Question	Control condition	Experimental condition
• Effects of praise?	No reinforcement	Praise
• Effects of adding points?	Praise	Praise + points

Arranging Appropriate Comparisons. This last example provides another opportunity to emphasize the difference between experimental or independent variable conditions versus control conditions. The distinction lies with the researcher's interests. If the researcher is interested in drawing conclusions about the effects of certain factors associated with a condition, this interest makes those factors the independent variable. If the researcher is not interested in drawing conclusions about any factors in a phase, this lack of interest makes it a control condition. However, a control condition must be more than just a baseline—the condition in which the independent variable is not present. It must also be constructed so that it serves as a control for a particular experimental condition, by including everything going on in that condition except the independent variable.

This specification means that it is important to avoid comparing data from two conditions in which the variables operating in one condition are largely replaced by a different set of variables in the other. For example, consider a study about the types of reinforcers used in discrete-trial training procedures with autistic children. Suppose that during a baseline phase the trainers use food reinforcers and in an intervention phase they discontinue using food and switch to social reinforcers. If the investigator is interested in drawing conclusions about the effects of social reinforcers, comparing the data from these two phases will present a problem. In order to evaluate the effects of the social reinforcer condition, we need a control condition that is essentially the same except for the use of social reinforcers. The problem here is that when the first phase ends, the food reinforcer procedures cease and are replaced by the social reinforcer procedures. This means that two changes occur at the same time. Assuming that the children's performance changes in the second phase, we will not know whether they behave differently because the food reinforcers were no longer earned or the social reinforcers were now being used. Although the way that responding changes might give us a hint, there would be no way to be sure. Table 10.2 shows this sequence of conditions as "original design."

The solution to this problem is making sure that all features of the two conditions being compared are the same except for the variables being evaluated. The sequence labeled "better design" in Table 10.2 illustrates one way to do this. Here, the food reinforcer condition continues throughout the social reinforcer condition. If any changes in responding are evident in the second condition, the only environmental factor that differed between the two

TABLE 10.2

Alternative control and experimental conditions for evaluating the effects of social reinforcers

Design alternatives	Conditions			
	First	Second	Third	Fourth
• Original design	Food	Social		
• Better design	Food	Food + social		
• Best design	No reinforcers	Food	No reinforcers	Social

conditions (adding social reinforcers to the contingency) would be the most likely explanation.

The sequence labeled "best design" in Table 10.2 shows still another option that would evaluate not just the effects of the social reinforcer condition but the effects of the food reinforcer condition as well. This sequence matches each reinforcement condition with a control condition that differs only in the absence of the reinforcement contingency. Comparison of the first pair of conditions allows a conclusion to be drawn about the effects of using food reinforcers, just as comparison of the second pair of conditions allows a conclusion to be drawn about the effects of social reinforcers. These comparisons make it easy to see if one reinforcer is more effective than the other.

Sequence of Conditions: Rationale. It is customary for the control condition to precede its matched experimental condition. This often makes practical sense because the control condition embodies all of the variables that will be operating in the experimental condition except for the independent variable. The control condition is therefore often used to fine-tune the general preparation. This way, any adjustments that might be needed can be made early in the project.

For example, it may be that some features of the procedures need to be changed so that they generate better responding. The researcher may learn that the response class definition can be improved, or that a different dimensional quantity should be measured. Early data may suggest that observational procedures should be revised. It is also not uncommon for the data to reveal unstable patterns of responding that will make it difficult to identify the effects of the treatment condition. The researcher may then need to identify and better control extraneous factors.

As any changes are made, the investigator can continue the control phase until it is clear that everything is working as intended. This flexible, repeated-measures approach is one of the major advantages of the steady-state strategy. Because control conditions establish a baseline that will be used to assess any effects of the independent variable, they are often called baseline conditions or just "baselines."

Another reason for the control condition to come first is that it is sometimes designed to give participants a particular kind of history they must have in order to prepare for the experimental condition. For example, a control condition is often used to generate a certain kind of performance because that performance is necessary to reveal the effects of the independent variable in the treatment condition. In other words, an initial control phase may be used to give participants a certain training experience.

Sometimes the desired training is somewhat indirect, as when participant behavior comes under the control of baseline procedures. This might be the case in a study in which individuals with mental retardation are serving in a study of prompting procedures. Among other things, each participant must learn to sit at a table and comply with the training procedure before this phase goes very far. On the other hand, sometimes the training objective is a key element of the experiment. This might be the case in a study of two staff management procedures. Para-professional staff might be trained during an initial phase to use certain intervention procedures with consumers. Their use of these skills would serve as the dependent variable used to assess the effects of the two types of staff management procedures.

In spite of these advantages of the control condition coming first, this sequence is not required. It can sometimes work just as well for the experimental condition to come first. When comparing steady-state responding under a matching pair of control and experimental conditions, their sequence does not change the experimental reasoning involved. Either way, the investigator winds up comparing responding in the absence versus the presence of the independent variable. In fact, many experimental designs involve comparisons between an experimental phase and a following control phase. Consider a design consisting of a control–intervention–control or ABA sequence of phases. These three phases will permit two comparisons of responding under control and experimental conditions. One comparison comes from the first two phases (control–intervention), and the other comes from the second and third phases (intervention–control).

Sequence of Conditions: Sequence Effects. Our discussion of sequences of phases indicates that one condition can be used to make responding more useful in identifying the effects of the next condition—a sequence effect. As we described in chapter 8, sequence effects are a likely outcome of within-subject designs because each participant experiences both control and intervention conditions one after the other.

Although sequence effects can be beneficial, they can also be problematic. In general, they are undesirable when the effects of the first condition interfere with seeing a clear picture of the effects of the second condition. The most common circumstance in which this might happen is when the changes in responding observed in an intervention phase depend on having experienced the prior control phase. In other words, if the changes observed in the intervention condition would have been different had the participant not been exposed to the prior condition, then those effects would at least partly depend on that sequence of conditions.

It is important to understand that just because one condition immediately follows another does not mean that exposure to the first condition will necessarily affect how participants respond under the second condition. Sequence effects may be negligible or transient, and there may be none at all. Although operant behavior is a function of both past experience and current conditions, the influence of conditioning history tends to be overtaken by the impact of current contingencies, which in turn become part of this accumulating history. Given the uncertainty surrounding sequence effects, researchers need to address two questions when designing experiments. First, how might sequence effects be created that will highlight the effects of treatment conditions? Second, how might sequence effects occur that could get in the way of identifying treatment effects?

Sequence of Conditions: Letter Designations. Finally, this discussion of sequences of phases may suggest that describing sequences of phases with words can sometimes get awkward if all we want to do is get across the sequence of conditions. To avoid this problem, researchers long ago started using the letters of the alphabet as a kind of shorthand. The rule is simple: Each different phase in temporal sequence is assigned successive letters of the alphabet. In other words, the first phase is labeled "A," the second phase is labeled "B," and so on. The label for the third phase will depend on whether it is a repeat of the first phase (A) or a new phase (C). Of course, these letters indicate nothing more than the temporal order of different phases.

Because a control or baseline condition is often the first phase in a study, it is common for baseline conditions to be labeled "A." What if an experiment starts with a treatment condition instead of a control condition, however? In this case, the treatment condition would be labeled "A" because it is the first phase. In other words, "A" does not designate a control or baseline phase. The letters merely indicate a sequence, not the nature of the condition in each phase. This becomes clear in experimental designs that include a number of phases for different control and treatment conditions. Although an initial control phase would be labeled "A," a different control phase later in the study might be labeled "C" or a subsequent letter.

Consider the sequence of phases in Table 10.3 describing a study of contingencies designed to reduce absenteeism among employees. The "ABABCB" sequence of letters suggests an experiment with two different independent variable conditions ("B" and "C") and their preceding and following control conditions. The phase descriptions below the letters clarify that an "ABA"

TABLE 10.3
Illustration of ABABCB design

Sequence of conditions

A	B	A	B	C	B
Control (1) Standard	Treatment 1 Public posting	Control (1) Standard	Control (2) Public posting	Treatment 2 Posting+lottery	Control (2) Public posting

sequence of phases allows comparisons of treatment 1 with its matching control condition, coming both before and after the intervention, and a following "BCB" sequence. The brief reference to the focus of each condition suggests that the initial control phase involved some standard condition relating to absenteeism already in effect in the workplace. This was followed by publicly posting absentee data in some manner, after which the same control condition was repeated. This ABA sequence allows two comparisons of A and B conditions. Next, the public posting condition was reinstated, but this time it served as the control condition for a subsequent intervention phase that involved adding a lottery contingency (every day that employees were at work their names were entered into a lottery) to the public posting procedure (treatment 2). Finally, this second type of intervention was followed by a return to the public posting condition, allowing a second comparison of C and B conditions. As you might imagine, this lettering system of summarizing sequences of phases in a study works well only for relatively simple experimental designs. The last section of this chapter will present a more broadly useful graphical notation.

Functional Relations

The goal of experimentation is to learn enough about the effects of the independent variable on the target behavior (the dependent variable) to show that particular changes in responding are a function of the independent variable and nothing else. This result is called a **functional relation**.

> **Functional relation.** An experimentally determined relation that shows that the dependent variable depends on or is a function of the independent variable and nothing else.

This goal is more demanding than it might seem. It is not necessarily difficult to show that responding changes in a particular way whenever an intervention condition is present, compared to its control condition. However, to say that those changes in responding are a function of the intervention alone requires confidence that no other factors are contributing to the effect. The only way in which researchers can convince themselves and others that the effects of the intervention are not due to extraneous factors is to control or eliminate likely candidates in some way.

Let us continue with our interest in studying procedures for helping businesses to address problems with employee absenteeism. In this example, let us assume that the procedures involve a system of monetary bonuses for good attendance. If the data for a manufacturing company show that absenteeism decreased after the bonus program started, can we be confident that the reduction was solely due to the bonus program?

As we look more closely at what actually happened in the study, we might be able to identify other factors that could have helped to reduce absenteeism

---

BOX 10.1

Levels of Empirical Elegance

A functional relation may be viewed as one end of a continuum of the elegance or completeness of empirical explanations. At the other end are investigations that take the form of *demonstrations*. A demonstration simply shows that something is possible. It can reveal the operation of a process or procedure that has not yet been fully defined and explained. Demonstration studies occupy an important position in the history of science. Demonstrating a relationship does not involve experimentally manipulating an independent variable or explaining why something works. However, a well-designed demonstration can eliminate arguments that a certain outcome is not possible. Demonstrations permit only an empirical statement in the form of "if . . . then" (if you do this, then you will get that outcome). Furthermore, a single demonstration only shows a relationship for the variables operating in that instance.

Correlations are in the middle on this continuum between demonstrations and functional relations. This form of investigation requires identifying and measuring multiple values of the variables in question, such as annual sales of single malt Scotch in the United States and annual professors' salaries. The resulting statements take the form "When X_1 occurs, Y_1 occurs." Because correlational studies do not involve manipulating variables, no statements should be made about the reasons for the correlation. Correlations merely show that two variables show some association.

Only the pursuit of *functional relations* involves actual experiments in which independent variables are manipulated in order to determine their effects on dependent variables. This leads to a kind of "co-relation" expressed as $y = f(x)$, where x is the independent variable of the function and y is the dependent variable. Although it is often useful to show that x is sufficient to produce y, it is more informative to show that x is necessary to produce y. Showing that y occurs *only if* x occurs is the most complete and elegant from of empirical inquiry in science.

---

during the bonus program. For instance, it might be that the publicity the management gave to the absenteeism issue throughout the bonus intervention period had a substantial effect on absenteeism. Let us assume that the researcher went beyond baseline and intervention phases to implement an "ABAB" design, following the initial intervention with a return to the original control condition and then returning to the intervention a second time. Let us also assume that the data again showed the same changes from higher absenteeism under no-bonus phases to lower absenteeism under bonus conditions.

Would these data allow the researcher to argue that they showed a functional relation between the bonus contingencies and absenteeism? The problem with this argument is that as long as the company made a big deal about absenteeism when the intervention was in place (but not when the program was not operating), the bonus contingencies would be confounded by the extra publicity. In order to look at the effects of the bonus contingencies alone, the researcher would have to convince management to stop calling attention to the absenteeism problem when the program was operating or to give equal attention to the absenteeism issue when it was not operating. It would take multiple phases, if not additional studies, looking at bonus intervention results with and without the publicity component to determine if the bonus contingencies were consistently responsible for reductions in absenteeism by themselves. The data might reveal that the publicity contributed to the decreased absenteeism.

From a practical perspective, of course, it might be useful if the extra attention to the absenteeism problem supplemented the effect of the bonuses. From an experimental perspective, however, it is important to learn whether the bonuses are effective by themselves, and it may also be valuable to assess the separate contribution of the extra publicity. When the results of the study are used by different companies, it will be important to know which factors have what effects. Consulting firms offering behavior analysis services to businesses need to know if bonus contingencies are functionally related to reductions in absenteeism or if they must be supplemented with a publicity program in order to obtain the desired outcome. Perhaps a publicity program will work just as well as bonuses.

This example suggests that showing that a particular behavioral outcome is solely the result of a certain independent variable—demonstrating a functional relation—will usually require more than a single experiment. It is not enough to show that a certain outcome is reliably associated with an intervention. Most intervention conditions, particularly in applied research, are confounded with some extraneous factors. It is risky to merely assume that those extraneous factors have no effect and to conclude that the independent variable is solely responsible for changes in responding. Proposing that an independent variable is functionally related to a particular behavioral outcome requires evidence that the relationship does not depend on any other factors.

Another way of making this point uses a logical argument that distinguishes between sufficiency and necessity. In the bonus program example, data showing that every time the bonus program was implemented absenteeism decreased might justify a statement that the program was *sufficient* to produce reduced absenteeism. If a series of experiments showed that the program had this effect even when likely extraneous factors were eliminated, however, they might justify a statement that the program was *necessary* to obtain this effect.

There is no clear standard for when it is appropriate to describe an experimental finding as a functional relation. What limits our certainty about making this kind of statement is the possibility that extraneous variables are contributing to the relationship. This means that although investigators may learn more and more about a relationship with each new study, they must still admit the possibility that someone will discover either conditions under which the relation does not hold because of factors yet to be identified or additional factors that are partly responsible for the relationship. It may be helpful,

---

BOX 10.2

Why Scientists Do Not Talk About Causes

Media reporters often seem frustrated when interviewing scientists. When reporters ask about some discovery, scientists tend to hedge their bets. They seem to qualify everything they say, using phrases such as "As far as we know . . . ," "Under such-and-such conditions . . . ," "There seems to be a relationship . . . ," "We're still not sure why . . . ," and so forth.

The reason for their caution is more than wanting to avoid embarrassment by being wrong. Scientists learn in graduate school that the world is a complex place and things are often not as simple as they seem. They learn to talk in conservative terms in order to avoid implying more than they know because they have learned that every research literature is a story of revisions of what we once thought was correct.

This is why scientists tend to avoid saying that one thing "causes" another. The notion of "cause" suggests that we know everything about the relationship, which is almost always untrue. This is the same reason why scientists do not talk about "proving" something. Instead of talking about causation, scientists may say that one variable is "related to" another. They may talk about a correlation between two variables. In fact, all we ever really know is that two variables are "co-related" in some way. In a way, it is almost impossible to show that no other factors are playing a contributing role in some relationship because it requires identifying all possible extraneous variables and then showing that they are not relevant. This is why science is better at disproving than proving.

---

therefore, to think of functional relations as a level of understanding that we approach only gradually as a result of a series of experiments.

Experimental Control

Rationale. At this point, it should be clear that the investigator must design and conduct an experiment in which the independent variable is the only thing that can explain changes in the dependent variable as the treatment condition is implemented and withdrawn, and also that these effects are clear and consistent. **Experimental control** refers to how successful the investigator is in this effort.

> **Experimental control.** The management or control of different variables in a study, including the independent variable and extraneous variables.

The pursuit of a high degree of experimental control is one of the hallmarks of the approach to experimentation described in this volume. This obligation pervades the investigator's decision-making from the outset. Decisions about the general procedures for a study that will constitute the context for responding, the desired characteristics of participants, the nature and dimensions of the target behavior that will be measured, and the measurement procedures themselves all affect how clearly the influence of the independent variable is revealed.

In addition, the details of the independent variable can have a substantial impact on how easy it is to identify its effects on responding. Designing an intervention that does not properly represent the variables of interest may fail to provide a good test of their potential impact. This might be the case, for example, if weak reinforcers are used as part of an otherwise sound procedure. In addition, selecting an intervention that is difficult to arrange or maintain from session to session may fail to provide a good test of its potential.

Implementation. Concern with issues of experimental control only starts with how a study is designed. Once the experiment is underway, the researcher must closely monitor the general procedures, the independent variable condition, measurement procedures, and the resulting data to evaluate these initial decisions. As we have already seen, one of the strengths of the steady-state strategy is that it insures ongoing opportunities to assess earlier decisions and adjust certain features to improve experimental control. Collecting repeated measures of the participant's behavior under each condition also provides the opportunity to react immediately to unanticipated factors that might interfere with seeing treatment effects clearly.

This ongoing monitoring often leads investigators to find things that require their attention as the study progresses. Sometimes they discover problems from simply observing what is going on. They may also find it useful to talk with individuals who are involved in the project in some way, including participants, those who are implementing procedures (staff members, for example), and observers. Finally, the data may sometimes suggest issues that need attention. Responding might be highly variable, for instance, or fail to change in ways that were anticipated.

The problems that investigators might identify are likely to fall into three general categories. First, there may be adjustments in how the target behavior is defined and measured that will generate more useful data. Altering the definition may be necessary to better reflect research interests or to improve observer accuracy. Changing observation times and durations may allow better sampling of the behavior.

Second, it may be necessary to modify some features of the control and independent variable conditions. Sometimes it may become evident that procedures should be adjusted to better represent key variables. For instance, it might be that the stimuli presented to participants on a computer screen need to be changed, enlarged, or rearranged to have the intended effect. More often, it is discovered that a procedure is not operating as intended. This is frequently the case when it requires certain individuals to behave in specific ways. For example, the procedure may involve teachers implementing a certain protocol, and it may become clear that they need additional training to do so correctly. Making sure that key features of the control or independent variable conditions are operating as designed is so important that investigators often go to the trouble of measuring those features so that they can verify that the procedure occurred as designed. This process is often described as insuring **treatment integrity**. These data may then be reported alongside participant data when the research is published (Peterson, Homer, & Wonderlick, 1982).

> **Treatment integrity.** The extent to which the independent variable is consistently implemented as designed.

Third, investigators may find that unanticipated extraneous factors are intruding on control and experimental conditions. Applied researchers are particularly likely to encounter problems with extraneous influences. The challenge is to determine which factors should be managed in some way and which can safely be allowed to vary. As we indicated in the discussion of steady-state issues in chapter 9, just because an extraneous variable is obvious does not mean that it is having a substantial impact on responding. As we noted, for instance, in a study conducted in an elementary classroom it might seem that a substitute teacher would have a major effect on student behavior, but student performance may be unchanged. On the other hand, less obvious factors such as unscheduled events happening outside of the classroom setting (a fight between two students during recess) can easily influence responding.

How Much Control? In sum, achieving sufficient experimental control involves attention to: (a) designing and implementing sound measurement procedures; (b) selecting and managing control and independent variable conditions; and (c) minimizing the contribution of extraneous variables. Our discussion also suggests that we can group these responsibilities into two categories: (a) those that can be anticipated from the outset and accommodated in how the study is designed; and (b) those that might be unexpected and that will have to be dealt with as the study progresses.

Let us take a closer look at these two options. Designing a study from the outset to minimize the intrusion of extraneous variables is relatively easy to do if the experimental question can be addressed under the relatively controlled conditions of a laboratory. For example, using laboratory animals such as rats means that genetic characteristics and environmental history can be fairly tightly specified. The researcher does not have to worry too much about how rats spend their time between sessions or what they eat, and experimental chambers provide a consistent and narrowly controlled research setting. Treatment variables can usually be arranged with computer-controlled precision, and data collection is comprehensive and automatic.

This extreme approach to experimental control works well for most basic research questions, but many research issues require human participants behaving under everyday circumstances. Even though the laboratory ideal is often inappropriate for these questions, it shows applied researchers what is possible. The challenge for researchers, then, is deciding how much control is necessary. The general answer involves a balance between two interests. On the one hand, there must be enough control over extraneous factors so that they do not interfere with drawing sound conclusions about the role of the independent variable. On the other hand, there must not be so much control that the preparation fails to reflect the circumstances needed to answer the question.

For instance, if an investigator wants to learn about procedures for training social skills in children with autism in small group settings using peers as trainers, it may be necessary to tolerate some extraneous factors associated with small groups of children in a preschool setting. As long as such factors have only minor effects on responding, this may not be a problem. It might be that the number of times when typical children serving as peer trainers provide appropriate prompts and consequences for social responses of autistic children varies a good bit from session to session. In other words, the number of training trials might not occur equally as often from day to day. This variation might result in variations in the performance of the autistic children. In addition, the peer trainers might sometimes interact with the autistic children in ways that are inconsistent with the intervention protocol. It might be feasible to address these problems by redesigning the study so that sessions are conducted in a training room with a single peer child interacting with a single autistic child. Although this approach might allow better control over the peer child's behavior, the contrived setting would no longer represent the circumstances required by the experimental question, which focuses on typical small group settings involving multiple peer and autistic children.

Managing Extraneous Variables. As we have pointed out, achieving sufficient experimental control requires attending to measurement issues, features of control and experimental conditions, and extraneous factors. Even in field research, investigators have some choice about the conditions of a study, as well as measurement procedures, so making sure that they are working as intended is usually a reasonable challenge. Managing extraneous factors can be more problematic. Although some extraneous influences may be considered from the outset, others may have nothing to do with the investigator's plans. There are three ways of managing extraneous variables. They can be: (a) eliminated entirely; (b) held constant across conditions; or (c) directly evaluated through experimental manipulations (see Table 10.4).

By definition, eliminating an extraneous factor is an effective tactic for insuring that it has no effect on responding. This option is not always feasible, but even when it is it can have undesirable consequences. As we just discussed, eliminating extraneous influences can change the features and circumstances of a study so that it does not adequately reflect the intended state of affairs. This outcome can be especially burdensome for applied studies when the extraneous factors are part of the applied situation itself.

TABLE 10.4
Managing extraneous variables

Tactic	Advantage	Disadvantage
• Eliminate	Effective	Limits generality of results
• Hold constant	Same for all phases	Influence still present
• Evaluate	Learn about variable	More time and resources

In other words, eliminating extraneous variables can make a study more contrived and less characteristic of the circumstances to which its findings are intended to apply. This means that it will be less clear how well the findings apply to less contrived (more real-world) situations. This gap between experimental and everyday circumstances must eventually be bridged by additional studies. So, achieving experimental control by eliminating extraneous factors may then require further research to examine the generality of the original findings. Although this requirement might seem to discourage this option, remember that the price for failing to deal with extraneous factors can be misleading results with poor generality.

The second tactic for managing extraneous factors is to hold them constant from one phase to another. If this can be done, the extraneous influences will be the same for each phase. In a study focusing on dietary compliance in diabetic children, for example, it might be important to hold attention from medical personnel constant across both control and intervention conditions. This would address any argument that dietary compliance under the intervention phase was partly due to extra attention from medical staff.

The problem with this tactic is that although the extraneous factors may be consistent, they are still having an impact. This is not always a problem, but it can be. For instance, consider a study of the effects of training procedures for individuals with mental retardation. If individuals were receiving various drugs that influenced their behavior, holding the drugs and dosages constant throughout the study would not mean that they had no effects on responding. Drug effects could interfere with seeing the impact of training procedures that might have occurred had the participants not been receiving the drugs.

Finally, a third tactic for managing extraneous variables is directly investigating them in order to evaluate their role. This can be done as part of the ongoing study or in a subsequent experiment. For example, a study evaluating a computer-based program for training basic academic skills with individuals with mental retardation may raise the question of whether the extra attention from a teacher helping participants respond to touch-screen stimuli contributes to their performance. The experimental question focuses on the effects of the computer program, so teacher attention is an extraneous factor. One way to determine whether the extra attention has a significant influence is to arrange conditions in which teacher attention is systematically varied as the independent variable.

Although directly investigating the extraneous variable can be a distraction from the original experimental agenda, it can lead to learning useful things about the variables in question. It might be learned that teacher attention is not influencing the target behavior, in which case it need not be controlled. This would also mean that the extra attention cannot explain the original treatment effects. On the other hand, if the investigation shows that the teacher attention does have a significant effect, the researcher can then decide how to take that fact into account.

Replication

Types. Replication means repetition, and repetition pervades every nook and cranny of scientific method. (In order to be clear about what is being repeated, it is helpful to use **replication** to refer to repeating procedures and **reproduction** to refer to repeating results.) Repeating things helps scientists to discover and correct their mistakes. There is a lot of repetition built into any single study, but it also occurs over time within an area of investigation as different investigators replicate parts of earlier studies to learn more about an issue.

One of the strengths of making experimental comparisons using repeated-measures designs with each participant is that there is a lot of repetition of important parts of a study. Let us distinguish between different types of repetitions. In some studies, for example, the basic procedure may be repeated a number of times in each session. This is called **within-session replication**. A study of prompts used in a discrete-trial training procedure with children with developmental delays might involve repeating the prompting feature on each trial during each session. In order for these repetitions to provide useful information about the consistency of the participant's responding across repetitions, however, it is necessary for the investigator to measure responding continuously during each session. Furthermore, the data must be displayed trial by trial so that the reproducibility of the performance can be examined. The basic research literature has many examples of this approach, in part because laboratory equipment makes it relatively easy to create moment-by-moment records of repeated cycles of the procedure and its effects on responding. For many years, standardized cumulative records were used to display the outcomes of within-session replication. Figure 8.1 shows examples of these kinds of displays.

Replication. Repetition of any parts of an experiment.

Reproduction. Repetition of results, usually as an outcome of repetition of procedures.

Within-session replication. Repetition of a basic element of a procedure throughout each session.

A second type of replication stems from the steady-state strategy. Obtaining repeated measures of responding under each condition means that each participant will be presented with the same condition many times in succession, usually once each day for a number of days. This is called **within-phase replication**. Chapter 9 described the value of data showing the consistency and durability of each participant's performance as the same conditions are repeated session after session with each phase.

A third type of replication repeats an even larger portion of the experiment. When the researcher repeats an entire phase, it is called **within-experiment replication**. That is, within the span of a study, a condition or phase may be repeated in order to evaluate the reliability of the effect observed when changing from one condition to another. For example, in an "ABA" design, the first phase is repeated following the intervention phase. This allows a second comparison between the "A" and "B" conditions. In an "ABAB" sequence, both conditions are repeated. This form of repetition is a key strength of within-subject design because it allows investigators to assess the reproducibility of an effect.

A fourth type of replication occurs within an area of research as different researchers repeat whole experiments. This may be called **within-literature replication**. Regardless of the care with which a study was done, the credibility of its findings will remain uncertain until other scientists repeat the experiment and are able to reproduce the original results. Researchers have learned that this is an important step because there are often unidentified factors unique to a particular research protocol or program that sometimes turn out to be crucial to obtaining the results. When other investigators replicate the original experiment but fail to reproduce the finding, it prompts a search for the hidden variables that may be responsible.

Finally, **across-research-literature replication** (i.e., replication across different fields of science) is the zenith of replication. When different fields of inquiry discover the same phenomena at work in similar ways under different conditions, these discoveries help to integrate our knowledge of how the world works. For example, Skinner (1975) suggested that the migratory patterns of certain species may involve replications of the basic process of shaping by gradually adjusting contingencies of reinforcement. This process is

---

Within-phase replication. Repetition of the same condition many times in succession throughout a phase.

Within-experiment replication. Repetition of an entire phase during the course of an experiment.

Within-literature replication. Repetition of an earlier experiment, usually by other researchers.

Across-research-literature replication. Repetition of phenomena under different conditions across different fields of science.

well understood at the level of individual organisms, but Skinner saw that the same process might operate across successive generations of a species. Given the now well-established understanding of how continental plates gradually move over very long periods of time, the migratory behavior of some species would have to gradually change accordingly. Data provided by Carr (1966) concerning sea turtles confirmed these predictions and helped to draw the fields of zoology and geophysics closer to the science of behavior.

Functions. Whatever the type of replication, it provides two general kinds of information. It assesses either the reliability of the original findings or the extent to which they might be obtained under somewhat different conditions (their generality). Although each of the above types of replication can be used to ask about either reliability or generality, investigators are probably most often interested in learning about the reliability and generality of each intervention condition on responding (within-experiment replication).

Information about the reliability of treatment effects answers the question of whether they will occur on demand under highly similar conditions if the same independent variable conditions are presented again. Researchers do not want to report findings to colleagues that cannot be consistently reproduced under the same conditions. In order to assess reliability, replications should be designed to repeat the original conditions as carefully as possible (Sidman, 1960, calls this a direct replication).

Of course, it is impossible to make a replication truly identical to the original procedure, but demonstrating reliability requires a close approximation. Trying to establish the reliability of experimental effects when the replication involves substantial changes from the original condition is a bit risky because if the effects are not reproduced the investigator may not know where to start looking for an explanation. If the replicated condition is highly similar to the original version, failing to reproduce the same effects directs the investigator to look for reasons why the same intervention does not consistently produce the same kind of change in responding. It might be, for example, that the original effects were actually due to extraneous factors, not the independent variable. However, if the replication incorporated a number of changes compared to the original condition, failure to reproduce the original findings could be due to having tampered with some key factors that were critical to the effect. In other words, if the replication involves significant changes, the investigator will not know if a failure to reproduce the original findings is due to having an inconsistent effect in the first place or having changed some critical variables.

It is important to understand the limitations of demonstrating the reliability of an effect. Even if the data show that repeating a condition results in the same behavioral outcomes, these data do not confirm that those effects were due to the independent variable. Reproducing an effect only shows that it is reliable. It still might be the case that extraneous factors associated with the intervention condition are partly or even entirely responsible for the effect.

For example, recall the earlier example of a study using a computer-based program for training individuals with mental retardation on basic academic skills. If the investigator wants to draw conclusions about the computer program as the independent variable, the attention from a teacher helping participants is an extraneous factor that is selectively associated with the intervention condition. Showing that the computer program (plus extra teacher attention) reliably changes the participant's performance in some way does not mean that this outcome is solely due to the computer program. They could also depend on the extra teacher attention. In other words, evidence that a finding is reproducible is primarily valuable in building confidence that the impact of an experimental condition on responding is worth further experimental attention.

Let us now turn to the second function of replication. Using replications to pursue the generality of treatment effects addresses the question of whether the same effects will still be obtained even if some features of the intervention are changed in some way. When replication is aimed at providing information about the generality of the effects, it does not help to try to replicate the original procedures exactly. This would not provide any information about whether the effects would still be found if certain procedural features were somewhat different. Answering this question requires making limited changes in the original conditions to assess whether those changes were important to the original findings (Sidman, 1960, calls this a systematic replication).

If the same findings are obtained even though certain features are changed, it suggests that those features may not be critical to getting the effects. Another way to say this is that the effects of the intervention condition on responding may be general to at least the extent of the changes. For example, when the same findings are obtained with different participants, it suggests that the effects did not depend on unique characteristics of the original participants. If one component of a complex procedure was dropped in a replication but the same findings were obtained, it suggests that the component may not be necessary for obtaining that outcome. As long as the same effects are found, the more changes incorporated in a replication, the broader the statement about generality that can be made.

This approach to learning about the generality of a finding involves some risk, however. If the replication changes a number of features of the original preparation and the original findings are not reproduced, it will probably be unclear which changes might be responsible. The researcher might then have to go back and investigate each factor separately to see what role each plays in the intervention effects.

In sum, demonstrating the reliability of the effects of an intervention tells us about the certainty of our knowledge, whereas demonstrating generality actually increases our knowledge. Information about generality suggests that certain features of the independent variable may not be required to get the same effect. As we will see in chapter 13, which will address the generality of findings more broadly, learning about factors that are and are not necessary to obtain a certain outcome is what enables us to predict the circumstances under which that outcome is likely to be found.

TABLE 10.5
Functions of replication

Function	Question	Procedure
• Reliability	If repeat procedure, get same effect?	Repeat exactly
• Generality	If change procedure, get same effect?	Repeat with changes

Issues. Replicating experimental conditions to see if their effects can be reproduced raises a number of questions. The first question concerns how to decide when an intervention should be replicated. Replications are more likely to be needed if: (a) the existing literature on the topic is small or weak; (b) the findings contradict the existing literature; (c) the researcher has little experience with the procedure; (d) there are obvious alternative explanations for the effects; (e) failure to reproduce the same outcome under other conditions is likely to be costly in some way; and (f) the replication will be relatively easy to do.

If a finding is not reliable or general, others will eventually discover these limitations as they attempt to use the results in some way. If the original investigator takes responsibility for reporting findings that are at least reliable, however, it improves the quality of the archival literature. If each researcher leaves this responsibility to others, published findings will sometimes be misleading, making it difficult for readers to distinguish between those results that can be reproduced and those that cannot be repeated.

A second question concerns whether to focus on establishing the reliability of the effects or pursuing their generality. In other words, the researcher must decide how similar the replication should be to the original condition. In addressing this question, remember that a result that is not reliable can have no useful generality, no matter how many attempts are made to reproduce it.

If interest lies primarily in the generality of a reliable outcome, the investigator must decide which variables should be changed in the replication. The particular circumstances of each study guide these decisions. One approach is to vary or even eliminate factors that the investigator suspects might not be critical to the effect. This might allow the intervention to be refined into a more efficient form. A contrasting approach would be to vary factors that are suspected of playing a critical role. Verifying their contribution would clarify the key features of a procedure.

A third question concerns the number of replications necessary to establish reliability or at least to suggest a certain degree of generality. Because replications that duplicate the original condition provide little information beyond the reliability of their effects, there is no point in continuing such replications. On the other hand, each replication that changes some variables creates the possibility of learning something new about the role of those factors. This kind of replication can be endlessly useful.

A fourth question asks how to determine when a replication is successful in reproducing the original results. That is, how close to the original results do the reproduced results need to be? It is unlikely that the reproduced results will duplicate the quantitative details of the original data, of course. The objective is to reproduce the form of the original relationship between the intervention condition and responding. For example, each participant may respond under control and intervention conditions in slightly different ways. One individual may respond more often than another under both conditions, or one may show a more rapid transition at the beginning of the intervention condition than another. These differences are usually unimportant, however, as long as responding is affected in the same way by the intervention condition. In other words, the standard for a successful reproduction of earlier results is obtaining the same form of the relationship.

Finally, there is the question of what to do when the replication does not reproduce the original results. If the replication was highly similar to the original effort, this failure suggests that the original findings might have been due to extraneous factors not present during the replication. If the replication focused on generality by incorporating changes from the original procedure, those changes must be examined more closely to assess their role in the original results. Either way, the researcher obviously has more work to do.

TABLE 10.6
Questions guiding replication decisions

- When should replications be pursued?
- Should replications focus on reliability or generality?
- How many replications are necessary?
- How close to the original results should the reproduced results be?
- What should be done if the original results are not reproduced?

Number of Participants

Rationale. As we have emphasized in earlier chapters, the fact that behavior is a phenomenon that occurs at the level of the individual organism means that investigators must address each participant separately throughout the experimental process. This means that many of the decisions involved in conducting an experiment must be made separately for each participant, including measuring the target behavior, making steady-state decisions, and analyzing data. It is almost as if each participant represents a separate experiment, even though it is usually practical to use multiple participants to get the most out of all the work involved in setting up a research project.

In fact, as long as a study is well done, only a single participant's data are necessary to justify conclusions that have every bit as much chance of being true as when the data represent the behavior of additional individuals. Although it could always be the case that any one individual is not typical of others with the same general characteristics (e.g., first graders learning to read), each participant's data reflect a relationship between the independent variable and his or her behavior. Even if one individual's reaction to the intervention was unusual compared to how other individuals responded, it would still be a real effect and no less credible than others. Indeed, sometimes it is especially important to learn why one participant responded differently from others.

If only a single participant is required to draw sound conclusions about the effects of an experimental condition, how can the investigator know if those conclusions are typical of how others would respond under the same condition? This is an important question, and chapter 13 will consider this topic more fully. However, we can point out now that adding a second or even a third participant to the roster does little to answer the question. The investigator has no way of knowing the extent to which the additional individuals are typical of the countless others who are not participating. Even if the second or third individuals react similarly to the intervention, though differently from the first participant, if does not mean that their results are "correct" and those of the first participant are "incorrect." Assuming accurate measurement, all three results are equally valid reflections of how individuals are affected by the intervention.

This point may be easier to grasp if we distinguish between the truthfulness of results and their generality to other individuals. The researcher's primary objective is to obtain data that truly represent the relationship between the independent variable and the dependent variable. If this is not accomplished, nothing else matters. Only when the findings are "true" does the question of their meaningfulness under other circumstances become relevant.

As we will see in chapter 13, the question about the generality of the results to other individuals is not a matter of how many participants are used in a study. Predictions about how well the findings will hold up with other individuals or under other circumstances depend on how well the investigator understands the factors that influence the effects of the intervention. If the investigator knows, for example, that changing a particular component of the intervention will substantially change its effects or that a certain characteristic of participants is necessary to get the effects, he or she is in a better position to make predictions about the circumstances under which the findings will hold. Learning these kinds of things does not depend on how many participants are used in a single study. Instead, it usually requires a series of experiments focused on identifying and evaluating key variables. This is one reason why statements about generality based on a single study should usually be considered speculative.

Practical Issues. If the number of participants in a study has little to do with the correctness or generality of its results, how does the investigator decide how many to use? It usually comes down to some fairly commonsense considerations. For example, it makes sense to take advantage of all the work of setting up an experiment by using more than just one or two participants. The more that are used, the more data will be available for analysis. Even though each participant's data will generally be treated as equally credible, it is valuable to see if the findings for each are similar or if some are noticeably

---

BOX 10.3

Why Psychology Likes Lots of Participants

In contrast with the requirements for good behavioral research, the style of experimentation that dominates psychology (and the social sciences in general) requires relatively large numbers of participants—the more the better. We consider the origins of this tradition in chapter 13, but it is largely based on a view of generality that turns out to be inappropriate for the study of behavior.

This approach to generality is encouraged by designing experiments in order to make comparisons between groups of participants. One group is typically exposed to a control condition and the other to an experimental condition. This allows the comparison to be made by using inferential statistical tests to decide whether there is a significant difference between the means of the groups. The mathematical theory underlying such statistics requires a certain minimum number of participants (usually comparatively large). The more participants used, the smaller the relative differences that will qualify as significant.

This conception of experimentation has led many researchers to view generality as a sampling issue. This approach to the question concerns whether, given the size of the difference between sample means, the sizes of the control and experimental groups as samples of the population of interest are sufficiently large to permit a statement about the likelihood of observing the effect in the population from which the samples were drawn. This is a straightforward mathematical question, but it is not really pertinent to the issue of generality.

Generality is about whether the effects of the experimental condition will be obtained under conditions that differ somewhat from those of the experiment. As chapter 13 will show, in order to know whether a particular result will be obtained for a participant in a later study or under applied circumstances, what we really need to know is what variables are necessary to make the effect occur, what variables will prevent it from occurring, and what variables will modulate the effect. This information cannot be learned by increasing the size of the control and experimental groups. It requires conducting a series of studies that identify and investigate such variables.

---

different from others. It is reassuring, of course, when all participants react in the same way as the intervention condition is initiated or withdrawn. When this is not the case, however, it may be no less useful to learn that reactions tend to vary. This outcome should encourage the investigator to try to figure out why, which often leads to discovering ways of strengthening the treatment condition, controlling extraneous factors, or selecting certain participant characteristics. In turn, these discoveries will lead to a clearer picture of the effects of the intervention condition, as well as possibly identifying some factors that improve predictions about the generality of the findings.

A second reason for using multiple participants is to accommodate the possibility that things may not go as planned. The investigator may intend to expose all participants to the same sequence of conditions, but the emerging data may suggest other alternatives. For example, it might prove tempting to use a couple of participants to assess the impact of eliminating an extraneous factor, while others continue the planned sequence of phases. The investigator might also wish to adjust an intervention condition to see if its effects can be strengthened. Although this can be done with all participants, it might be sufficient to use only two or three of them, again leaving the others to continue with the original experimental plan.

A third advantage of using a sufficient number of participants is to allow for the likelihood that some individuals will not complete the study for various reasons. These reasons are all too familiar to researchers, especially those who work in applied settings. Participants sometimes get sick, have transportation problems, move away, or just quit. Regardless of the reasons, if at any time participants fail to accumulate adequate exposure to a condition their data may not fully reflect its effects. Sometimes this means that the investigator must drop them from the study, or at least not include their data in the analysis. It is important to have enough participants to accommodate these losses without having to start the project all over again.

A fourth possibility is that some participants may not meet various performance criteria under pretraining conditions. A study might require participants to reach a certain standard of performance in an initial phase necessary for evaluating the impact of a subsequent intervention condition. For example, it might be necessary for preschool children to reach a certain level of competence in working match-to-sample problems using a computer touch screen before they are exposed to experimental conditions. Failing to master this performance might mean that a child's data would not be sensitive to the independent variable. Because such children should not be used, it may be wise to start a study with a few extra participants.

All of these considerations might seem to suggest that more participants are better than fewer participants. However, each additional participant involves some extra cost. Each individual must be recruited and permissions obtained. Depending on the nature of the project, each might need to be assessed in some way and pretrained. The number of participants involved also impacts the logistics of actually running the experiment. All of the methodological issues discussed in previous chapters must be addressed for each participant, including measurement, experimental control, and data analysis. Finally, simply running each participant through the various control and intervention phases involves time and resources, which are inevitably limited.

After all this is said and done, deciding on the number of participants needed comes down to educated guesses and compromises. Starting with the minimum of one, the investigator adds up the number that might be needed to accommodate different considerations. This number is then balanced against the costs and limitations involved. Most within-subject design studies use only a few participants, but a few more than that is not uncommon. On the other hand, it is fairly unusual for this type of study to include more than a dozen participants if the data are being analyzed individually.

TABLE 10.7
Reasons for using "additional" participants

- Take advantage of experimental preparations by assessing generality across participants
- Create possibility to pursue unplanned needs and opportunities with some participants
- Accommodate unintended loss of participants
- Accommodate loss of participants who do not meet standards

NOTATION OF EXPERIMENTAL DESIGNS

It is awkward to write about experimental designs using colloquial or even technical language, and it can be hard to follow such discussions. A notational system can help by providing a convenient graphical method of communicating the primary features of different designs. A notational system can also encourage researchers to consider different ways of setting up comparisons between control and intervention conditions. Perhaps even more importantly, it can help them consider how particular designs create or limit interpretations that might be made. This is useful not only in planning an experiment but in evaluating published studies.

The notational system presented here is intentionally limited in scope. It represents only those features of repeated-measures (within-subject) designs that determine the conclusions that are permissible, given ideal data. One strength of this approach is that it does not describe other features of an experiment, especially the nature of the data. It only shows the nature of the comparisons between control and intervention conditions. Although the data will obviously be a major influence on the conclusions, they cannot change the basic comparisons that are available. In other words, an experimental design allows certain comparison statements to be made, assuming the study was carefully conducted and there are no issues with the data. If there are problems with experimental preparations or data, the interpretive options may be limited. By focusing on the basic elements of these comparisons, this notational system allows investigators to review the interpretive possibilities of a particular design before they begin a study or as they consider changes to the original design during the course of the project.

The symbols in Table 10.8 specify the major features of any experimental design. These symbols can be combined to describe any variations of within-subject designs. A series of figures will illustrate these notational elements. Figure 10.2 shows an "ABAB" or reversal design often used to study behavioral effects of intervention conditions. The notation tells us that the design involves a participant identified as Subject 1, the target behavior of talking, and his home as the setting. An initial control or baseline condition is followed by an experimental condition labeled "token reinforcement." After the initial intervention phase, the control condition was repeated, and then the intervention condition was repeated as well.

TABLE 10.8
Symbols for notating experimental designs

- - - - - - - - -	A dotted line indicates that a control condition is present.
————————	A solid horizontal line indicates that an independent variable is present. The condition is described by a simple label underneath the line.
⌐	A vertical line extending upward a fixed distance from a horizontal line indicates the end of one condition and the beginning of another condition.
⌐	A vertical line extending downward a fixed distance from a horizontal line indicates the end of one condition and the beginning of a previously used condition.
}	A brace encloses labels identifying the participant, target behavior, and setting.
⊣ ⊢	This symbol indicates an interruption of a condition.

FIG. 10.2.   Notation of an "ABAB" design.

There are a few things to note in this first example. First, there is no need to repeat the label for the intervention condition the second time it occurs. That first "step" in the notation represents only that intervention phase whenever it is operating. Second, each horizontal line should be the same length. In other words, unless the study has already been conducted and the phases can be synchronized to the calendar (see Figure 10.5), the length of the line should not represent the duration of the phase. The reason for this convention is that the duration of the phase does not generally affect the nature of the comparisons, which is all that this notation attempts to do. We will later find an exception to this rule, however. Third, the height of the steps to new or old conditions is always the same as well. It is important that this feature does not represent anything about the nature of behavior change (increases or decreases) that might be anticipated or already obtained.

Figure 10.3 shows the notation of a design in which a single control condition alternates with three different treatment conditions. One feature that is

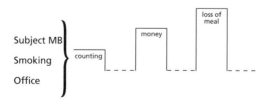

FIG. 10.3.   Notation of a control condition with different treatment conditions.

different in this example is that the initial phase (counting) is not viewed as a control condition, which means that it is represented by a solid line. This phase is followed by a condition that serves as a control for the different treatment conditions. The general rule is that the initial control condition is always on the "bottom" of the diagram, so the step to this control condition is downwards from the initial phase. With this exception, all new conditions are represented by horizontal lines located only above the initial control condition.

Figure 10.4 shows the notation of a design in which two participants are used in a coordinated way to create comparisons that would not otherwise be available. (This is called a multiple baseline design and will be described in chapter 11.) Because of the coordinated way in which these individuals are used, the notation represents each separately. The study uses the same target behavior and setting for each participant, so there is no need to repeat this identifying information to the left of the braces for the second participant.

What this notation shows is that each participant proceeds through the same "ABAB" sequence of conditions. However, SP starts and ends the counting phase some time after HJ, though both start the points phase at the same time. As we will see in chapter 11, this staggered exposure to the counting phase can be informative. In order to represent this important feature, we must create an exception to the rule that all phases are shown with the same-length lines (unless they can be synchronized with the calendar). To represent this staggered phase change, the initiation of the phase for the second participant should therefore be located in the middle of the phase for the first participant. Also, the termination of this phase and reintroduction of the original control condition is similarly located to represent this stagger. In order to catch up, so that both individuals can start the "points" phase at the same time, the second control phase for SP is depicted half as long as for HJ. Of course, these distances do not reflect how long each condition lasts but merely the fact that they are staggered.

Figure 10.5 depicts a design used in a study that has already been conducted. This allows the timing of phases to be synchronized with a calendar

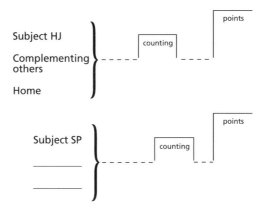

FIG. 10.4.   Notation of a design involving coordinated use of multiple participants.

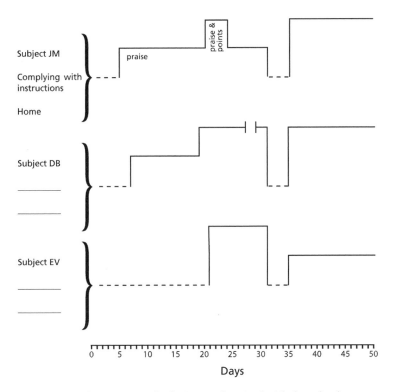

FIG. 10.5. Notation of a design synchronized with the calendar.

time scale. As in Figure 10.4, this design also involves multiple participants who encounter some phases in a staggered manner. In this case, the length of the phase lines exactly represents how long each individual was exposed to each condition. This permits us to see that although the "praise plus points" condition was introduced to each participant on different days, the stagger amounted to only a day or two.

Finally, these notational conventions are not sacred. Any features of this system should be adapted as necessary to represent these key features of experimental design in each case. What is important is that this notation should focus attention on how different control-treatment comparisons are arranged and what impact these arrangements have on interpreting experimental findings.

CHAPTER SUMMARY

1. The objective in an experiment is to determine the effects on responding of an experimental condition containing the independent variable compared to the effects of its control condition that does not include the independent variable. This is essential in determining whether the

changes in responding observed when the experimental condition is present, as compared to when it is absent, are due solely to the variable of interest in the treatment phase.

2. The key to identifying the effects of the independent variable in a study is making sure that the only thing that differs between an experimental condition and its matching control condition is the presence of the independent variable.

3. The researcher's interest in designing a control condition is selecting features that will help to highlight the effects of the independent variable. The resulting preparation must generate responding by participants that will be sensitive to any effects of the independent variable, while limiting the influence of extraneous factors.

4. It is customary for the control condition to precede its matched experimental condition. This allows the researcher to examine whether the procedures in place are working as intended. This sequence also allows the researcher to provide participants with a particular kind of history that may be required in order to prepare for the experimental condition.

5. The ordering of conditions may result in sequence effects, which may make responding more useful in indentifying the effects of the next condition. Although sequence effects can be beneficial, they can also be problematic. In general, they are undesirable when the effects of the first condition interfere with seeing a clear picture of the effects of the second condition.

6. The goal of experimentation is to learn enough about the effects of the independent variable on the target behavior to show that particular changes in responding are a function of the independent variable and not any extraneous factors.

7. Concerns over experimental control and how investigators might identify and modify these problems usually fall into three categories. First, there may be adjustments in how the target behavior is defined and measured. Second, it may be necessary to modify features of the control and independent variable conditions. Finally, investigators may find that unanticipated extraneous factors are intruding on control and experimental conditions.

8. Often in basic research, the investigators will design a study from the outset to minimize the intrusion of extraneous variables. However, applied research often involves less controlled conditions. The investigator should be sure that there is enough control over extraneous factors so that they do not interfere with drawing sound conclusions about the independent variable, but they must also make sure that there is not so much control that the preparation fails to reflect the circumstances needed to answer the question.

9. There are three ways of managing extraneous variables. They may be eliminated entirely, which is a good tactic but not always feasible, and could result in creating conditions that are not characteristic of the

circumstance. Extraneous variables could also be held constant across conditions, which assures us that they will be the same for each phase—but they will still have an impact. Finally, they may be directly evaluated through experimental manipulations.

10. Replication is useful because it helps the researcher to assess the reliability of the original findings, or the extent to which they might be obtained under somewhat different conditions (i.e., generality). Remember though, even if the data show that repeating a condition results in the same behavioral outcomes, these data do not confirm that those effects were due to the independent variable. Reproducing an effect only shows that it is reliable.

11. As long as a study is done well, only a single participant's data are necessary to justify conclusions that have as much chance of being true as when the data represent the behavior of additional individuals.

12. While the use of multiple participants has little to do with the correctness or generality of its results, there are advantages to using multiple participants, including the ability to analyze more data, which may lead to discovering new ways of strengthening treatment conditions and controlling extraneous factors. The use of additional participants is also helpful in case you have attrition or if your participants do not meet various performance criteria under pretraining conditions.

TEXT STUDY GUIDE

1. What is the shared feature of experimental, treatment, or independent variable conditions that distinguishes them from control conditions?

2. Explain why it is important that the only thing that differs between an experimental condition and its matching control condition is the independent variable itself.

3. What is the problem when the changes associated with an intervention condition are confounded with other changes?

4. What does the control condition control for?

5. Why must each experimental condition be compared to a "matching" control condition?

6. In addition to its control function, what is the other job for the control condition?

7. What problems would result if the features of a control condition were not continued throughout its matching intervention condition?

8. Describe two reasons why it is often useful to start a study with a control condition before introducing the treatment condition.

9. What is a sequence effect?

10. How can sequence effects be beneficial but also problematic?

11. What does the letter "A" represent in letter designations of experimental sequences?

12. What is a function relation?

13. Why might it often take multiple studies to identify a functional relationship?

14. Explain the concept of experimental control.

15. Explain how repeated-measures designs provide opportunities to improve experimental control.

16. How much experimental control might be too much?

17. Describe the three ways of managing extraneous variables and the pros and cons of each.

18. How do the authors recommend distinguishing between the terms replication and reproduction?

19. List and define five types of replication.

20. What are the two ways in which replication can be used?

21. When replicating a condition to assess reliability, how closely should the replication match the original condition and why?

22. When replicating a condition to assess generality, how closely should the replication match the original condition and why?

23. At best, what is learned by replicating a condition exactly and reproducing the original results? What does this fail to show?

24. Explain why replications in the pursuit of generality can help to identify controlling variables.

25. What factors bear on the decision about whether to focus on establishing reliability or pursuing generality?

26. What considerations are relevant to evaluating whether a replication has been successful in reproducing the original effects?

27. How many participants are minimally required to make a defensible statement about the effects of the intervention on the target behavior?

28. Why does adding additional participants not help the investigator to understand whether the findings will hold for all similar individuals?

29. List the practical considerations for deciding on the number of participants needed in a study.

30. What are the advantages of a notational system for describing experimental designs?

31. Draw the symbols for the following features of experimental designs: (a) beginning a condition; (b) baseline measurement; and (c) experimental condition in progress.

32. What information is enclosed by the brace?

BOX STUDY GUIDE

1. Describe a demonstration study and the information it provides.
2. Describe a correlation study and the information it provides.
3. What is required to show a functional relation?
4. Why do scientists not talk about causes?
5. Describe the typical design used in psychology experiments.
6. Contrast the approach to generality implicit in between-group designs using many participants and within-subject designs using a relatively small number of participants.

SUGGESTED READINGS

Johnston, J. M., & Pennypacker, H. S. (1993). *Readings for strategies and tactics of behavioral research* (2nd ed.). Hillsdale, NJ: Lawrence Erlbaum Associates. [Reading 7: Traditions of experimental design]

Sidman, M. (1960). *Tactics of scientific research*. New York: Basic Books. [Chapter 3: Direct replication]

Sidman, M. (1960). *Tactics of scientific research*. New York: Basic Books. [Chapter 4: Systematic replication]

DISCUSSION TOPICS

1. Select a published study in a behavioral journal and determine the independent variable. Discuss the extent to which the presence of the independent variable is the only thing that differed between control and experimental conditions.
2. Select a published study from a behavioral journal, and identify the independent variable condition. Describe the control condition associated with this experimental condition, and discuss how well it controls for all variables in the experimental condition except for the independent variable.
3. Provide the general outlines of a hypothetical study that might be conducted under field conditions. Designate the independent variable, and then discuss possible extraneous variables. Consider pros and cons of managing these extraneous factors by eliminating them, holding them constant, or directly studying their influence.

EXERCISES

1. Select three published studies from behavioral journals. Ask students to specify the independent variable for each study.

2. Using a behavioral journal, such as the *Journal of Applied Behavior Analysis,* find an example of a study in which one phase was intentionally used to create a sequence effect.

3. Select a study from a behavioral journal that does not use a multiple baseline or multi-element design and designate the sequence of phases using the letters of the alphabet.

4. Select different experiments from behavioral journals and diagram their design using the notational system.

Creating Experimental Designs

Someone remarked to me once: "Physicians shouldn't say, 'I have cured this man,' but 'this man didn't die under my care.'" In physics too, instead of saying, "I have explained such and such a phenomenon," one might say, "I have determined causes for it, the absurdity of which cannot be conclusively proved."

—George Christoph Lichenbergh

INTRODUCTION

Design Approach

There is no term or phrase that is universally used to refer to the approach to experimental design described in these chapters. One of the most common references is "within-subject design." This phrase emphasizes the fact that each participant serves as his or her own control. That is, each participant experiences both the control condition and the independent variable condition in turn. As we have already discussed, the advantage of this approach is that the unique characteristics of each participant are the same across both conditions. Unlike the alternative of exposing different participants to these two conditions, unique individual features are not differentially associated with only one of the conditions.

"Single-subject designs" is another common reference. It emphasizes that each participant constitutes a complete basis for legitimate conclusions, though without evidence of generality to other individuals. As we pointed out in chapter 10, using more than one participant certainly brings advantages and alternatives to a study. However, it is not the case that each additional participant increases the accuracy of any conclusions. More participants offer only the possibility of providing more of the same evidence already available from a single participant.

Other phrases that provide the same emphasis as single-subject designs are "N = 1 designs" and "small N designs." These are shorthand for indicating that only a single participant is necessary. Of course, the research literature representing this type of design typically involves multiple participants in each study, although not usually as many as used with between-group designs.

"Repeated-measures designs" is still another way of labeling this approach to experimentation. It emphasizes the steady-state strategy of giving each participant repeated exposure to each condition for a series of successive sessions before switching to the next condition.

Assumptions

It will aid discussion in this chapter if we make a few general assumptions. First, we will assume that there are no problems with measurement procedures. That is, in order to focus on what different types of designs can reveal, it helps to assume that the data sets being compared are fully accurate. Of course, this is not always the case in reality. When there are problems and weaknesses in measurement procedures, however, it means that the comparisons otherwise available in the design must be tempered by this limitation. Sometimes, measurement weaknesses are even sufficient to discourage drawing conclusions at all.

Second, we will also assume that the data show substantial and consistent differences in the target behavior between the two phases being compared. In other words, we will assume stable responding in each phase and orderly transitions between phases. Again, if this is not the case, the data can only limit the conclusions that the comparisons might otherwise justify.

Third, unless otherwise specified, we will assume that all variables are the same across the two phases being compared except that one condition includes the independent variable and the other does not. In other words, we will assume that the control condition is constructed so that it includes all of the factors operating in the treatment condition except for those factors defined by the researcher's interests as the independent variable.

In sum, in discussing experimental designs we will assume that all other aspects of the experiment are essentially perfect. Whatever these other features of actual studies, they cannot improve the interpretive possibilities created by the experimental design. That is, the comparisons in a design fully determine the conclusions that are legitimate, assuming that the study was otherwise well done. Any shortcomings that become evident in the real world, such as problems with measurement or weak effects, can only limit the conclusions that the design would otherwise allow.

Types of Designs

Finally, earlier editions of this text have avoided categorizing the infinite variety of experimental comparisons into formal types of designs. Our rationale for this position has been that a sound understanding of this approach to experimentation makes these categories unnecessary, if not distracting. Once students understand the reasoning underlying comparisons between control and experimental conditions, the different ways of creating these comparisons blossom into endless and creative possibilities. Imposing formal distinctions on this wealth of experimental options is largely arbitrary.

Nevertheless, the educational merit of discussing these experimental comparisons as design types may outweigh the risk that students will fail to appreciate the full array of experimental possibilities. The following discussion of types of within-subject designs attempts to minimize this risk by emphasizing the variations associated with each type of design, as well as the overlap between categories. In other words, it is important to understand how these types of comparisons work. This approach will show that all types of within-subject comparisons are fundamentally the same. Furthermore, it will become clear that in any single study different "types" of comparisons are often intermingled as needed.

SINGLE BASELINE DESIGNS

AB Designs

An **AB design** is the core of all within-subject comparisons. Recall that "A" simply designates the first condition in a sequence and "B" identifies the

> **AB design.** A within-subject experimental design composed of a control and an experimental condition.

second. Although the first condition is usually a control or baseline phase and the second is a treatment or intervention phase, the sequence can be the other way around. (In such a case, "A" would refer to the intervention condition and "B" to the control condition.) There are often practical reasons for a baseline-treatment sequence, but the comparison is between the same two data sets, regardless of the sequence.

An AB comparison is not without merit, but it is important to recognize its limitations. A comparison of data from matched control and experimental conditions in sequence provides evidence that in this one instance the two conditions generated differences in responding. This is not trivial, of course. It shows that although responding could have stayed the same when the conditions changed, the participant's performance changed as well.

If this is all there is, however, there are at least two important things we do not yet know. First, we do not know if this change in responding is a reliable outcome of switching between these two conditions. What if the AB sequence of conditions was repeated and the same changes were not observed? What would we conclude then about the result of implementing the intervention condition?

Second, we also do not know if the change in responding was due to the independent variable associated with the intervention condition. It may seem terribly likely that this is the case, but if we have only these two data sets we cannot be sure. This is often a difficult limitation to accept, especially for the investigator. After all, if everything was the same across the two conditions except for the independent variable, what else could explain why responding started changing when the experimental condition started and eventually stabilized at a different level of responding?

There are two possibilities. One is that an unrelated extraneous change in the environment just happened to occur at the same time the intervention started. Although this may seem unlikely, it is certainly possible. It is also possible that extraneous factors selectively associated with the treatment condition could supplement, or detract from, the effect of the independent variable. In other words, there is a not unlikely risk that the independent variable built into the intervention condition was not the only difference between the two conditions.

FIG. 11.1.   Notation of an AB design.

We have described a number of examples of this problem. For instance, in chapter 10 we explained how extra teacher attention (an extraneous variable) could influence student performance using a computer program (the independent variable). In this example, the extra teacher attention would only be present in the intervention phase when the computer program was being used. However much the investigator might believe that changes in academic performance were due to the computer program, it is possible that the extra teacher attention contributed to these changes as well. It is even possible that the extra attention was entirely responsible for the changes in responding and that the computer program had no influence at all. The risk that the independent variable is confounded with extraneous factors specifically associated with the intervention condition is especially likely in applied studies, where general preparations and intervention conditions involve complex environments.

In sum, an AB design is a weak basis for defensible conclusions about the influence of the independent variable because it only shows a single instance of changes in behavior corresponding to changes in conditions. It is an experiment because it measures a dependent variable under matched control and independent variable conditions, but it does not provide the kind of information necessary to conclude that the change in responding is functionally related to the independent variable. It will be important to keep the limited value of an AB comparison in mind as we later consider ways of integrating different types of designs in actual experiments.

Reversal Designs

Basic Features. In contrast to a simple AB design, reversal designs come in many variations. A **reversal design** involves a pair of control and experimental conditions in which one or both conditions repeat at least once. This replication is often described as reversing or going back to a prior condition. The simplest form of a reversal design may be described in letters as an ABA sequence (see Figure 11.2). This arrangement indicates that the first phase (for discussion purposes, we will assume that it is a control condition) is followed by an intervention phase, which is in turn followed by a return to the original control condition.

> **Reversal design.** A within-subject experimental design involving a pair of control and experimental conditions in which one or both conditions repeat at least once.

What information can a reversal design reveal? A reversal design begins with an AB design and therefore shows that introduction of a treatment condition corresponds to changes in responding. Repeating the original control condition adds the advantage of creating a second comparison between control and

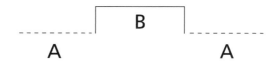

FIG. 11.2. Notation of an ABA reversal design.

intervention conditions. In other words, an AB design allows only one comparison, but an ABA design allows two such comparisons (AB and BA). Although the second comparison is between an intervention condition followed rather than preceded by the control condition, it is still the same kind of comparison. Both AB and BA comparisons allow a conclusion about the correspondence between the differences in the two phases and the differences in responding.

Given our working assumptions, this second comparison (BA) shows that the changes in responding occurring during the intervention condition "reverse" from intervention effects to the kind of responding observed under the original control condition. This evidence provides some encouragement that the behavioral changes occurring during the intervention condition are indeed related to something about that condition. It would be premature, however, to conclude that these changes are an effect of, the result of, due to, or caused by the independent variable itself. Replicating the control condition still does not address the second risk associated with a simple AB comparison—that the changes in responding associated with the intervention condition might be influenced by related extraneous factors. In other words, showing that changes in responding occur when the intervention starts, continue while it is ongoing, and end when the intervention terminates does not establish a functional relationship between the independent variable and related changes in behavior. Although an ABA version of a reversal design reveals preliminary evidence about the reliability of the effect seen under the treatment condition, it does no better than the AB design in revealing why responding changed.

What if we go further and replicate not just the control condition but the intervention condition as well—an ABAB design? What additional information does this extra phase provide? This repetition of the treatment condition adds still another AB comparison to our conclusions. We can now consider three such comparisons between these two phases (AB, BA, and AB again). At this point, we have even more evidence that the effect associated with the intervention condition is reliable. It comes and goes consistently with the presence and absence of the intervention phase, like water when turning a faucet on and off.

Unfortunately, the ABAB reversal design still does not eliminate a key alternative explanation for our findings. This design does not provide reassurance that the independent variable is solely responsible for the associated changes in responding. Someone could still argue that these behavioral changes are due to extraneous factors initiated by or selectively associated with the

FIG. 11.3.   Notation of an ABAB reversal design.

independent variable, and we would have no evidence for a convincing rebuttal. Again, investigators may sometimes find this a difficult constraint to accept. When you have labored to plan and implement a study and have watched everything closely from day to day, it is tempting to believe that the independent variable embedded in the intervention condition is solely responsible for the observed changes in responding. Even colleagues reading a published report of the study might want to make the same assumption, especially if they are also interested in a certain outcome. Nevertheless, the fact of the matter is that neither an ABA nor an ABAB design establishes a functional relation because it does not address the role of extraneous factors selectively associated with the independent variable.

Evaluating Extraneous Variables. What would it take to address alternative explanations involving extraneous influences attached to the independent variable? First, the investigator must examine the intervention condition with a clear understanding of how the independent variable itself is defined. As we have previously discussed, it is defined in terms of those factors that will be the basis for explaining why changes in behavior occurred. With a clear specification of the independent variable, the investigator must then identify any factors other than the independent variable that differ between the control and experimental conditions. Consider again the earlier example of a study of a computer program (the independent variable) for teaching academic skills to individuals with mental retardation. We suggested that extra teacher attention associated with using the computer program condition was an extraneous factor present only during the intervention condition.

In order to determine whether the extra teacher attention was contributing to the participant's performance measured during the intervention phase, we turn to the three options outlined in chapter 10 for managing extraneous variables. The investigator can: (a) change the procedures in the intervention condition to eliminate the extra teacher attention; (b) make sure that the amount of teacher attention is the same under both control and intervention conditions; or (c) arrange additional phases to test whether teacher attention has any influence on responding. The first two options are relatively straightforward. Let us consider the third alternative of evaluating teacher attention experimentally as part of the ongoing project.

With this aim in mind, the investigator might follow the ABAB design with phases specifically designed to test the role of teacher attention. For example, following the second intervention phase, a new phase might change the intervention procedure by eliminating extra teacher attention while leaving the computer protocol variables the same. (Because this is a new phase in the

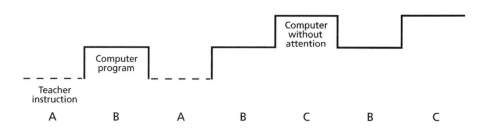

FIG. 11.4.   Notation of a reversal design that evaluates an extraneous factor.

study, it would be labeled C.) This phase could be followed by returning to the earlier intervention procedure that involved extra attention and then, in order to evaluate the reliability of the results, back to the computer program without attention. Figure 11.4 shows the resulting ABABCBC design.

This design (ABABCBC) would allow a comparison of the intervention condition with and without the extra attention. Note that, for these comparisons, the original intervention phase (B) now serves as the control condition for the revised intervention phase (C). If these comparisons show that the attention is not playing a significant role, the investigator is in a better position to argue that only the computer program was responsible for associated changes in behavior. If the comparisons indicate that the extra attention does influence responding, this would at least require conclusions that acknowledged the confounded influence of both factors. This extension of the original ABAB design manipulates extraneous factors to assess their contribution to intervention effects. This is the kind of experimental tactic that is necessary to make progress toward identifying a functional relation between the independent variable and the dependent variable. Being confident that a functional relation has been isolated often requires more than a single study as multiple extraneous factors are identified, controlled, or assessed. As a bonus, this approach often reveals how to strengthen the independent variable as well.

What if Responding Does Not Reverse? A reversal design makes it possible to see if the change in responding associated with the B condition of an ABA sequence ends when the B condition is terminated, and if responding then returns to patterns observed during the original A phase. (For ease of discussion, we continue to assume that ABA refers to a baseline–intervention–baseline sequence.) What if responding under the second baseline condition does not yield the same pattern of responding found in the original baseline phase? This would be a problem because the investigator would then have AB and BA comparisons that showed different behavioral outcomes.

This situation is depicted in Figure 11.5. Responding in the second baseline phase continues unchanged when the prior intervention ends, and fails to recover to the level originally observed in the first baseline phase. The AB comparison shows that responding is different under the two conditions, but the BA comparison shows that it is the same. This conflict weakens any

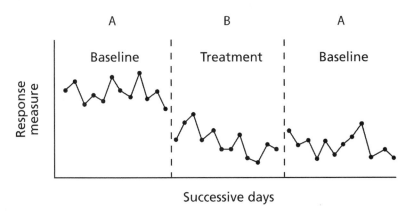

FIG. 11.5.   Hypothetical data from an ABA sequence in which responding does not return to original levels.

argument that the intervention condition is responsible for the change in responding compared to baseline.

In other words, reversal designs are informative only when responding reverts to the original baseline pattern after the intervention is withdrawn. Unfortunately, there are some credible reasons why baseline responding may sometimes not be recaptured when an intervention is terminated and baseline conditions are repeated. First, it is in the fundamental nature of behavior that responding at any one point in time is likely to be influenced by recent history. Second, repeated-measures designs optimize this historical influence by giving a participant repeated exposure to one condition before introducing another, thereby increasing the likelihood that responding will continue to be influenced by the first of the two conditions when it is withdrawn. Third, designs that expose a participant to different conditions in sequence set up the possibility that this historical influence will be revealed as a sequence effect.

Investigators contemplating a reversal design should consider these factors when deciding how to arrange comparisons for a particular study. Sometimes it may be obvious that the changes induced by an intervention will have an enduring effect on responding. For instance, if an intervention trains a skill, particularly one that is supported by natural contingencies, it would be unlikely that re-establishing baseline conditions would result in the skill suddenly being lost. In other cases, it might be clear that it would be difficult to arrange the original baseline conditions a second time. For example, if an intervention changed a child's behavior in a classroom in ways that changed how other children interacted with her, it would not be feasible to reconstruct the original baseline conditions because it would require getting the other children to interact with the participant as they did before the intervention.

When responding under a replicated baseline does not reverse to original patterns (as in Fig. 11.5), it is often tempting to argue that the intervention was responsible for the changes in responding but that those effects were simply durable and did not dissipate when baseline conditions were reinstituted. This position involves accepting the AB comparison as legitimate but treating the BA comparison as invalid. Although this argument could be true, it both reduces the experiment to an AB design and ignores conflicting evidence. Furthermore, another explanation may also be viable. It may be that extraneous factors, not the intervention, caused responding to change in the first place. If this were true, terminating the intervention might not result in those changes being lost. In other words, the evidence supports this alternative explanation.

This all means that an investigator is in a weak position when a reversal to a prior condition fails to generate a reasonable approximation of the prior pattern of responding. It is not proper to discount the BA comparison and accept the AB comparison as an adequate basis for concluding that the intervention was responsible for changes in responding. Instead, this situation unavoidably calls the impact of the intervention into question. The only recourse is to arrange other comparisons that will clarify the role of the intervention condition.

Multi-Element Designs

Definition. A **multi-element design** is a variation of a reversal design that exposes a participant first to one condition and then to another in some form of repeated alternation (Sidman, 1960). Each contact with each condition is typically brief, often a single session. The two (or more) conditions are the "elements" in a multi-element design. This type of design is also called an *alternating-treatments design*.

> **Multi-element design.** A variation of a reversal design that exposes a participant first to one condition and then to another in some form of repeated alternation. Also called an *alternating-treatments design*.

Multi-element designs are generally used to show a high degree of control over responding by repeatedly switching between two conditions. As always, it is important that one condition be a control condition for the other, its matched intervention condition. If this is the case, showing that responding abruptly changes in some way as soon as the conditions change can be an impressive demonstration of the reliability of an effect associated with the treatment condition. Of course, as with any design that only allows comparisons between a single pair of control and experimental conditions, the data cannot provide convincing evidence about exactly why behavior changes. As we have seen, this kind of information usually requires pursuing the role of extraneous factors that might be embedded in the treatment condition.

There are many ways of implementing a multi-element design. For example, a participant might alternate between one condition on one day and the other condition the next day. The conditions could also be alternated during each day, with one condition in a morning session and the other one in an afternoon session. Sometimes, the alternation involves repeatedly switching back and forth between conditions during each session. (As described by Sidman, 1960, this is similar to a multiple schedule of reinforcement, which was the origin of this approach to demonstrating stimulus control.) Furthermore, there may be three or more different conditions involved, and the rotation among them may not always be a simple alternation. Whatever these details, the repeated alternations should eventually accumulate a number of data points for each of the compared conditions.

Risks. If an investigator is unsure about the effects that will be observed when switching from a control condition to an intervention condition and back again, the multi-element design can be a risky choice. The rapid alternation feature of the multi-element design makes it especially important to know how responding changes when the treatment condition begins and how it continues to change with accumulating experience as treatment sessions are repeated for a number of successive sessions. As our discussion of steady states in chapter 9 pointed out, it is often the case that responding changes gradually as the features of the intervention condition begin to show their effect across repeated sessions. It is not unusual for responding to take a number of sessions over some time to reveal the full effects of the intervention. Furthermore, sometimes an initial transition to a different level of responding is only temporary, and responding eventually returns to baseline levels. As chapter 9 noted, distinguishing between transition states and transitory states requires extending a phase long enough to see if the changes initially observed are durable (see Fig. 9.9).

In other words, a multi-element design requires an investigator to be confident about two things: (a) that the transition in responding between control and treatment conditions will be immediate (occur in the first session); and (b) that the level of responding observed in a brief exposure to each condition is typical of the level found with uninterrupted exposure over a series of sessions. Together, these requirements mean that the switch between the two conditions must not create a sequence effect. If either of these requirements is not true, the multi-element design might provide a misleading picture of the differences in responding between the two conditions.

For example, although responding might be consistently higher in intervention sessions than in control sessions across repeated alternations, the increase could misrepresent the effects that might otherwise be expected if participants had contact with the intervention condition for an uninterrupted series of sessions. As illustrated by Fig. 11.6, repeated exposure to the intervention condition without intervening baseline sessions might show different effects. It might be that the increase in responding observed under the alternating conditions phase understates the effects of the intervention (data set *a*). On the other hand, repeated intervention sessions could mislead by showing an effect that actually wanes over time (data set *b*).

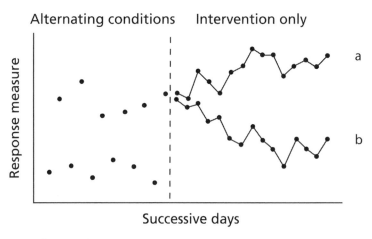

FIG. 11.6.   Data showing how multi-element design alternations can be misleading.

These risks can be minimized by obtaining stable responding under the control and intervention conditions being compared. Although this step could be taken after a period of rapidly alternating conditions, it makes more sense to do this prior to implementing a rapid alternation arrangement. If the steady-state effort showed a gradual change in responding when the treatment condition is implemented, this suggests that the multi-element approach would not be useful. Of course, if the steady-state effort showed that the initial change in responding was only temporary, the rapid alternation arrangement also would show a misleading picture.

Parametric and Changing Criterion Designs

Parametric and **changing criterion designs** are single baseline designs that combine AB and reversal sequences to identify the effects of changing a specific feature of an intervention. These features are typically defined very narrowly as a single parameter of a procedure or as a particular criterion for the performance of participants. For example, a parametric design might increase the dosage of a drug in a series of steps from one phase to another in order to see if changes in this parameter influence responding. A changing criterion

> **Changing criterion design.** A within-subject, single baseline design using AB and reversal sequences to identify effects of manipulating performance criteria.
>
> **Parametric design.** A within-subject, single baseline design using AB and reversal sequences to identify effects of manipulating a specific parameter of a procedure.

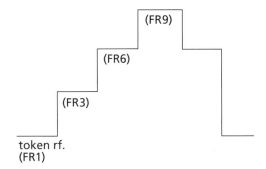

FIG. 11.7.   Notation of a parametric or changing criterion design.

design might similarly change the minimum number of arithmetic problems that must be done correctly in each phase in order to earn reinforcement.

There is no set sequence of control and intervention conditions that defines parametric and changing criterion designs. Their most typical feature is a sequence of phases in which a narrowly defined element of a more complex procedure is systematically varied from one value to another. In Figure 11.7, for example, a single parameter of a token reinforcement procedure (the value of a fixed ratio schedule of reinforcement of token delivery) is varied from FR1 to FR3, to FR10, to FR25, back to FR10, and back to FR1. The letter designation for this sequence is ABCDCA. In this case, the parameter is a criterion for student performance that will determine when tokens are earned. However, the parameter could be any variable of interest in an experiment.

Let us deconstruct this example to understand the nature of the comparisons in this type of design. The initial phase is clearly a control condition comprised of the token reinforcement contingency associated with the behavior of working problems in a classroom setting. This is a good control condition because all features of the condition continue throughout the second phase, in which only a single variable (the schedule of reinforcement for token delivery) changes (from FR1 to FR3). This is a straightforward AB design.

This same variable changes again in the third phase (from FR3 to FR10). If the FR10 phase is a new intervention condition, what is its control condition? Remember that a control condition controls for all of the factors in an intervention condition that are not the focus of interpretations. That is, all features of a control condition should continue throughout its matched intervention condition. Although the general token reinforcement procedure continues throughout all phases, the FR3 variable in the second phase ends and is replaced with the FR10 variable in the third phase. In other words, switching from the FR3 condition to the FR10 condition involves making two changes at the same time (terminating the FR3 value and starting the FR10 value). Technically, then, the FR3 condition is not a proper control condition for the FR10 phase. This same limitation applies to comparing the FR10 and FR25 conditions, as well as the two reversal conditions.

As we have already pointed out, comparisons between conditions in which one condition largely ends and is replaced by a different condition are usually risky. This is because it is not clear whether any effects are due to terminating the first condition or starting the second condition (or both). In the case of parametric and changing criterion designs, however, this kind of comparison can work because the changes are either very narrow or are specific changes in a single variable. In our example, the only thing that changes between the FR3 and FR10 conditions is the value of the token reinforcement schedule. If responding changes in predictable ways as this parameter is adjusted, there is often no question about why the change occurred. This specificity also eases the usual demand for replication to show that an effect is reproducible.

MULTIPLE BASELINE DESIGNS

Rationale

Single baseline designs are limiting in that the investigator can only arrange different conditions one at a time in sequence. This is because AB, reversal, multi-element, and parametric or changing criterion designs all use, at minimum, only a single participant, a single target behavior, and a single setting—in other words, a single "baseline." As we have noted, comparisons between control and experimental conditions are therefore made using the same participant, which means that the unique characteristics of the individual are more or less constant across conditions. Although multiple participants are often used in any single study as (discussed in chapter 10), each participant is treated separately as if he or she were the only individual in the study. In other words, additional participants allow more comparisons of the same kind.

Multiple baseline designs involve the same comparisons between control and experimental conditions as do single baseline designs, but additional baselines add some flexibility. This flexibility lies in allowing comparisons not only within one baseline but between two or more baselines.

Figure 11.8 illustrates this difference. The notation shows two baselines. In this case, we have simply designated them as 1 and 2, omitting the usual information about participants, target behaviors, and settings. The first baseline indicates that a control condition (A) is followed by a treatment condition (B). This allows a single comparison, here indicated by curved arrow number 1 pointing to the two phases being compared. This is a simple AB design, which, as we have seen, provides interesting but limited information about the effects of the B condition.

The second baseline sets up the same kind of comparison, putting aside the fact that the switch from control to treatment conditions occurs somewhat later than for the first baseline. The inclusion of the second baseline therefore adds a second AB comparison, indicated by curved arrow number 2. This replication with a second baseline is therefore twice as useful as a single AB design. So far, it would not matter if these two control–intervention sequences were coordinated in any way. One sequence could have been completed

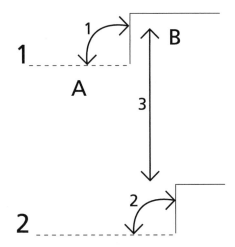

FIG. 11.8. Notation of multiple baseline comparisons.

before the other was even started, and the same two comparisons would still be available.

Coordinating the two AB arrangements as shown in the notation, however, provides a third comparison. By delaying or temporally staggering the introduction of the B condition in the second baseline relative to its introduction in the first baseline, the investigator creates an opportunity to compare responding under the control condition in the second baseline with responding under the treatment condition in the first baseline. Arrow number 3 connecting these two phases indicates this third AB comparison. Although this third comparison is between a control condition from one baseline and a treatment condition from a different baseline, it is still a straightforward AB comparison. One advantage of a multiple baseline design, then, is that two baselines involving simple AB sequences can be used to create a third AB comparison. Just by coordinating the two AB baselines in a temporally staggered arrangement, a third comparison becomes available without the trouble of setting up a third baseline.[1]

This bonus provides a further benefit because the extra comparison helps to make up for the inherent weakness of an AB design. Recall that although an AB design can provide useful information by showing that responding changes when conditions change, it does not tell us whether that relationship is reliable. Adding a reversal phase back to the original A condition begins to answer this question by providing an opportunity to see if the treatment effect ends and

---

[1] If the timing of the intervention condition in the second baseline is not staggered with reference to its introduction in the first baseline but occurs at the same time, this third comparison is not available. Without staggering, this arrangement would not be considered a multiple baseline design but merely two AB designs.

responding again looks like it did before the intervention started. Adding a reversal phase to an AB design is obviously a good idea in principle, but practical constraints sometimes get in the way. For example, we have already pointed out that sometimes a particular kind of intervention condition is likely to produce changes in responding that will continue when the condition ends and baseline responding will not be recovered. Furthermore, in applied research, as well as many clinical applications, it may be inadvisable, if not unethical, to terminate a treatment condition and therefore lose its beneficial effects.

A multiple baseline design can partially make up for not adding a reversal phase to a simple AB design because it offers not only a second baseline (and second AB comparison) but a third AB comparison. Although none of these comparisons show what would happen if the intervention condition were terminated, the fact that a single AB comparison is joined by two more can provide some reassurance that the change in responding is reliable.

Variations

A **multiple baseline design** uses two or more baselines in a coordinated way to allow control–treatment comparisons both within and across baselines. In this context, a baseline refers to a single participant, the target behavior being measured, and the setting in which it is measured. Most multiple baseline designs involve baselines that vary in one of these three ways. In each of these three variations, one component differs across the baselines and the other two are the same.

> **Multiple baseline design.** A within-subject design that uses two or more baselines in a coordinated way to allow control–treatment comparisons both within and across baselines.

First, each baseline in one study might involve a different participant. Figure 11.9 shows an example of this variation. In this case, there are not two but three participants. However, the study targets the same behavior for each child (interacting with peers) in the same setting (a preschool classroom). Each child first experiences a control condition and then an intervention condition. Measurement of the target behavior begins at the same time for all three children, but when the intervention starts for Jose, the other two children continue in the control phase. Liz starts the intervention phase somewhat later than Jose, and Chrissy starts it some time after Liz does. In other words, the introduction of the intervention phase is staggered in time across the three participants.

How many AB comparisons does this three-baseline, staggered arrangement create? There is one AB comparison for each baseline (numbered 1, 2, and 3), but there are also three more AB comparisons across the three baselines (numbered 4, 5, and 6). What if the three participants were exposed

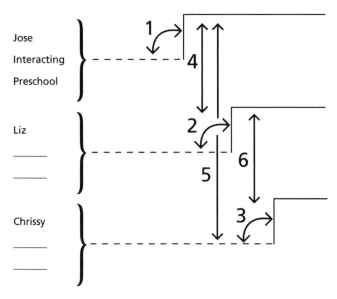

FIG. 11.9. Notation of a multiple baseline design across participants.

to the same AB sequence independently (e.g., Jose completing his participation in the project before Liz started hers, and Chrissy not starting until
Liz is finished)? This approach would create three separate AB designs and
only the three associated AB comparisons. By using the three participants
in a coordinated way, however, three additional AB comparisons become
available.

A second variation involves multiple baselines across target behaviors.
Figure 11.10 illustrates this approach. We can see that the study measures
two different behaviors (cursing and throwing things) for a single participant
(Ken) in a single setting (a group home). Both behaviors are initially measured

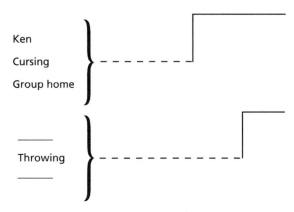

FIG. 11.10. Notation of a multiple baseline design across target behaviors.

under a control condition, but the treatment procedure is applied to cursing some time before it is applied to the behavior of throwing things. As we saw in Figure 11.8, this use of multiple baselines allows three AB comparisons, including one between throwing things under the control condition and cursing under the treatment condition.

A third variation involves multiple baselines across settings. Figure 11.11 shows a design in which Callie's tantrum behavior is measured both at home and at school. The notation shows the coordinated use of these two baselines in an ABA sequence of conditions in which both the onset and offset of the intervention phase are staggered in time with reference to each setting. Can you identify the six comparisons between control and intervention conditions built into this design?

BOX 11.1

Risks of Between-Subject Comparisons

Multiple baseline designs across participants raise a special issue. Comparing the performance of one individual in a control condition with that of a different individual in a treatment condition is not a within-subject comparison. This means that the performance of the two individuals might differ not just because they are experiencing different conditions but because they bring unique personal characteristics. The inherent risk of this kind of between-subject comparison is eased by the fact that the behavior of each individual is independently measured under otherwise similar conditions for repeated sessions. Furthermore, this comparison usually involves only two or three individuals.

Between-group designs also involve comparisons across individuals, but in a far more problematic manner. Each participant is typically assigned to only one condition—either control or experimental. The behavior of each participant is exposed to the assigned condition for the necessary period of time and then his or her behavior is measured in a single post-test. Of course, each individual is given the same amount of exposure to the assigned condition because no evidence is collected that would suggest that some individuals need more or less exposure to develop a complete reaction. This design approach further assigns a relatively large number of participants to each condition and analyzes the data collectively across all participants in each group. In other words, the comparison is between a control group and an experimental group.

The problems associated with this between-group approach lie in what the investigator is not able to learn. Because there is no measurement of each participant's behavior repeatedly during exposure to the assigned condition, there is no way to use variability to identify extraneous factors that might be operating for any one individual or even for the group. It will also not be possible to attend to different patterns of performance among either group of participants because of this lack of repeated measures. Although this approach will tell us something about the difference between group means, it is the individuals, not groups, that were behaving. In other words, it will not be possible to learn how the experimental condition affected behavior.

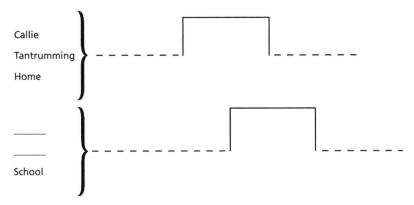

FIG. 11.11.   Notation of a multiple baseline design across settings.

Reasoning

We have already discussed the reasoning associated with comparisons between control and intervention conditions set up by single baseline designs. Each baseline in a multiple baseline design is made up of these same AB and reversal arrangements, and these comparisons allow the same conclusions that would follow if each baseline were a separate study. (Remember, throughout this chapter we are assuming sound measurement procedures and strong and consistent changes in responding.)

What multiple baseline designs add are comparisons of responding between two different baselines, typically a control condition in one baseline and an intervention condition in another baseline. Drawing conclusions from these cross-baseline comparisons raises some special issues. In order to understand these issues, consider the design in Figure 11.12 and the two different sets of results labeled A and B. The pair of graphs labeled A show that responding in the second baseline did not change until the intervention started for that baseline. However, the two graphs labeled B indicate that responding in the first phase of the second baseline changed when the intervention started in the first baseline. That is, responding in the second baseline changed even though the control condition was still operating and there was no change in conditions. Furthermore, this change occurred about when the intervention started in the first baseline.

For these results shown in the pair of B graphs, how might we explain why responding changed when it did in the second baseline? Although the change in responding occurred when the intervention started in the first baseline, the intervention procedures themselves could not be responsible because they were not operating for the second baseline. One possibility is that responding in the two baselines is dependent in some way. That is, for some unknown reason it might be that when responding in one baseline changes, responding also changes in the other baseline. For example, if

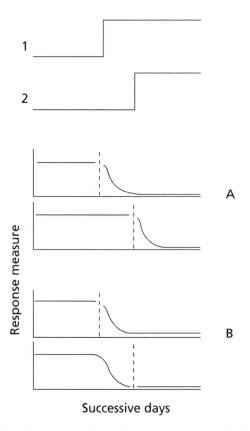

FIG. 11.12. Notation of a simple multiple baseline design (top) and stylized data illustrating different outcomes associated with a staggered introduction of the intervention condition.

the two baselines involved two different target behaviors for the same participant (getting out of seat and talking during study period), it might not be surprising that one behavior might change when the other did. Multiple baseline designs using the same participant across response classes or settings always involve this risk.

A second explanation might be that extraneous factors associated with the intervention in the first baseline influenced responding in the second baseline. Although the intervention itself could not be responsible, it could be that some related though extraneous factor contacted responding in the second baseline. This could explain why responding changed when it did. As an illustration, imagine that the baselines involve two children in the same classroom, even though they are in different phases at the same time. Factors present in the environment could be responsible for concurrent changes in the behavior of both children, independently of any effect of the treatment variable. Such an extraneous variable could be unrelated to or even associated with the treatment condition. In either case, it could influence the behavior of the child who is still in the control condition.

If an extraneous variable was responsible for the otherwise premature change in responding in the second baseline, we would have to wonder if that same extraneous factor might also explain the change in responding in the first baseline that was observed when the intervention started. In other words, we now have evidence consistent with the possibility that the intervention itself in the first baseline might have been only partly responsible for the associated change in responding, if it had any effect at all.

If the multiple baseline design represented in the pair of B graphs constitutes the entire experiment, we cannot evaluate these two alternative explanations. In this circumstance, we would have to conclude that the data do not support a conclusion that the intervention condition is selectively associated with an increase in responding. Instead, we should acknowledge that there is evidence that extraneous factors seem to be involved. In contrast, if the pair of A graphs were the outcome, we would be able to conclude that all three comparisons showed that the intervention was selectively related to an increase in responding. Of course, because these are only AB comparisons we would still not have the evidence to argue that the independent variable was solely responsible for this increase. This statement about a functional relation would require further manipulations investigating the role of extraneous factors that might be associated with the independent variable.

Requirements

Merely replicating an AB or even a reversal design in a temporally staggered fashion across multiple participants, target behaviors, or settings does not necessarily provide legitimate opportunities to make comparisons across baselines. So what does it take to turn multiple baselines into a multiple baseline design? There are five requirements that must be met.

First, each baseline must be independent. That is, responding in one baseline must not change just because responding in the other baseline does. In Figure 11.10, for example, if Ken's cursing behavior covaried with his throwing behavior for reasons having nothing to do with the control or treatment conditions, throwing would change when the intervention began for cursing, even though throwing had not yet contacted the intervention procedure. This would be a confusing outcome and would limit the value of making comparisons across baselines.

Second, it is important to eventually demonstrate the sensitivity of the second (or additional) baseline(s) to the intervention and associated variables. As we described above, our conclusions about the effects of the intervention condition partly depend on responding not changing in the control condition of each baseline until the intervention condition starts. When conclusions are based on the fact that responding did not change, it is necessary to show that it

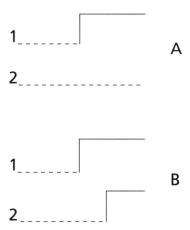

FIG. 11.13.   Notation of a design that does not test the sensitivity of a baseline (Panel A) and a design that assesses sensitivity by introducing the intervention in both baselines (Panel B).

did not fail to change merely because it was insensitive to the variables under investigation. Panel A in Figure 11.13 shows a design that would create this problem. This possibility can be tested by introducing the intervention condition for the second baseline at a later point, as shown in Panel B. This is typically done in multiple baseline designs, in part because it has the benefit of creating another AB comparison.

Third, when the intervention is ongoing in one baseline, the control condition must be ongoing in the other baseline(s) used for comparison. This might be obvious, given that the point of staggering the introduction of an intervention across two baselines is to compare responding under the intervention phase in one baseline with responding under the control condition in the other baseline. Panel A in Figure 11.14 shows this arrangement, which allows the necessary comparisons. Panel B shows the same two ABA sequences, except that the second baseline is not operating concurrently with the first. This lack of overlap means that it is not possible to see if responding changes under a control condition of one baseline when the intervention phase starts in the other baseline.

Fourth, not only must there be temporal overlap between control and intervention conditions in different baselines, but this overlap must be long enough to allow possible effects of extraneous variables associated with the intervention to emerge in the control phase. For example, if an AB sequence across each of two concurrent baselines was staggered by only 1 day, it would be fairly unlikely that any extraneous influences associated with initiating the intervention condition in one baseline would be evident by an immediate change in responding in the other baseline on that first day. It is simply in the nature of operant behavior that environmentally induced changes often take some time to develop, so a lag of only a day or two is not a fair test.

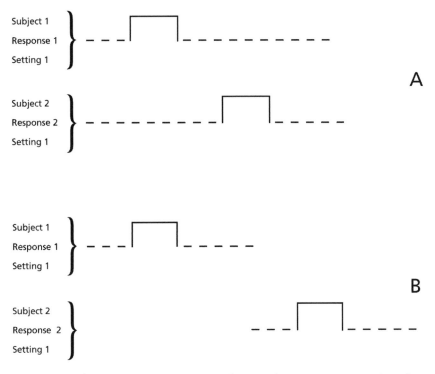

FIG. 11.14. Notation of comparisons showing the concurrent operation of control and experimental conditions in Panel A but not in Panel B.

The fifth requirement concerns those extraneous factors that might be associated with, or at least present during, the intervention condition and are not shared with the control condition. (Recall the example of the extra teacher attention that might be associated with a computer program for teaching academic skills to individuals with mental retardation.) In order to make valid comparisons between control and intervention conditions across baselines, these extraneous factors associated with the intervention condition must have the opportunity of influencing responding under the control condition in the second baseline. Without this possibility, there is no reason to worry about behavioral changes in the second baseline when the intervention is introduced in the first.

For instance, if different participants are used in the two baselines but the participant in the second baseline cannot possibly come into contact with these extraneous influences, then this does not allow a test of their possible contribution. So, if daily intervention sessions for one participant are conducted at one school and control sessions are conducted for the other participant at a different school, the second participant would presumably have no contact with any extraneous influences that might be associated with the intervention. As a result, it would hardly be surprising if there was no change in

TABLE 11.1
Requirements for comparing responding across multiple baselines

---

- Each baseline must be independent of the others
- The sensitivity of each baseline to the intervention must eventually be demonstrated
- When the intervention is ongoing in one baseline, the control condition must be ongoing in other baselines
- There must be sufficient temporal overlap between intervention and control conditions in different baselines to allow extraneous effects to develop
- Extraneous variables associated with the intervention condition must have the opportunity of influencing responding under the control condition

---

the performance of the second participant when the intervention started for the first participant.

This fifth requirement can be difficult to grasp. Remember that the reason for staggering the introduction of the intervention across a second baseline is to see if responding changes in the second baseline when, *but only when*, the intervention is later initiated. This is a meaningful question only if there is some reason why responding might substantially change prior to that point. As we have noted, there are only two reasons for such a "premature" behavioral change. First, it could be that responding in one baseline is tied to responding in the other for some reason (the first requirement addresses this issue). Second, it could be that responding in the second baseline is influenced by extraneous factors associated with the intervention condition in the first baseline. This fifth requirement specifies that these extraneous factors must, in some way, have an opportunity to have an effect.[2]

Collectively, these five requirements make comparisons of responding between an intervention condition in one baseline and a control condition in another baseline meaningful. If these requirements are not met, such comparisons may be misleading. Consider that when the intervention is initiated in one baseline while the control condition is operating in another baseline there are two possible outcomes that will influence the investigator's conclusions. Responding will either change in the control condition baseline at that point, or it will not. As we have described, conclusions about either of these outcomes need to focus on the role of extraneous factors tied to the intervention condition. These requirements help to make these conclusions valid.

---

[2] Watson and Workman (1981) propose a nonconcurrent version of multiple baseline designs in which this fifth requirement is explicitly not met. They argue that randomly assigning participants to each of several predetermined baseline lengths can allow experimenters to rule out the contribution of extraneous events. However, this position fails to account for extraneous factors associated with treatment conditions, which is a particularly likely source. We view nonconcurrent multiple baseline designs as failing this fifth requirement.

BOX 11.2

Experimentum Crucis

There is a longstanding tendency in psychology to try to learn too much from a single experiment, regardless of its complexity. An experiment offered as a grand and complete answer to a question is called an *experimentum crucis* or crucial experiment. Although it is tempting to imagine that one's study is grand and complete in some way, this almost always overstates its value—and a colleague will soon point this out, perhaps with some enthusiasm.

Perhaps we do not adequately appreciate that science works by taking very small steps. It is through the accumulation of little bits of very certain knowledge that science progresses. Science has been likened to creating a mosaic, with each tiny chip taking years to learn. The natural sciences have built a clear record of this conservative style of experimentation. Perhaps the relative absence of such a track record in the social and behavioral sciences prevents us from appreciating just how modest each experiment really is. This chapter shows that it takes much more than a few comparisons between control and experimental conditions to answer the deceptively simple question of whether an independent variable is responsible for changes in a target behavior.

TURNING DESIGNS INTO EXPERIMENTS

Building an Experimental Design

We have already pointed out that comparisons between responding under control and intervention conditions are fundamentally the same for all types of with-subject designs. In fact, the distinctions among AB, reversal, multi-element, parametric or changing criterion, and multi-baseline designs are more useful for training students than for guiding decisions about experimental design.

We also made it clear that in any single study researchers often combine or intermingle different types of "designs" as needed. For many studies, it would actually be difficult to describe the experimental design used as a single type. The AB design is obviously a component of all other types, for example. Reversal arrangements are often part of more complex designs. Although multiple baseline designs do not require reversal arrangements, an AB sequence in one or more of the baselines is often followed by a reversal to the original A condition.

What this means is that choosing a particular type of design is often only the first step in developing the experimental comparisons that will be used throughout all stages of a study. In fact, one of the strengths of this approach to arranging experimental comparisons is that it is not necessary to commit to a specific design before the study starts that cannot later be modified if circumstances warrant. Although investigators should certainly begin with specific experimental objectives and a clear plan for attaining them, there are often good reasons for modifying both the objectives of the study and the nature of the required comparisons as the study progresses.

Most often, the reason for adjusting the experimental plan is to accommodate emerging data. Suppose that an investigator plans to start a study with an ABAB sequence of conditions to assess the impact of an intervention procedure. This design presupposes that the intervention will have a clear effect and that the effect will come and go with reversal phases, showing it also to be reliable. What if the data from the first B phase fail to reveal a clear effect? The investigator may then choose to modify the intervention condition in some way to make it more powerful. This change would establish a new condition (C), which might then be evaluated with the same reversal sequence. The resulting design would then involve an ABCACA sequence of conditions.

Depending on the investigator's interests, this study could continue to evolve. Having determined that the modified procedure has useful effects on responding, the investigator might wish to determine whether a particular feature of the procedure is playing an important role. This question might be pursued by eliminating that feature and seeing if the procedure still produces the same effects. The revised procedure would be designated the D condition, and the C condition might serve as a good control condition for this comparison. The sequence of comparisons would now be described as ABCACACD. A further reversal back to C and then D phases would help to assess the reliability of the change induced by the D condition.

Figure 11.15 shows the notation for the experimental design resulting from these decisions. This example, perhaps still incomplete, shows how this within-subject approach to creating experimental designs provides researchers with the flexibility to modify original plans as circumstances require. As long as researchers understand the requirements for sound experimental comparisons, this approach encourages powerful and efficient designs that can lead to clear and reliable results with good generality.

Evaluating Alternative Explanations

Another reason for modifying original experimental plans is to evaluate any alternative explanations for the results. In order to appreciate alternative explanations, it helps to put yourself in the position of others in your field. It is perfectly appropriate for them to raise questions about your procedures and the results. After all, one of the key features of science is that it is a public

FIG. 11.15. Notation of an experimental design resulting from evolving circumstances.

exercise. When investigators publish their findings, colleagues can independently evaluate the study, perhaps going so far as to replicate some of its features in their own research or to attempt to use its findings as practitioners. This kind of replication is routine in science. It helps to uncover limitations of published findings, which over time improves the veracity of the scientific literature.

This process starts when an investigator submits a research report for publication in a scientific journal. The editor handling the manuscript asks three or four researchers who are familiar with the topic to review the paper. In addition to evaluating the study's methods and results, these reviewers consider how the results might be explained by factors other than those proposed by the investigator. If an alternative explanation seems sufficiently credible, and is not sufficiently resolved, the paper may not be accepted for publication.

In anticipation of this assessment, researchers learn to design their experiments in ways that avoid, or at least minimize, extraneous factors that could explain their results. When an alternative explanation remains viable, it may be worthwhile to evaluate its contribution to the results. This can be done by designing the study to include phases that test whether the extraneous factor in question is having any influence.

Consider a situation in which a medical researcher is studying the effects of a new drug. The literature suggests that if patients take the drug as prescribed, certain changes will occur in their medical condition. The drug has unpleasant side effects, however, and the researcher is worried whether participants will take the pills as required. If the participants do not follow the protocol, it could be argued that the data describing their medical condition under the drug phase represent the effects of unknown dosages taken on an unknown schedule.

This extraneous factor could be eliminated by having participants take the pills in the presence of research staff, but the investigator might be concerned that requiring participants to come to the hospital four times a day to take a pill would make it difficult to recruit participants. Instead, the investigator might decide to take advantage of the fact that certain byproducts of the drug can be measured in the patient's urine for limited periods. Requiring participants to come by the hospital once each week to provide a urine sample will allow a test of whether compliance with the drug protocol could be a factor in interpreting the effects of the drug on the medical condition.

If the data describing the drug byproducts in urine change appropriately when the drug regimen starts and remain stable throughout the drug phase, the investigator can argue that noncompliance with the protocol is not a credible alternative explanation for the medical data concerning the participant's condition, leaving the drug as the most likely explanation.

How Many Comparisons are Enough?

As an experiment progresses and comparison phases accumulate, it is fair to ask how many comparisons are needed. In general, the answer is always,

---

BOX 11.3

Do Experimental Designs Have to be Perfect?

It may seem that chapters 10 and 11 lay out some pretty tough standards for good experimental designs. Among other guidelines, for instance, these standards emphasize matching each experimental condition with a control condition that is the same except for the independent variable. They also worry incessantly about extraneous variables and all the ways in which they can confound and mislead. The risk of some shortfall between the ideals described here and the reality of actual research projects, especially in applied settings, makes it reasonable to ask just how close to these standards researchers have to come in order to conduct credible studies.

In answering this question, keep in mind that in writing a textbook we must not compromise when describing the proper relationship between control and experimental conditions or the most effective way to handle extraneous variables. In fact, it is not necessarily difficult to achieve these ideals, and even when there are practical limitations good approximations are usually possible. Understanding what it takes to create sound experimental comparisons helps investigators to appreciate the choices involved, as well as the consequences for experimental conclusions when some standard cannot be met.

Fortunately, if a comparison is not based on perfectly matched control and experimental conditions, it does not mean that conclusions about treatment effects will necessarily be invalid. However, the extent and nature of the mismatch might mean that the investigator and others need to qualify their conclusions. Furthermore, just because extraneous factors are unavoidable and can ruin a study does not mean that failing to chase every one down will significantly depreciate the value of a project. Many extraneous variables have no ill effects, and powerful treatment effects can help to justify unambiguous conclusions.

In other words, experimental designs certainly need not be perfect in order to lead to sound conclusions. On the other hand, weak designs can certainly result in misleading and even incorrect interpretations. Furthermore, hoping that large treatment effects will rescue a weak design can lead to disappointment when strong effects fail to materialize. As chapter 13 explains, there is no algorithm for weighing up these and other methodological strengths and weaknesses in deciding what conclusions are legitimate. This suggests that in designing an experiment it is wise for researchers to consider the highest standards, to compromise only when necessary, and then be willing to live with the interpretive consequences.

"As many as it takes to be reasonably confident about what the data have to say." No researcher wants to publish findings that later turn out to be incorrect. The challenge is balancing the limitations of research resources with the ideal of continuing to refine results. An investigator might like to extend a study for an additional month or two, but limitations in funding or access to a research setting or participants may make this a luxury, if not impossible.

The above rule is pretty vague, so we need to be more specific about the decisions that investigators face. There are three tactics that are especially important. First, it is important to understand the general nature of control-intervention comparisons and to keep interpretive statements within those limits. This is easier said than done. Investigators often find it difficult to be conservative about the conclusions that their procedures and data allow.

For example, we have already pointed out that a simple AB comparison only shows that responding changed when conditions changed. This comparison does not justify concluding that the change in conditions "caused" responding to change, no matter how likely it might be that this was the case. Although adding a reversal phase (making it an ABA design) generates a second comparison between control and treatment conditions, this constraint still applies. The fact that responding changed systematically as the treatment condition started and stopped only shows that the relationship seems to be reliable. A reversal design does not justify a conclusion that the independent variable, which is only part of what is going on in the treatment condition, was solely responsible for the changes in responding. As we have seen, concluding that a functional relationship has been established between the independent and dependent variables requires manipulations that show that extraneous factors are not contributing to this relationship.

Second, it is important to consider the number of needed comparisons for each different independent variable condition, rather than for the study as a whole. That is, if a study has two different intervention conditions, the assessment of whether there are enough control-intervention comparisons should be made separately for each of the two independent variables. Consider the multiple baseline design notated in Figure 11.16. We will assume that the C condition involves a variation in some feature of the B condition, so there are two experimental conditions in this study. The lower case letters indicate control-intervention comparisons for each of the two intervention conditions. You can see that there are four comparisons (labeled *b*) between the original baseline (control) condition and the B condition. The B condition then serves as a control for the C condition, but there are only two B–C comparisons (labeled *c*). This means that there is not as strong a basis for conclusions about the effects of the C condition as for the B condition. There is a third C comparison,

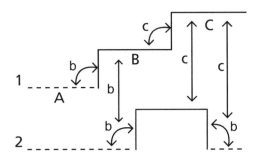

FIG. 11.16. Notation of an experimental design involving two interventions.

however, but with the original baseline, not the B condition, as a control. Assuming that this is a valid control condition, this comparison provides different information about the C condition.

Third, however many comparisons are available for each different independent variable, it is important to consider any differences in the nature of the comparisons. As we pointed out in the above example, there are two types of comparisons involving the C condition. One involves the B condition as a control and the other uses the A condition as a control. These different control conditions require different interpretations about any changes in responding under the C condition. Given that the C condition involves only a variation of the B condition, the B–C comparisons allow statements about the role of the variable that was changed in the C condition. However, the A–C comparison allows a statement about differences in responding when the C condition is operating versus when it is absent. (Note that there is only one of these comparisons, which therefore provides no information about the reliability of any effect.) This means that although there are three comparisons involving the C condition, they reveal two different kinds of information about the intervention.

The approach to experimental design described in chapters 10 and 11 is powerful, efficient, flexible, and elegant. It is consistent with the characteristics of behavior as a biological phenomenon, encourages a high level of experimental control, and promotes identification of the role of variables that enhance the generality of findings. Perhaps, most importantly, it has proven highly effective over many decades in identifying lawful behavior–environment relationships and a powerful technology.

CHAPTER SUMMARY

1. An AB design is the core of all within-subject comparisons. In these designs, the investigator compares data from a sequence of phases representing matched control (often labeled "A") and experimental (e.g., "B") conditions to determine if there was a difference in responding between the two conditions. Although beneficial, this design fails to inform the investigator if the change in responding is a reliable outcome of switching between these two conditions, and it does not inform us if the change in responding was due to the independent variable.

2. A reversal design involves a pair of control and experimental conditions in which one or both conditions repeat at least once. Unlike an AB design, repeating the original control condition adds the advantage of creating a second comparison between control and intervention conditions.

3. While a reversal design may provide encouragement that the behavioral changes occurring during the intervention condition are indeed related to something about that condition, it does not establish a functional relationship between the independent variable and related changes in behavior.

4. The reversal design is informative only when responding reverts to the original baseline pattern after the intervention is withdrawn. If a behavior is not likely to revert back to original baseline responding (e.g., due to sequence effects), a reversal design may not be the most effective way to assess the effects of the independent variable. Additionally, the investigator must consider whether it would be ethically appropriate to remove an intervention if it has been shown to be effective in treating a potentially life-threatening behavior (e.g., pica, SIB).

5. A multi-element design is a variation of a reversal design that exposes a participant to one condition and then another in some form of repeated alternation. These designs are generally used to show a high degree of control over responding by switching between two or more conditions. Of course, as with any design that only allows comparisons between a single pair of control and experimental conditions, the data cannot provide convincing evidence about exactly why behavior changes.

6. In deciding whether or not to use a multi-element design, the researcher must be confident about two things: (a) the transition in responding between control and intervention conditions will be immediate; and (b) the level of responding observed in a brief exposure to each condition is typical of the level found with uninterrupted exposure over a series of sessions.

7. Parametric and changing criterion designs are single baseline designs that combine AB and reversal sequences to identify the effects of changing a specific feature of an intervention. Their most typical feature is a sequence of phases in which a narrowly defined element of a more complex procedure is systematically varied from one value to another.

8. Single baseline designs are limiting in that the investigator can only arrange different conditions one at a time in sequence. Multiple baseline designs (across subjects, settings, or behaviors) involve the same comparisons between control and experimental conditions as do single baseline designs, but by adding additional baselines it allows the investigator to compare not only within one baseline but between two or more baselines.

9. By delaying or temporally staggering the introduction of the intervention condition in the second baseline, the investigator creates an opportunity to compare responding under the control condition in the second baseline with responding under the treatment condition in the first baseline.

10. Merely replicating an AB or a reversal design in a temporally staggered fashion across multiple participants, target behaviors, or settings does not necessarily provide legitimate opportunities to make comparisons across baselines. Multiple baseline designs must meet five requirements.

11. The first requirement in multiple baseline designs is that each baseline must be independent. That is, responding in one baseline must not change just because responding in the other baseline does. Second, it is important to demonstrate the sensitivity of the additional baseline(s) to the intervention. Any time you base conclusions on the fact that responding did not

change, you must show that behavior did not fail to change simply because it was insensitive to the variables under investigation.

12. The third requirement is that when the intervention is ongoing in one baseline, the control condition must be ongoing in the other baseline(s) used for comparison. Fourth, this overlap must be long enough to allow possible effects of extraneous variables associated with the intervention to emerge in the control phase. Finally, extraneous factors associated with the intervention condition must have the opportunity of influencing responding under the control condition in the second baseline.

13. Choosing a particular type of design is often only the first step in developing the experimental comparisons that will be used throughout all stages of a study. One of the strengths of this approach is that it is not necessary to commit to a specific design before the study starts that cannot later be modified if circumstances warrant.

TEXT STUDY GUIDE

1. Why is this approach to experimental design described as "within subject."

2. What is the rationale for within-subject comparisons?

3. Name three additional terms for within-subject designs.

4. What do "A" and "B" refer to when discussing AB designs?

5. What two things do you not know when comparing responding under a control and an experimental condition?

6. Why is an AB design a weak basis for drawing conclusions about the effects of an independent variable?

7. How is a reversal design better than an AB design?

8. What does a reversal design not tell you?

9. How is an ABAB design better than an ABA design?

10. What does an ABAB design not tell you?

11. What are three ways of evaluating the contribution of extraneous factors associated with the intervention condition?

12. Provide three reasons why responding might not reverse to earlier patterns when a condition is terminated and a prior condition is reinstated.

13. When responding does not reverse when a prior condition is reinstated, what can the researcher conclude about the effects of the intervention?

14. Describe a multi-element design.

15. What is the risk associated with a multi-element design?

16. How can this risk be minimized?

17. Distinguish between parametric and changing criterion designs.

18. How are multiple baseline designs fundamentally similar to single baseline designs?

19. What is the benefit of staggering the introduction of the intervention condition in the second baseline relative to its introduction in the first baseline?

20. Describe three common variations in multiple baseline designs.

21. Provide two reasons why responding would change in the control phase of a second baseline at the point when the intervention condition starts in the first baseline.

22. List the five requirements for making comparisons across baselines in multiple baseline designs. Explain the rationale for each requirement.

23. What is an alternative explanation?

24. List three factors that influence designs about how many comparisons are needed in a study.

BOX STUDY GUIDE

1. Describe the problems associated with between-subject designs that assign each participant to one condition and analyze grouped data using inferential statistics.

2. What is the risk of designing experiments that try to do too much, or assuming that the results completely resolve a behavioral issue?

SUGGESTED READINGS

Johnston, J. M. (1988). Strategic and tactical limits of comparison studies. *The Behavior Analyst, 11*, 1–9.

Sidman, M. (1960). *Tactics of scientific research*. New York: Basic Books. [Chapter 11: Selection of an appropriate baseline]

Sidman, M. (1960). *Tactics of scientific research*. New York: Basic Books. [Chapter 12: Control techniques]

Sidman, M. (1960). *Tactics of scientific research*. New York: Basic Books. [Chapter 13: Control techniques (continued)]

DISCUSSION TOPICS

1. Discuss why an AB design does not provide information about what variables were responsible for any change in responding. Consider why an ABAB design involves the same limitation.

2. Select a published study in a behavioral journal that uses a single baseline design and shows a clear effect of the intervention condition. Discuss possible extraneous variables that could explain the results and different ways of addressing these alternative explanations.

3. Discuss the requirements for comparing responding under control and experimental conditions across baselines in multiple baseline designs.

EXERCISES

1. Using the design notation introduced in chapter 10, notate a single baseline design from a study published in a behavioral journal such as the *Journal of Applied Behavior Analysis*. Identify the comparisons available for each treatment condition. For conditions where there are more than one comparison, determine whether the comparisons are the same or different.

2. Select examples of multiple baseline designs from published studies and evaluate their adherence to the requirements for making comparisons across baselines.

PART FOUR

INTERPRETATION

Analyzing Behavioral Data

Artists can colour the sky red because they know it's blue. Those of us who aren't artists must colour things the way they really are or people might think we're stupid.

—Jules Feiffer

DATA ANALYSIS STRATEGIES

Data Analysis as Stimulus Control

However a target behavior is observed and recorded, once each response has been measured, the resulting data are often the only source of information available about a participant's earlier actions. A participant's responses are present only momentarily, but the data permanently preserve their key features. These data, together with other features of the study, serve as stimuli that influence the investigator's reactions to what is going on during the project, as well as later interpretations about what the study's results mean.

In other words, analyzing behavioral data is a matter of arranging the data in ways that encourage investigators to manage the project effectively along the way and then to draw conclusions that are going to hold up when others use them. From this perspective, data analysis is a matter of bringing the investigator's reactions under the control of appropriate stimuli. These stimuli partly result from different ways of manipulating the data describing each participant's behavior under each phase of the study.

Of course, there are endless ways of manipulating data, both mathematically and graphically. Viewing data analysis as a stimulus control problem means that the choice of data analysis techniques is not just a matter of whether a particular statistic or graph is correctly calculated or constructed. The more important issue is whether it encourages the researcher, and eventually others, to make good decisions and draw sound conclusions. A graph may be properly constructed or a statistic correctly calculated, but either may still prompt misleading interpretations.

For example, suppose that a researcher plots a participant's performance using a histogram or bar graph in which a single column represents the average measure of responding for all sessions in each phase. Anyone looking at this kind of graph will not be able to see how responding changed from session to session throughout each phase. Displaying the same data using a line graph showing responding for each session in each phase provides a very different picture. These two displays might well prompt somewhat different interpretations.

Figure 12.1 rearranges the panels in Figure 8.4 to show such a case. The bar graph in Panel A shows that the average performance across all sessions was higher in the experimental condition than in the control condition. Putting aside the limitations of this AB design, this interpretation might encourage the conclusion that the experimental condition was responsible for this increase. However, the line graph in Panel B reveals that this difference resulted from an upward trend in the data in the control condition that continued throughout the experimental condition. This pattern of increasing responding across both phases is troublesome because each phase supposedly represented a constant set of conditions, which should have generated stable responding under each condition. The fact that responding increased throughout both conditions suggests that some extraneous factors were operating to produce this ongoing

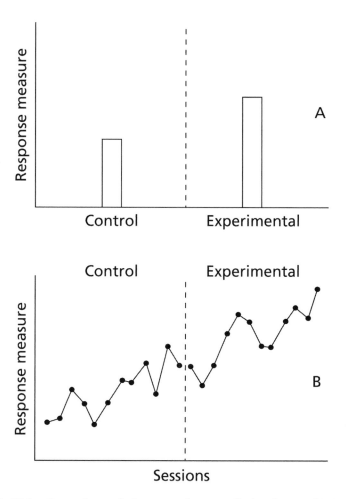

FIG. 12.1. Comparison of the same data set displayed as a histogram summarizing responding in each phase (Panel A) and as a line graph showing session-by-session responding throughout each phase (Panel B).

chance in responding. This likely possibility prevents a clear comparison between the effects of these two conditions.

In other words, although both graphs are correctly constructed, they would likely evoke different reactions from readers, even though they represent the same behavioral events. Choosing the best graph is a matter of figuring out what features of the data are most important and how to highlight those characteristics. The different pictures created by these two graphs should remind us why chapter 9, as well as other chapters, emphasized the tactic of first examining the ebb and flow of responding in each phase in order to assess the stability of responding under each set of conditions. A bar graph might be a useful way of summarizing responding across different conditions once it is clear from examining session-by-session data from each phase that there is something to be gained from this kind of summary.

Selecting Analytical Procedures

Exploring the Data. There are countless statistical and graphical ways of manipulating data, so how do researchers and practitioners choose? Although it may be clear how a quantitative or graphical construction works and what it does to the data, this is not the same as knowing what impact it will have on someone interpreting the outcome. In general, there is no way you can know exactly what any particular calculation or graph will show without trying it out.

There are some guidelines for selecting analytical procedures, however. One such guideline concerns the idea of exploration. The goal of data analysis is to discover variability in the data that helps to answer the experimental question. Each different way of looking at the data will reveal a somewhat different view of variability. In doing so, each picture will obscure other aspects of variability, as the two graphs in Figure 12.1 illustrate. The investigator needs to be aware of what each picture of variability may be hiding, even as it shows something else. The safest way to be sure about what is being missed is to look at alternative pictures of the same data. This tactic turns data analysis into an exploratory process in which the researcher looks into every promising nook and cranny.

Exploring what data have to say may sound straightforward, but preconceptions and biases can get in the way. Concerned that data analysis was too often approached as a matter of confirming a priori hypotheses instead of exploring broader possibilities in the data, Tukey (1977) described an analytical style that he called **exploratory data analysis** or **EDA**. This approach emphasizes largely graphical analytical techniques that focus on discovering order and structure in data. Over the years, other researchers have further developed this approach (Hoaglin, Mosteller, & Tukey, 1985; Velleman, & Hoaglin, 1981), which is generally consistent with the analytical style long used in the study of operant behavior, as described by Sidman (1960) and in this volume.

> **Exploratory data analysis (EDA).** An approach to data analysis that emphasizes largely graphical techniques focusing on discovering order and structure in the data. EDA may be contrasted with confirmatory data analysis or hypothesis testing.

In spite of the risk of allowing preconceptions to bias the selection of analytical procedures, investigators must approach this task with at least some idea of what the data might reveal. The challenge then becomes one of figuring out which calculations or kinds of graphs might highlight suspected features. In the case of behavioral data, looking at the ebb and flow of responding as each phase unfolds is usually a good place to start. Although session-by-session graphical displays are excellent ways of seeing this kind of information, there are many choices about how data are organized and how graphs might be constructed. Once an investigator has identified a few graphical alternatives, it may just be a matter of trying them out. Today's researchers usually store data in digital form, so the effort required to review two or three different kinds of graphs of the same data is not much more than a few keystrokes.

BOX 12.1

How Science Deals with Subjectivity

Many people think of science as a highly objective enterprise. Scientists are seen as unusually impartial in their approach to their subject matter and able to put personal and even professional biases aside in the interest of scientific discovery.

Scientists, and those who study how science really works, know better. As Boxes 1.1 and 3.3 suggest, scientists often have well-established prejudices about what they are looking for, and these biases can color their perception of what they find. Although it is true that science is a way of learning about the world that is demonstrably more effective than any alternatives, it is far from objective.

Why, then, does science work so well? First, scientists are indeed trained to identify and acknowledge their biases. They are even encouraged to put them aside to some extent, or at least to limit their impact on experimental and interpretive decisions. This training helps, but it hardly produces neutral observers of nature. In fact, preconceptions about the topic of an experiment are not only inevitable but also desirable. If a researcher does not know enough to understand what previous investigators have discovered and to develop some educated guesses about what to look for, he or she is probably not ready to conduct a study. These preconceptions are important in suggesting how to approach the topic and to design and conduct the experiment. The "biases" (perhaps it would be better to just call them opinions) are also important when drawing conclusions. There are usually different ways of interpreting a study's outcomes, and it is not always certain which way is right.

In part, this subjectivity is permitted by the flexibility of experimental methods. It is also limited by another important characteristic of science—its public nature. Although experiments are relatively private exercises, their methods and results must be shared for all to see. Publication of procedures, data, and conclusions mean that everyone else is welcome to assess the project and draw their own conclusions. Other investigators can even repeat the study to see if they obtain similar results. Replication is a key feature of scientific method. It helps to limit the impact of personal bias and corrects erroneous findings that do make it into the archival literature.

In summary, scientific methods accommodate subjectivity not only because it is unavoidable but also because it is valuable. Experimental methods encourage creativity and original thinking while guarding against excessive ignorance and intentional dishonesty.

Simple to Complex. A second guideline concerns the sequence of analytical choices. In general, it is a good idea for data analysis to proceed from relatively simple techniques to more complex procedures. Collecting repeated measures of performance under each of several conditions in sequence makes it useful to begin data analysis as soon as there are data to analyze. Behavioral researchers typically add each day's data to simple graphic displays that then reveal an increasingly complete picture of responding as each phase continues. Of course, this is done separately for each participant. As we pointed out in previous chapters, the primary benefit of analyzing data from the outset is that it helps the investigator to manage the course of the study. Based on the emerging data, the investigator can then correct problems with measurement procedures, adjust experimental conditions, or even revise a planned sequence of phases.

As control and intervention phases are completed and comparisons become possible, there may be a need for more complex analytical options. The investigator might wonder how the comparison would come out if the same data were displayed in different ways so as to highlight different features. Figure 12.2 shows such an example using data from the research program we have already mentioned, concerning the behavior of ruminating in individuals diagnosed with mental retardation (Rast, Johnston Ellinger-Allen, & Lubin, 1988). This particular study investigated whether getting participants to engage in supplementary oral stimulation (chewing bubble gum) immediately prior to meals might decrease the amount of ruminating after meals.

Panel A shows the number of ruminating responses for one individual after eating regular lunch and supper meals. In the first phase (S, involving satiation meals), he did not ruminate. In the second phase (N1, involving normal size meals), he did not chew gum before meals. In the third phase (G, also involving normal size meals), he chewed gum a predetermined number of times immediately before meals. The fourth phase (N2) was a return to the original procedure not involving gum chewing. The graph uses box and whisker plots to summarize the number of responses in each phase (Tukey, 1977). In this type of display, a box encloses the middle 50% of the data in a phase, and the line inside the box represents the median. The distance between the top and bottom of the box represents a measure of central variability. The dashed bars (whiskers) locate those values furthest away from the box (the range).

Panel B shows the frequency of responding of the same participant across the same phases. The top of the graph shows ruminating responses after lunches, and the bottom shows ruminating after suppers.

The graphs in Panel A and Panel B show different aspects of the participant's rumination behavior. In Panel A, the data show the number of responses in sessions as summarized in the box and whisker format. In Panel B, the data show the frequency of responding session by session throughout each phase. In other words, the two graphs represent different dimensional quantities (count versus frequency), summarize the data across different time frames (phases versus sessions), and display this information in different formats (box and whisker plot versus line graph).

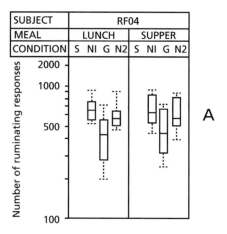

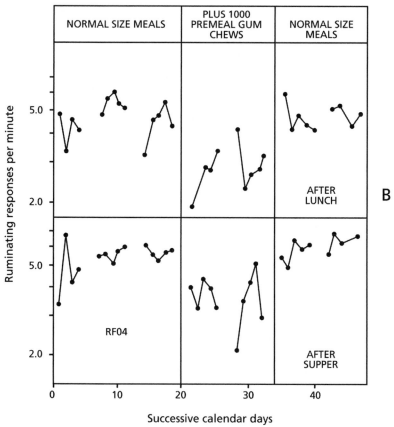

FIG. 12.2. Example of complex data analysis options. The data are adapted from Rast et al. (1988). Reproduced by permission of the American Association on Intellectual and Developmental Disabilities.

Although both panels show a decrease in responding in the premeal chewing condition, their information is not redundant. Count and frequency are different quantities and could have been differently affected by the premeal chewing procedure, although they were not. Panel A shows a number of facts about how many ruminating responses occurred during sessions, whereas Panel B shows how often these responses occurred. These two displays therefore provide much more analytical detail to the researcher than either alone. This is a good example of exploring data.

Risk of Intrusive Analytical Techniques. A third guideline is cautionary in nature. The more an analytical technique changes the picture of the participant's behavior as it actually happened, the greater the risk that interpretations may be swayed more by the analytical technique than by what actually happened. For example, calculating a descriptive statistic such as a mean or a median summarizing a participant's behavior over a series of sessions reduces those individual values to a single number. Although this outcome may be exactly what an investigator wants, it nevertheless greatly changes the picture of how the individual responded over time.

We saw this contrast in Figure 12.1, which suggested that calculating a measure of central tendency across all sessions in a phase prevents viewers from seeing the less processed picture of the participant's behavior session by session. Calculating a descriptive statistic such as a mean or median is the simplest of manipulations, however. Later in this chapter we briefly consider inferential statistical techniques such as analysis of variance and other statistical methods that involve processing behavioral data in ways that lose meaningful contact with more straightforward views of how a participant responded over time. These techniques come with specific rules for how the outcomes must be interpreted, and these rules tend to have more impact on interpretations than the direct evidence of what actually happened with the participant's behavior.

Summarizing Data

Within Participants. Exploring behavioral data often involves summarizing responding in different ways, as discussion and examples have already illustrated. It is important to remember that summarizing data can simultaneously reveal and obscure important features of the data. When we summarize a set of data, we change what readers are looking at, whether the resulting picture is graphical or numerical. Although we construct a summary because we want to see a different picture, it is unavoidable that the summarized representation prevents us from seeing unsummarized views of the same data. Of course, if we already know what the unsummarized data reveal, this may not be a problem.

One kind of summarization collates data separately for each participant. As we have emphasized all along, this can be important because the impact of variables on behavior occurs only at the level of the individual. The same treatment procedure may affect different participants in different ways. Summarizing within participants has the advantage of insuring that the resulting picture represents real behavioral effects.

Summarizing data within participants may take two forms. The most familiar form involves summarizing over periods of time. In order to consider the possibilities, we must start with the only picture of responding that does not involve summarization—displays that show each response in a real time sequence. Figure 8.1 shows some examples. The most common level of summarization over time shows individual responses collated for each session, usually displayed in sequence within a phase. Panel B of Figure 12.1 shows this type of display.

A second way to summarize is across environmental variables, rather than time. That is, a participant's performance might be collated across similar conditions, even though the resulting data are no longer in their original temporal sequence. For example, if the same condition is repeated multiple times then the data could be summarized across like phases. In an ABAB design, for instance, data from the two A phases might be combined and contrasted with data from the combined B phases. As a different example, an analysis might summarize data only for those days on which an extraneous factor was operating, such as looking at worker performance for all days in which the temperature was above a certain level in a manufacturing plant.

Across Participants. Collating data across participants is not merely another approach to summarization. As we have pointed out in many chapters, because behavior is an intraorganism phenomenon, orderly relationships between behavior and environmental variables can only be seen clearly by looking at the behavior of individuals. This does not mean that investigators should not summarize data across participants. However, this approach sets up some limitations on the conditions under which they do so, as well as on what may be said based on grouped data.

Certainly, investigators should not group data across participants until they have analyzed the data for each participant separately. Any uses of group data should only supplement analyses of individual data. One reason for this guideline is that group data obscure individual patterns of responding. Regardless of whether the collated data present an interesting picture, it does not necessarily represent what happened with each individual in the group. Remember, there is no such phenomenon as "group behavior" because there is no such organism as a "group" or an "average participant." If an effect appears in grouped data but not in individual records, it should not be considered as the sole result of a treatment condition. For example, calculating a group mean for all participants for each session may permit extreme values from some individuals to push mean values in a direction that suggests a treatment effect that is not characteristic of most participants. The individual data may show that the group "effect" is not apparent in the performance of any single individual.

The data in Figure 12.3 exemplify this kind of situation. The top graph displays data obtained by averaging the data from the four graphs below, representing the performance of four participants. The group data suggest that the responding in the first phase was followed by a gradually increasing and then stabilized performance in a second phase. Inspection of the individual graphs, however, shows that this description does not describe the pattern of responding for any of the participants. These schematic displays have been calculated to show just how much individual data sets can vary from one another while still showing an average picture that represents none of the individual cases.

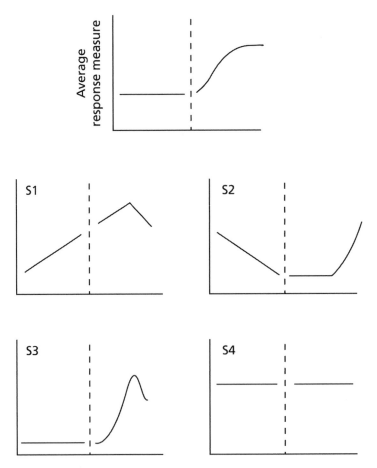

FIG. 12.3.   Schematic graphic representations of the individual performance of four individuals and the resulting average (top).

Discarding Data

Not all data are worthy of analysis. As the data from a study accumulate, researchers must decide if each value or series of values can be meaningfully interpreted. Those data that do not qualify should be discarded and eliminated from future analysis. In other words, experimental data should not be presented to the scientific community until the researcher decides that they warrant this kind of attention. Investigators have an obligation to their discipline to insure that published data are meaningful and important. When data are known to violate basic standards of measurement or represent circumstances that were different than those that were supposed to be operating, the investigator should consider eliminating the offending data from analysis so that they cannot mislead or confuse.

The reasons why some data might be misleading or confusing are familiar to any investigator. A participant may have been ill or emotionally upset for some sessions. A particular extraneous factor may have been operating, in spite of the investigator's best efforts. Observers may have had serious problems adhering to measurement procedures for some reason. Equipment may have malfunctioned. The procedures in control or treatment conditions may have deviated from the study's protocol. The list sometimes seems endless.

What qualifies data for being discarded is that some aspect of their measurement was unacceptable or they were collected in the presence of unacceptable variables. In other words, in determining whether data should be discarded, only the circumstances surrounding the data should be considered. Whether the data are consistent with the investigator's preconceptions or interests is not a legitimate criterion for keep or throwing out data. If unacceptable circumstances arise concerning data from certain sessions, the data should be set aside and not considered further, even if they appear acceptable. If no such circumstances are evident, the data should be considered in the analysis even if they appear unusual. Whether the investigator "likes" the data should be irrelevant to this decision.

In examining this guideline, let us consider a study involving some children in an elementary classroom. Assume that the teacher's behavior is a key feature of the procedure and he has been carefully trained to follow a specific protocol. What if the teacher is occasionally absent and is replaced by a substitute teacher (not trained on the protocol) on those days? Should the data (collected by research staff) be discarded for those days when there is a substitute teacher? What if the data show that the children's performance was not generally different when the substitute teacher was on duty?

Our guideline indicates that the data from substitute teacher days should be discarded, regardless of whether they suggested that the children's behavior was affected by this deviation from standard procedures. These data were collected under circumstances that were substantially different from those operating when other data were collected because the research protocol was not followed. They should not be interpreted as reflecting the conditions operating when the trained teacher was present. The fact that the data failed to suggest that the absence of the trained teacher had any effects should not encourage the investigator to use these data. Because the untrained substitute teacher could not have followed the study's protocol, the data collected on those days could not have reflected the effects of the protocol.

Selecting Representative Data

Within-subject experimental designs encourage repeated measurement of the behavior of each participant under each condition. As a result, these designs usually generate lots of data, even though there may be a relatively small number of participants. After using the data to figure out what interpretations they support, the researcher must decide how to communicate the findings to colleagues.

In considering how to describe a study's findings, an experienced researcher knows that scientific journals are interested in a report that describes the study as efficiently as possible. Journals struggle to balance their budgets, and editors have to make sure that every point of discussion and graph is necessary to communicate key findings. If an editor believes that a point can be made with smaller or fewer graphs, the researcher will be asked to revise a submitted paper and make appropriate reductions. This pressure may be relieved by the trend to on-line journal publication, but even then economy of expression and data display will remain a priority in scientific communication.

Researchers are also aware that every data point from every participant is not equally important. For example, many data points represent transition states at the beginning of a phase and may not always be important in describing the eventual impact of an intervention. As the discussion about discarding data suggested, some phases may include values that might be distracting to viewers because they represent flawed measurement practices that were subsequently improved, extraneous influences that were later controlled, or deviations from protocol that were corrected after being discovered.

It is also the case that every data point from every participant is usually not necessary to describe the outcome of each comparison between control and intervention conditions. Because multiple participants are usually exposed to each condition, there are often a number of duplicate records for each interpretive point the researcher might wish to make. Although these replications are valuable to the researcher, it may not be necessary to display all of the data when communicating findings to colleagues. The scientific community needs to see only sufficient data to support the proposed findings.

A tactic that accommodates these points involves selecting records from individual participants that represent each interpretive issue the researcher wants to address. A record is some portion of the data from a participant. In showing the behavioral outcomes of a study, it is important to look for records, not participants, that represent what really happened. It may not be the case that the data from a single participant best represents each of the different findings supported by the data from other participants.

In order to appreciate this point, consider a study in which two different treatment conditions are investigated using five participants who experience both treatments. The researcher will be interested in drawing conclusions about each of these two interventions. Let us assume that four of the participants responded to Treatment 1 in much the same way. It might be that data from any of these four participants would properly represent the performance of the other three. However, it might be a mistake to ignore the performance of the fifth participant. Even though we will assume that this performance was markedly different from the reactions of the others, it could be just as legitimate an outcome and should only be ignored if there is clear evidence that the data are misleading for some reason. In this case, then, the researcher might need two records to represent the effects of Treatment 1— one from any of the four who showed the same outcome and one from the participant who showed the different outcome.

For Treatment 2, however, assume that two participants showed one kind of effect, two showed a different effect, and the fifth was often absent and had insufficient contact with the condition. After deciding to discard the data from the fifth participant, the researcher will need to select one record from each pair to represent the two kinds of outcomes. These records need not be from either participant whose data were used to represent Treatment 1 effects, however. Again, the point is to select records, not participants, that represent the data not being presented, given that it is not feasible to present all pertinent data from all participants.

Finally, when selected records are used to represent data not presented, viewers are at a disadvantage in not being able to see how well the presented data reflect the data not being presented. In order to provide at least a limited picture of the remaining data, it is customary to present some kind of summary. Figure 12.4 shows one example of how this might be done. It shows the last 8 days of responding under each condition from one individual selected to represent the findings supported by the data from other participants but includes a summary of the other participant's data in the form of averages and ranges.

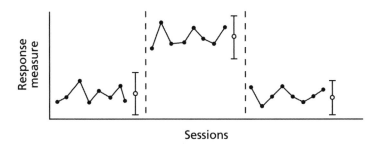

Sessions

FIG. 12.4. Data showing a representative record from three phases and the average and range for all of the data that this record represents.

BOX 12.2

Do We Need Data Analysis Police?

The preference for graphical analytical procedures as a way of deciding what
experimental data reveal sometimes bothers researchers who are more accustomed to inferential statistical analyses. In particular, they worry that the lack of
clear interpretive rules that force or limit graphically based conclusions invites
innocent or even malicious misinterpretation. They would rather have an
unambiguous set of regulations that police this kind of interpretation. From
this perspective, the outcome of data analysis procedures should be relatively
inflexible, with conclusions required by rules that leave little room for idiosyncratic reactions. In effect, this view is that data analysis procedures should
protect researchers from themselves.

The approach to data analysis described in this volume, as well as in many
other sources, contrasts sharply with this perspective. The approach that has
worked well in the natural sciences acknowledges that scientific investigation
is an uncertain and necessarily idiosyncratic process. Ambiguity and bias are not
only the norm but also are desirable within limits (see Box 12.1). Experimentation is a journey of discovery into unknown territory. There is no choice but
to trust the motivations and actions of individual investigators. It is possible to
create and enforce rigid interpretive rules, but it is not possible to guarantee the
propriety of each investigator's actions throughout the experiment. In short, if a
researcher really wants to cheat, it is easier to fake the data in the first place than
to bias the analysis. And if a researcher is unaware of his or her prejudices, their
impact will be embedded in how the study is conceived and implemented, not
just at the stage of data analysis.

Finally, fixed interpretive rules would not guarantee accurate conclusions
anyway. Because of their general and inflexible character, they would sometimes
force acceptance of problematic data. Furthermore, as we emphasize in chapter
13, good interpretation is not just about analyzing data. The meaningfulness of
data cannot be understood without evaluating the entire context in which they
were obtained.

GRAPHICAL ANALYTICAL TACTICS

Constructing Graphs

What Information Should be Represented? Most graphs are constructed using the Cartesian convention of representing two dimensions with
a pair of horizontal and vertical lines joined at one end to form a right angle.[1]
The resulting lines are described as the horizontal and vertical axes.

---

[1] Although this type of graphical display is quite common, there are endless alternatives that may
be more effective, as well as more efficient. Four volumes by Tufte (1983, 1990, 1997, 2006)
explore these possibilities and encourage researchers to think more creatively about ways of
displaying quantitative information.

In behavioral research, the horizontal axis typically represents values of: (a) some experimental variable (different experimental conditions); (b) measures of time over which responding occurred (hours, days, or weeks); or (c) events corresponding to time (sessions). The vertical axis customarily represents measures of responding—the dependent variable in a study. This means that the vertical axis is usually labeled with a dimensional quantity, such as number or count of responses, duration of responding in minutes, or response frequency (responses per minute). The label may also indicate a dimensionless quantity such as percent.

When measures of responding are plotted across time or experimental conditions in a straightforward and uncomplicated manner, it is usually easy for viewers to understand the relationship between the two kinds of information represented on the two axes. As previous sections have emphasized, however, a single graph is unlikely to communicate everything the data might have to offer. One reason is that the same data may prompt different insights when displayed in different ways. Another is that most studies generate data describing different features of a procedure and related participant reactions that help the researcher and others to understand what happened. This means that even simple projects often justify more than one graph to communicate outcomes.

What Measurement Scales Should be Used? Once a decision is made about what features will be displayed on each axis, numerical scales need to be selected that will allow specific values to be located on the axes. Although there are a number of possibilities (see Reading 10 in Johnston & Pennypacker, 1993b), the most common types of measurement scales used in behavioral research are linear and logarithmic interval scales.

Linear interval scales allow descriptions of events that show how much they differ in terms of equal intervals between values. Most of the ways in which we are accustomed to measuring things in everyday life involve linear interval scales. When you weigh yourself, differences from one occasion to another are distinguished in terms of equal intervals. In other words, the difference between 300 kilograms and 301 kilograms is represented by the same distance on a linear interval scale as the difference between 301 and 302 kilograms.

Logarithmic interval scales allow descriptions of events that show how much they differ in terms of equal ratios between values. This kind of scale represents equal ratios by equal differences on the scale. For example, an

---

Linear interval scale. A measurement scale that allows descriptions of events that show how much they differ in terms of equal intervals between values.

Logarithmic interval scale. A measurement scale that allows descriptions of events that show how much they differ in terms of equal ratios between values.

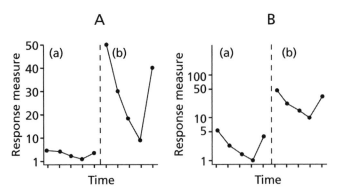

FIG. 12.5.   Comparison of the same data sets on linear and logarithmic interval scales.

increase in the frequency of responding from 4 cycles per minute to 12 cycles per minute is proportionally equivalent to an increase from 40 cycles per minute to 120 cycles per minute. This is because the difference between two values on a logarithmic scale is equivalent to a ratio of the two values.

These differences may be easier to appreciate by looking at the same data set plotted on both types of scales. Figure 12.5 shows two sets of values (a: 5, 3, 2, 1, 4; b: 50, 30, 20, 10, 40) representing responding in two phases. Panel A displays these values on a linear interval scale, and Panel B displays them on a logarithmic interval scale. The two scales obviously result in different pictures of the same data. Although the linear scale is probably more familiar to most people, the logarithmic scale highlights the fact that the values in the second data set are ten times greater than those in the first data set by showing the same pattern of the values in each set. (Additional information about using logarithmic interval scales to display behavioral data may be found in Pennypacker, Gutierrez, & Lindsley, 2003.)

The contrast between these two graphs emphasizes how different displays of the same data can have different effects on viewers. In this case, Figure 12.5 illustrates how different measurement scales may highlight different aspects of the data. Once again, it is not just a matter of whether a display is correct, but whether it encourages sound interpretations.

How Should Scales be Applied to Axes?   In addition to selecting the type of measurement scale that will be applied to horizontal and vertical axes, the investigator must choose the range of values that will be needed and how those ranges will be applied. This is usually a fairly straightforward decision. The lowest and highest values in the data set determine the minimum range that each axis must display. Then it becomes more complicated.

First, let us first consider the horizontal axis. If it represents some measure of time, the investigator must first decide what unit of time is most appropriate. This choice is something like selecting the lens on a microscope to produce different degrees of magnification. In general, the smaller the time unit, the

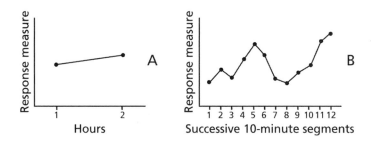

FIG. 12.6. Graphs showing data displayed over longer (hours in Panel A) and shorter (10-minute periods in Panel B) intervals of time.

more variability will be seen. Figure 12.6 makes this point by comparing the same data across hours versus successive 10-minute intervals. Using 10-minute units of time (Panel B) shows more information about responding than using hours (Panel A). This advantage partly results from the fact that smaller time units simply show more values than larger time units.

A second issue in representing time on the horizontal axis concerns whether it is represented continuously or discontinuously. Of course, time is a continuous dimension, and a participant's behavior throughout a study can be located along this dimension. However, any depiction of a participant's behavior that omits periods of time when behavior did not occur may make it more difficult for readers to understand how responding was distributed over time. Figure 12.7 illustrates this point by showing the same data plotted on two graphs. Panel A shows a graph in which time is applied to the horizontal axis in terms of successive sessions. This means that any days on which there were no sessions are omitted on the axis. Although this approach saves space on the axis, the cost lies in failing to show responding as it actually occurred over time.

Panel B shows the correct temporal distribution for these data. In this example, by including on the axis the time when sessions did not occur, the data in Panel B reveal a fairly regular pattern not evident in Panel A. In the first session following a day or two without sessions, responding was usually higher than in subsequent sessions. Knowing this allows us to ask why. If these data came from an actual study, we would be able to consider possible explanations for this pattern. If sessions were not held on weekends, for instance, this could mean that something about weekend activities was affecting responding on Mondays. The point is that the behavior of participants during sessions can be influenced by events occurring between sessions. Displaying data across continuous representations of time such as successive calendar days facilitates the discovery of such influences.

A third aspect of how dimensional units are mapped onto axes applies to both vertical and horizontal axes. Different ways of spacing intervals on the axis unavoidably affect the slopes of connecting lines. Figure 12.8 illustrates this impact by showing the same two values on two graphs in which time is

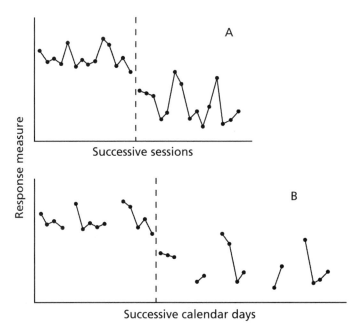

FIG. 12.7. Graphs showing data displayed across discontinuous (Panel A) and continuous (Panel B) representations of time on the horizontal axis.

mapped differently on the horizontal axis. In the graph on the left a year's time is displayed in successive months, whereas in the graph on the right the same year is divided into four 3-month seasons. In this case, however, the larger units of time are mapped onto the axis with shorter spaces between intervals. As a result, the slope of the line is steeper on the right graph than on the left. Both ways of constructing these axes are acceptable, but viewers might respond differently to each depending on what the data represent.

A fourth issue is most often relevant to the vertical axis. In selecting the range needed to display the data, it is important to create a display that suggests a fair and meaningful interpretation. It is not appropriate to use this opportunity

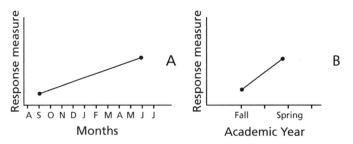

FIG. 12.8. Graphs illustrating the impact of interval spacing on the slopes of lines connecting data points.

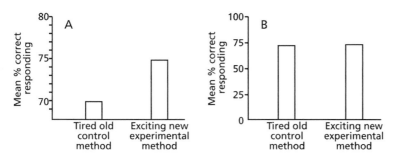

FIG. 12.9. Graphs illustrating the impact of range on interpretations of data.

to encourage conclusions that might be considered misleading. Figure 12.9 shows such an example. The range of values on the vertical axis in Panel A implies that there is an important difference in the outcomes of two procedures. Panel B shows the same data plotted against a different range, which might encourage a conclusion that the size of the difference between the two procedures is not important. Neither graph is necessarily improper, but which is more appropriate depends on what the difference in responding means in the context of the study's procedures and the literature.

Finally, it is generally improper to insert a break in the vertical axis, especially to accommodate outliers. (An outlier is a value that deviates substantially from other values.) When a data set includes one or more outliers, it can be tempting to apply scale values to the axis to highlight the majority of the values and locate the outliers on the other side of a break in the axis. Figure 12.10 shows this approach in Panel A. A break in the scale values above 45 allows the two outliers to be plotted in a way that does not require compressing the scale for the remaining values. The problem is that this treatment distorts the location of the outliers in relation to the other values. Panel B shows the same data without

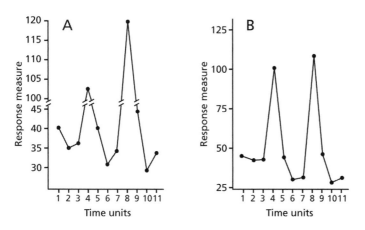

FIG. 12.10. Graphs illustrating improper (Panel A) and correct (Panel B) displays of data sets containing outlier values.

a break. Accommodating the outliers in a graph of the same size places the outliers in the correct spatial relation to the remaining values.

How Should Data be Plotted? Even after the axes of a graph have been drawn, some issues remain before the investigator can plot data. One decision concerns how to represent each value, and computer graphing software usually provides a variety of options. The most common choices include representing values with a symbol such as a dot connected by lines (creating a line graph) or with a column or bar (creating a histogram). In general, line graphs will customarily work, but histograms are only useful when the data set does not include too many values. Plotting larger data sets in a histogram format tends to require lots of relatively narrow bars. The key information communicated in a bar is usually its height relative to the vertical axis, yet it requires long vertical lines connecting that value to the horizontal axis. If one criterion for graphic efficiency is the amount of ink necessary to show the data compared to the total amount of ink actually used (Tufte, 1983), histograms are less efficient than line graphs.

Ease of interpretation can also be an issue with line graphs. Problems can arise when multiple data sets are displayed on the same graph. If the data sets do not overlap very much, it can be very useful to show two or three different functions (lines) on the same graph. However, as the number of lines increases, particularly if they overlap somewhat, it can be difficult to follow individual functions. Figure 12.11 illustrates this problem. When this is the case, separate graphs are required.

A few plotting conventions have evolved in the behavioral research literature that concern when to connect or not to connect data points. One rule is that data points should not be connected across phase changes. That is, the last data point in one phase should not be connected to the first data point in the next phase. This rule helps to highlight the break between two phases.

Another plotting convention concerns whether to connect data points across intervening days when no data were collected, assuming that the horizontal axis represents consecutive calendar days. Here is the rule. If the target behavior could not possibly have occurred on one or more days, the

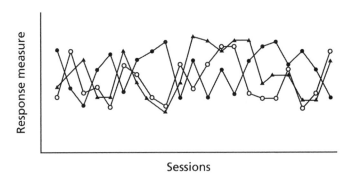

FIG. 12.11.   Illustration of a line graph showing three overlapping functions.

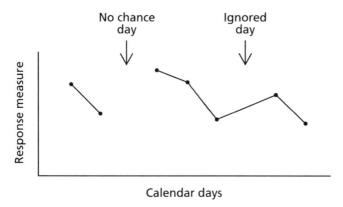

FIG. 12.12. Illustration of plotting conventions for no chance (Panel A) and ignored (Panel B) days.

bracketing data points should not be connected. These are called **no chance days** (Pennypacker, Gutierrez, & Lindsley, 2003). However, if the behavior could have occurred but measurement did not take place, the adjacent data points should be connected across the days with no values. These are termed **ignored days** (Pennypacker et al., 2003). Figure 12.12 illustrates these two situations.

> **No chance day.** A plotting convention referring to days on which the target behavior could not have occurred. Data points bracketing such days should not be connected in line graphs.
>
> **Ignored day.** A plotting convention referring to days on which the target behavior could have occurred but was not measured. Data points bracketing such days should be connected in line graphs.

The reasoning underlying this convention is that if the target behavior could have occurred but was not measured, it is reasonable to imply an estimate. This estimate is where the line connecting the adjacent values crosses the vertical line on which the missing value would have been placed. If the behavior could not have occurred, no such implication is appropriate. Therefore, the preceding and following data points should not be connected. This convention has the advantage of permitting viewers to distinguish between these two types of situations.

Finally, all of the examples thus far have plotted each value independently of previous values. However, there is another plotting rule that provides a very different picture by adding each new value to the previous total and plotting the new total value. The result is a cumulative picture of responding and is a type of display that has a long history in the study of behavior (Skinner, 1956). Using data sets representing two conditions, Panel A in Figure 12.13 shows a cumulative plot across both phases, and Panel B shows a non-cumulative plot.

Control data: 2, 3, 4, 3, 0, 0, 2, 1, 3, 3
Experimental data: 4, 6, 10, 8, 2, 1, 0, 1, 0, 0

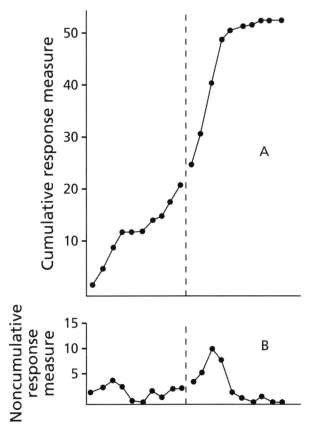

FIG. 12.13. Illustration of data displayed in cumulative (Panel A) and non-cumulative (Panel B) plots.

In a cumulative graph, successive data points can never go lower on the vertical axis than the last value, even if a new value is zero. In fact, if no responses are recorded for a series of days, the total response measure will not change and the same value will be plotted each day, resulting in a horizontal line. As a result, interpreting cumulative graphs requires learning how to assess variations in the positive slope of a line. Nevertheless, this type of plotting rule can nicely highlight the variability in some data sets. For example, it is probably easier to see the ebb and flow of responding in Panel A in Figure 12.13 than in Panel B.

BOX 12.3

The Cumulative Recorder

Plotting data cumulatively on the vertical axis has a special history in the study of behavior because, as Skinner (1956) described it, "Some people are lucky" (p. 224). In his earliest experimental efforts, he discovered that he could automatically draw a cumulative record of food deliveries using part of the food delivery apparatus. Further work led to the invention of the cumulative recorder. This device became a standard way of displaying operant behavior in laboratory settings, much as electrocardiograms (ECGs) use standard axes for displaying heart activity.

What makes the cumulative recorder valuable is not so much the cumulative picture it creates but the fact that it locates individual responses on a horizontal axis representing continuous time. In standard usage, one of the recorder's pens steps upward a small distance for each response. Because the paper rolls underneath the pen at a constant rate, the result is a graph of the cumulative number of responses over time, thereby showing the temporal distribution of individual responses (see Fig. 8.1, Panel A).

This picture of responding provides the most basic level of analysis of a participant's behavior. Skinner and later generations of his students used this kind of display to reveal the intricate relations between behavior and environmental variables. Just as physicians learn to read the data from the standard ECG format, behavioral researchers learn to interpret this standard format showing variations in the slope of the line drawn by accumulating responses. These slopes are a graphic representation of the frequency of responding, so the cumulative record provides a moment-to-moment picture of changes in response frequency. This analytical technique is especially useful when brief experimental contingencies cycle repeatedly throughout a session, a common arrangement in much laboratory research.

The cumulative recorder is a laboratory device that has never been much used in applied settings. Today, data collection and display are computer-based in laboratory settings, and portable microprocessor devices allow practitioners similar options. Of course, cumulative graphs remain one of many graphic options.

Analyzing Graphed Data

Analyzing graphed data is remarkably intuitive, which may be why graphical data analysis is widespread in the natural sciences. When researchers and practitioners study properly graphed data, they usually feel little uncertainty about how to react. This comfort can be misleading, however. There is one step that must be completed before interpreting the data's message.

Because data analysis is a matter of arranging visual stimuli that influence the reader's interpretive behavior, it is important that readers are fully aware of the features of a graph. The goal is to figure out exactly how each feature contributes to the effect that a graph has on viewer reactions. Without this understanding, readers may be unable to judge whether each feature usefully contributes to describing what the data reveal or encourages problematic interpretations. The risk is not just that conclusions may be unsound in some way and therefore misleading, but that the reader may be unaware of this possibility.

The previous section described a number of graphical features, the choices they offer, and the issues they raise. Whether constructing a graph and plotting data on it or studying a graph put together by someone else, there are many aspects of graphical data displays that unavoidably affect interpretive reactions. Identifying these features allows users to decide how to react. If the display seems to facilitate reaching the appropriate conclusions about what the data show, nothing may need to be done.

On the other hand, it may be that the features of the graph and how the data are plotted make it difficult to see clearly those aspects of responding that might be important. If the researcher or practitioner conducting the project discovers this problem, it is easy to modify the graph as needed. Others have no access to the raw data, however, so changing the display is often not possible. In these cases, there may be no alternative to judging the graph fatally flawed and inappropriate for interpretation. This can be a frustrating assessment when you are interested in a study and its findings, but there is no point in drawing conclusions based on data displays that do not clearly reveal what happened.

In sum, although analyzing graphical data displays can be straightforward and productive, these benefits require some technical knowledge about graphs and experience with graphical analysis as both an originator and an end user. The value of experience lies in playing with lots of data collected in different projects. This experience provides an appreciation for how powerfully various features of graphical data displays influence interpretive reactions. In turn, this lesson provides the motivation to create, or demand from colleagues, displays that are effective for each set of data.

STATISTICAL ANALYTICAL TACTICS

Consideration of statistical analytical tactics must first distinguish between descriptive versus inferential statistical techniques. Descriptive statistics range from simple (calculating a mean) to complex (time series analysis). However, they share a focus generally limited to describing certain features of data. They do not involve a formal mechanism for deciding whether the independent variable was responsible for the obtained outcomes. Many descriptive statistical calculations are broadly useful and widely used in all fields of science.

In contrast, inferential statistics (e.g., analysis of variance) focus on detailed rules for framing the experimental question, conducting the experiment, and deciding whether there are any effects of the independent variable. Data

> ## BOX 12.4
>
> ### Does a Graphic Approach to Data Analysis Need Defending?
>
> Psychology developed more as a social than a natural science. As a result, its methodological style was dominated by the development of inferential statistical procedures. These were first described by Fisher in 1935 and quickly adopted by a young discipline eager for the status associated by mathematical methods. Over the years, this quantitative approach to conceptualizing, conducting, and interpreting psychological data has come to so completely dominate social science research methods that alternative approaches are unavoidably in a defensive position.
>
> From a broader scientific perspective, however, no such defense is required. With certain exceptions in the life sciences, the natural sciences were far less taken with a statistical approach to experimental design and analysis. Natural science researchers had a clearer, more thorough, and more certain understanding of their subject matters and methods than their social science colleagues, which made them less inclined to use inferential statistics as a default approach to experimental design. As a result, today, inferential statistics are used more narrowly and appropriately in the natural than in the social sciences.
>
> Is graphic analysis an effective interpretive approach for behavioral research? The answer lies in its track record. These methods have consistently characterized the field of behavior analysis since its inception. The real test of scientific literature is evidence that the findings are sufficiently complete and accurate descriptions of nature that they can be depended on in daily practice. The widespread application of applied behavior analysis procedures (e.g., Austin & Carr, 2000), as well as independent reviews of its effectiveness (e.g., New York State Department of Health, 1999), provides the reassuring answer to this question.

analysis based on these rules requires certain assumptions about the nature of the data, particular manipulations of the data, and limitations on conclusions about the outcomes of a study.

A quantitative approach to interpreting experiment data based on objective rules might seem appealing. However, behavioral researchers have fully considered the role of inferential statistical methods for the study of behavior (see, for example, Ator, 1999; Baron, 1999; Branch, 1999; Crosbie, 1999; Davison, 1999; Hopkins, Cole, & Mason, 1998; Johnston & Pennypacker, 1993b; Perone, 1999; Shull, 1999). Their assessment is that the interests of a science of behavior are often not well served by inferential statistical methods. Boxes 2.7, 3.4, 3.5, 9.1, 10.3, 11.1, 12.2, 13.3, and 13.5 collectively summarize some of the problems associated with using inferential statistics as a methodological framework for learning about behavior. The concerns that many behavior researchers have with inferential statistical methods are more substantive than these short discussions, however, and require some background in inferential statistics in order to appreciate them.

Both types of quantitative analysis are thoroughly described in many professional volumes and classroom textbooks, and an adequate consideration of their features and consequences is well beyond the limits of this volume. In spite of concerns about the appropriateness of inferential statistics as a methodological foundation for the study of behavior, it should be clear that these methods do what they do perfectly well and have many valuable applications in science.

CHAPTER SUMMARY

1. Analyzing behavioral data is a matter of arranging the data in ways that encourage investigators to manage the project effectively along the way and then to draw conclusions that are going to hold up when others use them.

2. The goal of data analysis is to discover variability in the data that helps to answer the experimental question. Each of the multiple ways of collecting and viewing data will reveal a somewhat different view of variability. In doing so, each will obscure other aspects of variability that the investigator must be aware of. The safest way to be sure about what is being missed is to look at alternative viewpoints of the same data.

3. In spite of the risk of allowing preconceptions to bias the selection of analytical procedures, investigators must approach this task with at least some idea of what the data might reveal. In selecting an analytical procedure, researchers should usually proceed from relatively simple techniques to more complex procedures. Collecting repeated measures of performance under several conditions in sequence makes it useful to begin data analysis as soon as there are data to analyze. As control and intervention phases are completed and comparisons become possible, there may be a need for more complex analytical options.

4. The more that an analytical technique changes the picture of the participant's behavior as it actually happened, the greater the risk that interpretations may be swayed more by the technique than by what actually happened.

5. It is important to remember that summarizing data can simultaneously reveal and obscure important features of the data. Although we construct a summary because we want to see a different picture, it is unavoidable that the summarized representation prevents seeing unsummarized views of the same data.

6. Because behavior is an intraorganism phenomenon, orderly relationships between behavior and environmental variables can only be seen clearly by looking at the behavior of individuals. This does not mean that investigators should not summarize data across participants. However, it sets up some limitations on the conditions under which they do so, as well as on what they can say based on grouped data.

7. Not all data are worthy of analysis. Investigators have an obligation to their discipline to insure that published data are meaningful and important. Whether the data are consistent with the investigator's preconceptions or interests is not a legitimate criterion for keeping or throwing out data. If unacceptable circumstances arise concerning data from certain sessions, they should be set aside and not considered further, even if they appear acceptable. If no such circumstances are evident, data should be considered in the analysis, even if they appear unusual.

8. In behavioral research, the horizontal axis typically represents values of some experimental variable (different experimental conditions) or measures of time over which responding occurred (e.g., hours, days, weeks). The vertical axis customarily represents measures of responding (dependent variable) in a study.

9. The lowest and highest values in the data set determine the minimum range that each axis must display. In determining how to examine data on the horizontal axis, the investigator first must decide what unit of time is most appropriate. In general, the smaller the time unit, the more variability will be seen.

10. In addition to determining the range, the investigator must decide how to space the intervals on the axis to allow the slopes of the data to be as representative and informative as possible. In addressing this issue, it is important to remember that it is generally improper to insert a break in the vertical axis, especially to accommodate outliers. The problem in doing so is that it distorts the location of the outliers in relation to the other values.

11. Analyzing graphed data is remarkably intuitive, which may be why graphical data analysis is widespread in the natural sciences. Although data analysis can be straightforward and productive, these benefits require some technical knowledge about graphs and experience with graphical analysis as both a designer and a reader. This experience provides an appreciation for how various features of graphical data displays influence interpretive reactions.

TEXT STUDY GUIDE

1. What is the benefit of viewing data analysis as a stimulus control problem?
2. What is exploratory data analysis?
3. Explain the rationale for starting data analysis with simple options and gradually moving to more complex options.
4. What is the risk of using increasingly complex analytical procedures?
5. What is the basic effect of summarizing data?
6. Describe two general forms of summarizing data within participants.

7. How is summarizing data across participants fundamentally different than summarizing within participants?
8. What interpretive constraints apply when summarizing data across participants?
9. Provide some reasons why it might be appropriate to discard data.
10. What is the general guideline for when to discard or keep data?
11. Why can it be appropriate to select representative data?
12. What is the difference between the selection of representative participants versus selecting representative records?
13. What information is usually represented on the horizontal and vertical axes in behavioral research?
14. What is the difference between linear and logarithmic interval scales?
15. What is the effect of representing different units of time on the horizontal axis?
16. Describe the consequences of representing time on the horizontal axis continuously versus discontinuously.
17. How can the spacing of time units on the horizontal axis affect the slope of the lines connecting data points?
18. Why is it improper to break the vertical axis in order to accommodate outlier values?
19. When are histograms a poor choice as a plotting format?
20. What is the convention for connecting data points across phase changes?
21. Explain the plotting conventions for no chance and ignored days.
22. Explain how data points are calculated in a cumulative graph.
23. What is the difference between descriptive and inferential statistics

BOX STUDY GUIDE

1. How can experimenter bias be useful? How is it limited by the scientific process?
2. Why would it not improve interpretive decisions to have rigid interpretive rules that all researchers had to follow?
3. What made the cumulative recorder a valuable recording format for early researchers?

SUGGESTED READINGS

Hopkins, B. L., Cole, B. L., & Mason, T. L. (1998). A critique of the usefulness of inferential statistics in applied behavior analysis. *The Behavior Analyst, 21*, 125–137.

Pennypacker, H. S., Gutierrez, A., Jr., & Lindsley, O. R. (2003). *Handbook of the standard celeration chart*. Gainesville, AL: Xerographics Inc.

Tufte, E. R. (1990). *Envisioning information*. Cheshire, CN: Graphics Press.

DISCUSSION TOPICS

1. Discuss the impact on interpretations for summarizing data within versus between participants.

2. Select a graph from a published study in a behavioral journal. Critique the graph using the standards discussed in this chapter. Consider how any shortcomings might affect interpretations.

EXERCISES

1. Select a graph from a published study in a behavioral journal. Estimate each of the values in each phase. Replot these values using a graphic format that differs in some way. Compare the picture presented by the two graphs and consider how the differences might impact the interpretations.

2. Make up a data set of about 20 values or use a data set that is already available. Plot the data on a graph using a linear interval scale on the vertical axis and also on a graph using a logarithmic interval scale. Consider how the different displays might influence interpretations.

Interpreting Experiments

Across Species
Evidence
EVALUATING INTERPRETATIONS

Data can be negative only in terms of a prediction. When one simply asks a question of nature, the answer is always positive.
—Murray Sidman

INTERPRETIVE BEHAVIOR

Throughout this volume, we have viewed the scientist as a behaving organism, and we have described the behavior of researchers in the same conceptual framework as used for participants. In this chapter, we focus on the interpretive behavior of researchers and those who read published studies. Although it might seem that the data are the most important outcome of a research project, this quantitative information is almost worthless unless it leads to interpretations by the investigator or others that prompt people to behave more effectively. In effect, when anyone interprets a study, he or she is translating the language of nature (data) into the language of the culture. This, in turn, enables people to interact successfully with nature without having to accumulate personal experiences. So, we can learn that smoking is unhealthy by reading reports of scientific findings without having to smoke for many years to discover this the hard way.

The primary challenge in interpreting a study is to decide how each of its features might have affected the data. The researcher must then decide how each factor should influence interpretive statements. Interpreting a study requires many judgments about how each element of control and experimental conditions, as well as data collection procedures, should guide statements about what has been learned about the issues under study. In making this assessment, we must start by considering all of the possible sources of control over the investigator's interpretive reactions.

SOURCES OF CONTROL

Pre-Experimental

Theory. Some influences on the researcher's interpretive reactions are also likely to have played a significant role when the study was designed. For example, the researcher's general theoretical perspective toward behavior and the specific topic under investigation typically influences early decisions. How the experimental question is framed, measurement procedures are set up, experimental comparisons are arranged, and data are analyzed are activities typically guided by the researcher's general approach to behavior as a scientific subject matter. This influence therefore both establishes and limits the experimental procedures and data that are available for interpretation.

As a source of control over interpretations, the researcher's theoretical persuasion cannot be prejudged as inherently helpful or harmful. In one instance, it may help by prompting reactions to the data that others might fail to detect. In another case, however, it might prevent the researcher from seeing flaws in experimental procedures. Whatever the impact of theoretical orientation, it may help if researchers can step back and appreciate how their perspective toward behavior could be influencing their reactions to a study.

Literature. As with theory, the scientific literature concerning the experimental question likely influenced how the researcher framed the question and designed the study in the first place (see chapter 3). After the project is completed, the literature provides the context for its results. For instance, how the study's findings are described may partly depend on whether they support or conflict with published research. An important feature of this assessment is comparing the methods of the present study with those in the literature. If the results of the present study seem to differ from those already published, these differences would be considered in evaluating what the new study might contribute.

Extra-Experimental Contingencies. As we noted in chapter 3, scientific research is not conducted in the sterile context some people might imagine. There are many potential influences on a researcher's interpretations that have nothing to do with the experiment itself. It is important, though often difficult, to assess whether these factors are appropriate and helpful.

One possible problem is that by the time a study is completed the researcher has usually invested considerable time, money, and effort in the project. It may be as punishing to draw conclusions unfavorable to these interests as it is reinforcing to reach favorable conclusions. This kind of contingency can lead to what we have called advocacy research (Box 3.7), in which the investigator biases the design and conduct of a study toward a preordained outcome. It is this kind of bias that makes it important for studies to be replicated by other experimenters.

The degree of fame and fortune that may accrue to researchers who report certain outcomes is another possible influence on interpretive reactions. The fact that scientists are often deprived of both only means that such deprivations are easily satisfied. At the very least, publication in peer-reviewed journals brings a small and temporary measure of recognition for those in academia. The riches may be institutional rather than personal. Obtaining or maintaining funding for a line of research is often contingent on obtaining a certain kind of finding. Access to research settings or participants can also depend on a project's outcomes.

We might agree that these influences on the conclusions that an investigator draws can be problematic. However, it is not as clear whether the planned uses of a study's findings should be considered when deciding how results should be described. One argument is that the procedures and data of an experiment should be interpreted without regard to how the findings might be used by others. On the other hand, it could also be argued that a study's outcomes might be described with more or less caution depending on their application. For example, if a study's results will be used to encourage nationwide dissemination of a new treatment procedure, it may be wise to be more cautious than if the likely use of a study's conclusions is merely to guide further experimentation.

Experimental Question. We discuss in chapter 3 the pervasive role of the experimental question in interpreting a study. The question concisely summarizes the investigator's interests, and determining how well the project is able to answer the question is therefore a natural focus of interpretation. This influence is an important constraint. Because the question guided decisions about how the experiment was designed and conducted, it places certain limits on what the procedures and data can reveal. If interpretations exceed these limits, it may mean that conclusions are too strongly influenced by other factors, such as extra-experimental considerations.

On the other hand, too slavish a devotion to the experimental question can blind the investigator to the possibility of discovering outcomes that were not forecast by the question. Box 3.7 points out the importance of serendipity in science, and the question should not discourage examining the data for unanticipated discoveries.

Measurement

Response Class Definition. It is risky to interpret data without knowing exactly what they represent and how they were obtained. Each of the elements of behavioral measurement provide information essential to understanding what the data might reveal. In chapter 4, we considered how different ways of defining target behaviors can affect the nature of the data. There are a number of questions whose answers should be used to guide interpretations:

1. Is the selected target behavior appropriate and useful for answering the experimental question?
2. Did the definition capture the behavior of individual participants or some form of grouped behavior of multiple participants?
3. Was the target behavior defined in functional or topographical terms (or both)? What are the implications of this choice for interpretation?
4. Was the level of specificity in the definition appropriate for the study?

Dimensional Quantities and Units. Another influence on interpretations concerns the dimensional quantities and the units of measurement that were the focus of measurement. The treatment of these choices in chapter 5

BOX 13.1

When You Cannot Get There From Here

As chapter 3 points out, one of psychology's biggest methodological headaches comes from asking questions that cannot be clearly answered. Such questions often share a focus on hypothesized mental "events." (The reason for putting "events" in quotes is because they are not real, physical events.) Questions about mental activity can only be approached by working with behavior and environmental variables, which are very much in the physical world. The problem with this approach is knowing whether the behavior measured in a study and the environmental variables actually manipulated have anything to do with the mental "events" that are the focus of the experimental question.

Consider as an example a question that asks whether self-esteem in previously unsuccessful students changes as a result of positive learning experiences. Self-esteem might be measured in multiple ways, such as with a questionnaire and by counting the occurrence of positive self-statements. The experimental procedure may involve arranging learning tasks in which success is assured.

What is actually measured in each case is not self-esteem, but verbal behavior. The researcher might like to assume that the questionnaire and positive self-statements represent self-esteem, but how are we to know this? Although the experimental manipulations may be clear, all we can say with certainty is that they were followed by certain changes in questionnaire-answering behavior and positive self-statements. This assessment does not answer our question about whether these changes represent self-esteem. In other words, questions about "phenomena" that are not known to exist force researchers to assume that there is a relationship between the conceptual elements in the question and the operational elements in the experiment.

Asking questions about behavior, clearly a physical event, helps to minimize this problem, although this approach does not always avoid it. When the question asks about behavior that is not directly measured, the same issue can arise. For instance, a question may ask about the impact of different ratios of work and leisure time on recycling behaviors such as separating trash. However, what if the experiment is conducted in a laboratory setting in which participants "work" by pushing buttons and "recycle" points under different ratios of "work" and "leisure" periods during each session? Although the investigator may want these conditions to represent what goes on in everyday life, it will not be clear whether the experiment really has anything to do with recycling.

---

raises a number of questions that should be answered in considering what the data might reveal:

1. Was the chosen dimensional quantity adequately sensitive to treatment conditions? Would different dimensional quantities have been more appropriate?

2. What limits does the selected quantity place on the characteristics of responding that were observed?

3. Does the quantity reflect variability that is informative and useful?

4. If a compound dimensional quantity was used, is it important to look at the contributing quantities separately?

5. Were the units of measurement used to describe the amounts of the observed dimensional quantities standard and absolute? If not, what are the resulting constraints on interpretations?

Observing and Recording. The data available for interpretation depend on how the observation was conducted, and we considered this topic in detail in chapter 6. Here are some of the questions that must be answered:

1. Did the observation procedure accommodate the needs of the question and the characteristics of the target behavior?

2. Was the frequency and duration of observation adequate?

3. If incomplete observation procedures were used, what limitations should they place on interpretations?

4. If human observers were used, were they properly selected, trained, and evaluated?

5. What kind of evidence was gathered about the observation and recording process? Does the evidence reveal the accuracy and reliability of observations or only agreement among observers?

Evaluating Measurement Procedures and Data. Finally, the investigator and others evaluating a study must be satisfied about the quality of the data generated by these measurement procedures. The investigator has presumably been making this assessment all along and by this late stage should be content with his or her decisions and their impact on the data. Others can only judge measurement procedures and the resulting data as a completed package.

Nevertheless, the decision must be multi-faceted, taking into account all aspects of measurement. Anyone interpreting a study should be able to take a single data point and, in a single sentence, state precisely what it represents. For example, consider the two following statements:

1. This data point represents the average number of functionally defined compliance statements per minute (accuracy unknown) of a single participant observed by a single observer during a 45-minute period in the clinic.

2. This data point represents the mean number of 20-second intervals out of consecutive 30-second periods for five participants scored as containing at least one topographically defined disruptive response (accuracy unknown) observed by a single observer during a 15-minute period in a classroom setting.

This is not only a good exercise for students when reviewing a published study, but it is also a realistic standard for experienced researchers. It forces a summary evaluation of measurement components in a way that highlights their consequences for interpretation.

Experimental Comparisons

Independent Variable. At this point, we will assume that a study's measurement procedures and the resulting data have been judged acceptable and therefore worthy of interpretation. Interest may now turn to whether the independent variable is appropriate for the experimental question and how well it was managed during the project. This assessment helps to reveal whether comparing responding under the experimental condition and its matched control condition is likely to make any progress toward answering the question.

The first issue can sometimes be complex, and there are no simple rules to guide an evaluation of whether the designated independent variable will help to answer the question. As an example of this challenge, consider once again a series of studies addressing the question of why consuming satiation quantities of food at meals has the effect of immediately and substantially reducing frequencies of postmeal ruminating in individuals with mental retardation (Rast, Johnston, & Drum, 1984; Rast, Johnston, Drum, & Conrin, 1981; Rast, Johnston, Ellinger-Allen, & Lubin, 1988; Johnston, Greene, Rawal, Winston, Vazin, & Rossi, 1991). The basic research literature suggests that increases in oropharyngeal and esophageal stimulation from chewing and swallowing, glycogen in the blood, and stomach distention might contribute to this effect. Each of these variables was separately manipulated in a series of experiments, in each case requiring a procedure that would represent the variable in question. What complicated this challenge was that in order to separate the effects of these three variables, each had to be manipulated while the other two were held constant.

To manipulate chewing and swallowing, the participants were encouraged to chew sugarless bubble gum before eating. Because these severely and profoundly mentally retarded participants would immediately swallow a piece of gum, it was placed in a strip of gauze, and staff held the ends of the gauze to prevent the gum from being swallowed. The staff also counted the number of chewing and swallowing responses (periodically swapping old gum for fresh) until they matched the average number of chews and swallows taken to consume a satiation quantity meal. This procedure did not affect the other two variables.

To evaluate the role of increased glycogen, participants were fed single-portion meals that had the caloric density of a satiation sized meal. This was done by preparing otherwise typical meals using high calorie ingredients. In other words, under this condition they experienced the nutritional effects of eating satiation quantities of food without increasing the amount of chewing and swallowing or the extent of stomach distention.

To assess the effects of increased stomach distention, participants were fed regular single-portion meals followed by supplementary dietary fiber. The amount of fiber was calculated to mimic the stomach distention effect of satiation sized meals.

These experiments were intended to reveal whether each variable had an effect on frequencies of ruminating, which were easily measured as each condition was introduced and withdrawn. Although the data clearly showed a decrease in ruminating when each procedure was implemented, it is fair to ask if these effects were due to the intended independent variables. That is, it was reasonably clear that the effects were due to the procedure, but did the procedure properly represent the variables of interest? For example, perhaps feeding supplementary fiber did not properly mimic the stomach-distending effect of consuming a very large meal. In other words, the fact that a procedure apparently changed behavior does not clarify why the change occurred or what it might mean for the experimental question.

The second issue, concerning how well the independent variable was managed during the study, is easier to assess but is no less important. The primary concern is that the independent variable and general preparation in which it is embedded were implemented as designed and that they were consistent from session to session. For research conducted in highly controlled settings such as laboratories, this fidelity and consistency is usually assured. Researchers using applied settings, on the other hand, often struggle to make sure that the procedures in both control and treatment conditions operate as intended. It is often the case, for instance, that these procedures require personnel working in a setting to comply with specific protocols. As we suggested in chapter 8, for example, classroom teachers might have to follow detailed rules in how they interact with students serving as participants. Care-givers in a group home might have to adhere to intervention rules 7 days a week across two daily shifts.

Under such circumstances, it is often useful to collect evidence specifically to verify that the procedures happened as designed (Peterson, Homer, & Wonderlick, 1982). For example, the investigator might measure the teachers' compliance with experimental protocols and present these data alongside those showing participant performance. Figure 13.1 shows an example of this practice from a study evaluating the feasibility of school personnel conducting functional analysis procedures in classroom settings (Northup et al., 1994). The figure shows functional analysis data for one student, together with treatment integrity data showing teacher adherence to treatment procedures.

Control Condition and Extraneous Variables. It is not enough to determine that the independent variable was appropriate and properly implemented. The same issues of appropriateness and consistency must be addressed for the control condition. We have identified the role of the control condition as controlling for all of the factors operating in an intervention

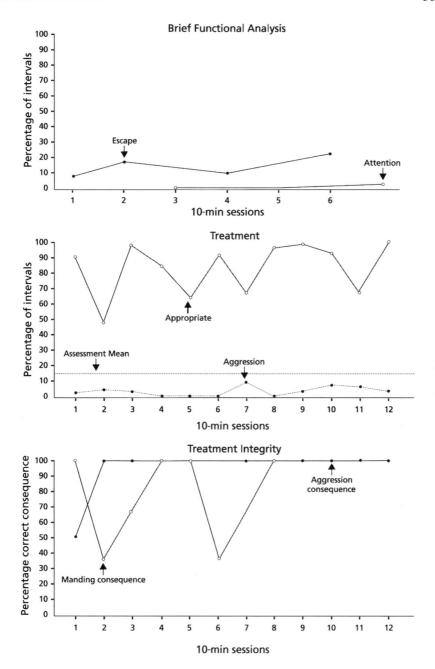

FIG. 13.1. Example of data showing participant outcomes (top two graphs) and teacher implementation of treatment procedures (bottom graph). Adapted from Northup, J., Wacker, D. P., Berg, W. K., Kelly, L., Sasso, G., & DeRaad, A. (1994). The treatment of severe behavior problems in school settings using a technical assistance model. *Journal of Applied Behavior Analysis*, 27, 33–47, p. 41. Copyright 1994 by the Society for the Experimental Analysis of Behavior, Inc. Used by permission.

condition except the independent variable. That is, if all of the variables present in the control condition are also present in an intervention condition, the only thing that differs between the two conditions will be the independent variable. This means that the independent variable will be the only reasonable explanation for any differences in responding (the dependent variable) between the two conditions.

This reasoning means that the researcher must first be sure that the control condition is appropriate for its task. As we noted in chapter 10, it must establish environmental conditions that are likely to help reveal the effects of the independent variable, and also control for those factors present in the treatment condition that are not part of the independent variable itself. Anyone interpreting a study, then, must evaluate the appropriateness of the control condition in serving these two functions.

As with the treatment condition, it is important that the control condition is implemented as designed and is consistent in its features from session to session. For example, it might be clear that a control condition is well designed for its two functions. However, if it is also evident that the condition is not well managed, the condition may not provide a good basis for evaluating the effects of the independent variable. This is why it may be useful to collect evidence about procedural integrity not only for the treatment condition but for the control condition as well.

Finally, how well the control and treatment conditions have been selected and managed is not the only interpretive concern about a study's procedures. Extraneous variables that are not taken into account by the control condition can come and go at any point during a project. For example, a participant may be sick one day or a field trip in the morning of one day may affect a participant's behavior in an afternoon session. Whether such events influence a participant's performance is often not obvious. Sometimes an apparently significant event (such as a weather incident) will not clearly disrupt the usual performance. On the other hand, performance may be affected by less obvious extraneous factors.

Occasional extraneous anomalies are not necessarily a serious threat to sound comparisons of control and experimental conditions. Nevertheless, interpreting a study requires making a judgment about whether extraneous factors had frequent and powerful effects on responding. If so, the data would reflect an intermingling of their effects with those of the control and experimental conditions. This might encourage conclusions that fail to hold up when others attempt to use them.

Evaluating Experimental Comparisons. When it is clear that the control and independent variable conditions of the study were appropriately designed and well managed, attention can turn to assessing the comparisons themselves. This is relatively straightforward in an ABA or reversal design. There are only two comparisons, and they involve a single treatment condition compared twice with the same control condition. However, many experimental designs involve more than one kind of treatment condition.

Furthermore, pairs of control and treatment conditions may be repeated, perhaps more than once.

In studies involving more than one kind of independent variable condition, each independent variable may be evaluated in terms of the number of control-treatment comparisons available. That is, a study should be evaluated not on the basis of how many comparisons are included overall but on how many comparisons are available for each different independent variable under examination. (This was the point of the discussion in chapter 11 concerning Fig. 11.16.) For example, a project examining two independent variables may include four control-treatment comparisons for one but only one such comparison for the other. Having only a single comparison means that this independent variable is examined with only an AB comparison, which is insufficient to make statements about the reliability of any effect or whether it was due to the independent variable itself.

Finally, interpreting a study requires more than determining whether each particular control-treatment comparison was replicated and showed consistent results. There is also the matter of deciding what each comparison says about the influence of the independent variable and, more broadly, the experimental question. This is often a complex judgment, and no simple rules will help. This complexity is evident in the fact that the comparisons in a particular experiment may prompt somewhat different interpretations by different readers, each of whom may judge some factors differently. This is why even reasonably clear findings should usually be expressed tentatively out of respect for what we may not yet know. Of course, one thing we do not know is whether a particular conclusion is correct. We learn this only with future investigations.

Experimental Data

Analytical Procedures. In turning to the data as an influence over interpretive reactions, the first question is how data analysis procedures might affect our reactions. We examined this topic in some detail in chapter 12, and it should be clear that how data are processed and presented can easily sway how readers interpret a study.

With the advantage of access to the raw data, the researcher should have considered all of the relevant options and chosen procedures that helped to reveal the data's message. Others are not obligated to agree with the researcher's analytical decisions, however. They may judge the selected quantitative or graphical techniques as limiting in some way, for example, perhaps preventing them from making an analysis that they would prefer. It is perfectly appropriate for them to request unpublished information about procedures and data from the researcher so they can conduct their own analysis. This involves a substantial investment in time, however, and is not routinely done. More practically, the researcher's peers satisfy themselves with evaluating the impact of the researcher's analytical choices on their own interpretations.

BOX 13.2

Internal and External Validity

In 1966, Campbell and Stanley published a slim volume about experimental designs in which they introduced a distinction between internal and external validity. These terms caught on because they referred to important influences on the legitimacy of experimental inferences.

Internal validity refers to the appropriateness of attributing a causal role to independent variables. It can be threatened by a variety of extraneous factors, as we have described in different chapters. For example, the *history* that participants bring to a study, especially events in their lives during the course of the study, can influence their performance. *Maturational changes* can occur in studies that last for long periods (e.g., a 2-year study with rats) and can confound the effects of treatment variables. If participants perform differently on a post-test because of their prior exposure to the pretest, then *testing* is another threat to internal validity. *Instrumentation* refers to the possibility that measurement operations may change over time, thus contributing error to the data. *Statistical regression* refers to the tendency of extreme scores to regress toward the mean with subsequent testing, a statistical phenomenon that means that they often become less extreme. *Selection biases* can plague between-group designs in which different participants are exposed to control and experimental conditions if participant characteristics are not properly matched. *Attrition* can also be a problem in group designs when participants drop out during the study, thereby creating the impression that the group performance has changed. *Diffusion of treatment* refers to situations in which control and experimental conditions do not remain distinct but become confounded in some way. This might be the case when a trainer is supposed to behave differently under two conditions but fails to comply fully.

External validity refers to the extent that the results of a study can be generalized to other circumstances. There are a number of questions that may be asked about whether features of the study limit generality. We have already discussed *generality across participants, settings, and response classes. Generality across times* refers to the possible influence of the time at which the experiment was conducted and whether variables associated with it contributed to the results and might therefore limit generality. *Generality across behavior change agents* asks the same kind of question about individuals who interacted with participants as part of the experimental procedures. If individuals behave differently because of their status as participants, it is called *reactive experimental arrangements. Reactive assessment* refers to what is also called measurement reactivity, or the effects of the participant's performance of being measured. *Pretest sensitization* concerns the possibility that participants will react differently to the experimental condition because of the effects of a pretest. *Multiple-treatment interference* or sequence effects are possible if one condition influences responding in a subsequent condition.

BOX 13.3

Inferential Statistics as Interpretation

When experiments are designed in accordance with the requirements of inferential statistical tests of significance, the interpretive process is largely dictated by the mathematical and logical rules underlying this approach. The most common statistical test used in the social sciences is analysis of variance (ANOVA). The process begins with a null hypothesis (see Box 3.5), which is a prediction that there will be no differences among the mean performances of control and experimental groups. The alternative hypothesis predicts that there will be differences and attributes them to the independent variable. In other words, there is actually no formal question, only predictions. The focus of attention lies in whether there are statistically significant differences among the performances of the groups.

After the experiment is complete and the data have been subjected to the mathematics of ANOVA, the interpretive process finally begins. (This contrasts with the approach described in this volume, in which it begins as soon as there are data, early in the experiment.) If the F ratio is smaller than would be expected by chance (as defined by the alpha level chosen), this means that there is not a significant difference between the groups. The null hypothesis must then be accepted, and the investigator can only speculate about why the independent variable did not have the anticipated effects. If the test shows that there are differences, the investigator must reject the null hypothesis and turn to the alternative hypothesis as the best explanation of the difference.

Whether the researcher concludes that the independent variable influenced the behavior of participants is formally determined by the outcome of the test in relation to the alpha level selected. A significant result would be thrown out only if there were serious problems with the design or in the conduct of the study. In practice, a significant result licenses considerable interpretive discussion about why the result was obtained and what it means, even though the procedures of between-group studies do not usually create sound evidence for this discussion.

Aside from many other problems (see Reading 13 in Johnston & Pennypacker, 1993b), what is worrisome about this interpretive approach is that it places excessive credence on obtaining statistical significance. Because this tactic is a dominant tradition in the social sciences and is dignified by an unambiguous mathematical process that seems immune from subjective bias, there is a tendency to treat all significant results as true, meaningful, and important. Although some certainly are, that status is not the result of the interpretive process itself. Many outcomes that survive the same analysis may be inaccurate, confounded, and trivial, in spite of being statistically significant. Interpreting experiments is simply a more complex activity than this tradition acknowledges.

Variability. After being sure that the study's analytical procedures will help to identify sound interpretations, it is finally appropriate to evaluate the data. Before trying to understand what the data say about intervention conditions and the experimental question, however, it is important to look at the nature of the variability in the data.

One important consideration follows from having already evaluated the study's measurement and analytical procedures. It is possible that problems with these procedures produced data that do not represent what actually happened. As discussed in chapter 6, the pattern of data points on a graph, for instance, could partly reflect observer error. There are also ways in which discontinuous observing procedures might generate misleading values. In addition, chapter 12 showed that decisions about how to construct graphs can distort the values displayed. These possibilities make it important to decide the extent to which the data show variability that really happened versus variability that is merely illusory. Unfortunately, if this assessment is discouraging, there is often nothing that can be done, other than to put the study aside.

A second way of looking at the variability in the data follows from evaluating the pattern of responding within phases. We identified in chapter 9 the most important issue—whether stable responding was adequately achieved in each phase. The evidence on this point indicates the level of experimental control attained and the extent to which extraneous factors intruded. As we have already stressed, whether differences in responding between control and treatment conditions justify conclusions about the effects of independent variables depends not only on the size of the differences but also on the characteristics of responding in each of the two phases being compared.

Finally, if the study was well designed and conducted, the variability between phases ideally represents the effects of only the independent variable. The interpretive issues here concern the characteristics of changes in responding as the intervention condition is initiated and withdrawn. Although it is common to focus on differences in the "level" of responding (how much increase or decrease was found), this is not the only feature that might be important. Changes in variability under control versus treatment conditions are often evident and might be relevant to the experimental question. For example, it might be that one effect of the treatment condition is to reduce variability compared to the control condition. Another effect that can be important is the nature of the transition when initiating the treatment condition. Whether the transition to a stable pattern of responding is rapid or slow is often relevant to practical interests, for instance.

Conclusions. At this point in the interpretive process, there is finally nothing left to do but judge what the data reveal about the effects of the independent variable and how these effects might help to answer the experimental question. Before trying to draw these conclusions, however, a summary assessment is required.

Identifying a study's outcomes is only appropriate if the project's procedures and data are worthy of interpretation. Although all of the factors discussed in this and the prior chapters bear on this decision, it comes down to a dichotomous judgment. All factors considered, the study is either good enough to warrant conclusions or it is fatally flawed and therefore cannot support conclusions. There really is no middle ground. If the procedures are only somewhat weak in certain ways, proceeding to interpret the study may be worthwhile if conclusions are sufficiently qualified and cautious. If some aspects of measurement decisions and procedures are seriously problematic, however, ignoring these flaws and drawing conclusions anyway may only insure that the conclusions are misleading and not useful.

Deciding whether a study justifies conclusions is easy when it has been well done. However, after going to the trouble of carefully evaluating all a study's

---

BOX 13.4

Do Attitudes Toward Interpretation Vary Across Disciplines?

There are many differences between the social sciences and the natural sciences (see Reading 1 in Johnston & Pennypacker, 1993b). The natural sciences have been around a good bit longer than the social sciences and have settled many methodological issues. They have accumulated a sophisticated literature describing how the world of matter works. They have learned that there is no point in using weak or inappropriate methods or drawing inaccurate and self-serving conclusions. In fact, they tend not to tolerate much conceptual, methodological, or interpretive sloppiness.

Their methodological progress has been rewarded by an increasingly broad and sound foundation of scientific laws. Scientists can see the relationship between good experimental methods and outcomes because they reap the benefits every day. As a result, interpretation seems to be approached with the highest concern about finding truth, whatever its consequences for theory or individuals. Although these are crude generalities with inevitable exceptions, the influence of theory literature and extra-experimental factors in the natural sciences seems distinctly secondary to experimental procedures and data.

Do the social sciences generally approach interpretation with different attitudes? After all, they are relatively young and are still struggling with the most basic methodological issues, such as the nature of their subject matter. Although their literatures are large, they do not yet reflect a sound, well-developed, and broadly accepted understanding about how behavior works. In fact, they reveal diverse conceptual and methodological approaches to the same fundamental phenomena. The uncertain state of these literatures is reflected by the fact that there are few effective technologies that have emerged from a century of research (Estes, 1979), and progress seems to be represented by new literature replacing, rather than building on, old ones.

It should not be surprising, therefore, that social scientists cannot see a clear relationship between the quality of experimental methods and the likelihood of accurate and important findings. As a result, interpretation may more often be a self-serving exercise than in the natural sciences. The ideal of seeking truth often seems subservient to the influence of theory, literature, and extra-experimental factors. Because there is not yet much of a track record showing that the nature of experimental methods and interpretation makes a big difference in the advancement of the science, it may be understandable if social scientists approach interpretation somewhat differently than do natural scientists.

features, it is often difficult to put it aside because fatal flaws in its procedures or data have become evident. This is especially true when you are interested in the topic and the particular question posed by the project. Our natural tendency is to accept the implicit opinion of the journal's reviewers and editors, who decided it was at least worth publishing, and draw conclusions about what the study showed, even though we know it has serious problems.

Nevertheless, researchers and practitioners in all experimental fields learn that publication in a peer-reviewed journal does not guarantee that a study is methodologically sound or that the author's conclusions are valid. It may be more difficult to admit that ignoring serious weaknesses in a study, or failing to recognize them in the first place, risks conclusions that will not hold up when they are used in some way. In other words, although we may honestly believe (or at least hope) that the researcher's conclusions, or our own, are reasonably accurate, the real test comes when we or others act on them. If a practitioner improperly concludes that a study showed that a certain procedure was more effective than it actually was, for example, it may not work as well as expected when it is used in a treatment program.

More optimistically, let us now assume that a study is at least generally sound and warrants our attention. Having examined the methodological features of a study, as well as its data, the essential task remaining is to decide what the data have to say about the effects of the independent variable. Of course, the independent variable was selected because it might shed light on the experimental question, so this assessment should license an attempt to answer the question.

Once again, there are no simple rules for coming up with this answer. One reason why this is a complex process is that studies often lead to not a single answer but several. Even in a simple study with only a single independent variable, the data may reveal more than one outcome. For example, measuring more than one target behavior or multiple dimensional quantities creates the possibility that a treatment condition had somewhat different effects depending on which measures are examined. One behavior may have increased during the treatment condition, but another may have decreased. Frequency of responding may have decreased while the aggregate duration of responses increased. In studies investigating more than one treatment condition, conclusions must also take account of how the effects of each condition bear on the experimental question.

Even when a study's conclusions are clear, part of the interpretation involves considering what those conclusions mean in the context of the published literature. It is not unusual for readers to agree on what a particular study shows but disagree about what those conclusions might mean for a certain issue or larger question. It might seem problematic that interpretation of experimental findings is not more tightly bound by firm rules. However, it is actually important that each reader bring his or her unique histories to this task. After all, even well done experiments may generate misleading outcomes, and scientists have learned to avoid thinking that any experiment proves some unimpeachable truth. The fact is that when experienced researchers disagree about the conclusions of a sound study or their implications for larger issues, no one can be sure of who is right. Only more research will answer this question. Such disagreements are an important feature of the scientific process.

In sum, interpreting a study involves complex judgments subject to many influences, and it takes both training and experience to master this skill. Perhaps the most valuable guidance is to remember that *the task is not just to interpret the data, but to interpret the entire experiment*. It is tempting to "read" an article by scanning the methods section and looking more closely at the graphs. However, data cannot be meaningfully interpreted without a detailed appreciation of all of the factors that led to the data and were involved in their analysis.

GENERALITY

Definition

Thus far, we have discussed interpretation only in terms of what happened in an experiment and what the results might mean for the experimental question. Research interests are usually more general than this, however. After all, if a study's results had no value beyond its unique features, there would be little point in having conducted the project. Extending experimental findings beyond the special circumstances that generated them is therefore an important part of interpretation.

Deciding what a study showed is grounded in what was done and how that affected the dependent variable. By contrast, speculating about what these findings might mean for somewhat different situations is somewhat riskier and raises some new issues. They concern what is called the **generality** of a study's effects.

> **Generality.** The meaningfulness of experimental interpretations under circumstances different from those that generated the data.

Generality has to do with the meaningfulness of interpretations under circumstances that are at least somewhat different from those that generated the data. Unlike variability, for example, generality is not a characteristic of data. It is simply a way of referring to the predictions inherent in our interpretations that address future uses of research findings. In a sense, data do not actually "mean" anything by themselves. Their only role, together with the details of experimental procedures, is to prompt the investigator and readers to say things about the relationship between the independent and dependent variables. In other words, when we talk about the generality of a study, we are not speculating about a quality of the data or even their meaning. We are

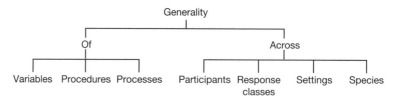

FIG. 13.2. Dimensions of generality.

talking about the predictions implicit in our interpretations about whether they apply to different circumstances.

These predictions are sometimes fairly specific or narrow, such as when we speculate about whether the study's findings would hold if the same procedures were applied to participants with different characteristics. For example, will the findings of a project conducted with typical first graders also be obtained if the same procedures are used with 6-year-old children who are developmentally delayed? We might also guess what would happen if the procedures in a study were slightly modified or if their effects would be the same with a different target behavior.

Conjectures about a study's findings are often relatively broad, however. For instance, when a practitioner uses the findings from a published study in deciding on how to construct a clinical intervention, he or she makes an implicit prediction about the applicability of the study to the clinical circumstances of interest. In such cases, there are probably many details in the clinical situation that are different from those in the research project. Factors associated with the setting, staff, consumers, and procedures will be determined by the practical situation and are likely to differ, sometimes substantially, from those used in the research project.

In sum, asking about the generality of our interpretations addresses the question: "If experimental findings are used under circumstances that are somewhat different, will the same kind of effects be obtained?" This question is similar to the question raised by curiosity about the reliability of a study's outcomes, but it is not the same. Reliability asks: "If experimental procedures are repeated, will the same effects be obtained?" We make this same distinction in discussing replication in chapter 10. In both instances we are making predictions, but the basis for these predictions is different. Concluding that a study's effects are reliable predicts that the same results would be obtained if the procedures were repeated more or less exactly. Concluding that our interpretations are general predicts that the same kind of results would be obtained even if certain features of the study were somewhat different.

TABLE 13.1
Distinguishing between the reliability and the generality of experimental findings

• Reliability	Asks about getting the same outcomes if procedures were repeated exactly
• Generality	Asks about getting the same outcomes if procedures were somewhat different

Interests in Generality

Generality Of and Generality Across. Every study has many different features or elements, of course. There are always two kinds of interests that make up our curiosity about generality. We are interested in the generality *of* some aspect of a study *across* changes in some other feature. In other words, in speculating about generality there must be some elements of the study whose "generalness" is in question, and there must be other features of the study that, if changed, would provide a test of whether the element of interest is general.

Suppose, for example, that a practitioner is interested in using the findings of a published research study as a basis for developing an intervention procedure that will change a consumer's behavior in some way. The practitioner might be able to faithfully duplicate the procedure described in the study. However, the question remains as to whether the published outcomes depended on the characteristics of the participants in the study. If so, the practitioner's consumer might well not share those characteristics and therefore not show the same effects of the procedure. On the other hand, if the study's results did not depend on the characteristics of the participants, the practitioner might expect to get the same results. In this example, we would say that the practitioner was interested in the generality *of* a procedure *across* different individuals. As we have seen, this is a way of asking if the feature that differs between the original study and some other circumstance (such as a clinical application) is critical to obtaining the same results.

Of Variables. Interest in the generality of variables helps to integrate and systematize a literature. When researchers can show that a particular variable is relevant beyond the confines of a certain experiment or even an area of literature, it advances our knowledge of behavior. Discovering such similarities is one of the goals of a science. Although differences are easier to discover, they are only signs of our ignorance.

A good example of a variable in the science of behavior is conditioned reinforcement (reinforcement by stimuli that have become conditioned reinforcers through pairings with other reinforcers). This variable has been shown to have excellent generality across species, individuals, response classes, settings, and other dimensions. The subject index of basic research journals such as the *Journal of the Experimental Analysis of Behavior* provides a long list of variables whose generality continues to be examined.

Of Procedures. Most behavioral research is directed toward the generality of methods of controlling behavior. This is a natural focus for applied research, of course, because the practical goal is often to develop techniques that will be effective in changing behavior under widely varying circumstances. Although this is an ideal outcome, a procedure can be quite valuable even though it is effective under a narrow range of conditions, as long as we know what those conditions are. Whatever the range of effectiveness of a procedure, it is important to know its limits.

What determines the conditions under which a procedure will be effective is the status of its components, as well as the status of other factors operating when it is implemented. Learning about the generality of a procedure requires identifying which of its components may be varied and by how much without weakening the effectiveness of the procedure. It is possible that certain components are critical and must not be tampered with at all, whereas others are unimportant and could even be omitted without risking the procedure's effectiveness.

The procedure known as "time out from positive reinforcement" provides a good example. A summary of the "time out" literature described in Johnston and Pennypacker (1980, chapter 15) showed how accumulated studies over the years demonstrated that many facets of the basic "time out" procedure may be varied without losing its effectiveness as a way of decreasing a target behavior.

Of Processes. A behavioral process may be defined as the result of an ordered series of steps. Sidman (1960) described two meanings of behavioral processes. First, behavior that results from the interactions of two or more different variables or procedures can be called a behavioral process. Perhaps the clearest example here is the process called discrimination, which results from a combination of reinforcement and extinction procedures.

A second type of behavioral process results from applying a wide range of quantitative values of a particular variable. An example is the decreasing number of presentations of a new word necessary to meet a criterion for verbal imitation by an autistic child as a function of the number of presentations of other new words already mastered (Lovaas, Berberich, Perloff, & Schaeffer, 1974). The fact that the number of presentations of a new word required to meet a performance standard is a decreasing function of the words already learned makes this a behavioral process.

Across Individuals. Whether focusing on variables, procedures, or processes, perhaps the most common curiosity about generality concerns whether the findings will be obtained across individuals. This interest follows from the fact that each individual brings together many factors that can modulate the impact of experimental variables. Even individuals who are similar in some obvious ways (e.g., children diagnosed with autism spectrum

TABLE 13.2
Evidence for generality

Evidence	Conclusions
• Showing that the same results are obtained when a variable is changed	Variable does not limit generality
• Showing that the results change when a variable is changed	Variable does limit generality

disorders) may differ in gender and other biological features, reinforcement history of target behaviors, particular features of their repertoire, level of functioning, sensitivity to experimental variables, and many other characteristics. The question about generality is whether the results of a study depended on the status of any of these factors among the participants. If this is true, and if individuals to whom these results are applied differ in these features from the original participants, the study's results may be difficult to reproduce.

The discussion of replication in chapter 10 suggested that generality across individuals may be assessed by repeating a study with different participants. Reproducing the original results may imply that they did not depend on any characteristics that are different from those of the original participant characteristics. Failure to obtain the original results, however, might then require the more selective approach of systematically varying particular characteristics to see which ones influence experimental outcomes.

Across Response Classes. Although the target behavior used as the dependent variable in a study might be considered an individual characteristic, particular response classes often have consistent characteristics across different individuals. This means that it is reasonable to wonder if a study's results would still be obtained if a different response class were used. For example, using biofeedback techniques to treat medically related behaviors has been shown to produce varying degrees of effectiveness depending on the behavior targeted. As a case in point, reports have suggested that biofeedback procedures may work better to decrease pain behavior associated with migraine headaches than when aimed at decreasing systolic blood pressure (Taylor, 1982).

Although practitioners hope that behavior change procedures will be as broadly effective as possible, they must be aware of any limits on a procedure's generality across target behaviors. It is especially important to answer this question when the study at issue was conducted in a laboratory setting using an arbitrary response class such as button pushing or touching a computer screen. These response classes are selected because they are simple and usually lack a meaningful reinforcement history. This may be an advantage in some basic research projects, but it often leaves applied researchers and practitioners wondering whether the same results would be obtained with more practically relevant behaviors.

Across Settings. Practitioners have a similar interest in the generality of findings across settings. Even in applied research projects, experimental circumstances are usually somewhat different from the situations in which practical applications might take place. In this context, "setting" is a broad reference not just to a physical location but to everything that comes with that location. This might include social factors associated with nonparticipants (peers, for example, or care-givers) or things going on in a setting that have nothing to do with the intervention procedure (a school fire-drill).

BOX 13.5

Are We Preoccupied with Generality Across Individuals?

In most psychological research, the paramount interest in generality is whether the findings will hold for all individuals in a class (such as all individuals diagnosed with a certain mental illness) or even all human beings. This focus stems from the widespread use of inferential statistics, which reduces the search for generality across participants to an actuarial or sampling issue (see Reading 13 in Johnston & Pennypacker, 1993b). From this perspective, the question is how well the control and experimental group samples represent the population.

This preoccupation with generality across individuals also confuses our desire that a finding be as universal as possible with our obligation to establish generality through experimental manipulations of controlling variables. Parametric tests of statistical significance encourage the confusion by providing a simple method that appears to enhance generality while increasing the likelihood of getting a significant result—increasing the number of participants in control and experimental groups. Unfortunately, this only further discourages a distinction between assessing versus obtaining generality across individuals. The drive to evaluate generality across individuals at the conclusion of the study by making it a sampling question takes attention away from the more important matter of determining what needs to be learned from future experiments about the role of individual characteristics.

Because behavior is an intraorganism phenomenon, our real interest should be in the individual, not the population. When we understand what factors produce a certain outcome at this level, we are in a much better position to assess whether that outcome will be obtained for other individuals or classes of individuals. Furthermore, it is important to understand that no aspect of generality can be fully resolved with a single study. Identifying the participant variables that influence the impact of a procedure requires a series of experiments in which those variations are systematically manipulated. This approach also helps to refocus attention away from an uncritical desire for generality across a broad range of individuals and toward an interest in identifying those characteristics that will reliably predict success or failure in each case.

It is interesting that in research conducted in the methodological framework of this book, generality across individuals is not regarded with special attention and is easily addressed as a matter of routine. This does not reflect a lack of interest in this aspect of generality but an appreciation of its proper place among our scientific curiosities. Furthermore, behavioral researchers have learned that when sufficient attention is given to issues of experimental control, generality across participants (and eventually other individuals) is relatively easy to demonstrate. In fact, behavioral researchers are accustomed to finding that most, if not all, participants in a study show the same kind of effects.

In contrast, between-group designs tend to put the cart before the horse. The tactics of exposing different levels of the independent variable to different groups, insuring that these groups contain a large number of participants, and treating their responses collectively provide comparisons that describe no member of any group. By failing to focus on individuals with careful attention to experimental control, these traditional methods greatly decrease the chances of discovering orderly relations in the first place. This makes the question of generality across individuals moot.

For example, a research publication may show that a parenting skills course was effective in getting foster parents to use certain procedures with their children in the home. The report indicates that the course was taught to six foster parents in the early afternoon at the county offices of the department of human resources by two trainers assisted by two graduate students in five weekly 3-hour classes. For the practitioner interested in using this parenting skills curriculum, the question is whether presenting the same curriculum will yield the same outcomes if the circumstances are somewhat different. What if the class is taught in the evening or there is only one trainer? What if the classes are only 1 hour long and taught over 15 weeks? What if they are held in a community college classroom? The question, then, is whether any of these features in the published study contributed to the effectiveness of the curriculum.

Across Species. Behavioral scientists are interested in discovering relationships that hold across the widest variety of circumstances, including different species. The most common form of this question is whether the findings of research conducted with nonhuman species will be found when they are extended to humans. Overall, the basic processes of conditioning have shown strong generality across species. As a result, it has been possible to build a behavior change technology strongly rooted in basic science. Of course, the generality of specific studies with nonhuman species to human behavior depends on the details of each prediction.

Evidence

The best evidence about the generality of a study's findings should be the nature of the study's procedures and data. There are two aspects of a study that are important. First, the stronger a study's methods and data, the greater the foundation for predictions about its generality. If a study is methodologically weak or generates equivocal data, it should not encourage speculations about the generality of its outcomes. If the basic outcomes are themselves debatable, questions about generality should be put aside.

Second, the more directly a study addresses issues of generality, the greater the opportunity for interpretations about the extent to which its findings will hold under different conditions. For example, if an experiment included only a single set of control and intervention conditions (as in an ABAB design, for example), there may be little basis for proposing that its results should be obtained when certain features are varied. On the other hand, if a study included systematic variations in particular features, the data may provide a solid basis for statements about whether those features will be important under other circumstances. Similarly, if a project used only two participants, there may be scant evidence about whether its results would be obtained with participants exhibiting different characteristics.

This second feature of research projects raises a useful distinction in the basis for statements about generality. On the one hand, such statements may be largely speculative when there is little or no evidence in a study about whether its results will be reproduced if some of its features are changed. In contrast, they may be well founded when a study included systematic or even unsystematic variations in some of its features so that the data provide support for certain predictions.

In other words, we might distinguish between interpretations that merely speculate about generality versus those that rest on clear evidence about generality. Such evidence usually takes one of two forms: (a) showing that the same results are obtained even when a certain variable is changed, suggesting that it does not limit generality; and (b) showing that the results change when a certain variable is changed, suggesting that it can limit generality. Perhaps the most direct approach to collecting such evidence is to systematically manipulate the variable in question and identify any effects.

Finally, although this section focuses on generality, what we really want to know about is whether certain variables are important or unimportant in obtaining a certain outcome. Once we know about the role of each factor, we will be in a good position to predict what is required to obtain that same outcome under widely varying circumstances. That is, when we wonder about the generality of a study's findings, what we really want to know is how much each of its features contributed to its results. If we understand the role of these variables, we would then know what it takes to produce those results, as well as what would prevent us from obtaining those results.

In other words, the real objective is not to develop procedures or outcomes that are "general" but to understand the role of contributing variables. As a way of making this point, imagine that someone had discovered a technique that was highly effective for treating 25% of the cases of self-injurious behavior. With this track record, we might say that the technique had weak generality across individuals. However, what if we had identified the participant variables that allowed practitioners to identify in advance those individuals with whom the technique would always work? With this knowledge, how might we assess the generality of the procedure? We could now say that its generality to individuals sharing certain characteristics is excellent. This example makes the point that questions about the generality of research findings disappear when we understand the variables underlying experimental effects.

EVALUATING INTERPRETATIONS

When we interpret a research study, our statements about what happened and what it means probably fall short of perfect accuracy and completeness. We do not know how far short, of course, which often leads to disagreements among readers considering the same study. These differences of opinion might tempt some to search for fixed interpretive rules that require certain conclusions under certain conditions, but this approach would represent a misunderstanding of the problem.

In fact, interpretive disagreements are an inevitable and important part of the scientific process. After all, science addresses questions that are just beyond the limits of our knowledge, and individual experiments do not usually provide completely unambiguous answers. As we have already noted, when readers disagree about a study's findings, it is not usually clear who is right. Differing interpretations of a study are therefore not a problem so much as a prompt for replication and additional research. Interpretive issues are eventually resolved as more is learned about the phenomenon.

Does this mean that there is no way to be sure if our interpretations of a research project are correct? In a word: "Yes." When analyzing a study, the best that can be done is to be aware of the influences discussed in this chapter. Regardless of our level of confidence, there is no way to be sure whether our interpretations are correct, much less whether they will hold up under different circumstances. Interpretations are no more than the verbal behavior of individuals. They are influenced by many different factors and may or may not be accurate or complete. This assessment applies regardless of the general analytical approach or particular techniques used.

This does not mean that we can draw whatever conclusions we like without fear of contradiction, however. There is a kind of yardstick that ultimately measures the soundness of all interpretations. This standard is the *reproducibility* of the original findings. Let us say, for instance, that a practitioner concludes that a published study showed that a particular procedure was effective in changing behavior in a certain way. If this interpretation is correct, when the practitioner uses that procedure there is a good chance that the same result will be obtained. If so, being able to reproduce that result implies that the interpretation of the study was correct. If the procedure does not work as expected, it may suggest that the interpretation was incorrect in some way. Of course, things are not this simple. The practitioner's success will also depend on how well the application embodies the critical factors at work in the research study. In other words, this standard for evaluating interpretations is not perfect. It does not test our interpretations until we use them in some way, and even then the assessment is complicated by how they are used.

The standard of reproducibility is at least unavoidable, however. Even if an investigator does not replicate his or her own study, sooner or later others will replicate it or use its findings in some way. Other researchers might base experiments on the original results, and practitioners might use the findings in service settings. This likelihood creates a contingency between our interpretations and their consequences for those who use them. This contingency encourages everyone to base their interpretations on a careful consideration of experimental methods and the data.

This example of how the contingencies embedded in experimental methods influence the behavior of scientists has been a theme throughout this book. It reminds us that scientific methods were not invented by early scientists by some rational process. The history of science shows that they slowly evolved, experiment by experiment, over many years. Some practices were shaped and maintained because they often produced reinforcing consequences in the form of an increased ability to predict and control natural events. Other practices were abandoned because they failed to do so. In other words, what might appear as a set of rules about "how to do science" is really just a way of summarizing a long history of the impact of contingencies between the researcher's behavior and the subject matter.

Although the strategies and tactics outlined in this book are certainly important guidelines, following them will not guarantee experimental success any more than violating them will assure failure. Each experimental challenge is unique, and creativity is often more important than blind compliance with methodological rules. Every experimental action has its consequences, however, and skilled researchers understand these relationships well.

CHAPTER SUMMARY

1. The primary challenge in interpreting a study is to decide how each of its features might have affected the data. The researcher must then decide how each factor should influence interpretive statements. In making this assessment, the investigator must start by considering all of the possible sources of control over their interpretive reactions.

2. Some influences on the researcher's interpretive reactions are also likely to have played a significant role when the study was designed. Variables such as a researcher's theoretical perspective, the scientific literature, and available resources are likely to have influenced how the experimental question has been framed.

3. Because the experimental question guides decisions about how the experiment is designed and conducted, it places certain limits on what the procedures and data can reveal. If interpretations exceed these limits, it may mean that conclusions are too strongly influenced by other factors, such as extra-experimental considerations. However, too slavish a devotion to the experimental question can blind the investigator to the possibility of discovering outcomes that were not forecast by the question.

4. In comparing responding under the experimental condition and its matched control condition, we are attempting to assess if any change in responding is due to the introduction of the independent variable. In deciding if this is the case, the reader must determine whether the independent variable was appropriate for the experimental question and how well it was managed during the project.

5. It is not enough to determine that the independent variable was appropriate and properly implemented. The same issues of appropriateness and consistency must be addressed for the control condition. Additionally, extraneous variables that are not taken into account by the control condition must be considered when evaluating the results.

6. Interpreting a study requires more than determining whether each particular control–treatment comparison was replicated and showed

consistent results. There is also the matter of deciding what each comparison says about the influence of the independent variable and, more broadly, the experimental question. This is often a complex judgment in which no simple rules will help.

7. In considering what the data say about intervention conditions, it is important to look at the nature of the variability in the data. It is possible that problems with the study's measurement and analytical procedures have produced data that do not accurately represent what actually occurred. However, if the study was well designed and conducted, the variability between phases presumably represents the effects of the independent variable. Once we are confident that this is the case, we can then judge what the data reveal about the effects of the independent variable and how these effects might help to answer the experimental question.

8. Generality has to do with the meaningfulness of interpretations under circumstances that are at least somewhat different from those that generated the data. There are always two kinds of interests that make up our curiosity about generality. We are interested in the generality of some aspect of a study (e.g., variables, procedures, processes) across changes in some other feature (e.g., individuals, response classes, settings). Each area of interest contributes to our understanding of specific techniques and variables and aids us in integrating and expanding the literature on these topics.

9. When we interpret a research study, our statements about what happened and what it means probably fall short of perfect accuracy and completeness. This may lead to interpretive disagreements, which are an inevitable and important part of the scientific process. Differing interpretations of a study are not a problem so much as a prompt for replication and additional research.

10. Regardless of our level of confidence, there is no way to know whether our interpretations are correct, much less whether they will hold up under different circumstances. Interpretations are no more than the verbal behavior of individuals. They are influenced by many different factors and may or may not be accurate or complete. This assessment applies regardless of the general analytical approach or particular techniques used.

11. Although the strategies and tactics outlined in this book are certainly important guidelines, following them will not guarantee experimental success any more than violating them will assure failure. Each experimental challenge is unique, and an investigator's creativity is often more important and valuable than blind compliance with methodological rules. Every experimental action has its consequences, however, and skilled researchers understand these relationships well.

TEXT STUDY GUIDE

1. What is the function of interpretations for the culture?
2. How can an investigator's theoretical persuasion affect interpretations?
3. List some extra-experimental contingencies that may influence interpretations.
4. How can focusing on the experimental question sometimes be a harmful influence on interpretations?
5. Why is it important to assess, one at a time, each of the components of measurement?
6. Provide some aspects of response class definitions that should guide interpretations.
7. Describe some issues concerning dimensional quantities and units of measurement that are relevant to interpretations.
8. List some features of observing and recording that should be considered when drawing conclusions.
9. What is the point of the exercise of describing in one sentence what a single data point represents?
10. Make up an example showing how an independent variable could be inappropriate for an experimental question.
11. Under what experimental circumstances might it be important to measure how well the control and treatment conditions were implemented?
12. What are the requirements that a control condition must satisfy?
13. Why does it matter how many instances of each control-experimental comparisons are available?
14. What features of the data should be evaluated before drawing conclusions about what they mean?
15. Under what circumstances might you decide to reject a study because it does not warrant interpretation?
16. Explain the dictum ". . . the task is not just to interpret the data, but to interpret the entire experiment."
17. What is generality, and what is it not?
18. How is the generality of a study's findings different from its reliability?
19. Explain the two main interests in generality.
20. What is it that must be learned in order to predict the conditions under which a study's findings will or will not be obtained under other circumstances?
21. Explain the standard by which all interpretations are eventually evaluated.

BOX STUDY GUIDE

1. What is the main problem associated with experimental questions that ask about mental events?

2. Define and distinguish between internal and external validity.

3. Why is statistical significance an outcome of limited importance?

4. Why might attitudes toward interpretation differ between the social sciences and the natural sciences?

5. How does a preoccupation with generality across individuals confuse interest in the broad applicability of a finding with the requirement to establish generality experimentally?

6. How will a sound understanding of individual characteristics that influence the effects of a procedure help to predict whether those effects will be found with other individuals?

7. Why is generality across individuals not the primary goal of experimentation for behavioral researchers?

8. Why can between-group designs make it difficult to establish generality across individuals?

SUGGESTED READINGS

Johnston, J. M. (1979). On the relation between generality and generalization. *The Behavior Analyst, 2*, 1–6.

Terrell, D. J., & Johnston, J. M. (1989). Logic, reasoning, and verbal behavior. *The Behavior Analyst, 12*, 35–44.

DISCUSSION TOPICS

1. Select and study a research report published in a behavioral journal such as the *Journal of Applied Behavior Analysis*. Debate the interpretations that are defensible, given the methodological features of the study.

2. Discuss the contrast between generality as discussed in this chapter and as it is treated in research based on inferential statistics.

EXERCISES

1. Select a research report published in a behavioral journal. Assess the study in terms of the number of questions concerning response class definition, dimensional quantities and units, and observing and recording. How should this assessment affect interpretations of the data?

2. Select a research report published in a behavioral journal. Describe in a single sentence exactly what a single data point represents.

3. Select a research report published in a behavioral journal. Identify the specific features of the study about which there might be interest in generality.

Glossary

AB design. A within-subject experimental design composed of a control and an experimental condition.

Absolute unit. A unit of measurement whose value is defined in a fixed or unvarying manner independently of the phenomenon being measured.

Accuracy. The extent to which observed values approximate to the events that actually occurred.

Across-research-literature replication. Repetition of phenomena under different conditions across different fields of science.

Advocacy research. A style of research in which an investigator's primary goal is to generate support for a predetermined outcome or hypothesis. See Boxes 3.1 and 3.3.

Alternative hypothesis. In contrast to the null hypothesis, a prediction that there are differences between the populations of which the experimental control groups are samples and that the differences are due to the independent variable. See *Null hypothesis*. See Box 3.5.

Antecedent event. An environmental event that occurs immediately before a response. Used generically when it is not certain what function the event serves.

Applied behavior analysis. A phrase that may refer to: (a) the field of research that focuses on applying the findings of a basic science (the Experimental Analysis of Behavior) concerning fundamental processes of conditioning to address the need for changing behavior under everyday circumstances; (b) the behavior change technology developed by applied researchers; or (c) the field encompassed by applied research and delivery of the resulting technology.

Baseline condition. A condition or phase of an experiment in which the independent variable is not present. Also called a *control condition*.

Behavioral variability. Variations in features of responding within a single response class, as well as variations in summary measures of that class.

Believability. The extent to which the investigator can, in the absence of direct evidence, convince others to believe that the data are good enough for interpretation.

Does not involve direct evidence about the relationship between data and the events they are intended to represent.

Between-group design.   A method of arranging comparisons between control and experimental conditions in which different groups of subjects are exposed to control and experimental conditions so that the data represent the combined performance of individual participants who have experienced only one of the conditions.

Blind.   A reference to being unaware of the goals of an experiment, the nature of experimental or control conditions, or the outcomes of each condition. May apply to the experimenter, observers, or participants. If both experimenter and participants are blind, it is called a *double-blind* experiment.

Calibration.   Evaluating the accuracy and reliability of data produced by a measurement procedure and, if necessary, using these findings to improve the procedure so that it meets desired standards.

Celeration.   A dimensional quantity that describes change in the frequency of responding over time.

Changing criterion design.   A within-subject design using AB and reversal sequences to identify effects of manipulating performance criteria. See *Parametric design*.

Classical conditioning.   The processes involved in creating conditioned reflexes from unconditioned reflexes. Also called *respondent* or *Pavlovian conditioning*.

Comparison.   Using descriptions of multiple individual events to identify differences among them.

Complete observation.   A schedule of observation that allows detection of all responses in the defined class.

Conditioned reflex.   A reflex in which the class of eliciting stimuli have acquired this function because of a history of being paired with unconditioned stimuli.

Conditioning.   The process of changing a behavior that involves interactions between responses and environmental events whose effects depend on the processes of reinforcement and punishment.

Consequent event.   An environmental event that occurs immediately after a response. Used generically when it is not certain what function the event serves.

Contingency.   A relationship between a class of responses and a class (or classes) of stimuli. Implies nothing about the nature of the relationship or its effects.

Continuous observation.   Observation procedures in which all target responses can be detected during observation periods.

Control condition.   A condition or phase of an experiment in which the independent variable is not present. Also called a *baseline condition*.

Countability.   A dimensional quantity reflecting the property of repeatability that refers to the occurrence of the event being measured and is measured in terms of cycles.

Cycle.   A repeating pattern of local variability, often involving sequences of increasing and decreasing trends (in either order). *Also*, a unit of measurement for the dimensional quantity of countability.

Cycles per unit time.   The unit of measurement for the dimensional quantity of frequency. In the study of behavior, minutes is most often the time unit used (e.g., 1.5 cycles per minute).

Cycles per unit time per unit time.   The unit of measurement for celeration.

Dead Man's Test.   An informal test of whether a particular event is a behavior. The test is that if a dead man can do it, it is not behavior. See Box 2.2.

Demonstration research.   A style of research in which the primary goal is to show that a certain outcome is possible. See Box 3.1 and *Explanatory research*.

Dependent variable. In behavioral research, usually a response class. The objective is to see if changes in the dependent variable depend on manipulations of the independent variable.

Description. Attaching a number to an event to distinguish it from other events.

Dimensional measurement. An approach to measurement that involves attaching a number representing the observed extent of a dimensional quantity to an appropriate unit of measurement.

Dimensional quantity. A quantifiable dimension of a property of a natural phenomenon. Also referred to as a *quantity*.

Dimensionless quantity. A unitless or scalar number that results from calculations whose components share the same dimensional quantities.

Direct measurement. Measurement practices in which the events measured are the same as those about which conclusions will be drawn. See *Indirect measurement*.

Discontinuous observation. Observation procedures in which all target responses are not necessarily detected and recorded.

Discriminated operant. A class of responses that are functionally related to classes of both antecedent and consequent stimuli.

Discriminative stimuli. Stimuli that have acquired the function of setting the occasion for a behavior to occur. A behavior is more likely to occur in the presence of a discriminative stimulus than in its absence. Abbreviated S^D.

Duration. A dimensional quantity that refers to the elapsed time between the beginning and ending of an event, such as a single response.

Environment. The complex of physical circumstances in which the organism or referenced part of the organism exists. This includes any physical even or set of events that is not part of a behavior and may include other aspects of the organism.

Episode. A relatively brief period of responding defined by the relatively frequent occurrence of one or more specific response classes and which is distinguished from other such bouts by relatively extended periods in which the targeted responses do not occur.

Event-response latency. In the study of behavior, a type of latency representing the time between an environmental event and a response.

Exact agreement. A procedure for calculating interobserver agreement that involves dividing the observation period into intervals in which two observers record the actual number of responses. To obtain percent agreement, only intervals in which the two observers agreed on the exact count are considered agreements.

Experimental condition. A condition or phase in which the independent variable is present. Also called a *treatment, intervention*, or *independent variable condition*.

Experimental control. The management or control of different variables in a study, including the independent variable and extraneous variables.

Experimental design. Arrangement of control and treatment conditions that permit comparisons that help to identify the effects of the independent variable on the dependent variable.

Explanatory research. A style of research in which the primary goal is to understand the nature or mechanisms of the relationship between the independent and dependent variable. See Box 3.1 and *Demonstration research*.

Exploratory data analysis (EDA). An approach to data analysis that emphasizes largely graphical techniques focusing on discovering order and structure in the data. EDA may be contrasted with confirmatory data analysis or hypothesis testing.

Extraneous variables. Environmental events that are not of interest to the researcher but may influence the participant's behavior in ways that obscure the effects of the independent variable.

Extrinsic variability. The assumption that variability in behavior is describable, explainable, and predictable in terms of variation in other phenomena, whether biological or environmental. See *Intrinsic variability.*

Frequency. A compound dimensional quantity describing the average number of events per unit of time. In the study of behavior, calculated by dividing total count by either total IRT or by the total time during which responses occurred. Also called *rate.* See Box 5.1.

Functional relation. An experimentally determined relation that shows that the dependent variable depends on or is a function of the independent variable and nothing else.

Functional response class definition. A definition of a response class based on the functional relations between its responses and classes of antecedent and consequent environmental events.

Generality. The meaningfulness of experimental interpretations under circumstances different from those that generated the data.

Group behavior. The mathematical result of combining the data from multiple individuals who are related in some way (e.g., exposure to an experimental condition or applied intervention). Does not refer to a natural phenomenon distinct from the behavior of an individual organism.

Hypothesis. A speculation, prediction, or guess about the outcome of an experiment. May refer to a formal, written statement or to an informal statement. See Box 3.4.

Hypothetico-deductive method. An approach to experimental reasoning in which reasoning is from a set of general postulates or axioms to a series of specific theorems that can then be verified by experiment. See Box 3.6.

Ignored day. A plotting convention referring to days on which the target behavior could have occurred but was not measured. Data points bracketing such days should be connected in line graphs.

Incomplete observation. A schedule of observation that samples from the population of responses in the defined class.

Independent research. A style of research in which a researcher conceives of a study independently of any coordinated research program or even the existing literature. See Boxes 3.1 and 3.2 and *Thematic research.*

Independent variable. Environmental event or events whose presence or absence is manipulated by the investigator in order to determine their effects on the dependent variable.

Independent variable condition. A condition or phase in which the independent variable is present. Also called an *experimental, treatment,* or *intervention condition.*

Indirect measurement. Measurement practices in which the events measured are not the same as those about which conclusions will be drawn. See *Direct measurement.* See Box 6.2.

In-house research. A style of research in which a study is designed to serve strictly local purposes and is not intended to be published in the archival literature. See Box 3.1.

Interobserver agreement. A procedure for enhancing the believability of data that involves comparing simultaneous but independent observations from two or more observers. Provides no information about accuracy or reliability.

Interresponse time (IRT).   A dimensional quantity referring to the time elapsing between two successive responses.

Intersubject variability.   Differences in responding between participants.

Interval agreement.   A procedure for calculating interobserver agreement when interval recording or time sampling is used. Each interval scored by two observers is counted as an agreement, and each interval that is scored by neither observer is also called an agreement. Intervals for which only one observer scored the behavior are counted as disagreements.

Interval recording.   A discontinuous observation procedure in which observation periods are divided into equal intervals, which are scored according to some rule if the target behavior occurs.

Intervention condition.   A condition or phase in which the independent variable is present. Also called an *experimental, treatment,* or *independent variable* condition.

Intraorganism.   A reference to the individual organism as a level of analysis (e.g., behavior is an intraorganism phenomenon in that it involves only relations between the individual organism and its environment).

Intrinsic variability.   The assumption that variability in behavior is in one way or another inherent or built into the nature of organisms. See *Extrinsic variability.*

IRTs per opportunity.   A dimensional quantity that reflects the likelihood of occurrence of specific IRT values that accounts for the mutual exclusivity of all shorter IRTs in each instance of a given IRT range.

Latency.   A dimensional quantity that refers to the time between two events. In the study of behavior, the second event is usually a response and the first event may be a response or an environment event.

Learning.   The relatively enduring changes in behavior that result from conditioning processes.

Linear interval scale.   A measurement scale that allows descriptions of events that show how much they differ in terms of equal intervals between values.

Logarithmic interval scale.   A measurement scale that allows descriptions of events that show how much they differ in terms of equal ratios between values.

Measurement reactivity.   The effects of measurement procedures on a participant's behavior. See Box 6.3.

Momentary time sampling.   A discontinuous observation procedure in which observation periods are divided into equal intervals, but the observer only notes the momentary status of the target behavior at the end of each interval.

Multi-element design.   A within-subject design in which each participant is repeatedly exposed to one or more conditions in an alternating sequence. Also called an *alternating-treatment design.*

Multiple baseline design.   A within-subject design that uses two or more baselines in a coordinated way to allow control–treatment comparisons both within and across baselines.

Negative punishers.   A class of stimuli that are terminated immediately following responding, resulting in a decrease in some aspect of the response class over baseline levels.

Negative punishment.   A procedure involving the termination of a stimulus immediately following responding that results in a decrease in some aspect of the response class over baseline levels.

Negative reinforcement.   A procedure involving the termination of a stimulus immediately following responding that results in an increase in some aspect of the response class over baseline levels.

Negative reinforcers. A class of stimuli that are terminated immediately following responding, resulting in an increase in some aspect of the response class over baseline levels.

No chance day. A plotting convention referring to days on which the target behavior could not have occurred. Data points bracketing such days should not be connected in line graphs.

Null hypothesis. A prediction required by the logic of inferential statistics that there are no differences among the populations of which the experimental and control groups are samples. See *Alternative hypothesis*. See Box 3.5.

Observed values. Values resulting from observation and recording procedures used to collect the data for a study.

Observer drift. A change in the accuracy of an observer's performance, often gradual and for unknown reasons.

Occurrence/nonoccurrence agreement. A conservative approach to calculating interobserver agreement when interval recording or time sampling is used that involves calculating and reporting agreement separately for both occurrences (scored intervals) and nonoccurrences (unscored intervals).

Operant. A class of responses defined by a functional relation with a particular class of environmental stimuli that immediately follow these responses.

Operant conditioning. The processes involved in changing operant behavior based on its environmental consequences.

Operational definition. A definition in terms of the operations used to produce and measure a phenomenon. Especially associated with nonobservable constructs in an attempt to clarify their reference. See Box 4.5.

Parametric design. A within-subject design using AB and reversal sequences to identify effects of manipulating a specific parameter of a procedure. See *Changing criterion design*.

Partial interval recording. A form of interval recording in which an interval is scored if at least one target response (or even part of a response) occurs during the interval.

Pavlovian conditioning. See *Classical* or *Respondent conditioning*.

Pilot research. A style of research in which a study is primarily intended to test certain aspects of a procedure before conducting a formal experiment. See Box 3.1.

Positive punishers. A class of stimuli that occur immediately following responding, resulting in a decrease in some aspect of the response class over baseline levels.

Positive punishment. A class of procedures involving the occurrence of a stimulus immediately following responding that results in a decrease in some aspect of the response class over baseline levels.

Positive reinforcement. A class of procedures involving the occurrence of a stimulus immediately following responding that results in an increase in some aspect of the response class over baseline levels.

Positive reinforcers. A class of stimuli that occur immediately following responding, resulting in an increase in some aspect of the response class over baseline levels.

Prediction. Making repeated descriptions of an event taken over time in order to predict the outcome of a future measurement.

Property. A fundamental quality of a natural phenomenon. See *Dimensional quantity*.

Quarter-life. A dimensional quantity reflecting the time required to emit 25% of the responses that occur during an interval of time (most often under a fixed-interval schedule of reinforcement). Provides a way of quantifying the curvature of a cumulative record of responding throughout an interval. See Box 5.3.

Range.   A measure of variability defined by the highest and lowest values in a data set.

Reflex.   A class of stimulus–response relationships in which certain environmental events consistently elicit specific responses.

Reliability.   The stability of the relationship between observed values and the events that actually occurred.

Repeatability.   A property of events that can recur. In the study of behavior, a property of a class of functionally equivalent responses. Described in terms of the dimensional quantity of countability.

Replication.   Repetition of any parts of an experiment.

Reproduction.   Repetition of results, usually as an outcome of repetition of procedures.

Respondent.   A class of responses elicited by particular unconditioned or conditioned antecedent stimuli.

Respondent conditioning.   See *Classical conditioning*. Also called *Pavlovian conditioning*.

Response.   A single instance of a response class.

Response class.   A collection of individual responses that have common sources of influence in the environment. Also called a behavior.

Response products.   The tangible or intangible environmental effects of responding that are more than transitory in duration.

Reversal design.   A within-subject experimental design involving a pair of control and experimental conditions in which one or both conditions repeat at least once.

Scientific method.   The established practices of scientific communities that have evolved over time because of their effectiveness in studying natural phenomena.

Sequence effect.   An effect of a participant's behavior resulting from exposure to a prior condition.

Serendipity.   In science, the discovery of useful findings that were not being looked for. See Box 3.8.

Steady state.   A pattern of responding that shows relatively little variation in its measured dimensional quantities over some period of time.

Steady-state strategy.   An approach to making experimental comparisons that involves measuring responding for each participant repeatedly under each condition in an effort to assess and manage extraneous influences and thereby obtain a stable pattern of responding that represents the full effects of each condition.

Temporal extent.   A property of any phenomenon that occurs in time. Described in terms of the dimensional quantity of duration.

Temporal locus.   A property of any phenomenon that occurs in time. Described in terms of the dimensional quantity of latency.

Thematic research.   A style of research in which experiments are designed so that they are related to other studies in specific ways. See Boxes 3.1 and 3.2 and *Independent research*.

Three-term contingency.   A set of functional relationships among distinct classes of antecedent stimuli, responses, and consequent stimuli that together constitute the model of how behavior is influenced by the environment.

Time per cycle.   The unit of measurement for interresponse time.

Topographical response class definition.   A definition of a response class based on the form of responses in three-dimensional space.

Total agreement.   A procedure for calculating interobserver agreement typically used with dimensional quantities such as count, duration, and latency that involves summing the total count for each of two observers, dividing the smaller total by the larger total, and multiplying the result by 100 to arrive at the percentage agreement.

Transition state.   A pattern of responding involving change from one steady state to a different steady state.

Transitory state.   A pattern of responding involving a deviation from a steady state that ends in a return to the same steady state.

Treatment condition.   A condition or phase in which the independent variable is present. Also called an *experimental, intervention,* or *independent variable condition.*

Treatment integrity.   The extent to which the independent variable is consistently implemented as designed.

Trend.   A relatively consistent change in the data in a single direction.

True values.   Values resulting from special observation and recording procedures that are somewhat different from those used to collect the data being evaluated and that involve special efforts to minimize error.

Unconditioned reflex.   A reflex in which the class of eliciting stimuli serve this function without a history of being paired with unconditioned stimuli.

Unit of analysis.   A constituent part of a whole phenomenon that serves as a basis for experimental study. In the study of behavior, the unit of analysis is the response class.

Unit of measurement.   A determinate amount of a dimensional quantity of the phenomenon being measured.

Validity.   The extent to which observed values represent the events they are supposed to represent and that will be the focus of interpretation.

Whole interval recording.   A form of interval recording in which an interval is scored if the target behavior occurs without ceasing throughout the entire interval.

Within-experiment replication.   Repetition of an entire phase during the course of an experiment.

Within-literature replication.   Repetition of an earlier experiment, usually by other researchers.

Within-phase replication.   Repetition of the same condition many times in succession throughout a phase.

Within-session replication.   Repetition of a basic element of procedure throughout each session.

Within-subject design.   A method of arranging comparisons between control and experimental conditions in which each subject is exposed to both control and experimental conditions in sequence so that the data represent the performance of individual participants. Also referred to as *single-subject, N = 1,* and *repeated-measures design.*

References

Ator, N. A. (1999). Statistical inference in behavior analysis: Environmental determinants? *The Behavior Analyst, 22*, 93-97.

Austin, J., & Carr, J. E. (2000). *Handbook of applied behavior analysis*. Reno, NV: Context Press.

Azrin, N. H., Rubin, H., O'Brien, F., Ayllon, T., & Roll, D. (1968). Behavioral engineering: Postural control by a portable apparatus. *Journal of Applied Behavior Analysis, 1*, 99-108.

Bailey, J. S., & Burch, M. R. (2002). *Research methods in applied behavior analysis*. Thousand Oaks, CA: Sage Publications.

Barenblatt, G. I. (1987). *Dimensional analysis*. New York: Gordon & Breach.

Barlow, D. H., Becker, R., Leitenberg, H., & Agras, W. S. (1970). A mechanical strain gauge for recording penile circumference change. *Journal of Applied Behavior Analysis, 3*, 73-76.

Baron, A. (1999). Statistical inference in behavior analysis: Friend or foe? *The Behavior Analyst, 22*, 83-85.

Barrett, B. H. (1962). Reduction in rate of multiple tics by free operant conditioning methods. *Journal of Nervous and Mental Disease, 135*, 187-195.

Baum, W. M. (2005). *Understanding behaviorism* (2nd ed.). Malden, MA: Blackwell Publishing.

Bijou, S. W., Peterson, R. F., Harris, F. R., Allen, K. E., & Johnston, M. S. (1969). Methodology for experimental studies of young children in natural settings. *Psychological Record, 19*, 177-210.

Branch, M. N. (1999). Statistical inference in behavior analysis: Some things significance testing does and does not do. *The Behavior Analyst, 22*, 87-92.

Branch, M. N., & Vollmer, T. R. (2004). Two suggestions for the verbal behavior(s) of organisms (i.e., authors). *The Behavior Analyst, 27*, 95-98.

Bridgeman, P. W. (1927). *The logic of modern physics*. New York: Macmillan.

Campbell, D. T., & Stanley, J. C. (1966). *Experimental and quasi-experimental designs for research*. Chicago: Rand McNally.

Carr, A. (1966). Adaptation aspects of the scheduled travel of *Chelonia*. In *Annual orientation and navigation*. Corvallis: Oregon State University Press.

Catania, A. C. (2007). *Learning* (4th ed.). Cornwall-on-Hudson, NY: Sloan Publishing.

Catania, A. C., Shimoff, E., & Mathews, B. A. (1989). An experimental analysis of rule-governed behavior. In S. C. Hayes, (Ed.), *Rule-governed behavior: Cognition, contingencies, and instructional control* (pp. 119-150). New York: Plenum Press.

Chertov, A. G. (1964). *Units of measurement of physical quantities*. New Haven, CT: Hayden.

363

Connell, J. E., & Witt, J. C. (2004). Applications of computer-based instruction: Using specialized software to aid letter-name and letter-sound recognition. *Journal of Applied Behavior Analysis, 37,* 67-71.

Cooper, J. O., Heron, T. E., & Heward, W. L. (1987). *Applied behavior analysis.* Columbus, OH: Merrill Publishing.

Crosbie, J. (1999). Statistical inference in behavior analysis: Useful friend. *The Behavior Analyst, 22,* 105-108.

Davison, M. (1999). Statistical inference in behavior analysis: Having my cake and eating it? *The Behavior Analyst, 22,* 99-103.

Deguchi, H. (1984). Observational learning from a radical-behavioristic viewpoint. *The Behavior Analyst, 7,* 83-95.

Durbin, P. T. (1968). *Logic and scientific inquiry.* Milwaukee, WI: Brice Publishing.

Epstein, R. (1980). *Notebooks, B. F. Skinner.* Englewood Cliffs, NJ: Prentice-Hall.

Estes, W. K. (1979). Experimental psychology: An overview. In E. Hearst (Ed.), *The first century of experimental psychology* (pp. 623-667). Hillsdale, NJ: Lawrence Erlbaum Associates.

Falk, J. (1961). Production of polydipsia as a function of fixed interval length. *Journal of the Experimental Analysis of Behavior, 9,* 37-39.

Falk, J. (1971). The nature and determinants of adjunctive behavior. *Physiology and Behavior, 6,* 557-588.

Falk, J. (1981). The environmental generation of excessive behavior. In S. J. Mule (Ed.), *Behavior in excess: An examination of the volitional disorders* (pp. 313-337). New York: Free Press.

Fisher, R. A. (1935). *The design of experiments.* London: Oliver & Boyd.

Fisher, W., Piazza, C. C., Bowman, L. G., Hagopian, L. P., Owens, J. C., & Slevin, I. (1992). A comparison of two approaches for identifying reinforcers for persons with severe and profound disabilities. *Journal of Applied Behavior Analysis, 25,* 491-498.

Fuller, P. R. (1949). Operant conditioning of a vegetative organism. *American Journal of Psychology, 62,* 587-590.

Gardenier, N. C., MacDonald, R., & Green, G. (2004). Comparison of direct observational methods for measuring stereotypic behavior in children with autism spectrum disorders. *Research in Developmental Disabilities, 25,* 99-118.

Glenn, I. M., & Dallery, J. (2007). Effects of internet-based voucher reinforcement and a transdermal nicotine patch on cigarette smoking. *Journal of Applied Behavior Analysis, 40,* 1-13.

Green, S. B., McCoy, J. F., Burns, K. P., & Smith, A. C. (1982). Accuracy of observational data with whole interval, partial interval, and momentary time-sampling recording techniques. *Journal of Behavioral Assessment, 4,* 103-118.

Handley, G. P., Iwata, B. A., & McCord, B. E. (2003). Functional analysis of problem behavior: A review. *Journal of Applied Behavior Analysis, 36,* 147-185.

Harrop, A., & Daniels, M. (1986). Methods of time sampling: A reappraisal of momentary time sampling and partial interval recording. *Journal of Applied Behavior Analysis, 19,* 73-76.

Hawkins, R. P., & Dotson, V. A. (1975). Reliability scores that delude: An Alice In Wonderland trip through the misleading characteristics of interobserver agreement scores in interval recording. In E. Ramp & G. Semb (Eds.), *Behavior analysis: Areas of research and application* (pp. 359-376). Englewood Cliffs, NJ: Prentice-Hall.

Hefferline, R. F., & Keenan, B. (1963). Amplitude-induction gradient of a small-scale (covert) operant. *Journal of the Experimental Analysis of Behavior, 6,* 307-315.

Henson, D. E., & Rubin, H. B. (1971). Voluntary control of eroticism. *Journal of Applied Behavior Analysis, 4,* 37-44.

Hoaglin, D. C. Mosteller, R., & Tukey, J. W. (1985). *Exploring data tables, trends and shapes.* New York: John Wiley & Sons.

Hopkins, B. L., Cole, B. L., & Mason, T. L. (1998). A critique of the usefulness of inferential statistics in applied behavior analysis. *The Behavior Analyst, 21,* 125-137.

Hull, C. L. (1940). *Mathematico-deductive theory of rote learning: A study in scientific methodology.* New York: Appleton-Century.

Hull, C. L. (1943). *Principles of behavior.* New York: Appleton-Century.

Ipsen, D. C. (1960). *Units, dimensions, and dimensionless numbers.* New York: McGraw-Hill.

Iwata, B. A., Vollmer, T. R., & Zarcone, J. R. (1990). The experimental (functional) analysis of behavior disorders: Methodology, applications, and limitations. In A. C. Repp & N. N. Singh (Eds.), *Perspectives on the use of nonaversive and aversive interventions for persons with developmental disabilities* (pp. 301-330). DeKalb, IL: Sycamore Press.

Johnson, K. R., & Layng, T. V. J. (1992). Breaking the structuralist barrier: Literary and numeracy with fluency. *American Psychologist, 47*, 1475-1490.

Johnson, L. M., & Morris, E. K. (1987). When speaking of probability in behavior analysis. *Behaviorism, 15*, 107-129.

Johnston, J. M. (1979). On the relation between generality and generalization. *The Behavior Analyst, 2*, 1-6.

Johnston, J. M. (1988). Strategic and tactical limits of comparison studies. *The Behavior Analyst, 11*, 1-9.

Johnston, J. M. (1996). Distinguishing between applied research and practice. *The Behavior Analyst, 19*, 35-47.

Johnston, J. M., Greene, K., Rawal, A., Winston, M., Vazin, T., & Rossi, M. (1991). The effects of caloric density on ruminating. *Journal of Applied Behavior Analysis, 24*, 597-603.

Johnston, J. M., O'Neill, G. W., Walters, W. M., & Rasheed, J. A. (1975). The measurement and analysis of college student study behavior. Tactics and procedures for research. In J. M. Johnston (Ed.), *Behavior research and technology in higher education* (pp. 387-398). Springfield, IL: Charles C. Thomas.

Johnston, J. M., & Pennypacker, H. S. (1980). *Strategies and tactics of human behavioral research*. Hillsdale, NJ: Lawrence Erlbaum Associates.

Johnston, J. M., & Pennypacker, H. S. (1993a). *Strategies and tactics of behavioral research*. Hillsdale, NJ: Lawrence Erlbaum Associates.

Johnson, J. M., & Pennypacker, H. S. (1993b). *Readings for strategies and tactics of behavioral research*. Hillsdale, NJ: Lawrence Erlbaum Associates.

Kantor, J. R. (1945). *Psychology and logic, Vol. 1*. Bloomington, IN: Principia Press.

Kennedy, C. H. (2005). *Single-case designs for educational research*. Boston, MA: Pearson Education.

Koch, S. (1954). Clark L. Hull. In W. K. Estes et al. (Eds.), *Modern learning theory: A critical analysis of five examples*. New York: Appleton-Century-Crofts.

Lalli, J. S., Browder, D. M., Mace, F. C., & Brown, D. K. (1993). Teacher use of descriptive analysis data to implement interventions to decrease students' problem behaviors. *Journal of Applied Behavior Analysis, 26*, 227-238.

Lee, V. L. (1981). Terminological and conceptual revision in the experimental analysis of language development: Why. *Behaviorism, 9*, 25-53.

Lovaas, I. O., Berberich, J. P., Perloff, B. F., & Schaeffer, B. (1974). Acquisition of imitative speech by schizophrenic children. In I. O. Lovaas & B. D. Bucher (Eds.), *Perspectives in behavior modification with deviant children* (pp. 161-183). Hillsdale, NJ: Lawrence Erlbaum Associates.

Lowe, C. F. (1979). Determinants of human operant behavour. In M. D. Zeiler & P. Harzem (Eds.), Reinforcement and the organization of behaviour (pp. 159-192). New York: John Wiley & Sons.

Mahoney, M. J. (1976). *Scientist as subject: The psychological imperative*. Cambridge, MS: Balinger Publishing.

Moore, J. (1975). On the principle of operationism in a science of behavior. *Behaviorism, 3*, 120-138.

Moore, J. (2008). *Conceptual foundations of radical behaviorism*. Cornwall-on-Hudson, NY: Sloan Publishing.

Murphy, G., & Goodall, E. (1980). Measurement error in direct observations: A comparison or common recording methods. *Behavior Research and Therapy, 18*, 147-150.

New York State Department of Health (1999). *Report of the recommendations: Autism/pervasive developmental disorders*. Albany, NY: New York State Department of Health.

Northup, J., Wacker, D. P., Berg, W. K., Kelly, L., Sasso, G., & DeRaad, A. (1994). The treatment of severe behavior problems in school settings using a technical assistance model. *Journal of Applied Behavior Analysis, 27*, 33-47.

O'Brien, F., Azrin, N. H., & Bugle, C. (1972). Training profoundly retarded children to stop crawling. *Journal of Applied Behavior Analysis, 5*, 131-137.

O'Neill, G. W., Walters, W. M., Rasheed, J. A., & Johnston, J. M. (1975). The measurement and analysis of college student study behavior. Validity of the study reporting system—II. In J. M. Johnston (Ed.), *Behavior research and technology in higher education* (pp. 411–420). Springfield, IL: Charles C. Thomas.

Pennypacker, H. S., Gutierrez, A., Jr., & Lindsley, O. R. (2003). *Handbook of the standard celeration chart*. Gainesville, AL: Xerographics.

Perone, M. (1999). Statistical inference in behavior anaysis: Experimental control is better. *The Behavior Analyst, 22*, 109–116.

Peterson, H., Homer, A. L., & Wonderlick, S. A. (1982). The integrity of independent variables in behavior analysis. *Journal of Applied Behavior Analysis, 15*, 474–493.

Powell, J., Martindale, A., & Kulp, S. (1975). An evaluation of time-sample measures of behavior. *Journal of Applied Behavior Analysis, 8*, 463–469.

Powell, J., Martindale, B., Kulp, S., Martindale, A., & Bauman, R. (1977). Taking a closer look: Time sampling and measurement error. *Journal of Applied Behavior Analysis, 10*, 325–332.

Rast, J., Johnston, J. M., & Drum, C. (1984). A parametric analysis of the relationship between food quantity and rumination. *Journal of the Experimental Analysis of Behavior, 41*, 125–134.

Rast, J., Johnston, J. M., Drum, C. & Conrin, J. (1981). The relation of food quantity to rumination behavior. *Journal of Applied Behavior Analysis, 14*, 121–130.

Rast, J., Johnston, J. M., Ellinger-Allen, J., & Lubin, D. (1988). Effects of pre-meal chewing on ruminative behavior. *American Journal of Mental Retardation, 93*, 67–74.

Reid, D. H., & Hurlbut, B. (1977). Teaching nonvocal communication skills to multihandicapped retarded adults. *Journal of Applied Behavior Analysis, 10*, 591–603.

Repp, A. C., Deitz, D.E.D., Boles, S.M., Deitz, S. M., & Repp, C. F. (1976). Differences among common methods for calculating interobserver agreement. *Journal of Applied Behavior Analysis, 9*, 109–113.

Repp, A. C., Roberts, D. M., Slack, D. J., Repp, C. F., & Berkler, M. S. (1976). A comparison of frequency, interval and time-sampling methods of data collection. *Journal of Applied Behavior Analysis, 9*, 501–508.

Salmon, W. C. (1966). *The foundation of scientific inference*. Pittsburgh: University of Pittsburgh Press.

Schnelle, J. F., Kirchner, R. E., Casey, J. D., Uselton, P. H., & McNees, M. P. (1977). Patrol evaluation research: A multiple baseline analysis of saturation police patrolling during day and night hours. *Journal of Applied Behavior Analysis, 10*, 33–40.

Schwartz, B., & Gamzu, E. (1977). Pavlovian control of operant behavior. In W. K. Honig & J. E. R. Staddon (Eds.), *Handbook of operant behavior* (pp. 53–97). Englewood Cliffs, NJ: Plenum Press.

Shook, G. L., Johnston, J. M., & Mellichamp, F. H. (2004). Determining essential content for applied behavior analyst practitioners. *The Behavior Analyst, 27*, 67–94.

Shull, R. L. (1999). Statistical inference in behavior analysis: Discussant's remarks. *The Behavior Analyst, 22*, 117–121.

Sidman, M. (1960). *Tactics of scientific research*. New York: Basic Books.

Sidman, M. (1994). *Equivalence relations and behavior: A research story*. Boston: Author's Cooperative.

Skinner, B. F. (1935). The generic nature of the concepts of stimulus and response. *Journal of General Psychology, 12*, 40–65.

Skinner, B. F. (1938). *The behavior of organisms*. New York: Appleton-Century-Crofts.

Skinner, B. F. (1945). Operational analysis of psychological terms. *Psychological Review, 52*, 270–281.

Skinner, B. F. (1953). *Science and human behavior*. New York: Free Press.

Skinner, B. F. (1956). A case history in scientific method. *American Psychologist, 11*, 221–233.

Skinner, B. F. (1961). *Cumulative record*. New York: Appleton-Century-Crofts.

Skinner, B. F. (1971). *Beyond freedom and dignity*. New York: Alfred A. Knopf.

Skinner, B. F. (1974). *About behaviorism*. New York: Alfred A. Knopf.

Skinner, B. F. (1975). The shaping of phylogenic behavior. *Journal of the Experimental Analysis of Behavior, 24*, 117.

Skinner, B. F. (1976). *Particulars of my life*. New York: Alfred A. Knopf.

Skinner, B. F. (1979). *The shaping of a behaviorist*. New York: Alfred A. Knopf.

Skinner, B. F. (1983). *A matter of consequences*. New York: Alfred A. Knopf.

Stoerzinger, A., Johnston, J. M., Pisor, K., & Monroe, C. M. (1978). Implementation and evaluation of a feedback system for employees in a salvage operation. *Journal of Organizational Behavior Management, 1*, 268-280.

Taylor, C. B. (1982). Adult medical disorders. In A. S Bellack, M. Herson, & A. E. Kazdin (Eds.). *International handbook of behavior modification and therapy* (pp. 467-499). New York: Plenum Press.

Terrell, D. J., & Johnston, J. M. (1989). Logic, reasoning, and verbal behavior. *The Behavior Analyst, 12*, 35-44.

Thompson, T., & Lubinski, D. (1986). Units of analysis and kinetic structure of behavioral repertoires. *Journal of the Experimental Analysis of Behavior, 46*, 219-242.

Trap, J. J., Milner-Davis, P., Joseph, S., & Cooper, J. O. (1978). The effects of feedback and consequences on transitional cursive letter formation. *Journal of Applied Behavior Analysis, 11*, 381-393.

Tufte, E. R. (1983). *The visual display of quantitative information*. Cheshire, CN: Graphics Press.

Tufte, E. R. (1990). *Envisioning information*. Cheshire, CN: Graphics Press.

Tufte, E. R. (1997). *Visual explanations*. Cheshire, CN: Graphics Press.

Tufte, E. R. (2006). *Beautiful evidence*. Cheshire, CN: Graphics Press.

Tukey, J. W. (1977). *EDA: Exploratory data analysis*. Reading, MA: Addison-Wesley.

Van Houten, R., Nau, P. S., MacKenzie-Keating, S. E., Sameoto, D., & Colavecchia, B. (1982). An analysis of some variables influencing the effectiveness of reprimands. *Journal of Applied Behavior Analysis, 15*, 65-83.

Velleman, P., & Hoaglin, D. C. (1981). *The ABC's of EDA: Applications, basics, and computing of exploratory data analysis*. Boston, MA: Duxbury.

Walters, W. M., O'Neill, G. W., Rasheed, J. A., & Johnston, J. M. (1975). The measurement and analysis of college student study behavior. Validity of the study reporting system—I. In J. M. Johnston (Ed.), *Behavior research and technology in higher education* (pp. 399-410) Springfield, IL: Charles C. Thomas.

Watson, P. J., & Workman, E. A. (1981). The non-concurrent multiple baseline across-individuals design: An extension of the tradition multiple baseline design. *Journal of Behavior Therapy and Experimental Psychiatry, 12*, 257-259.

Wittenborn, J. R. (1972). Reliability, validity, and objectivity of symptom-rating scales. *Journal of Nervous and Mental Disease, 2*, 159-170.

Zeiler, M. D. (1984). The sleeping giant: Reinforcement schedules. *Journal of the Experimental Analysis of Behavior, 42*, 485-493.

Author Index

Subject Index